Playing Fair

Recent Titles in

Studies in Penal Theory and Philosophy
R.A. Duff, Michael Tonry, General Editors

Popular Punishment
On the Normative Significance of Public Opinion
Jesper Ryberg and Julian V. Roberts

Just Sentencing
Principles and Procedures for a Workable System
Richard S. Frase

Punishment, Participatory Democracy, and the Jury
Albert W. Dzur

Retributivism Has a Past
Has It a Future?
Edited by Michael Tonry

Taming the Presumption of Innocence
Richard Lippke

Sentencing Multiple Crimes
Edited by Jesper Ryberg, Julian V. Roberts and Jan W. de Keijser

Playing Fair
Political Obligation and the Problems of Punishment
Richard Dagger

Playing Fair

Political Obligation and the Problems of Punishment

RICHARD DAGGER

OXFORD
UNIVERSITY PRESS

Oxford University Press is a department of the University of Oxford. It furthers the University's objective of excellence in research, scholarship, and education by publishing worldwide. Oxford is a registered trade mark of Oxford University Press in the UK and certain other countries.

Published in the United States of America by Oxford University Press
198 Madison Avenue, New York, NY 10016, United States of America.

© Oxford University Press 2018

All rights reserved. No part of this publication may be reproduced, stored in a retrieval system, or transmitted, in any form or by any means, without the prior permission in writing of Oxford University Press, or as expressly permitted by law, by license, or under terms agreed with the appropriate reproduction rights organization. Inquiries concerning reproduction outside the scope of the above should be sent to the Rights Department, Oxford University Press, at the address above.

You must not circulate this work in any other form
and you must impose this same condition on any acquirer.

Library of Congress Cataloging-in-Publication Data
Names: Dagger, Richard.
Title: Playing fair : political obligation and the
problems of punishment / Richard Dagger.
Description: New York, NY : Oxford University Press, 2018. |
Series: Studies in penal theory and philosophy |
Includes bibliographical references and index.
Identifiers: LCCN 2017054226 | ISBN 9780199388837 (hardback) |
ISBN 9780199388844 (updf) | ISBN 9780190884789 (epub)
Subjects: LCSH: Political obligation. | Civil society. |
Punishment—Philosophy. | BISAC: PHILOSOPHY / Political. |
POLITICAL SCIENCE / History & Theory. | LAW / Jurisprudence.
Classification: LCC JC329.5.D34 2018 | DDC 320.01/1—dc23
LC record available at https://lccn.loc.gov/2017054226

1 3 5 7 9 8 6 4 2
Printed by Sheridan Books, Inc., United States of America

For Barbara, Emily, Elizabeth, and Julia

CONTENTS

Acknowledgments ix

Introduction 1

PART I POLITICAL OBLIGATION AS FAIR PLAY

1. Political Obligation: Concepts and Challenges 15
2. Fair Play and Cooperative Practices 42
3. Fair Play and Its Rivals 68
4. Political Obligation as Fair Play: Elaboration and Defense 101

PART II PUNISHMENT AS FAIR PLAY

5. Justifying Punishment: Concepts and Challenges 139
6. Playing Fair with Punishment: Elaboration and Defense 176
7. Punishing Fairly 204

PART III FAIR PLAY AND THE POLITY

8. Authority, Deference, and Fair Play 261
9. Political Obligation, Punishment, and the Polity 283

Index 297

ACKNOWLEDGMENTS

Like many an author of a book long in the making, I have accumulated numerous debts in the years I have been drafting, or not, this book. If I fail to acknowledge the assistance of some who deserve notice here, as I no doubt will, I hope the neglected parties will attribute this oversight to a lapse of memory rather than a lack of gratitude.

For I am grateful indeed to the many institutions and people who contributed in various ways to the publication of this book. In addition to the editorial staff at Oxford University Press for their assistance, I am indebted to Arizona State University and the University of Richmond for sabbatical leaves and summer fellowships that enabled me to begin the book and finally bring it to completion. Even more important was the support I received from the Center for Ethics and Public Affairs at Tulane University, which granted me a research fellowship for 2005–06, the year in which I started to forge a few articles and scattered thoughts into a book. Before I could set to work at Tulane, however, Hurricane Katrina drove my wife and me, along with hundreds of thousands of others, out of New Orleans. In the ensuing chaos, the CEPA staff went far beyond the call of duty as they worked to salvage the year for its 2005–06 research fellows: Allison Denham, Jonathan Quong, Elaine Sternberg, and myself. We all owe a profound debt to the Center's Director, Rick Teichgraeber, and Assistant Director, Meg Keenan, for their supererogatory efforts on our behalf.

Among other amazing deeds, Rick secured a new home for the CEPA Fellows when it became clear that Tulane would not reopen until the spring semester of 2006, at the earliest. Thus it was that, three weeks after Katrina struck New Orleans, my wife and I found ourselves in Lexington, Virginia, where Washington and Lee University was to prove a most gracious host for the next eight months. The faculty and staff of W&L, and the people of Lexington in general, went out of their way to help the refugees from New Orleans, and for their kind assistance I shall always be grateful. In particular, I am indebted to Bob Strong of the Political Science Department, who worked with Rick and Meg to bring the CEPA Fellows to W&L, and to the indefatigable Greg Cooper of the Philosophy Department, who was the principal liaison between the CEPA Fellows and the W&L administration throughout the year. It is not too much to say that these four people were largely responsible for turning a catastrophe into a remarkably pleasant and productive stay in the Shenandoah Valley. Three other members of the W&L Philosophy Department—Melina Bell, James Mahon, and Lad Sessions—also contributed greatly to our intellectual and emotional well-being through those months in Lexington.

During the three weeks between New Orleans and Lexington, my wife and I were the unexpected guests of Steve and Sue Oehmen of Germantown, Tennessee, old friends with whom we had almost fallen out of contact. We had the Oehmens' telephone number with us in New Orleans, however, and one phone call as we drove north on Interstate 55 through Mississippi brought their unhesitating invitation to stay with them as long as necessary. For their generosity, hospitality, and good cheer in those uncertain days in the Memphis area, I remain deeply appreciative.

Among those who helped more directly with the writing of this book, my foremost debts are to Antony Duff, George Klosko, and Jeffrie Murphy. None of them agrees completely with the ideas expressed within these pages—not even George, who has often joked that he and I formed a two-person "fairness network"—but each has been indispensable to the development of the arguments to be found in them. In addition to many conversations and exchanges over the last quarter century, George also read the penultimate draft of the chapters on political obligation and offered numerous acute comments and helpful suggestions. Antony and Jeff have both encouraged and refined my writing on punishment for many years now, through the example of their own distinguished scholarship, in conversation, and by the comments they have provided on the many papers and drafts that eventually found their way into this book. To them and to George, I am most grateful.

Others who have contributed to this book, in some cases before I even was thinking of writing it, are Terry Ball, Chris Bennett, Samantha Besson, David Boonin, Jack Crittenden, Bill Edmundson, John Horton, Zach Hoskins, Youngjae Lee, Claudio Lopez-Guerra, Daniel MacDermott, David Mapel, Sandra Marshall, Matt Matravers, David Miller, Herbert Morris, Jon Quong, George Sher, Mary Sigler, Avital Simhony, Peter Steinberger, and Kit Wellman. To all I am grateful, as I am to those who joined in the discussion of early drafts of parts of the book I presented at the *Centro de Investigacion y Docencia Economia* in Mexico City, to the Society for Applied Philosophy in Manchester, England, to a workshop on political authority and obligation sponsored by the Manchester Center for Political Theory, and to a conference on legal philosophy at the University of Stirling. I owe a special debt to the anonymous reviewers for Oxford University Press, whose comments pressed me to strengthen and stretch the arguments of this book, and to David Lefkowitz, Massimo Renzo, and Justin Tosi, whose comments and suggestions in recent years have proved especially helpful. Maria Psarakis provided valuable assistance during her senior year at the University of Richmond, including most of the work on the book's index. None of these good people is responsible, I hasten to add, for any mistakes of fact, reasoning, or judgment the reader will find in this book, for that is a responsibility that falls squarely on me.

I owe debts of a different kind to Barbara Dagger, who has not only traveled with me from Tempe to New Orleans to Memphis to Lexington to Tempe to Memphis to Richmond, but who has also provided technical assistance at various times. To her, and to our daughters and granddaughter, I dedicate *Playing Fair*.

Portions of the following articles and chapters I have written, often much revised and rearranged, are included in this book, and I am grateful to the publishers for permission to use them here:

"Playing Fair with Punishment," *Ethics* 103 (1993): 473–88. Reprinted by permission of the University of Chicago Press.

"Review of Christopher Heath Wellman and A. John Simmons, *Is There a Duty to Obey the Law?*," *Ethics* 118 (2007): 184–88.

"Individualism and the Claims of Community," in *Contemporary Debates in Political Philosophy*, ed. Thomas Christiano and John Christman (Malden, MA: Wiley-Blackwell, 2009). Reprinted with permission of John Wiley & Sons Inc.

"Republicanism and the Foundations of Criminal Law," in *Philosophical Foundations of Criminal Law*, ed. R. A. Duff and S. P. Green (Oxford: Oxford University Press, 2011). Reprinted by permission of Oxford University Press.

Civic Virtues: Rights, Citizenship, and Republican Liberalism (New York: Oxford University Press, 1997). Reprinted by permission of Oxford University Press.

"Playing Fair with Imprisonment," in *Democratic Theory and Mass Incarceration*, ed. A. Dzur, I. Loader, and R. Sparks (Oxford: Oxford University Press, 2016). Reprinted by permission of Oxford University Press.

"Membership, Fair Play, and Political Obligation," *Political Studies* 48 (2000): 105–12. Reprinted by permission of Wiley Publishing.

"Jean Hampton's Theory of Punishment: A Critical Appreciation," *American Philosophical Association Newsletter on Philosophy and Law* 10 (2011): 6–11. Reprinted by permission of the American Philosophical Association.

"Punishment as Fair Play," *Res Publica* 14 (2008): 259–75. Reprinted by permission of Springer Publishing.

"Playing Fair with Recidivists," in *Recidivist Punishment: The Philosopher's View*, ed. C. Tamburrini and J. Ryberg (Lanham, MD: Lexington Books, 2012). Reprinted by permission of Rowman & Littlefield.

"Restitution: Pure or Punitive?," *Criminal Justice Ethics* 10 (1991): 29–39. Reprinted by permission of Taylor & Francis Publishers.

Playing Fair

Introduction

This book addresses two longstanding concerns of political and legal philosophy: the problems of political obligation and of punishment. So longstanding are these concerns, in fact, and so extensive the literature on each of them, that it may seem imprudent to attempt to resolve both in a single book. Perhaps it is. But there is also reason to think that there is much to gain by addressing these two vexing problems in a single volume, each in the light of the other. After all, political obligation and punishment do seem to pose closely related problems. According to a common view, we are justified in punishing people who break the law because their lawbreaking is wrong; we even call them "wrongdoers." What makes lawbreaking wrong, according to another common view, is that it is a breach of duty—a violation of the moral obligation to obey the law. Putting these two common views together, then, leads to the conclusion that we have a right to punish lawbreakers because we have a right to expect people to live up to their political obligations.

So stated, of course, this argument is much too short and far too simple. It lacks a *ceteris paribus* provision to allow for exceptional circumstances, and it assumes far too much—for instance, that punishment is the proper response to lawbreaking, that we really do have an obligation to obey the law, and that this obligation is moral in nature. Nevertheless, this simple argument is essentially correct. That, at least, is the proposition I shall put to the test in this book. If I am right, it follows that a theory that provides a satisfactory answer to one of these age-old problems should also provide the basis for a satisfactory answer to the other. To show that I am right, I shall have to make the case for a theory that supplies a firm grounding both for political obligation—understood as the claim that the members of a reasonably just polity have a general obligation to obey its laws—and for punishment sanctioned by law.

The theory in question rests on the principle of fair play. According to this theory, as developed by H. L. A. Hart and others, those people who participate in a cooperative enterprise have an obligation to one another to bear a fair share of the burdens of the enterprise in return for a fair share of its benefits.[1] Applied to the political order, the principle holds that a reasonably just polity is a cooperative enterprise in that its members receive benefits under the rule of law that they can enjoy only because other members obey the law, for the most part, even when they find obedience to be disagreeable. In John Rawls's words, reasonable persons desire "a social world in which they, as free and equal, can cooperate with others on terms all can accept. They insist that reciprocity should hold within that world so that each benefits along with others."[2] According to the principle of fair play, then, the members of a reasonably just polity have an obligation to obey its laws because they have an obligation of reciprocity or fair play to one another.[3] Those who break the laws fail to discharge this obligation, and their failure justifies the law-abiding members, acting through the proper authorities, in punishing the lawbreakers.

Such, in brief, is the argument I shall elaborate and defend in this book. The argument will not be entirely original, nor will it be free from difficulties. In addition to Hart and Rawls, other philosophers have advocated the principle of fair play, most notably George Klosko with regard to political obligation and Herbert Morris and George Sher with regard to punishment.[4] Whatever originality I can claim derives largely from three features of my project: first, the attempt to justify political obligation *and* punishment as two aspects of the same fundamental concern for sustaining a polity that can be reasonably regarded as a cooperative enterprise; second, the emphasis I shall place on the rule of law as

---

[1] Hart, "Are There Any Natural Rights?," *Philosophical Review* 64 (April 1955): 175–91.

[2] Rawls, *Political Liberalism*, expanded ed. (New York: Columbia University Press, 2005), p. 50.

[3] Strictly speaking, as Justin Tosi notes, duties of fair play are a subset of the broader category of duties of reciprocity, but here I follow Rawls's terms. See Tosi, "A Fair Play Account of Legitimate Political Authority," *Legal Theory* 23 (2017): 7.

[4] Klosko, *The Principle of Fairness and Political Obligation*, 2nd ed. (Lanham, MD: Rowman & Littlefield, 2004); *Political Obligations* (Oxford: Oxford University Press, 2005); and Morris, "Persons and Punishment," *The Monist* 52 (October 1968): 475–95. Morris does not refer to the principle of fair play (or fairness) in this essay, or elsewhere, so far as I am aware, but commentators frequently place his argument in this category. In *The Problem of Punishment* (Cambridge, UK: Cambridge University Press, 2008), for instance, David Boonin says (p. 119, n. 32) that the "fairness-based version of retributivism is perhaps most widely associated with Herbert Morris's influential paper 'Persons and Punishment' (1968) and George Sher's widely discussed book *Desert* (1987)." Sher identifies his position with the fair-play approach in "Deserved Punishment Revisited," in Sher, *Approximate Justice: Studies in Non-Ideal Theory* (Lanham, MD: Rowman & Littlefield, 1997). Other philosophers who approach punishment from the perspective of fair-play theory include Michael Davis, *To Make the Punishment Fit the Crime* (Boulder, CO: Westview Press, 1992); John Finnis, "Retribution: Punishment's Formative Aim," *American Journal of Jurisprudence* 44 (1999): 91–103; and Peter Westen, "Retributive Desert as Fair Play," in Kimberly Kessler Ferzan and Stephen J. Morse, eds., *Legal, Moral, and Metaphysical Truths: The Philosophy of Michael S. Moore* (Oxford: Oxford University Press, 2016).

essential to the existence of fair-play obligations to obey the law; and third, the development of the critical, aspirational dimension of fair-play theory. By this last feature, I mean that the principle of fair play rests on the conception of the political and legal order as a cooperative, rule-governed enterprise. Such a conception sets an ideal standard against which we may, and should, assess actual political and legal systems. Such assessments will undoubtedly lead to the conclusion that no polity fully realizes the ideal of a cooperative enterprise under law and that some do not even qualify as polities in which the principle of fair play applies. All those that fall short, whether by a little or a lot, ought to be subjected to criticism and pressed to do better.

In these three respects I believe that this book constitutes an original contribution to legal and political philosophy.[5] Originality, however, is not as important as developing a compelling theory, and to do that I shall have to confront serious objections to the use of fair play as a way of grounding political obligation and justifying legal punishment. Even Rawls, concerned as he was with "the idea of society as a system of fair cooperation over time, from one generation to the next," concluded that citizens generally have no obligation of fairness to obey the law.[6] Robert Nozick reached the same conclusion by a different route, and others, such as A. John Simmons and Robert Paul Wolff, have gone so far as to embrace "philosophical anarchism"—that is, the belief that neither fair play nor any other consideration can justify the claim that citizens generally have an obligation to obey the law.[7]

---

[5] The two works that pursue projects most similar to mine are articles by Dan Markel and Zachary Hoskins. Markel's lengthy essay, "Retributive Justice and the Demands of Democratic Citizenship" (*Virginia Journal of Criminal Law* 1 [2012]: 1–134), presses the connection between political obligation, grounded not in fair play but in "democratic fidelity," and criminal law, but not specifically punishment. Hoskins's essay, "Fair Play, Political Obligation, and Punishment" (*Criminal Law and Philosophy* 5 [2011]: 53–71) links the justification of punishment to political obligation by way of fair-play theory, but his approach differs from mine—indeed, he criticizes earlier statements of my position—in ways to be noted below (n. 8). In "Fairness-Based Retributivism Reconsidered," Göran Duus-Otterström remarks that one "noteworthy and attractive feature of FBR [i.e., fairness-based retributivism] is that it is unusually clear about the connection between punishment and political philosophy," and in particular "the theory of political obligation from which FBR flows, the *fair play theory*" (*Criminal Law and Philosophy* 11 [2017]: 483; emphasis in original). As Duus-Otterström's discussion reveals, however, this connection he notices is one that has largely escaped the scholars he cites, who in almost every case concentrate their attention either on political obligation or on the justification of punishment.

[6] For the quotation, see Rawls, *Political Liberalism*, p. 15; for the conclusion, see Rawls, *A Theory of Justice*, rev. ed. (Cambridge, MA: Harvard University Press, 1999), §§18 and 52.

[7] Nozick, *Anarchy, State, and Utopia* (New York: Basic Books, 1974), pp. 90–95; Simmons, *Moral Principles and Political Obligations* (Princeton, NJ: Princeton University Press, 1979); Wolff, *In Defense of Anarchism*, 3rd ed. (Berkeley and Los Angeles: University of California Press, 1998).

Similar difficulties arise with regard to punishment. As with political obligation, the objections are in some cases specific—that is, appeals to fair play cannot ground a satisfactory theory of punishment—while in other cases they take the form of general rejections of the practice of legal punishment.[8] Responding to these objections and overcoming these difficulties will not be easy, but these challenges must be met if the fair-play account of political obligation and punishment is to prove compelling.

In the case of punishment, as the book's title indicates, there is more than one problem to address. There is, first, the problem to which I have been referring—that is, of *how to justify* legal punishment. But there is also the problem of *how to punish*. In this respect the theory of punishment resembles just-war theory, with its distinction between *jus ad bellum*—the conditions under which war is justified—and *jus in bello*—the standards of just conduct in warfare. Among other things, this distinction reveals that we may know whether a war is just without knowing whether a certain tactic used in the course of the war also satisfies the requirements of justice. In much the same way, we may find that the practice of punishment is justified but not know whether certain forms or manners of punishment are justified, or to what extent it is proper to punish someone who has committed a particular crime. It will not be enough, then, to show that the principle of fair play provides an answer to the first problem of punishment—that is, of how to justify legal punishment. It will be necessary also to show that the principle offers valuable guidance when we confront the second problem—that is, of how, or even whether, to punish those who have broken the law.[9] Part of this attempt to bring the principle of fair play to bear on this second problem of punishment will consist in an argument for punitive restitution as a form of punishment that is especially conducive to the aim of repairing the relationship between criminals and their victims, including the indirect victims of their crimes—a category, I shall argue, that comprises all those whose law-abiding cooperation makes it possible for the lawbreakers to enjoy the benefits of the rule of law. Other concerns that arise in this context involve the proper

---

[8] For the specific objection, see, e.g., Boonin, *The Problem of Punishment*, pp. 119–43, Richard Burgh, "Do the Guilty Deserve Punishment?," *Journal of Philosophy* 79 (1982): 193–210, and R. A. Duff, *Trials and Punishments* (Cambridge, UK: Cambridge University Press, 1986), chap. 8. For the general rejection of punishment, see, e.g., Karl Menninger, *The Crime of Punishment* (New York: Viking Press, 1968), Geoffrey Sayre-McCord, "Criminal Justice and Legal Reparations as an Alternative to Punishment," *Philosophical Issues, 11: Social, Political, and Legal Philosophy* (special issue of *Noüs*, 2001): 502–29, and Boonin, *The Problem of Punishment*, passim.

[9] Here is where the differences between my position and Hoskins's (n. 3, *supra*) become apparent. On his view, fair-play theory can do no more than establish that states may be permitted to punish; it offers no positive justification for punishment and no guidance to the sentencing of offenders (p. 54 et passim).

treatment of recidivists, the voting rights (if any) of felons and ex-felons, and the possibility that "penal populism" or some other force has generated an unacceptable degree of imprisonment in recent decades, most notably in the United States. I shall also have something to say about how far the criminal law should reach, or how much of our lives should fall within its scope.

Fair play is thus the unifying theme in this attempt to solve the problems of political obligation, which is the focus of Part I, and of punishment, which is the concern of Part II. I do not turn directly to fair play, however, until Chapter 2, which follows an examination of the problem of political obligation in general in the first chapter. What is political obligation, in other words, and why is it the subject of so much disagreement? In particular, why have a number of prominent political philosophers come to think that there is no general obligation to obey the laws of even a reasonably just polity? I offer reasons to reject this dismissive position in Chapter 1, but a complete refutation requires the development of a satisfactory theory of political obligation. That task I take up in the three remaining chapters of Part I of the book. In Chapter 2 I explicate the principle of fair play and explain how it grounds, at least in some circumstances, a general obligation to obey the law. In explicating the principle I give particular attention to the crucial concept of a cooperative practice—what Hart called "a joint enterprise according to rules"—one feature of which is the participants' right to be respected as equals.[10] Chapter 3 then turns directly to objections lodged against the principle of fair play as the grounding of the obligation to obey the law. Some of these objections have been raised by political philosophers who deny that such grounding has been or can be found; others have been raised by advocates of rival theories of political obligation, especially those based on membership (or association) or on an appeal to some kind of "natural duty," such as the duty to be a good Samaritan.[11] Whatever their provenance, I believe that the fair-play theory is not vulnerable to these objections—at least not when the theory is properly stated—and I explain why in Chapter 3. In Chapter 4, which concludes Part I, I restate the fair-play theory of political obligation with an emphasis on the central part the rule of law plays in the theory. This restatement helps to

---

[10] Hart, "Are There Any Natural Rights?," p. 64.

[11] For the membership or associative account, see, e.g., John Horton, *Political Obligation*, 2nd ed. (Basingstoke: Palgrave Macmillan, 2010), chaps. 6 and 7, and Yael Tamir, *Liberal Nationalism* (Princeton, NJ: Princeton University Press, 1993); for samaritanism, see Christopher Heath Wellman, "Samaritanism and the Duty to Obey the Law," in Wellman and A. John Simmons, *Is There a Duty to Obey the Law?* (Cambridge, UK: Cambridge University Press, 2005); and for other "natural duty" accounts, see Anna Stilz, *Liberal Loyalty: Freedom, Obligation, and the State* (Princeton, NJ: Princeton University Press, 2009); Jeremy Waldron, "Special Ties and Natural Duties," *Philosophy and Public Affairs* 22 (1993): 3–30; and Thomas Christiano, *The Constitution of Equality: Democratic Authority and Its Limits* (Oxford: Oxford University Press, 2008).

explain how and why my explication of the theory differs from that of other fair-play proponents. In this case I am particularly concerned to demonstrate that fair play is the only principle necessary to solve the problem of political obligation, properly understood, and not one of the "multiple principles" that Klosko and Jonathan Wolff hold to be required.[12] I also stress in this chapter the critical aspect of fair play as a theory of political obligation that explains not only how there can be a general obligation to obey the law in some circumstances but also why there is no such obligation in others.

I should note that my aim in these chapters is not to provide a survey of the arguments for and against political obligation. Excellent and up-to-date surveys of this sort are already available, wherein the author canvasses the theories on offer before defending the one, or the combination of theories, that he or she thinks best.[13] I shall refer to these surveys in the course of this work, but I do not aim to compete with them. My purpose is to elaborate and defend a theory of political obligation grounded in the principle of fair play, and I shall attend to other theories primarily as a way of clarifying the fair-play account and calling attention to its merits.

The same point holds with regard to the discussion of punishment in Part II. What punishment is and how, or whether, it is to be justified have been the subjects of vigorous and wide-ranging debate in recent years—so much so, in fact, that one commentator has dubbed the period from 1957 to 2007 the "golden half century" of punishment theory.[14] Within this half century, and beyond, the proponents of retributivism, deterrence, moral education, republicanism, rights-forfeiture, and other approaches to punishment have devoted considerable effort and ingenuity to exposing the defects of one another's attempts to justify punishment while defending their own against the critical onslaught. I shall be concerned to locate the fair-play account within these debates, but only to the extent necessary to distinguish that account from its rivals and to strengthen the arguments in its favor. But I shall not attempt a comprehensive

---

[12] Klosko, *Political Obligations*, esp. chap. 5; Wolff, "Political Obligation, Fairness, and Independence," *Ratio* 8 (1995): 87–99; and "Political Obligation: A Pluralistic Approach," in *Pluralism: The Politics and Philosophy of Diversity*, ed. M. Baghramian and A. Ingram (London: Routledge, 2000).

[13] See Horton, *Political Obligation*; Dudley Knowles, *Political Obligation: A Critical Introduction* (Abingdon, Oxon: Routledge, 2010); and Dorota Mokrosińska, *Rethinking Political Obligation: Moral Principles, Communal Ties, Citizenship* (Basingstoke: Palgrave Macmillan, 2012). For shorter surveys, see William A. Edmundson, "The State of the Art: The Duty to Obey the Law," *Legal Theory* 18 (2004): 215–59; and David Lefkowitz, "The Duty to Obey the Law," *Philosophy Compass* 6 (2006): 571–98.

[14] Michael Davis, "Punishment Theory's Golden Half Century: A Survey of Developments from (About) 1957–2007," *Journal of Ethics* 13 (2009): 73–100.

survey of the various theories of punishment. As with political obligation, such surveys are available elsewhere.[15]

In the three chapters of Part II, then, my aim is to bring the principle of fair play to bear on the problems of punishment. Chapter 5 takes up the conceptual and definitional issues surrounding punishment under the law—what is punishment, how can it be justified as a practice, and what form or forms should it take? I also locate the principle of fair play within the time-honored debate between consequentialist and retributivist approaches to the justification of punishment, arguing that fair play provides an essentially retributive theory of punishment that nevertheless accommodates the forward-looking considerations—particularly the concern for deterrence and crime prevention—usually associated with consequentialism. Chapter 6 then takes up and responds to the various objections that critics have lodged against fair play as a theory of punishment. One objection, for instance, is that the fair-play theory cannot explain why such serious crimes as rape and murder should be subject to more severe punishment than, say, tax evasion and littering. If crime is essentially a matter of taking unfair advantage of the law-abiding members of society, as the fair-play theory suggests, then it seems that murder is no more unfair than tax evasion; in fact, it may be less so, for most people find the temptation to cheat on their taxes much more powerful than the temptation to commit murder.[16] Hence the fair-play view, according to the critics, is simply counterintuitive. As one of them says, "It is very difficult to believe that just punishment is based on unfairly benefiting from a system of rules."[17]

In response to this and other objections, I elaborate and refine in Chapter 6 the fair-play account of punishment. All crimes are indeed crimes of unfairness, I argue, and that is why the members of a polity are justified in punishing those who break the law. But the members of a polity—a body politic that may be reasonably regarded as a cooperative enterprise governed by and administering the rule of law—bear some responsibility for the laws under which they live, and thus the responsibility to declare that some infractions are more weighty, and subject to more severe sanctions, than others. Not all political and legal systems, however, are polities in this full sense of the word. Does that mean that they

---

[15] In addition to Davis's "Punishment Theory's Golden Half Century," see R. A. Duff's lengthy article, "Penal Communications: Recent Work in the Philosophy of Punishment," *Crime and Justice* 20 (1996): 1–97; Boonin, *The Problem of Punishment*; Thom Brooks, *Punishment* (New York: Routledge, 2012); and David Wood's three-part essay, "Punishment: Consequentialism"; "Punishment: Nonconsequentialism"; and "Punishment: The Future," *Philosophy Compass* 5 (2010): 455–91.

[16] Richard Burgh, "Do the Guilty Deserve Punishment?," esp. pp. 207–10.

[17] Victor Tadros, *The Ends of Harm: The Moral Foundations of Criminal Law* (Oxford: Oxford University Press, 2011, p. 27, n. 6). Note also that Brooks's *Punishment* dismisses what he calls the "unfair advantage" form of retributivism in three short paragraphs (pp. 30–31).

lack the authority to punish wrongdoers altogether? This question I also address in Chapter 6, arguing that even highly imperfect polities retain the authority to punish those who commit not only *mala in se* offenses but also various *mala prohibita* ones, such as violations of traffic laws.

Chapter 7 then follows with an exploration of the question of how best to punish those who break the law. I do not pretend to offer either a precise or a comprehensive answer to this question, but I do make a case for fair play as a theory that is congenial to attempts to restore criminals to, or reintegrate them into, society. In particular, I try to show (1) that the principle of fair play cannot condone the epidemic of over-incarceration that has afflicted the United States, at least, in recent decades; (2) that programs requiring offenders to make restitution to their victims—including the polity as a whole—should count as forms of punishment rather than alternatives to it; (3) that there is a basis in fair play for imposing harsher penalties on recidivists than on first-time offenders; and (4) that fair-play theory may justify the disenfranchisement of felons while they are imprisoned but not when they have completed their sentences. Here and in previous chapters, I also try to enlist one of the most trenchant critics of the fair-play approach to punishment in its cause by showing how fair-play considerations can enrich R. A. Duff's powerful "communicative" theory of punishment.[18]

For the most part, the discussion of punishment in Part II of the book proceeds without reference to the discussion of political obligation in Part I. In Part III, however, I bring these two concerns together, and I do this in two ways. First, I argue that the ability of the principle of fair play to provide solutions to the problems of political obligation and of punishment displays a special strength of the theory. This will be true, of course, in the straightforward sense in which a theory that solves two problems is stronger than a theory that solves only one. But there is also a special strength in the way that the two aspects of the fair-play theory prove to be mutually supporting. The fact that fair play can ground a justification of punishment is especially important for what it says to those who believe that there is no general obligation to obey the law; indeed, those who take this position are especially vulnerable where punishment is concerned. Presumably they do not want lawbreakers to go unpunished, for they clearly believe that laws have some significant value. If there is no obligation to obey the law, however, it is not easy to see how the state or government can have a right

---

[18] Duff, *Punishment, Communication, and Community* (Oxford: Oxford University Press, 2001). I shall also draw a connection to Jean Hampton's expressive retributivism, which Hampton advanced, in part, as a superior alternative to the fair-play account of punishment. See Hampton, "An Expressive Theory of Retribution," in *Retributivism and Its Critics*, ed. Wesley Cragg (Stuttgart: F. Steiner, Verlag, 1992), pp. 1–25.

to punish those who break it. By providing the basis for an explanation of this right to punish, the principle of fair play stands as a rebuke to those who deny the possibility, even within a reasonably just polity, of a general obligation to obey the law.

The second way in which the two chapters of Part III bring together the concerns of political obligation and punishment is by addressing these concerns in light of questions about the nature of political authority. In recent years several philosophers have concluded that there is something wrong with the traditional understanding of authority, according to which those who hold authority have a right to issue orders that those subject to their authority have a duty to obey.[19] Their reasons for rejecting the traditional understanding vary, but in every case they call into question the traditional linkage between political authority and political obligation. Other philosophers have tried to rescue political obligation, albeit in a weakened form, without defending the traditional conception of authority.[20] Such attempts to divorce authority from obligation, or at least to weaken the ties that bind them, are mistaken, in my view, for reasons I set out in Chapter 8. In particular, I defend the traditional understanding of authority against perhaps its most influential critic, Joseph Raz, by way of a countercriticism of his own "service conception" of authority. I then go on to argue that attempts to show that citizens have a duty to *respect* or *defer to* the law, rather than an obligation to obey it, are neither necessary nor desirable substitutes for the general obligation to obey the laws of a reasonably just polity.

As the attentive reader may have noticed, here and elsewhere I have used the term 'polity' rather than the more common 'state' or 'government.' For the most part I employ 'polity' rather than the other terms because the others tend to divert attention from the body politic to the agency or agencies that are supposed to serve that body. To say that a citizen has an obligation to obey the state or government leaves the false impression that the obligation is owed to some monolith that stands above and apart from the citizenry. On the fair-play theory, talk of an obligation to the state or government can be nothing more than an elliptical way of saying that a citizen has an obligation to her fellow citizens—a point that is better made by speaking of an obligation to the polity.

---

[19] See, e.g., Joseph Raz, *The Authority of Law: Essays on Law and Morality* (Oxford: Oxford University Press, 1979); Leslie Green, *The Authority of the State* (Oxford: Oxford University Press, 1988); Rolf Sartorius, "Political Authority and Political Obligation," *Virginia Law Review* 67 (1981): 3–17; David Copp, "The Idea of a Legitimate State," *Philosophy & Public Affairs* 28 (1999): 3–45.

[20] Ruth C. A. Higgins, *The Moral Limits of Law: Obedience, Respect, and Legitimacy* (Oxford: Oxford University Press, 2004); and Philip Soper, *The Ethics of Deference: Learning from Law's Morals* (Cambridge, UK: Cambridge University Press, 2002).

To be sure, fair play is not the only theory to insist that political obligations are owed to other persons rather than to the state or government as such. Those who advocate natural-duty and associative theories make a similar point, as Chapter 3 should make clear. In ordinary language, moreover, we commonly talk about punishment as a way of making criminals pay their "debt to society"—not to "the state" or "the government" but to "society." But here also I see a reason to prefer the term 'polity,' and to prefer it not only to 'state' or 'government' but also to 'society' or 'community.' That reason has to do with the association of 'polity' with the rule of law. Polities differ from societies and communities because they are, to varying degrees, law-governed associations of people, taking 'law' to mean something more deliberate and formal than customs or norms of behavior. Polities also differ from communities in that they do not require the shared commitment to a conception of the good or the multifaceted relationships that define communities, at least on a strict definition of 'community.'[21] A polity may be a community, but it need not be. It is more likely, nowadays, to consist of people who have widely varying conceptions of the good and who are largely unknown to one another. What matters is that they are bound together by a system of laws.

To put the point another way, 'polity' is the word that best fits the idea of a body politic as a cooperative enterprise according to rules. This is a point I shall develop throughout, but especially in the concluding chapter, which brings together the main arguments of the book. In doing so, I hope to show that issues usually consigned to the province of legal philosophers are also part of the purview of political philosophy. I shall also try to convince the reader that attending to considerations of fair play is more than a matter of bringing benefits and burdens into balance. My claim, in fact, is that these considerations form the core of a sound and robust political philosophy.

As an exercise in political and legal philosophy, this book is less concerned with timely matters than with longstanding problems. But that is not to say that it lacks relevance to pressing issues of the day. Whether one does or does not have a political obligation may be a question that occupies philosophers much more than it does jurists, politicians, and ordinary citizens in liberal democracies these days, but there is no reason to think that the debates of the 1960s and 1970s settled the question once and for all. To the contrary, one suspects that it would have been as fiercely debated a question in the first decade of this century

---

[21] I refer here, first, to John Rawls's definition of 'community' as "a special kind of association, one united by a comprehensive doctrine, for example, a church" (*Political Liberalism*, p. 40, n. 43); and second, to Michael Taylor's definition of 'community' as "characterized by shared values and beliefs, direct and many-sided relations, and the practice of reciprocity" (Taylor, *Community, Anarchy and Liberty* [Cambridge, UK: Cambridge University Press, 1982], p. 32).

as it was forty and fifty years ago if military conscription had remained in force in the United States. Should a change in circumstances make it more difficult for people to evade or ignore the question of their duty to obey the laws of their country, we should expect it once again to be a matter of widespread and probably heated contention. There are, indeed, reasons to believe that the problem of political obligation may once again become the subject of public debate as a result of controversies over environmental policies, economic inequality, racial justice, and immigration. The "Black Lives Matter" movement within the United States and the "Blue Lives Matter" reaction to it, for example, suggest that the questions of when and whether one has an obligation to obey the law are not far from the surface of public life.

In the case of punishment, moreover, there is no doubt that the arguments of this book bear more or less directly on much-discussed issues of contemporary public policy. Should felons retain the right to vote, or have it restored to them upon completion of their sentences? Should the punishment for recidivists be more severe than it is for first-time offenders? Can we justify the seven-fold increase in the rate of incarceration in the United States between 1970 and 2010, to the point where a country with 5% of the world's population has 25% of its prisoners—and 37% of those prisoners are from a racial category, African-American, that constitutes only 13% of the country's population?[22] These and related questions about crime and punishment have been the subject of ongoing concern not only among scholars but also in electoral campaigns, legislative bodies, and the popular press. There is no doubt, then, that what I have to say in these pages about punishment will be timely. For the most part, though, my intent will be informative and analytical rather than narrowly prescriptive. The aim, in other words, is not to advance straightforward recommendations for public policies but to demonstrate how the principle of fair play provides a way of approaching these problems that can, and should, inform public policy with regard to crime and punishment.

That said, I must acknowledge that some potential readers are likely to find that this book, appearing as it does in a series of Studies on Penal Theory and Philosophy, contains much less of penal theory and much more of philosophy, and of analytical philosophy in particular, than they would like. If so, I have both an excuse and a two-fold justification for the philosophical and analytical nature of the following chapters. The excuse is that my profession is political philosophy, not penology or criminology, and I believe that writers should confine

---

[22] George Will, "Seeking Sense on Sentencing," *Richmond Times-Dispatch* (June 7, 2013), p. A11; also at the opinion section of WashingtonPost.com for June 5, 2013. Will's unattributed data are consistent with those published in the *Sourcebook of Criminal Justice Statistics* (http://www.albany.edu/sourcebook/pdf/t6132011.pdf).

themselves to topics and approaches in which they are well versed. Occasionally I will refer to historical evidence or empirical data of other kinds to clarify or support a point, as I have done in the preceding paragraph, but more often I will proceed by way of analogies and criticisms of others' arguments, as my education and profession have prepared me to do. With regard to the justification for proceeding in this way, there are two points to make. The first, as I have already noted, is that the two problems with which this book is deeply concerned are longstanding and important topics within political and legal philosophy, and as such they require a philosophical response. The second point is that I am not the only writer in recent decades to venture a response to one or the other of these problems, and these responses have often taken the form of lively discussions and debates within analytical philosophy about political obligation and/or punishment. In the case of political obligation, in fact, it is difficult to see how anyone could join the discussion of the subject without engaging in analysis of the concept or critical examination of the claims put forward in arguing for or against its existence, its justification, or its limits.

My hope, in any case, is that everyone who is interested in these topics will read on, and that those who do will find this book to be a genuine contribution to the philosophical exploration of topics that are both timely and of lasting importance. Whether that hope is realized is, of course, for the reader to judge 200 pages or so from this point.

PART I

POLITICAL OBLIGATION AS FAIR PLAY

1

Political Obligation

Concepts and Challenges

As a term of political discourse, 'political obligation' is apparently no older than T. H. Green's use of the term in his lectures on the principles of political obligation at Oxford University in 1879–80.[1] The two words from which Green formed the phrase are much older, of course, and there was nothing novel about the problem that Green addressed in his lectures: "to discover the true ground or justification for obedience to law."[2] Political obligation, in fact, is one of the oldest problems of political life, appearing at least as far back as Sophocles' *Antigone* in the middle of the fifth century BCE and the trial and death of Socrates at the beginning of the fourth century. In its most fundamental sense, the problem has to do with the relation of the individual to the political society that claims him or her as a member subject to its rules. In its most common expression, the question it raises is whether I, or anyone similarly situated, have a moral duty to comply with the law's demands. In more formal terms, the question is this: "Is there a general, *prima facie* moral duty to obey the law simply because it is the law, such that the subject of the law in any given case (say, a citizen) would have the burden of providing sufficient reasons to override this duty?"[3]

---

[1] Alexander Passerin D'Entrèves, *The Medieval Contribution to Political Thought* (London: Oxford University Press, 1939), p. 3.

[2] Green, *Lectures on the Principles of Political Obligation and Other Writings*, ed. Paul Harris and John Morrow (Cambridge, UK: Cambridge University Press, 1986), p. 13. Green's lectures begin (ibid., p. 13) with the following words: "I have entitled the subject of the course 'political obligation'. I mean that term to include both the obligation of the subject towards the sovereign, of the citizen towards the state, and the obligations of individuals to each other as enforced by a political superior. My purpose is to consider the moral function or object served by law, or by the system of rights and obligations which the law enforces, and in so doing to discover the true ground or justification for obedience to law."

[3] Abner S. Greene, *Against Obligation: The Multiple Sources of Authority in a Liberal Democracy* (Cambridge, MA: Harvard University Press, 2012), pp. 14–15.

As the examples of Antigone and Socrates attest, this question is often raised in turbulent times and dramatic circumstances, when lives and cherished beliefs are at stake. Thus it was that political obligation became a pressing problem for Christians commanded to worship Caesar; for Protestants living under Catholic regimes in the sixteenth century; for Thomas Hobbes, John Locke, and others caught in the upheavals of seventeenth-century England; for Henry David Thoreau, whose country endorsed slavery and launched a war he considered unjust; for Mohandas Gandhi, Martin Luther King, Jr., and all of the others who have had to decide whether the struggle against oppression justified them in breaking the law of the land. Political obligation is not simply an academic matter, in short, but a real and inescapable problem for many people over the centuries, and sometimes quite literally a life-or-death concern.[4]

It is important, though, to note that the problem also has its quotidian aspect. So it has seemed, at least, to a number of car-driving philosophers provoked by traffic signals that direct them to stop, no matter how obviously deserted the streets may be.[5] Do we really have an obligation to obey the law, they have asked, even when it is virtually certain that no harm will follow from disobedience? The complaint implicit in this question may seem petty, especially when compared to those cases where life and conscience are involved, but the traffic-signal example makes an important point about the problem of political obligation—namely, that it concerns laws, and laws are meant to be obeyed. They do not invite the people who are supposedly subject to them to examine a law's content before deciding whether to obey or disobey it, and they do not present themselves as either very important laws that one must obey, regardless of the circumstances, or not-so-important laws that one may disobey whenever the circumstances allow. Those who are charged with enforcing the law may draw such a distinction, but those who make the laws do not.[6] If obedience seems foolish at times and appears to serve no good purpose, this sense that the law demands too much, or

---

[4] For a personal statement of how political obligation can be both a practical problem and an academic concern, see Dorota Mokrosińska's preface to her *Rethinking Political Obligation: Moral Principles, Communal Ties, Citizenship* (Basingstoke: Palgrave Macmillan, 2012).

[5] One collection of essays on political obligation even displays a picture of a stop sign on the cover of its paperback edition. See William A. Edmundson, ed., *The Duty to Obey the Law: Selected Philosophical Readings* (Lanham, MD: Rowman & Littlefield, 1999). In some cases the stop sign is in the desert and the driver approaches it at dawn. The example may seem trivial, as Edmundson acknowledges in another work, "but the type of case it represents is a huge class. If our background morality prefers liberty to constraint, lack of a consensus intuition about the stop sign case would appear to count against the party of constraint—here, the party intuiting a duty to obey in the thin desert air" (William A. Edmundson, *Three Anarchical Fallacies: An Essay on Political Authority* [Cambridge, UK: Cambridge University Press, 1998], p. 28).

[6] In saying this, I refer only to those laws that impose duties on people, and not to those that confer powers. On this distinction, see H. L. A. Hart, *The Concept of Law*, 2nd ed. (Oxford: Oxford

that it is unreasonably inflexible, may do as much to raise doubts about the obligation to obey the law as do dramatic cases of deep moral conflict.

Indeed, trivial cases may do more to raise these doubts than the dramatic ones. In the case of *Antigone*, for example, Sophocles may be saying that Antigone is right to disobey Creon's decree, but he does not seem to doubt that law carries some obligatory force. Nor have those women and men who have engaged in civil disobedience typically challenged the claim that one has a duty to obey the laws of a just polity; what they have challenged is either the justice of the existing regime or of one or more of its laws or policies. Sweeping challenges to the authority of the state and its laws are the province of anarchists, who seem to be motivated at least as much by what they regard as coercive interference in their everyday lives—taxation, conscription, rules and regulations of all kinds—as by particular acts or incidents. In recent years, moreover, the anarchists have been joined by a number of prominent political philosophers who hold, not that states and legal systems are necessarily immoral, but that there is no general obligation to obey the law, not even on the part of the citizens of a reasonably just polity in relatively placid times. How these philosophers have reached this near-anarchist conclusion and whether they are wrong to do so are questions I take up in this chapter.

If these questions are to be properly posed and answered, however, it is necessary first to attend to various conceptual matters involved in the problem of political obligation. What *is* a political obligation, for instance, and how does it differ from related obligations? These and other points must be settled before we can assess the claim that there is, or is not, an obligation to obey the law.

Political Obligation: Conceptual Concerns

When Green set out in his *Lectures* "to discover the true ground or justification for obedience to law," he was looking for more than a merely prudential answer could provide. "You ought to obey the law because you will suffer if you do not" may be a powerful reason for obedience, but it is not a reason that speaks to "the moral function or object served by law" that was Green's concern.[7] For Green and for almost everyone else who has pondered it, the problem of political obligation is a moral problem, and the obligation in question is a moral obligation. It will be a legal obligation too, for it is an obligation to obey the law; but it will be a

---

University Press, 1994), p. 81. See also Kent Greenawalt, *Conflicts of Law and Morality* (Oxford: Oxford University Press, 1987), pp. 9–10.

[7] Green, *Lectures on the Principles of Political Obligation*, p. 13.

legal obligation that one has a moral duty to discharge, at least when there are no overriding moral duties that permit, or perhaps even require, civil disobedience.

Obligation and Duty

As the previous sentence suggests, obligations are also duties. That is true, at any rate, when the obligation under discussion is a political obligation. To be sure, some philosophers have uncovered differences between obligations and duties, the most important of which is that obligations must be voluntarily undertaken or incurred, but duties need not be.[8] The obligation to keep a promise or fulfill a contract, for example, arises only when one has done something that generates the obligation—made a promise or signed a contract—but the duties of charity and truth-telling supposedly fall on us regardless of what, if anything, we voluntarily consent to do. John Rawls relies on this distinction when he argues that most citizens of a reasonably just political society have no general obligation to obey its laws, even though they do have a "natural duty" to support just institutions— a duty that has the general effect of requiring them to obey.[9] For the most part, however, the distinction between obligation and duty has played no significant role in the debates over the supposed moral responsibility to obey the law. To invoke the distinction here would run counter to the tendency in both ordinary language and philosophical discussion to use the terms interchangeably, as we do when we speak of the "duty" to keep a promise or an "obligation" to tell the truth. It would also work against those who maintain that political obligations need not be acquired voluntarily, perhaps because they believe that the duty to obey the law is a "role obligation" akin to the "obligations" imposed by membership in a family.[10] Furthermore, those who follow the Rawlsian natural-duty approach typically argue that political *obligation* is grounded in a natural *duty* of some sort. In short, there seems to be nothing to gain from insisting on a sharp distinction between obligations and duties in this context. I will proceed, then, like almost everyone who writes on the subject, on the understanding that a political obligation, if it exists, is a moral duty to obey the law.

Obligation itself is for the most part a straightforward concept. To have an obligation is to be bound to do or not do something, as the etymological connection to the Latin *ligare* indicates; and to have a political obligation is to be bound to obey the law. But what is the force of this obligation? And why is

---

[8] Richard Brandt, "The Concepts of Obligation and Duty," *Mind* 73 (1964): 374–93; H. L. A. Hart, "Legal and Moral Obligation," in *Essays in Moral Philosophy*, ed. A. I. Melden (Seattle: University of Washington Press, 1958).

[9] Rawls, *A Theory of Justice*, rev. ed. (Cambridge, MA: Harvard University Press, 1999), p. 97.

[10] See, e.g., Michael Hardimon, "Role Obligations," *Journal of Philosophy* 91 (1994): 333–63.

it a *political* rather than a *legal* obligation? Both of these questions have proved troublesome.

Obligation and Morality

In the case of the first question, the problem is to determine whether the obligation to obey the law outweighs, overrides, or excludes competing moral considerations. If there is an obligation or duty to obey the law *as such*, simply because it is the law, then it is an obligation to obey no matter what the content of a particular law may be. For the most part, those who have entered the debate over political obligation, whether they speak for it or against it, have taken political obligations to have this *content-independent* character.[11] Even so, few people will say that someone who exceeds the speed limit while driving a desperately ill person to the hospital is acting immorally; and many will say that some laws, such as those prohibiting consensual homosexual activity or recreational drug use, are themselves immoral. We may grant that the law carries moral force, in other words, but we cannot grant that it holds a monopoly on that kind of force. Whether one ought to obey the law in a particular case is something that must be decided *all things considered*—that is, in light of other moral considerations that may arise. But what kind of an *obligation* is it that may be overridden or outweighed in this manner?

There are three responses to this question, broadly speaking. The first and most common is to hold that political obligations, if they exist, are morally binding, but not absolutely or unconditionally so. They are, instead, *prima facie* or *pro tanto* obligations.[12] Like the obligation to keep a promise or meet the terms of a contract, the obligation to obey the law binds one to obedience, *ceteris paribus*, but it may be overridden in special circumstances. Nevertheless, the obligation is both presumptive and, at least on some accounts, quite strong. According to M. B. E. Smith's definition, for instance, "a person S has a prima facie obligation to do an act X if, and only if, there is a moral reason for S to do X which is such that, unless he has a moral reason not to do X at least as strong as his reason to do X, S's failure to do X is wrong."[13] Others will allow that the

---

[11] For a notable exception see George Klosko, "Are Political Obligations Content Independent?," *Political Theory* 39 (2011): 498–523. I consider and respond to Klosko's arguments in chap. 5.

[12] These terms are not synonymous, and recent discussions tend to favor the use of *pro tanto* to indicate that the reason or obligation in question is not merely apparent—that is, one that seems to be true or binding on its face when it may not be—but a genuine, albeit limited, obligation. For a helpful brief discussion of this distinction, see Dudley Knowles, *Political Obligation: A Critical Introduction* (Abingdon, Oxon: Routledge, 2010), pp. 14–16. *Prima facie* remains in use, however, and I shall use the two terms together, for the most part.

[13] Smith, "Is There a Prima Facie Obligation to Obey the Law?," *Yale Law Journal* 82 (1973): 950–76; reprinted in Edmundson, ed., *The Duty to Obey the Law*, where the quoted passage is on p. 76.

overriding reason need not be strictly moral, as in the case of friends who break a law against gambling on their weekly poker night. On either account, though, there will be a presumption that one ought to obey the law. Someone who is under a political obligation thus should presume that she has a duty to obey the laws of her polity, and she should consider disobedience only when it seems that obeying a particular law may be, on balance, the wrong course of conduct. To have a political obligation, then, is not to have an obligation to obey laws *a*, *b*, and *c*, but perhaps not law *d*; it is to have a general obligation to obey the laws of one's polity as such. This general obligation, though, will not always require obedience to particular laws when all things are considered.

A second response is to maintain that political obligations may be overridden because they are not (fully) moral obligations. As Margaret Gilbert argues, political obligations fall between "the dictates of morality," on the one hand, and "one's inclinations and . . . self-interest," on the other.[14] A political obligation is thus a "genuine obligation," in Gilbert's terms, but it is not in itself a moral requirement. Like all genuine obligations, a political obligation has binding force—in this case, binding the obligated person to obey a lawful command even when his inclinations and/or self-interest lead him toward disobedience. "Yet it may be," Gilbert says, "that one need not, all things considered, obey that command. One may, indeed, be morally required *not* to do so."[15]

The third response is to hold that a *prima facie* or *pro tanto* obligation is not really an obligation at all. As one writer tempted by this view says, with particular reference to political obligation, it "makes little sense to insist there is such an obligation if those who stand under it are entitled to exercise their own moral discretion regarding the propriety of their obedience to law."[16] Either we have an obligation to do (or not do) X, in which case we are simply and absolutely bound to do (or not do) it, or we do not. Those who take this view must conclude, therefore, either that anyone who has a political obligation should always obey the law, being guilty of immoral conduct if he does not, or that no one ever has been or will be under a political obligation. Given the reasons already noted for believing disobedience to be morally justified in some circumstances, few of those who take obligations to be absolutely binding will be inclined to draw the first conclusion. To conceive of obligations as necessarily absolute is thus to slide

---

[14] Gilbert, *A Theory of Political Obligation* (Oxford: Oxford University Press, 2006), p. 293.

[15] Ibid. See also her *Joint Commitment: How We Make the Social World* (Oxford: Oxford University Press, 2013), p. 395, where Gilbert distinguishes between "two radically different kinds of obligation": "moral requirement, on the one hand, and owing, on the other." As she goes on to say, political obligations are owing-obligations that give those who bear them "sufficient reason to fulfill them," and are "forces to be reckoned with," without being morally required obligations.

[16] Craig Carr, "Fairness and Political Obligation," *Social Theory and Practice* 28 (2002): 2.

toward the conviction that there is no duty to obey the law as such, at least not if this duty is understood as a general obligation to obey the law of one's polity.

What, then, is the force of a political obligation? Is it "merely" a *prima facie* or *pro tanto* obligation, or is it, if it exists at all, absolutely binding? Or is it a genuine but non-moral obligation, as Gilbert seems to think? The advantage of Gilbert's position is that it avoids the problem of resolving the question of whether the obligation is or is not absolute. That is, one may acknowledge that political obligations are truly binding, so that anyone who has such an obligation is bound in some sense to obey the law, but also acknowledge that this obligation must give way when it conflicts with moral obligations. The disadvantage, however, is that Gilbert's position appears to deny what seems to be the common belief—namely, that all genuine obligations carry some moral force. To be sure, it may be easy to think of cases in which morality requires us to break promises or vows, but these cases are not evidence that the promise or vow is devoid of moral content—not unless we take a moral obligation to be an all-things-considered requirement. But if we allow that all genuine obligations carry some moral force, if not enough to be always dispositive, then we are in effect accepting the distinction between *prima facie* (or *pro tanto*) obligations and absolute obligations. Either that or we need to introduce a related distinction between genuine obligations, which are moral but subject to being overridden, and some other kind of moral requirement, responsibility, or "ought" that is capable of overriding moral obligations.

Or we could take the third route and insist that genuine obligations, including political obligations, must be absolutely binding. To do so, however, is to require more of political obligation than almost any obligation can bear. In fact, the usual candidates for absolutely binding moral requirements are highly abstract and truly fundamental—to do God's will in all of one's actions, to do good and avoid evil, to promote the greatest happiness of the greatest number, to submit only to laws that one makes for oneself, and the like. Unless one holds the implausible view that the obligation to obey the law is a fundamental requirement of this kind—that is, the moral duty from which all other moral duties derive—there is no good reason to deny that political obligations are as liable to be overridden as almost all of our other obligations, such as those that follow from promises, contracts, oaths, and vows.

In the end, my view is that we should not be troubled by the charge that "it makes little sense to insist there is such an obligation [i.e., a political obligation] if those who stand under it are entitled to exercise their own moral discretion regarding the propriety of their obedience to law."[17] It is true that the law does

---

[17] Ibid.

not invite us to examine its content before deciding whether to obey, nor does it typically present us with a set of options from which to choose. As Joseph Raz and others have observed, the law claims exclusive or ultimate authority within its domain.[18] From the standpoint of moral or political philosophy, however, there is no reason to cede such authority to "the law." We may not want people to stop in their tracks so that they can ponder the moral implications of obedience each and every time the law directs them to do something, but neither should we want them to obey unquestioningly whatever is presented to them as a law. Political obligation resembles military duty in this respect. Anyone who believes that a military force is necessary will almost certainly accept the need for a chain of command, which entails a duty on the part of subordinates to obey the orders of those who outrank them. To undermine the requisite sense of duty is to weaken, and perhaps to destroy, the effectiveness of a military unit. Yet we do not take "I was only following orders" to justify blind obedience. The soldier's duty to obey orders is no doubt a general and powerful obligation, but there are nevertheless circumstances in which it may and should be overridden. In the same way, the obligation to obey the law can be genuine and powerful, if it exists at all, even though it is a *prima facie* (or defeasible) or *pro tanto* (or limited) obligation.

Obligation, Political and Legal

What does this defeasible or limited nature of political obligation imply by way of an answer to the second question I raised earlier, which concerns the distinction between political and legal obligation? If those who have a political obligation have a duty to obey the law, *ceteris paribus*, then why not call it a *legal* obligation? Or why not conclude, with Bhikhu Parekh, that the question of whether we have a duty to obey the law is really a matter of *civil obligation*—that is, "the obligation to respect and uphold the legitimately constituted civil authority"—that entails *legal obligations* "to obey the laws enacted by the civil authority" rather than political obligation?[19] 'Political' is the broadest term, according to Parekh, and someone who has a truly *political* obligation will owe her polity more than mere obedience to its laws or respect for legitimate authority. Such a person will have a positive duty to take steps to secure the safety and advance the interests of her country. Following Parekh's distinction, then, we may say that someone who pays taxes discharges a legal obligation, no matter how grudgingly she pays them, but someone who pays taxes *and* contributes voluntarily to public projects fulfills a truly political obligation.

---

[18] Raz, *The Authority of Law* (Oxford: Oxford University Press, 1979), pp. 22–27.
[19] Parekh, "A Misconceived Discourse on Political Obligation," *Political Studies* 41 (1993): 240.

Other philosophers also distinguish political from legal obligation, but not in the far-reaching way that Parekh does. Nor is there anything to gain, so far as I can see, from adopting his unconventional set of distinctions. Parekh has an important point to make about the difference between passively obeying laws and actively contributing to the good of the polity, but we already have a term, 'civic duty,' that does the work he wants to assign to 'political obligation.' The exhortations to do one's civic duty that are commonplace in many countries make this point quite clearly. Such exhortations would have us vote in elections and be well-informed voters; buy government bonds; limit our use of water and other scarce resources; donate blood, service, or money (beyond what we may owe in taxes) in times of crisis; and generally contribute in an active way to the common good. Whether we really have a civic duty to do any of these things may be a matter of dispute, but appeals to civic duty are certainly quite common, and it is not at all evident that there is something to be gained by reclassifying them as appeals to political obligation. It is no doubt true that "an exclusive focus on obedience to the law will often be too narrow to capture all that is at stake in complex discourses of political obligation."[20] But there is no need for 'political obligation' to displace 'civic duty' within these complex discourses; nor is there reason to doubt that the focus of debates about political obligation—even if it is not the *exclusive* focus—has long been on questions of obedience to law.

How, then, do others draw the distinction between political and legal obligation? In general, the difference seems to be that political obligations attach to membership in or belonging to a political society and legal obligations apply to anyone who is subject to the law. Political philosophers, as I have noted, typically take the problem of political obligation to be the problem of determining whether there is a ground or justification for obedience to the law—not this or that law in particular but the law in general of one's state or polity. Political philosophers thus have worried less about whether a particular law is binding than about the conditions under which one has an obligation to obey the laws as such. They look upon the system of laws as an aspect of the polity, albeit a vital one, and their question is, What kind of polity can rightly claim that its members have a moral duty to obey its laws? Their answers have varied, of course, from Hobbes at one extreme, insisting that there is an obligation to obey the dictates of anyone who can maintain order, to anarchists at the other. Yet their concern has been the general or systemic one of establishing the grounds for obeying the laws of one's body politic.

---

[20] John Horton, *Political Obligation*, 2nd ed. (Basingstoke: Palgrave Macmillan, 2010), p. 189; see also p. 14.

For legal philosophers, however, the binding nature of laws in general is usually something to be assumed. The law claims ultimate or exclusive authority within its domain, and anyone who acknowledges that a legal system is in place must also acknowledge that its laws are binding. The obligation, though, is *legal*—that is, an obligation from the law's point of view—and need not carry moral force. According to legal positivists, in fact, a law will be morally binding only when it requires those subject to it to do what morality independently requires of them. Thus the laws that prohibit robbery, murder, and other acts that are *mala in se* are laws that people have both a moral and a legal obligation to obey; while laws that are otherwise morally indifferent, such as driving on the left-hand side of the road in Great Britain, are merely legal obligations. For most legal philosophers, it seems, the claim that a person has a legal obligation is simply a descriptive claim—a statement of a social or institutional fact. Whether the person who is subject to the legal obligation has a moral reason to obey the law depends on whether she has a distinct moral duty—a political obligation—as a member of the political society.

Many legal philosophers reject positivism, however, and those who do typically hold that genuine legal obligations are also moral obligations.[21] I am inclined to agree with them, for reasons that should become clear in later chapters. Even so, one need not be a positivist to recognize the difference between political and legal obligations. The value of this distinction is that it allows one to hold that a person may be subject to a legal obligation even though she has no political obligation to obey the laws of the regime in power. There are at least two kinds of cases in which doing so can prove helpful. In the first, the regime is tyrannical, inept, or simply so unjust that only a Hobbesian would maintain that those subject to its commands have a moral obligation to obey those commands. Nevertheless, people in this unhappy country manage to drive cars on roads that the regime maintains and to marry according to its rules. In such a situation we can acknowledge that people have legal obligations to obey certain laws—those that govern traffic and marriage—despite the absence of a political obligation to obey the laws as such. In the second, happier kind of case, we can acknowledge that the citizen of one country, to which she owes a political obligation, has a legal obligation to obey the laws of another country that she is visiting. This legal obligation lapses, however, when she returns to her own country, whereas the political obligation to her country is something she carries with her. If she is truly under a political obligation, she may be morally bound to pay taxes to her

---

[21] For a clear example, see Edward Harris, "Fighting Philosophical Anarchism with Fairness: The Moral Claims of Law in the Liberal State," *Columbia Law Review* 91 (1991): 929, n. 44: "Like political obligation, legal obligation constitutes a moral constraint upon the individual's actions and provides a moral reason to comply with a law."

polity while abroad, and perhaps even to return home to perform military or some other kind of service.[22]

Political and legal obligations are related, in short, but they are not one and the same. A political obligation is a moral duty that only a citizen or perhaps a permanent resident can have, for it is an obligation that attaches only to members of a polity. Legal obligations, by contrast, attach themselves to anyone who is subject to the pertinent law or laws, including tourists who owe no allegiance to the country they happen to be visiting.

To appreciate the value of this distinction, and of the way I have drawn it, it may help to consider §119 of John Locke's *Second Treatise of Government*. There Locke insists that the obligation to obey the laws of a political society extends not only to those who have expressly consented to obey but also to anyone who owns property in that society, lodges within its borders for a week, or travels freely on its highways—indeed, "it reaches as far as the very being of any one within the territories of that government." If the obligation in question is a political obligation, then Locke would find himself in the embarrassing position of holding that the person who sneaks into a country with the aim of subverting it nevertheless has a moral duty to obey its laws. In Locke's terms, this person would be tacitly consenting to obey the laws of a political society she is trying to overthrow—an odd form of consent, indeed. Such a position may not be absurd, but it is difficult to see how the "very being" of someone within the boundaries of a country can place her under a *political* obligation to obey the laws of a regime she abhors. If Locke were to distinguish political from legal obligation, though, he could say that the subversive is under a legal but not political obligation while within the territory of the regime she seeks to destroy. While there, in other words, she will be subject to its laws, at least in the eyes of those who enforce them, and thus under a legal obligation to obey the laws that apply to her. But the subversive will not be under a political obligation, for she will have no moral duty, as a non-member, to obey the laws of the political system of which she is not a part and to which she thoroughly objects. To be sure, Locke does not explicitly draw a distinction between political and legal obligations, but he may have something of the sort in mind when he distinguishes "perfect members" of a political society, who expressly consent to place themselves under an obligation, from those whose tacit consent makes them merely temporary subjects of it.[23]

---

[22] David Lefkowitz makes much the same point in "The Nature of Fairness and Political Obligation: A Response to Carr," *Social Theory and Practice* 30 (2004): 6, but without explicitly distinguishing political from legal obligations. I am grateful to Professor Lefkowitz for valuable discussions of the nature of this distinction.

[23] Locke, *Second Treatise of Government*, §§119–22, esp. §122: "And thus we see, that *foreigners*, by living all their lives under another government, and enjoying the privileges and protections of it,

Generality and Particularity

Two final conceptual points, already touched on, concern the *generality* and the *particularity* of political obligations. In this context, 'generality' (or sometimes 'universality') carries a two-fold meaning. That is, political obligations are usually taken to be general in the sense of applying to the entire body of laws of a polity—to the law *as such*. Moreover, this obligation falls upon every citizen or member of the polity. There are, of course, likely to be laws that bear on some members but not others; laws requiring the registration of automobiles, for example, only apply to those who own automobiles or are thinking of buying one. Nevertheless, political obligations are general in that they apply to everyone in the class they define—everyone who may purchase an automobile, in this case—and in the sense that all the members of the polity have a moral duty to obey all of its laws that apply to them.[24]

The final point concerns what John Simmons has called the "particularity requirement."[25] The point is simple but important. Political obligations are not free-floating duties, like jellyfish that may attach themselves anywhere, but moral bonds to some particular group or entity—some state or government or polity—to which one has a special relationship. A citizen of the United States thus will have an obligation to obey the laws of other countries when she is on business or holiday in them—a legal obligation, as I have called it—but her only *political* obligation will be to the United States, her country of citizenship.[26] This requirement fits neatly within most theories of political obligation, which try to show how consent or membership or fair play or some other consideration places people under an obligation to obey the laws of a particular political entity. As Simmons shows, however, the particularity requirement poses a serious problem for utilitarian and natural-duty approaches to political obligation—a point to which I shall return in Chapter 5.[27]

---

though they are bound, even in conscience, to submit to its administration, as far forth as any denison [i.e., denizen]; yet do not thereby come to be *subjects or members of that common-wealth*" (emphasis in original).

[24] For a dissenting view on this point, see Joseph Raz, "The Obligation to Obey: Revision and Tradition," *Notre Dame Journal of Law, Ethics, and Public Policy* 1 (1984): 139–55; reprinted in Edmundson, ed., *The Duty to Obey the Law*, where Raz says (p. 169): "the extent of the duty to obey the law in a relatively just country varies from person to person and from one range of cases to another.... It may depend on the expertise of the individual citizen." Raz's position relates to his "service conception" of authority, which I criticize in chap. 8 *infra*.

[25] Simmons, *Moral Principles and Political Obligations*, pp. 31–35.

[26] Unless, perhaps, she holds dual citizenship with another country.

[27] Simmons, *Moral Principles and Political Obligations*, p. 48 and pp. 155–56.

Adding the particularity requirement to the preceding account leads to the paradoxical conclusion that a political obligation is both general (because it is an obligation not to obey one or another law but the laws as such) and particular (because it is an obligation to obey the law of one's country, state, government, or polity). Political obligation differs in this way from other moral duties, such as duties of charity or benevolence (which are general but not particular), and from promises and contracts (which are particular but not general).

Other conceptual concerns relating to political obligation remain, such as the distinction between perfect and imperfect duties and the question of whether there are "institutional" or "positional" duties that lack moral content. It seems best, though, to take these up as they arise in the course of subsequent chapters. At this point, with the conceptual groundwork established, we may turn to the arguments of those who deny that political obligations really exist, either at all or to any significant extent.

Anarchist Challenges to Political Obligation

According to the foregoing analysis, a political obligation is a systemic, *prima facie* (or *pro tanto*) moral duty to obey the laws of one's polity. But does such an obligation really exist or obtain in any general or widespread sense? Most political philosophers have assumed that the answer is yes, and many of them have devoted their efforts to discovering what T. H. Green called "the true ground or justification for obedience to law." Some philosophers in the middle years of the twentieth century even asserted, on conceptual grounds, that political obligation needs no justification. As one of them declared, "to ask why I should obey any laws is to ask whether there might be a political society without political obligations, which is absurd. For we mean by political society, groups of people organized according to rules enforced by some of their number."[28] This view did not long prevail, nor should it, but it testifies to the strength of the tendency to believe that citizens surely have an obligation to obey the laws of their country, at least if it is reasonably just.

---

[28] Margaret Macdonald, "The Language of Political Theory," in *Logic and Language*, 1st series, ed. A. G. N. Flew (Oxford: Basil Blackwell, 1951), p. 192. See also Thomas McPherson, *Political Obligation* (London: Routledge & Kegan Paul, 1967), esp. p. 64, and, more subtly, Hanna Pitkin, "Obligation and Consent, Parts I and II," *American Political Science Review* 59 (1965): 990–99, and 60 (1966): 39–52. For criticism of this conceptual argument, see Carole Pateman, "Political Obligation and Conceptual Analysis," *Political Studies* 21 (1973): 199–218, and John Horton, *Political Obligation*, 2nd ed. (Basingstoke: Palgrave Macmillan, 2010), pp. 138–46. For a more sympathetic critique, see Mokrosińska, *Rethinking Political Obligation*, pp. 33–38.

There have been dissenters, though, and in recent years they have come to occupy a prominent place among political philosophers. As they see it, there is no general obligation to obey the law, not even on the part of the citizens of a reasonably just polity. Some of them even suggest that this view is widespread among citizens in general.[29] The most thorough-going of these dissenters have been anarchists in the traditional sense of the term—that is, those persons who insist that states and governments are wickedly coercive institutions that ought to be abolished. Yet other skeptics or dissenters have concluded that the all-out anarchist is wrong about the need for the state but right about the obligation to obey the law. Like the anarchist proper, these "philosophical anarchists" hold that the state is illegitimate, but they deny that its illegitimacy entails "a strong moral imperative to oppose or eliminate states; rather they typically take state illegitimacy simply to remove any strong moral presumption in favor of obedience to, compliance with, or support for our own or other existing states."[30]

The upshot is that those who believe in the existence of political obligation, in the sense I have outlined above, must now respond to challenges from two different kinds of anarchists. On the one hand, to use terms that have become conventional, are the *political anarchists* who call for the eradication of the state or any coercive law-enforcing regime; on the other hand are those who, as noted above, call themselves *philosophical anarchists*. Both groups are mistaken, in my view, but their arguments require attention. The arguments of the philosophical anarchists present the greater challenge, however, for they may appeal to the great many people who find anarchism proper too radical or implausible to be taken seriously. I begin, therefore, with some brief comments on political anarchism before turning to a more thorough consideration of their "philosophical" counterparts. In both cases, there is an important internal division to take into account.

Political Anarchism

In the case of political anarchism the internal division is between the *individualist* and the *communal* anarchists. The members of both groups agree that states and governments are coercive and evil institutions that can and should be replaced by some form of voluntary, noncoercive association. They disagree sharply,

---

[29] For opposing views on this contested point, see Leslie Green, "Who Believes in Political Obligation?," in *For and Against the State: New Essays*, ed. J. T. Sanders and J. Narveson (Lanham, MD: Rowman & Littlefield, 1996), and George Klosko, *Political Obligations* (Oxford: Oxford University Press, 2005), chaps. 9 and 10.

[30] A. John Simmons, "Philosophical Anarchism," in Simmons, *Justification and Legitimacy: Essays on Rights and Obligations* (Cambridge, UK: Cambridge University Press, 2001), p. 104.

however, on the nature and form of such an association. The individualists—or anarcho-capitalists, or libertarian anarchists—believe that the state is an entirely unnecessary evil that should give way to a form of association in which individuals are free to govern their lives by means of private enterprise and contractual relationships. The communal anarchists, by contrast, believe that men and women are thoroughly social creatures, so that any freedom we enjoy is more a matter of freedom through cooperation than freedom to go one's way. Their economic views, moreover, are firmly opposed to capitalism, which they take to be an exploitative and oppressive system—an enemy of individual freedom, as they see it, rather than a means to its realization. Both groups of political anarchists deny the authority of the state over individuals, to be sure, and both reject the claim that anyone has a general obligation to obey the law. Their reasons for taking these positions are different, though, and each group requires a response of its own.

In the case of the communal anarchists, the aim is to replace the coercive state with some form of spontaneous, cooperative social order—one in which people will live together freely and peacefully, for the most part, without the need for political authority. When decisions affecting more than a few people are necessary, they will be made by the consensus of those most directly involved. When disputes arise, they will be settled by appeal to some neutral party, or perhaps by the informal authority of neighbors or colleagues, who will make sure that the disputants adhere to the judgment the others have reached. Those who use violence against others will face the spontaneous response of society—in the rare cases in which such a response is necessary—and either learn the lessons of wrongdoing or face banishment. The details vary from one version of anarcho-communism to another, but the vision is largely the same.

But is this vision at all realistic? Perhaps it is possible for a small, stable community to govern itself in this spontaneous fashion, but even then its chances of success will be greatest when the members of the community share a commitment to some overarching conception of the good, such as a religion. Such a form of community, however, is anathema to many of the communal anarchists. According to Emma Goldman, for example, anarchism "really stands for the liberation of the human mind from the dominion of religion; the liberation of the human body from the dominion of property; liberation from the shackles and restraint of government."[31] If anarcho-communism is to succeed

---

[31] Goldman, "Anarchism: What It Really Stands For," in Goldman, *Anarchism and Other Essays* (New York: Mother Earth Association Publishers, 1910); reprinted in *Ideals and Ideologies: A Reader*, 8th ed., ed. Terence Ball and Richard Dagger (New York: Pearson Longman, 2011), with the quotation appearing at p. 261.

without the benefits of religion, or of unthinking devotion to the customary ways, then it seems that one or the other of two things will have to happen.

One possibility is that human beings will undergo a transformation—perhaps as they cast off the trammels of religion, property, and government, or perhaps subsequently—that will enable everyone to live together in peace and harmony. Such a transformation will either eliminate or drastically diminish the problem of crime, for crime, as Goldman says, "is naught but misdirected energy."[32] Once religion, property, and government have been swept away, that energy will find its natural outlet in

> a social order based on the free grouping of individuals for the purpose of producing real social wealth; an order that will guarantee to every human being free access to the earth and full enjoyment of the necessities of life, according to individual desires, tastes, and inclinations.[33]

If one finds this picture more pleasant than plausible, there is another possibility, which is, forgoing spontaneity, to spell out the procedures by which anarcho-communist societies can deal with crime and other forms of "misdirected energy." It will also be necessary to find procedures for coordinating the activities of people who cannot rely entirely on spontaneous order, at least not in anything larger than a very small and stable community. Once we begin to spell out these procedures, however, we find ourselves on a path that leads very quickly to formal authority—that is, to government and law. If these procedures are to have the force of social pressure behind them, furthermore, the anarcho-communist will have introduced into his scheme the coercion that he had set out to avoid. The choice for the anarcho-communist, in sum, seems to be a choice between an unrealistic conception of what will happen once anarchy is achieved, on the one hand, and a more plausible order, on the other, that falls short of what communal anarchism is supposed to be. Because it involves political authority, that more plausible order also implies, and perhaps entails, the existence of political obligation.

In the case of individualist anarchists there is no need to worry about the plausibility of their view of human transformation. Aside from the expectation that the too-common tendency to bow to authority will fade away, the anarcho-capitalists expect human nature to remain much as it has been.[34] In fact,

---

[32] Ibid., p. 260.

[33] Ibid., p. 261.

[34] See, e.g., Michael Huemer, *The Problem of Political Authority: An Examination of the Right to Coerce and the Duty to Obey* (Basingstoke: Palgrave Macmillan, 2013), pp. 109–36 and 187–94. Other books professing individualist anarchism include Randy Barnett, *The Structure of Liberty: Justice and the Rule of Law* (Oxford: Oxford University Press, 2000); David Friedman, *The Machinery of*

they seem to believe that life will go on much as it typically does within liberal democracies, except that it will go much better once individuals are altogether free from the heavy hand of government interference, regulation, and coercion. If their vision is implausible, then, it will not be the fault of an unrealistic belief in the possibility of human transformation.

Nevertheless, the anarcho-capitalist vision is in two ways implausible. The first is that the logic of the libertarian anarchists' argument does not necessarily lead to a stateless condition; and the second is that such a condition, were it to exist, could not sustain itself.

With regard to the first point, anarcho-capitalists are caught up in an intramural dispute with other libertarians on the question of whether some kind of state would or would not emerge from a hypothetical stateless condition. They all agree that individuals in such a condition would take steps to protect their persons and property against force and fraud, which they would do by forming or paying for the services of private protective agencies. The question is whether competitive pressures would lead to the emergence of a dominant protective agency and then to a minimal state, as Robert Nozick famously argues in *Anarchy, State, and Utopia*, or whether the free market in protection would remain open and competitive.[35] As someone who stands apart from both of these camps, I shall not pretend to settle this intramural dispute here. But it is telling, I think, that the libertarian anarchists have met such resistance from so many who share their individualistic premises and commitment to free enterprise.

Let us suppose, though, that the individualist anarchists manage to convince the other libertarians to abandon their commitment to the minimal state in favor of anarcho-capitalism. In that case they would still face the second problem I alluded to, which is to show that an association based entirely on contractual relationships could be self-sustaining. The arguments here quickly become intricate, and it would take me too far afield to explore them in these pages.[36] The problem, in brief, is that the anarcho-capitalists must show that the free market and individual contracts can supply everything essential to a decent life that we now look to government to provide, including the benefits of law, defense against invaders as well as neighbors, provisions for public health, and protection of the physical environment. For all the ingenuity they have mustered in defense

---

Freedom: Guide to a Radical Capitalism (LaSalle, IL: Open Court, 1989); and Murray Rothbard, *For a New Liberty* (New York: Macmillan, 1973).

[35] Nozick, *Anarchy, State, and Utopia* (New York: Basic Books, 1974).

[36] For helpful—and to my mind persuasive—discussions of these matters, see George Klosko, *Political Obligations* (Oxford: Oxford University Press, 2005), pp. 21–51, and Gregory Kavka, "Why Even Morally Perfect People Would Need Government," in *For and Against the State*, ed. Sanders and Narveson.

of their unorthodox position, the anarcho-capitalists have not overcome the doubts of those who believe that market failures will lead to the underprovision of essential public goods—and thus to the collapse of the anarcho-capitalist associations. It is more than mere rule or authority worship, in other words, that leads most people to believe in the necessity of political authority.

Both of the problems I have identified, I should note, are problems that arise within the general premises of individualist anarchism. Those who find these atomistic premises less than compelling, as I do, will have an additional reason to reject anarcho-capitalism. To put the point simply, libertarian anarchists exaggerate the extent to which people are rational and discount the extent to which we are dependent. In doing so, their anarchism "inclines toward a picture of human relations that is neither metaphysically nor morally persuasive."[37] In this respect, they have much in common with the "philosophical" anarchists.

Philosophical Anarchism

This "philosophical" branch of anarchism comprises political philosophers who profess no desire to overthrow or eradicate the state, but who have concluded that the political anarchists are right to insist that there is no hope of providing a satisfactory account of political obligation. According to these philosophers, the typical citizen of any political society—even the best, the most just of such societies—has no general, *prima facie* or *pro tanto* obligation to obey its laws. The typical citizen may have good reasons, moral as well as prudential, for obeying the law in many or even most cases, but no obligation to obey the law as such. The search for a satisfactory account of political obligation is simply bound to be fruitless.[38]

As with the political anarchists, the arguments of these philosophical anarchists fall into two categories. In John Simmons's terms, these are the *a priori* and *a posteriori* forms of philosophical anarchism.[39] Arguments of the first sort try to show that it is impossible in principle to provide a satisfactory account of

---

[37] Horton, *Political Obligation*, p. 116. Horton effectively elaborates this point in his discussion of individualist anarchism, pp. 113–16.

[38] See, *inter alia*, Robert Paul Wolff, *In Defense of Anarchism*, 3rd ed. (New York: Harper and Row, 1998 [1970]); M. B. E. Smith, "Is There a Prima Facie Obligation to Obey the Law?," *Yale Law Journal* 82 (1973): 950–76, reprinted in Edmundson, ed., *Is There a Duty to Obey the Law?*; A. John Simmons, *Moral Principles and Political Obligations*; Joseph Raz, "The Obligation to Obey the Law," in Raz, *The Authority of Law* (New York: Oxford University Press, 1979); Rolf Sartorius, "Political Authority and Political Obligation," *Virginia Law Review* 67 (1981): 3–17, reprinted in Edmundson, ed., *Is There a Duty to Obey the Law?*; and Leslie Green, *The Authority of the State* (Oxford: Oxford University Press, 1988), pp. 220–47.

[39] "Philosophical Anarchism," in Simmons, *Justification and Legitimacy*, pp. 104–106.

a general obligation to obey the law. This is the position Robert Paul Wolff takes in his *In Defense of Anarchism*. Arguments of the second sort are more modest in their aims but no less devastating in their conclusions. In this case the aim is not to show that a satisfactory defense of political obligation is impossible but that such a defense, despite the efforts of some of the best minds in the history of philosophy, has yet to be mounted. Those who take this *a posteriori* approach usually proceed by raising objections to the various attempts to justify political obligation, including those based on fair play. All of these attempts have failed, the *a posteriori* anarchists maintain, so we must conclude that only those relatively few people who have explicitly committed themselves to obey the law, perhaps by swearing allegiance as part of an oath of citizenship, have anything like a general obligation to obey the laws under which they live.

This conclusion is wrong, I believe, as is Wolff's more sweeping conclusion about the impossibility of a satisfactory account of political obligation. To see why they are wrong, however, we shall have to look more closely at these two arguments against political obligation.

According to Wolff, the principal advocate of *a priori* philosophical anarchism, there can be no general obligation to obey the law because any such obligation would violate the "primary obligation" of autonomy, which is "the refusal to be ruled."[40] As Wolff defines it, autonomy combines freedom with responsibility. To be autonomous, someone must have the capacity for choice, and therefore for freedom; but the person who has this capacity also has the responsibility to exercise it—to act autonomously. Failing to do so is to fail to fulfill this "primary obligation" of autonomy.

This primary obligation dooms any attempt to develop a theory of political obligation, Wolff argues, except in the highly unlikely case of a direct democracy in which every law has the unanimous approval of the citizenry. Under any other form of government, autonomy and authority are simply incompatible. As Wolff defines it, authority is "the right to command, and correlatively, the right to be obeyed."[41] Someone who has authority over us thus has the right to give us orders, while we have the correlative obligation to obey. But if we acknowledge such an obligation, we allow someone else to rule our lives, thereby violating our fundamental obligation to act autonomously. We must therefore reject the claim that we have an obligation to obey the orders of those who purport to hold authority over us and conclude that there can be no general obligation to obey the laws of any polity that falls short of a unanimous direct democracy.

---

[40] Wolff, *In Defense of Anarchism*, p. 18.
[41] Ibid., p. 4.

The arguments against Wolff's philosophical anarchism usually concentrate on his conception of autonomy and its relation to authority. In brief, Wolff's critics argue that he is wrong to insist that moral autonomy is our "primary" or "fundamental" obligation, for taking this position would require us

> to think that autonomy will always over-ride values such as not harming other people, supporting loved ones, doing a favour for a friend or even more mundane desires, such as that for a quiet life, with which this ideal of moral autonomy will from time to time conflict.[42]

Moreover, there is no reason to accept Wolff's claim that autonomy and authority are necessarily incompatible. Insofar as autonomy is a capacity, as Wolff says it is, autonomy is something that will need to be developed before it can be exercised, and various kinds of authority—including political authority—will foster its development and make its continued exercise possible.

Wolff fails to appreciate this point because of his hyper-individualistic approach. Despite a discussion of the importance of social roles in the third part of his book (pp. 72–78), he argues as if the individual is to achieve the highest possible degree of autonomy solely through her own efforts. But no one becomes or remains autonomous without the assistance and cooperation of parents, teachers, and other people.[43] In some cases this is plainly true. Someone who suffered so severely from headaches that she could no longer make choices has good reason to believe that the physician who found a way to stop the headaches or relieve the pain has enabled her to exercise autonomy once again, as would the person who overcomes disabling delusions with the help of a psychotherapist. Behind the physician and the psychotherapist in these examples are other individuals and institutions, of course, such as the medical researchers whose discoveries make it possible for the physician to treat the person with crippling headaches. Whether there is one person responsible or 1 million, however, the point is the same: some people plainly owe the exercise of their autonomy to the efforts of others.

These are unusual cases, to be sure, but there are less obvious respects in which all of those who exercise autonomy do so only because they can count

---

[42] John Horton, *Political Obligation* (London: Macmillan, 1992), p. 129. In the revised edition of this book (2010, p. 127), Horton says that autonomy "takes its place along with other moral ideals, for example those having to do with concern for other people, as one of many action-guiding principles that have to be weighed against each other in deciding how to act in the particular circumstances in which we find ourselves. It is, in fact, highly implausible to think that autonomy should invariably override all other values."

[43] The discussion in this and the following paragraphs condenses the criticism of Wolff's position in my *Civic Virtues*, pp. 62–69.

on the efforts of others. This is not to say that these "others" do what they do in order to enable the autonomous person to exercise his autonomy; in a great many cases the "others" will not even know the person or persons whom they help to act autonomously. Yet when "others" observe traffic laws or wait their turns in line, they expand our opportunities, even if this is not what they specifically intend to do. By doing so, they enhance our capacities to choose—that is, they make it possible for us to do, and therefore to choose to do, far more than we could without their help, intended or not. Even if neither we nor they are aware of it, in short, we often rely on the assistance of others when we exercise autonomy.

Is this a point that an *a priori* philosophical anarchist can simply shrug off? Why, in other words, can't Wolff agree that no one is autonomous entirely on her own, yet continue to claim that every individual has a primary obligation to act autonomously and therefore to refuse to bow to authority? Being grateful to those who help us become and remain autonomous, he might say, is not a reason to surrender that autonomy when someone in authority tells us what to do.

The problem with this reasoning is that it contradicts itself. If we acknowledge that the development and exercise of autonomy is not something individuals can achieve entirely on their own, we are soon led to the conclusion that the development and exercise of autonomy relies on the existence of authority. If the physician, the psychotherapist, and the medical researchers in the examples above are to take the steps that restore people to autonomy, they must be able to count on a high degree of order and security in their lives, and order and security require the existence of law and government—that is, political authority. The same is true of parents, teachers, and all of those whose actions intentionally or otherwise make the autonomy of others possible. Of course, Wolff could deny that political authority truly is necessary to provide order and security, but in that case he would be a political anarchist.[44] To take that line, however, would not only entail problems of its own, as we have seen; it would also place Wolff in a category he eschewed when he proclaimed himself to be a "philosophical" anarchist. He is left, as a result, in the awkward position of having to acknowledge the importance of authority to autonomy while simultaneously arguing that autonomy and authority are incompatible.

There is another escape route, though, and this one would keep Wolff within the philosophical anarchist camp. This route would require Wolff to give up the *a priori* claim that authority and autonomy are incompatible, but it would allow him to deny the legitimacy of political authority and the existence of political

---

[44] For a defense of philosophical anarchism as a kind of halfway house for those who are not yet prepared to embrace full-fledged anarchism, see chap. 7 of Michael Huemer, *The Problem of Political Authority*.

obligation, at least as a general obligation to obey the law as such. The route, that is, leads to the *a posteriori* version of philosophical anarchism, which rests on the conviction that no theory of political obligation has proved successful, despite the many efforts over the centuries to devise such a theory. Consent, gratitude, utilitarianism, membership, natural duty, fair play—all have been tried and found wanting, according to John Simmons, who has made a powerful case for philosophical anarchism on *a posteriori* grounds in *Moral Principles and Political Obligations* and in subsequent work.[45] Many have found Simmons's trenchant criticisms of the various theories of political obligation persuasive, and many others have been moved to defend and adjust their favored theories in response. Indeed, those who believe in political obligation must respond in this way, for the only conclusive argument against *a posteriori* philosophical anarchism is to produce a theory that withstands criticism. That is why the next three chapters of this book expound and defend a theory of political obligation grounded in the principle of fair play—and why I shall need to respond to Simmons and other critics of this theory in Chapter 4.

That said, there are reasons to be suspicious of this brand of philosophical anarchism even if we do not have a theory of political obligation ready to hand. These reasons begin with the general concern that this brand, like the libertarian anarchists' and Wolff's *a priori* commitment to philosophical anarchism, is excessively individualistic. For Simmons, the fact that we are "born into political communities" is much the same as "being 'dropped into' a cooperative scheme" that we have not consented to join.[46] This strikes me, for reasons I have developed elsewhere, as an artificial and atomistic way to think of the relationship between the individual and the community, society, or polity in which she finds herself.[47] As with Wolff and the anarcho-capitalists, the tendency here is to envision the individual as a fit and rational adult who is set apart from a community or cooperative scheme that is trying to impose its will on her. To be sure, there are times when that is exactly what is happening. Fit and rational adults do find themselves in situations in which those in authority within the society are trying to impose their will on those who want, perhaps quite rightly, to go their own way. But that is not always the case, even for fit and rational adults, who sometimes ought to bend their wills to those of their fellow citizens or colleagues or other members of society. And it is certainly not true of those who are yet to

---

[45] See especially the essays collected in Simmons's *Justification and Legitimacy* and his "The Duty to Obey and Our Natural Moral Duties," in C. H. Wellman and A. J. Simmons, *Is There a Duty to Obey the Law?* (Cambridge, UK: Cambridge University Press, 2005).

[46] Simmons, *Moral Principles and Political Obligations*, pp. 137–38.

[47] See my *Civic Virtues*, pp. 76–79.

become fit and rational adults, or those who may never achieve that condition. Such persons—that is, all of us at some point in our lives—will need the protection and assistance of community, society, and polity if we are to become fit and rational adults whose consent or lack of consent, or desire to go one's way, ought to be taken into account.

Beyond this general concern, there are three specific reasons to regard philosophical anarchism, even in its *a posteriori* form, with suspicion. The first is what Christopher Heath Wellman has dubbed the "bricks and bottles objection."[48] As Wellman points out in the course of his book-length debate with Simmons, philosophical anarchists are like political anarchists in rejecting the claim that there is a duty to obey the law as such, but unlike them in that they do not try to bring down the state or even question its right to exist. But, Wellman asks, how can they hold the first position without committing themselves to the second? Drawing an analogy to what he calls "philosophical abolitionism"—that is, the belief that "slaves have no moral obligation to obey their masters [while] denying that slavery is necessarily impermissible"—Wellman concludes that "it seems at the very least awkward" to maintain that "citizens have no moral obligation to obey the law" while denying "that there is anything morally problematic about imposing this law in the first place."[49] Like the political anarchists, in other words, the philosophical anarchists should be reaching for bricks and bottles to throw at the state. Either that or they should give up the pretense of anarchism and acknowledge that there is a duty to obey, according to Wellman, the just laws of a legitimate regime.

In responding to this objection, Simmons follows Locke in affirming "the natural right of all persons to enforce morality (by coercion, if necessary)."[50] This right extends to those who hold positions of political and legal authority, which means that these officials act wrongly only insofar as they preempt the rest of us from exercising our natural right to prevent wrongdoing and punish wrongdoers. To be sure, the officials will also act wrongly if they extend "the law's requirements beyond those actions that we also have independent moral reasons to perform," such as respecting the lives, liberty, and property of others.[51] When officials stay within these limits, however, the philosophical anarchist will

---

[48] Wellman, "Samaritanism and the Duty to Obey the Law," in Wellman and Simmons, *Is There a Duty to Obey the Law?*, p. 28. This and the following paragraph borrow from my review of the Wellman and Simmons book in *Ethics* 118 (October 2007): 184–88.

[49] Wellman, "Samaritanism and the Duty to Obey the Law," p. 28.

[50] Simmons, "The Duty to Obey and Our Natural Moral Duties," in Wellman and Simmons, *Is There a Duty to Obey the Law?*," p. 192.

[51] Ibid.

"embrace the commonsense judgment that states generally do no *serious moral wrong* by threatening and punishing murderers and rapists" while denying the rest of us this right to threaten and punish.[52] Ordinary state coercion is thus "nothing like the wrongs done by a master to a slave."[53] The philosophical anarchist is not, then, analogous to Wellman's "philosophical abolitionist." In fact, the philosophical anarchist holds that states that exceed their proper limits—that is, states that do more than prevent wrongdoing and punish wrongdoers—commit wrongs

> that are, in normal circumstances in decent states, *insufficiently serious* to justify risking the widespread misery and social upheaval that could be expected to flow from active or revolutionary resistance to the state (or to states generally).[54]

The philosophical anarchist, then, stands apart from the brick, bottle, or bomb throwing of the political anarchist.

Setting aside the Lockean foundation of Simmons's argument, there is a problem here that I have hinted at by twice using italics when quoting from his response to Wellman. As these passages indicate, Simmons believes that the state does wrong when it prevents others from threatening or punishing rapists, murderers, and the like, but this is not a *"serious moral wrong."* The wrong it does, however, when it extends "the law's requirements beyond those actions that we also have independent moral reasons to perform" is a serious wrong, but "in normal circumstances in decent states, *insufficiently serious*" to warrant "active or revolutionary resistance to the state (or to states generally)."[55] On its face, this language seems to suggest that there is a significant difference of degree between philosophical and political anarchists; while the latter are ready to regard any transgression as good reason to call for the abolition of the state, the former will do so only when those transgressions are grave and systematic, like the wrongs done by a master to a slave. But we should also notice the implicit concession that states perform valuable services, at least "in normal circumstances in decent states." Nor is there any suggestion that we could do better, or even as well, in dealing with rapists, murderers, and other wrongdoers if we were to abolish the state. If philosophical anarchists differ from their political counterparts, in other words, it is because they have a certain, perhaps grudging, respect for states and government. Whether they can combine that respect with a refusal

---

[52] Ibid.; emphasis added.
[53] Ibid.
[54] Ibid.; emphasis added.
[55] Ibid.

to acknowledge its authority—even if they stop short of taking up bricks and bottles—is doubtful.

The second and third reasons to be suspicious of philosophical anarchism both relate to its instability.[56] The second reason is that the philosophical anarchists' denial of political obligation will have a corrosive effect on the state's perceived authority—an effect that they both do and do not want to achieve.[57] That is, they want us to obey the law, at least most of the time, on the grounds that the law often forbids us to do what we have independent moral reasons for not doing—committing murder and assault, for example—and because people develop reasonable expectations about how to conduct their lives based on traffic regulations and other laws. Yet they also want us to recognize that the law as such has no authority over us. This is tantamount to pointing out that the emperor has no clothes while hoping that the people so informed will not mock or scorn him. Whether the skepticism they want us to adopt is compatible in the long run with the general obedience to the law they appear to approve is, once again, doubtful. Simmons argues that the likely outcome of this skepticism is a properly chastened and "less statelike" state, but it looks to others as if the widespread adoption of philosophical anarchism must weaken the state more drastically than these anarchists themselves desire.[58] As one critic remarks, a "democratic state can only be vitiated by popular doubts about its right to exist, and a weakened state is to that extent less able to do what only it can do, for example, protect the weak and the meek against the strong and loud."[59]

Let us grant, however, that the philosophical anarchists can accomplish the trick of undermining the state's perceived authority without rendering it ineffective. Even so, the third reason for suspicion remains. Assuming that the adoption of philosophical anarchism would not produce rampant disobedience, it would still have the effect of diminishing the polity and denigrating public service. The spread of this attitude among people who are supposedly self-governing poses two dangers. On the one hand, if everyone becomes a philosophical anarchist, there will be no one left to make the decisions and do the governing. On the other (and more likely) hand, if too many stand on the sidelines, government

---

[56] This and the next paragraph draw on my "Individualism and the Claims of Community," in *Contemporary Debates in Political Philosophy*, ed. Thomas Christiano and John Christman (Malden, MA: Wiley-Blackwell, 2009), p. 310.

[57] On this point, see Thomas Senor, "What If There Are No Political Obligations?," *Philosophy and Public Affairs* 16 (1987): 260–68, and Simmons, "The Anarchist Position: A Reply to Klosko and Senor," *Philosophy and Public Affairs* 16 (1987): 269–79. For a related criticism, see Horton, *Political Obligation*, p. 133.

[58] Simmons, "Philosophical Anarchism," in Simmons, *Justification and Legitimacy*, p. 118.

[59] Edmundson, *Three Anarchical Fallacies*, p. 1.

either will become so weak as to lose its ability to perform the useful duties that even the philosophical anarchists want it to perform, or it will fall into the hands of those who are all too eager to claim authority and wield power over the rest of us. Philosophical anarchism, in sum, appears to foster the insidious kind of individualism that Tocqueville deplored insofar as it encourages people to leave "the greater society to look after itself."[60] The result, as Tocqueville warned, is likely to be despotism, whether of a soft or hard form. In either case, the result will not be one that pleases anarchists—and certainly not anarchists of the philosophical kind.

There are reasons, then, to be suspicious of philosophical anarchism, including reasons that are grounded in the premises of philosophical anarchism itself. There are also reasons to reject the *a priori* form of philosophical anarchism outright, as I have argued. In fact, Simmons agrees that Wolff's *a priori* argument is a "failed attempt."[61] If we are to take the case against the *a posteriori* form of philosophical anarchism to its conclusion, however, it will be necessary to do more than raise suspicions about it. It will be necessary to prove it wrong by developing a satisfactory account of political obligation. That, indeed, will be the best response to any version of the anarchist challenge.

Conclusion

In the next three chapters I try to show that an account of political obligation grounded in the principle of fair play can withstand the criticisms of both philosophical anarchists and advocates of other theories of political obligation. If successful, I will have met not only the challenges of the political and *a priori* philosophical anarchists, but also that of the *a posteriori* school of philosophical anarchism. There is a further challenge to address, however, in the form of philosophers who raise conceptual considerations I have yet to take into account. According to these philosophers, the philosophical anarchists are right when they argue that there is no general obligation to obey the law, even within a reasonably just polity, but wrong to conclude that states necessarily lack authority or legitimacy.

This position, which occupies a kind of middle ground between philosophical anarchism and the traditional understanding of political authority and obligation, is mistaken, in my view, and it will be necessary to explain why. But that

---

[60] Alexis de Tocqueville, *Democracy in America*, trans. George Lawrence, ed. J. P. Mayer (Garden City, NY: Doubleday, 1969), p. 506.

[61] Simmons, "Philosophical Anarchism," in Simmons, *Justification and Legitimacy*, p. 111.

is a task that need not be taken up quite yet. Instead, I shall make the case for the fair-play theory of political obligation in the next three chapters, and follow that with a defense of the fair-play justification of punishment in Part II. Then in Part III, with a fully developed account of fair play as the grounding principle for both political obligation and punishment at hand, I shall take up this final challenge.

2

Fair Play and Cooperative Practices

As children are quick to learn, cooperative activities often give rise to questions of fairness. Indeed, complaints of unfair treatment and criticisms of those who fail to play fair are among the first signs that children are developing moral sensibilities. Such complaints and criticisms also suggest that a concern for fairness is one of the most basic and widely shared of moral intuitions. It should be no surprise, then, to find such a concern manifested in philosophical thinking about authority, punishment, and political obligation. Where exactly that concern should lead us is the subject of this chapter.

The topic is neither a new nor a neglected one. A hint of an argument from fairness or fair play appears as long ago as Plato's *Crito*, when Socrates asks Crito (50a), "if we leave here without the city's permission, are we mistreating people whom we should least mistreat?"[1] Explicit references to "the principle of fairness" and "the argument from fairness" are at least as old as C. D. Broad's 1916 essay "On the Function of False Hypotheses in Ethics."[2] Political obligation was not one of Broad's concerns, but it was certainly one of H. L. A. Hart's in his influential 1955 essay, "Are There Any Natural Rights?," and the argument he advanced there is usually taken to be the opening statement of the fair-play approach to political obligation. The core of the argument, as Hart puts it, is this: "when a number of persons conduct any joint enterprise according to rules and thus restrict their liberty, those who have submitted to these restrictions when required have a right to a similar submission from those who have benefited by their submission."[3] Hart's argument has not met with universal approval, of course, but it clearly has caught the attention of many political philosophers. According to one commentator's list, more than fifty items touching on the fair-play approach

---

[1] Plato, *The Trial and Death of Socrates*, 3rd ed., trans. G. M. A. Grube (Indianapolis, IN: Hackett Publishing, 2000), p. 50.

[2] Broad, "On the Function of False Hypotheses in Ethics," *International Journal of Ethics* 26 (1916): 377–97.

[3] Hart, "Are There Any Natural Rights?," *Philosophical Review* 64 (1955): 185.

to political obligation appeared in print between 1955 and 1999.[4] Included in that list is one full-length work, George Klosko's *The Principle of Fairness and Political Obligation*.[5] Nor has the fairness account of political obligation lacked for attention in the early years of the twenty-first century, as a bibliographical search will soon reveal. Fair-play arguments for political obligation are vigorously contested, to be sure, but hardly neglected.

Even so, something has been lacking in the various criticisms and defenses of the fair-play account. What I have in mind here is close attention to some of the fundamental elements of this account, most notably the related concepts of fair play and of a cooperative practice. Perhaps because fairness and cooperation are such basic features of widely shared moral intuitions, commentators seem to presume that little needs to be said about them. There is groundwork to be done here, however, if the case for the fair-play theory of political obligation is to be properly stated. Establishing this groundwork is the business of this chapter, beginning with the little-noted distinction between *fairness* and *fair play*.

Fairness or Fair Play?

Hart's appeal to what he called "mutuality of restrictions" may have been the first attempt to argue for fair play as a distinct basis for political obligation, but John Rawls's "Legal Obligation and the Duty of Fair Play" provided, a few years later, a more fully developed statement of the principle at work. According to Rawls,

> The principle of fair play may be defined as follows. Suppose there is a mutually beneficial and just scheme of social cooperation, and that the advantages it yields can only be obtained if everyone, or nearly everyone, cooperates. Suppose further that cooperation requires a certain sacrifice from each person, or at least involves a certain restriction of his liberty. Suppose finally that the benefits produced by cooperation are, up to a certain point, free: that is, the scheme of cooperation is unstable in the sense that if any one person knows that all (or nearly all) of the others will continue to do their part, he will still be able to share a gain from the scheme even if he does not do his part. Under these conditions a person who has accepted the benefits of the scheme is

---

[4] Govert den Hartogh, *Mutual Expectations: A Conventionalist Theory of Law* (Dordrecht, The Netherlands: Kluwer Law International, 2002), p. 81, n. 64.

[5] Klosko, *The Principle of Fairness and Political Obligation* (Lanham, MD: Rowman & Littlefield, 1992); reissued with a new introduction in 2004.

bound by a duty of fair play to do his part and not to take advantage of the free benefit by not cooperating.[6]

Rawls's statement is important, and worth quoting at length, for at least three reasons. The first is that it identifies clearly the main elements of the argument from fair play. Nowadays we are more likely to talk about collective-action problems and free riders than "unstable" schemes of cooperation, but the point remains the same. The statement is also important because, as I noted in the introductory chapter, Rawls subsequently backed away from the fair-play theory of the obligation to obey the law. And it is important, finally, for another change that Rawls introduced when he published *A Theory of Justice* in 1971. This is not a change that Rawls called to his readers' attention, and it may not even have been a change that he was aware of making. Nevertheless, there is some significance, I think, to the fact that "the principle of fair play" of his 1964 essay became "the principle of fairness" in §§18 and 19 of *A Theory of Justice*.

How much significance there is to this shift from "fair play" to "fairness" is difficult to determine. On the one hand, if someone as careful and self-conscious in his use of terms as Rawls saw no need to mark a difference between the two, then perhaps we should conclude that there is no difference worth marking. The fact that Klosko, the leading proponent of the principle's application to political obligation, writes consistently of the principle of "fairness" rather than "fair play" tends to reinforce the point. On the other hand, it is not hard to find examples where one of the two terms is appropriate and the other is not. This is particularly true in the case of cooperative practices, where the term "fair play" is clearly at home.

To appreciate this point, one need only consider some cases where talk of fair play is out of place. Anyone who is required to pass judgment on the conduct or achievements of others may find herself in a position where the *fairness* of her judgments is called into question, yet it would be odd indeed for her to be accused of not *playing fair*. An unhappy student may accuse a teacher of grading his work unfairly, for example, but only in unusual circumstances would it make sense for the student to claim that the teacher has not played fair with him. In the ordinary course of events, the two are not engaged in a cooperative practice

---

[6] Rawls, "Legal Obligation and the Duty of Fair Play," in *Law and Philosophy*, ed. Sidney Hook (New York: New York University Press, 1964), pp. 9–10. See also Rawls, *A Theory of Justice*, revised ed. (Cambridge, MA: Harvard University Press, 1999), p. 96: "The main idea is that when a number of persons engage in a mutually advantageous cooperative venture according to rules, and thus restrict their liberty in ways necessary to yield advantages for all, those who have submitted to these restrictions have a right to a similar acquiescence on the part of those who have benefited from their submission."

in which student and teacher are co-participants. There may be respects in which the student is engaged in a cooperative practice with his classmates, and is thus in a position to ride free on their efforts, but those considerations are not typically involved in the teacher's grading of his work. There may also be respects in which the teacher is open to complaints of not playing fair, but these complaints are likely to come from other teachers, who may believe that she is not bearing her fair share of the burdens in their school. Where the grading of her students is concerned, though, the teacher's duty is to treat them fairly according to the merits of their work, not to play fair with them. The same is true of judges in courts of law, in pie-eating contests, and in gymnastic competitions, among many other examples.

A similar point holds with regard to parents and children. When they have more than one child, parents frequently find themselves worrying about whether they are treating each child fairly. If Johnny has ten friends over for his birthday party, do they have to make sure that Janie has no more than ten for hers? If Janie is allowed to go to a movie with her friends, should Johnny be allowed to go to another movie with his (perhaps less trustworthy) friends? In these and many other instances considerations of fairness clearly arise, but not considerations of fair play. To be sure, there may be occasions in which it makes sense to think of the family as a cooperative practice—when they are gathered around the table or video console playing a game, for example—and there will be many more when the siblings will be involved in a cooperative activity with one another. In those circumstances it is appropriate to talk of fair and unfair play. But it is not appropriate to think that parents have a general duty of *fair play* to their children, no matter how important it is for them to treat their children fairly.

A third example of the importance of the distinction between fairness and fair play concerns the question of what is sometimes called "cosmic fairness." Why must some people suffer one setback after another when others seem to have every good thing that life can offer? Why do some live to a happy old age when others are afflicted with physical or mental burdens from the moment of birth? How can such disparities be fair? To this last question there are various answers, one of which is that fairness is not something we should expect from the cosmos. Another is that God has purposes that we can neither grasp nor compass with our ideas of fairness. Whatever the merits of these answers, they at least speak to the question in a way that an appeal to fair play cannot. For how can we conceive of the cosmos as a cooperative practice that is open to collective-action problems and free riding? God may be in charge of things, but we certainly cannot regard God as a co-participant, on an equal footing with us, in the great game of life. If we believe that God is in charge, in other words, we may have reason to search for the fairness that lies beneath the apparent unfairness of life, but no reason to expect God or the cosmos to play fair with us.

A final set of examples arises whenever there appears to be a discrepancy between fairness and fair play. Two cases in point are the presidential elections of 2000 and 2016 in the United States, when Al Gore and Hillary Rodham Clinton respectively won the popular vote—by a margin of nearly 3 million votes in Clinton's case—yet lost to candidates who obtained a majority of the votes within the electoral college as required by the US Constitution.[7] Were these outcomes, as many asked at the time, fair ones? A common reply to the question was "yes and no." That is, "yes" because one could hold that the election of George W. Bush in 2000 and that of Donald Trump in 2016 were proper or fair within the rules that governed the election; but "no" because one could also hold that the rules themselves were unfair. As the example illustrates, fair play occurs within or under the rules of a cooperative practice, and it does not settle the question of whether the rules of the practice are as they should be. The same point emerges from similar examples in games and sports, such as the lawsuit instigated by a professional golfer, Casey Martin, whose congenital leg disease made it virtually necessary for him to use a golf cart while playing.[8] Under the rules of the Professional Golfers' Association, however, competitors in PGA Tour events were required to walk from one hole to another during tournaments. Martin's complaint, then, was not that the other golfers were not playing fair with him, since the others were abiding by the rules; it was that the rule banning the use of golf carts was not fair to him and others in similar circumstances.

Whether she intended to do so or not, Shirley Jackson provided an especially striking example of the possible discrepancy between fairness and fair play in her widely read short story, "The Lottery."[9] In the story Jackson depicts a group of villagers who assemble to carry out a longstanding ritual. As she gradually reveals, the ritual involves an annual drawing to select one villager to be stoned to death by the others. At the end of the story Tessie Hutchinson, the woman whose name is drawn from the lottery box, is screaming "it isn't fair," and "it isn't fair, it isn't right," while her neighbors are pelting her with stones. But is Tessie right? As Jackson tells the story, there is no reason to think that anyone has rigged the lottery; nor is there any reason to think that Tessie herself refused to join in the stoning in previous years or made any effort to alter or abolish the ritual. From the standpoint of fair play, in fact, it seems that Tessie has no grounds for complaint. If she is right when she screams "it isn't fair," she is right because the

---

[7] I set aside here the complications arising from the conduct of the election in Florida 2000 and from the subsequent decision of the Supreme Court in the case of *Gore v. Bush* (2000), as I also do with regard to the various complaints about the fairness of the campaigns in 2016.

[8] *PGA Tour, Inc. v. Martin* (2000). For an interesting discussion of this case, see Michael Sandel, *Justice: What's the Right Thing to Do?* (New York: Farrar, Straus & Giroux, 2009), chap. 8.

[9] Jackson, "The Lottery," *The New Yorker* (June 16, 1948): 25–28.

ritual itself is in some way unfair. If there is unfairness here, the unfairness lies in the misguided nature of the practice, not in the failure of the participants to play fair.

Jackson's story could be embarrassing for proponents of fair-play theory, for reasons to be discussed later in this chapter. For the present, though, I take it that "The Lottery" and the preceding examples are enough to establish that there is a distinction of some significance between fairness and fair play. Fairness is the broader term, as I see it, with fair play having a narrower range of application. Fair play has its place *within* those "mutually beneficial and just scheme[s] of social cooperation" to which Rawls refers, including political society itself. That is why I believe it makes sense to ground political obligation in the principle of *fair play*. Whether a scheme truly is "mutually beneficial and just" is thus a matter of both fairness and fair play. But these are points that require elaboration, and the elaboration begins with a closer look at the contexts in which considerations of fair play most often arise.

Most of us, I suspect, first learn about fair play in the context of games. One of the first things we learn, even in such simple games as tag and hide-and-seek, is that "turnabout is fair play." Unpacking those four words reveals several important features of fair play. One is that these games involve rules of some sort, even if they are nothing more than informal norms. Another is reciprocity. If you are to enjoy the playing of the game, you must be willing to abide by the rules so that the others can enjoy it too. Solitaire is an exception, of course, but in the great majority of games reciprocity is required. If I have the first move in checkers, then I must wait for you to make the second, and you for me to make the third. Reciprocity, moreover, brings rights and duties into the picture, for reciprocity is what we owe to one another as participants in the game. If I have a right to a turn at bat in a softball game, then you and the other players have a duty to allow me that turn; but I also have a duty to respect your right to bat when your turn comes. "Turnabout is fair play" even involves a sense of equality. This is not equal skill, of course, for some will be much better at any game than others are. Every participant has equal standing simply as a player of the game, though, with the rules applying equally to all. If the rules themselves seem to put some of the players at an advantage or disadvantage, then the standard of equal treatment may lead some to call for a change in the rules. But this, as I have argued, takes us from fair play, strictly construed, into the broader realm of fairness.

There are two further points to spell out here, with the first being implicit in the preceding remarks. That is, understood as a duty, fair play is something owed to other persons. I may sometimes worry that I am not treating one of my dogs fairly when I give the other more attention or more food, but this is not a matter of fair or unfair play. Fair play presupposes that the participants in a cooperative practice have certain abilities, such as the ability to grasp and follow rules, to make choices, and to understand the point of reciprocity, and these are abilities that we find only in persons. Like fairness more broadly, in other words, fair play is grounded in respect for persons. There is even a sense in which fair play helps to reinforce respect for persons by cultivating this respect among those who learn, usually as children, the value of fair play. It is true that athletes sometimes talk about the importance of "respecting the game," but that seems to be an elliptical way of talking about respect for those people who play the game, including those who played it in the past and those who will play it in the future.

The final point concerns the relationship of fair play to morality. On this point I disagree with Craig Carr, who sees an ambiguity in the concept of fair play—and, indeed, in the concept of fairness generally, which Carr does not distinguish from fair play as I have done.[10] According to Carr, the ambiguity obscures the difference between a generic notion of fairness that does not involve moral considerations and a "more specific one" that does.[11] Comments about "fair weather" and someone's "fair hair" or "fair complexion" exemplify the former, while objections to "unfair grading" and praise of someone's "commitment to fairness" are instances of the latter. From this point Carr goes on to draw a related distinction between two kinds of fair play: "Sometimes it refers to proper or appropriate play (fairness in the general sense), and sometimes it indicates a certain commitment to the spirit of competition, a concern not to cheat, and so forth."[12] But here is where I take issue with Carr's analysis. "In the first instance," he says, "fair play can be juxtaposed with something like 'foul play,' where deviations from the standards of fair play constitute a foul or breach of the rules."[13] This seems to me to confuse "foul play" with "poor" or "unsuccessful" play. To accuse someone of foul play is to accuse him not of a poor or clumsy performance but of acting wrongfully. It is true, as Carr points out, that a breach of the rules of a game is often called a foul, and basketball players frequently commit fouls even when they are doing their best to stay within the rules. There are even occasions in which one player will intentionally foul another, and perhaps be told to do so by her coach, in order to prevent the opponents from scoring easily. But these fouls are usually either inadvertent, in the case of ordinary fouls, or acceptable tactics within the game. They are not examples of foul play. When the intentional foul goes too far, however, to the point where it poses a threat of physical injury to an opponent, it becomes a "flagrant foul," and talk of foul

---

[10] Carr, *On Fairness* (Burlington, VT: Ashgate Publishing, 2000), pp. 8–10.
[11] Ibid., p. 9.
[12] Ibid., p. 9.
[13] Ibid., p. 9.

play becomes appropriate. But that is to say that moral criticism or condemnation of the one who commits the flagrant foul is then appropriate. Fair play is always morally correct play, in short, and foul play is never so.[14] An innocent foul is not a violation of fair play.

I do not mean to deny that occasional ambiguities arise when we talk of fair play. If I ask you what kind of bridge player Jones is, and you say in response that he is a "fair player," I may not know at first whether you are commenting on his level of skill or on his ethics. That is merely an ambiguity of expression, though, not an ambiguity in the concept itself. If I ask you whether Jones is someone who is known for fair play, your answer is almost certain to be an assessment of his ethical conduct. Carr is right, in sum, to note that there are both moral and non-moral forms of fairness, but he is wrong to carry that distinction over to fair play. Fair play is always a matter of morality.

If I am right about this final point, then we have yet another reason to draw a distinction between fairness—which has a place in both moral and non-moral contexts—and fair play. But how significant is this distinction? Is it weighty enough to lead us to abandon the term "principle of fairness" in order to replace it with "principle of fair play" in our debates about political obligation? The latter is the better term, in my view, for it draws an immediate connection between the putative obligation and the idea of a cooperative practice. Yet that is not a strong enough reason to reject appeals to the "principle of fairness." To see why, we should consider those cases in which we are likely to have doubts about what counts as fair play. Suppose that the game we are playing includes a mixed group of adults and children. Does fair play require everyone involved to follow the same rules, or does it require adjustments to the rules that will help to "level the playing field" for the young participants? In this and many similar cases, it seems that the desire to play fair leads to more general considerations of fair treatment. Fair play occurs within the rules, as I have said, but the rules are subject to evaluation in terms of their fairness.

So long as we are concerned with political obligation, however, we will be concerned with fair play within cooperative practices. That is why I prefer to speak of the principle of *fair play*. That is also why it is necessary to examine more closely the idea of a cooperative practice.

---

[14] The intricacies of fair and foul play are among the subjects of Tom Stoppard's "Professional Foul," a teleplay published in his *Every Good Boy Deserves Favor and Professional Foul* (New York: Grove Press, 1977). See also the discussion of "the implicit labelling of actions as 'wrongful' by use of the word 'foul,' though fouling is part of what competent players are expected to do," in Kent Greenawalt, *Conflicts of Law and Morality* (Oxford: Oxford University Press, 1987), p. 11.

Cooperative Practices

Whether we refer to it as fairness or fair play, the principle in question clearly does not apply in all times and circumstances. Masters and slaves are not bound to one another by duties of fairness, nor do the victims of exploitation in general owe a duty of fair play to those who exploit them. The same point applies, even in the case of benign enterprises, when the relationship between insiders and outsiders comes into question. If a group of people form two teams to play volleyball, the players will have a duty of fair play to one another. If someone wandering by asks to join the game, however, fairness need not enter into the players' response. There may be unusual circumstances in which it does, as the players may discover when they learn that the stranger who wants to join the game is a fellow participant in the group that maintains the park in which they are playing. Because she is related to them in a larger cooperative practice within which their volleyball game is nested, fairness to her becomes an appropriate consideration. If she is a complete and unconnected stranger, though, the moral principles the players should take into account when weighing her request—hospitality, the Golden Rule, utility, and perhaps others—will not include fairness or fair play. Considerations of fairness or fair play are of great import when and where they do apply, but they do not exhaust the moral universe.

Where fair play does apply, as already noted, is within cooperative practices: joint enterprises according to rules, in Hart's terms. Failure to appreciate this point led to one of the earliest and most sweeping criticisms of the principle. This is the criticism Robert Nozick advanced in *Anarchy, State, and Utopia* when he argued that the principle of fair play implies that others can place us under obligations to them simply by conferring benefits on us. Someone who sweeps the sidewalk in front of my house or throws desirable books through my open window without asking my consent is providing a benefit to me and, according to the principle, apparently placing me under a duty of fair play to reciprocate in some way. But to say this, Nozick charged, is to say that others may foist obligations on us, which is contrary to our usual understanding of obligation. As Nozick concluded, "You may not decide to give me something ... and then grab money from me to pay for it, even if I have nothing better to spend the money on."[15]

Nozick's conclusion is surely correct, but it is beside the point. Neither Hart nor Rawls nor any other advocate of the principle has held that fair play requires us to reciprocate whenever someone does something to our benefit; it applies only to the benefits of a cooperative practice. Nozick has another criticism that

---

[15] Nozick, *Anarchy, State, and Utopia* (New York: Basic Books, 1974), p. 95.

comes closer to the mark, to be sure, and I shall respond to it in Chapter 5. At this point, though, it is necessary to look more closely at the elements of cooperative practices.

A convenient starting place is Klosko's set of "five main factors upon which the principle [of fairness] depends." These are:

1. the existence of a joint venture or cooperative scheme;
2. that cooperative effort coordinated by rules produces benefits for those who cooperate;
3. that cooperation requires submission to various restrictions and is therefore burdensome for the cooperators;
4. that the cooperation of some (generally most) but not all individuals is required to produce the benefits, and so there is a distinction between individuals who submit to the necessary restrictions and others, noncooperators, who do not;
5. that the noncooperators also receive benefits from the cooperative effort.[16]

The first factor Klosko identifies is important for two closely related reasons. One is that not all instances of cooperation involve joint ventures or cooperative schemes. Two strangers who help to push another's car out of a snow drift are cooperating while they are pushing, but they are not participating in a cooperative practice. They may accept the stranded motorist's thanks, and perhaps some money or other reward, when they have pushed the car onto the road, but they may go their own ways afterward and never see each other, or the motorist, again. There may be complaints of unfairness, of course, if one does almost all the pushing while the other accepts an equal share of the thanks, but neither of the helpers owes a duty of fair play to the other, or to the motorist, save in unusual circumstances. In one such circumstance the two might turn out to be members of a roadside-assistance cooperative, in which case considerations of fair play surely would apply. But in that case, they are clearly members of a cooperative practice rather than two strangers who happen to be good Samaritans. As the example indicates—and this is the second important point embedded in Klosko's first factor—joint ventures and cooperative schemes are or have been *ongoing*. There is no point to talking about joint enterprises *according to rules*, as Hart does, if the cooperation in question occurs only on a single occasion with no expectation of further cooperation in the future.

---

[16] Klosko, *The Principle of Fairness and Political Obligation*, p. 34. Cf. the similar list in den Hartogh, *Mutual Expectations*, pp. 80–81.

A possible exception is the group of people who find themselves in a pub following several vigorous volleyball matches. One pays for the first round of drinks, another pays for the second, and so on. What will the contributors say, at the end of the evening, if the only person not to have bought a round thanks them for the drinks and prepares to leave? No doubt they will accuse him of taking unfair advantage of them. But if this is the first time they have followed their volleyball games with a trip to a pub, and if no future trips of this kind have been planned, then my analysis seems to fail: either the contributors will be unreasonable to accuse the non-contributor of unfairness—which seems unlikely—or it is wrong to insist that a cooperative practice must be an ongoing activity or scheme. I do not think the analysis is wrong, however, even though I believe that those who have bought rounds are right to complain of the unfairness of the one who has not (and who has not "done his part" in some other way). The cooperative activity in question may not have a long history or a clear future, but there is enough of a pattern of interaction to regard it as sufficiently ongoing or extended. To begin with, all of the people in the example came to the pub from the volleyball court, so it is reasonable to regard their round-buying as an extension of their earlier cooperative activity. Moreover, their interaction at the pub suggests the possibility of future interactions of this sort following future volleyball matches. And there is, finally, the broader pattern of social interactions and expectations that teach us that "turnabout is fair play."[17] If such considerations are not enough to lead the person who drinks at others' expense to conclude that he has a duty of fair play toward the others, then we should expect that he will not be welcome to join in their future trips to the pub.

The principle of fair play has its point, then, when cooperation is an essential element in an ongoing practice. Such practices must produce benefits, as Klosko's second factor indicates, as a result of cooperation under rules that serve to coordinate the activities of the cooperators. Some enterprises will be small enough to make a success of cooperation without the kinds of rules that govern volleyball, chess, and legal systems, but they will rely on informal norms or understandings that are easily communicated. "You do your part, I'll do mine, and no shirking" will be sufficient when it is easy to see what one's part is. When it is not, something more formal—including someone with the authority to hand down rulings—will be necessary. Formal or informal, though, the production of benefits is a necessary feature of a cooperative practice. Whether the benefits of participating in such a practice must always outweigh the burdens is a question I take up in Chapter 5, but it is clear that no one has a duty of fair

---

[17] For a defense of the fair-play theory of political obligation that places special emphasis on the role of expectations, see den Hartogh, *Mutual Expectations*, chaps. 4 and 5.

play to contribute to a practice that neither provides nor has provided her with any benefits at all. Nor is there a point to a practice that produces no benefits for anyone. At worst we should expect a cooperative endeavor to satisfy the lesser-of-evils criterion. If our cooperation will leave us all in a bad way, in other words, we may still regard the endeavor as mutually beneficial as long as it prevents us from sinking into an even worse condition. If we will be better off without cooperation, however, and with everyone striking out on her own, we have no duty to cooperate—and no right to insist on the cooperation of the others.

The same point holds, paradoxically, with regard to burdens. If a cooperative activity produces nothing but benefits for its participants, considerations of fairness simply will not arise. If the members of a string quartet want nothing more than to play Mozart's Clarinet Quintet in A Major superbly, and they find a capable clarinetist who shares this desire, the five musicians will need to cooperate with one another to accomplish their shared aim. Because they want nothing more than to play this piece superbly, all five will be fully committed to doing whatever is necessary, even if that requires everyone working to the full extent of his or her talent and time. Nor will any of them regard this effort as burdensome, for all regard the practice and preparation as either enjoyable in itself or part and parcel of the ultimate benefit. In these circumstances, the principle of fair play has no part to play.

But these are rare circumstances indeed, at least among ongoing endeavors. In this case the musicians would require full agreement as to when and where to practice, who is to play first and who second violin, whose interpretation of tempo, tone, and dynamics is to govern, and so on. Burdens of some sort almost inevitably appear, even if they are nothing more than relatively painless restrictions of one's liberty. That is why Klosko rightly takes "submission to various restrictions" to be the third of the main factors involved in the principle of fairness.[18]

Concerning Klosko's fourth and fifth "main factors," little comment is necessary. The point of both factors is that the principle of fair play only applies to cooperative enterprises that pose potential collective-action problems. If *everyone* involved in the enterprise must contribute fully to its success, none of them has the opportunity to be a free rider. To be sure, they may quarrel over the fair distribution of the proceeds of their enterprise, with those who think themselves

---

[18] Another way to put this point is to say that the production of the benefits of a cooperative practice must be *costly*. For explorations of this point in the context of the possible application of the principle of fair play to public responsibility for children, see Paula Casal and Andrew Williams, "Equality of Resources and Procreative Justice," in *Dworkin and His Critics*, ed. J. Burley (Oxford: Blackwell Publishing, 2004), esp. pp. 156–59, and Serena Olsaretti, "Children as Public Goods?," *Philosophy and Public Affairs* 41 (Summer 2013), esp. pp. 239–47.

more talented or more experienced perhaps maintaining that they deserve a larger share than those who worked as hard but to less effect. As Hart's and Rawls's formulations indicate, however, the principle of fair play pertains not to divisible benefits but to *public* or *collective goods*—that is, goods that are indivisible, non-excludable, and non-rival, in the sense that one person's consumption of the good does not deprive another of an equal opportunity to consume it. Such goods, of course, are not likely to require universal cooperation to produce, as the classic examples of national defense and clean air make clear. They are, instead, the kind that noncooperators may enjoy every bit as much as those whose cooperative efforts produce the good in question. The noncooperators thus will enjoy the benefits as long as enough people cooperate to produce the good. In cases of this sort, as Rawls says, "a person who has accepted the benefits of the scheme is bound by a duty of fair play to do his part and not to take advantage of the free benefit by not cooperating."[19]

How far this principle extends and what counts as having "accepted the benefits of the scheme" are questions to be taken up in Chapter 5. At this point two other questions about the nature of cooperative practices need attention. John Horton raises both of them when he criticizes fair-play theory in his *Political Obligation*, and I shall address the first here and the second in the next section of this chapter.

Horton's first question is "what is meant by a scheme of social cooperation?"[20] What I have previously said in this chapter should go some way toward answering this question, but I have yet to speak to Horton's particular concern. There are obvious examples of social cooperation, he acknowledges, but there are also difficult cases where cooperation and competition are intermixed. For example, "are two teams playing football against each other engaged in a scheme of social cooperation? Or, are two firms in a competitive market, both trading legally, but each trying to drive the other out of business, engaged in a scheme of social cooperation?"[21]

The answer to both questions, in my view, is yes. In fact, an element of competition is often involved in cooperative practices. Not only is there competition between two football teams and two firms in a market, as Horton indicates, but there usually will be competition within each team and each firm. There is likely to be competition for a position on the team or with the firm, to begin with, and then competition for preferred positions among those selected for the team or firm. If the team or the firm is to succeed, however, this competition must take place within, and be governed by the spirit of, a cooperative enterprise. Much

---

[19] Rawls, "Legal Obligation and the Duty of Fair Play," p. 10.
[20] Horton, *Political Obligation*, p. 90.
[21] Ibid.

the same holds with regard to competition between two teams and two firms. In the case of the football teams, their competition will be pointless—that is, it will not be competition for victory in football—if they do not see themselves as being engaged in a "joint enterprise according to rules," to use Hart's terms. It is true that athletes and their coaches will sometimes stretch or break the rules to gain a victory or an advantage, but that is why umpires, referees, and other arbiters are necessary to the play of the game. It is also why appeals to fair play and "sportsmanship" are so common. Those who cheat are in effect trying to ride free on the cooperative efforts of those whose fair play makes the game a meaningful activity.[22]

The same is true of firms competing in the marketplace. However hard they work to increase their profits and share of the market, even to the point of driving competitors out of business, commercial firms are nevertheless subject to standards of fair play. The use of force and fraud are forbidden, and other activities, such as collusion, are at least discouraged. The marketplace must be a cooperative practice, in other words, subject to rules and Hart's "mutuality of restrictions," if it is to be something other than a no-holds-barred competition for wealth and power.[23]

These affirmative responses to Horton's questions about football teams and economic firms, however, are not enough to allay his concerns about the vagueness of the concept of a cooperative practice. As he points out, we might say that two competing firms are engaged in a cooperative practice under law, and even note their "mutual respect for the law," but we "might equally say that two states at war, if they are scrupulous in observing the various conventions and rules of war, are also engaged in a cooperative scheme. War [though] is not mutually beneficial to the two states, and nor, necessarily, is a competitive market to the two firms."[24] If cooperative practices must be mutually

---

[22] It may be more accurate to say that the cheater is trying to be a *parasite* rather than a free rider. That is, the cheater is not only trying to take advantage of those who abide by the rules; he is also trying to *gain an advantage* on them. If he is successful, in other words, the cheater's actions will serve to worsen the situation of his opponent(s) in the game, and that is what distinguishes parasites from free riders, whose actions do not directly worsen the situation of others. On this point, see David Gauthier, *Morals by Agreement* (Oxford: Oxford University Press, 1987), p. 96. In my example, however, the cheater's situation is complicated in two ways. First, his cheating may not worsen the situation of his rule-following teammates; and second, his cheating may fail to worsen the situation of his opponents, who may win despite his violation of the rules. In these cases, it seems proper to refer to him as a free rider.

[23] For a related point about the importance of "the cooperative practice of honest dealing" to "a successful market economy," see Richard Arneson, "Paternalism and the Principle of Fairness," in *Paternalism: Theory and Practice* (Cambridge, UK: Cambridge University Press, 2013), p. 139. For insightful comments on the cooperative aspects of athletic competition that bear on fair-play theory, see Edward Song, "Acceptance, Fairness, and Political Obligation," *Legal Theory* 18 (2012): 216–18.

[24] Horton, *Political Obligation*, p. 90.

beneficial, as they must according to Rawls's definition, then it is difficult to see how competing firms and warring states could be engaged in schemes of social cooperation.

Horton here poses an important challenge to fair-play theory. He is, in effect, all but denying that it is reasonable to regard any kind of extensive social practice—anything more extensive than the crew of a ship, the members of a club, and other forms of small-scale cooperation—as an instance of a cooperative practice. He is certainly casting doubt on the reasonableness of holding a political society under the rule of law to be such a practice. As he says, "so much of politics is about coercion and the threat of coercion, about managing fundamental conflicts of value and interest, that it sits uneasily with what appears to be an overly comfortable and optimistic conception of political relations as a scheme of social cooperation."[25]

This complaint—that it is not reasonable to regard a political society as a cooperative endeavor—is perhaps the most formidable objection to the fair-play account of political obligation. I shall return to it in Chapter 5, with particular attention to M. B. E. Smith's and John Simmons's statements of the objection. I can make a beginning here, however, with three points about the nature of cooperative practices.

The first point is that cooperative practices are multiform. They come in various sizes and shapes, from a few people playing a game to sprawling political systems, including schemes of international cooperation. They include groups in which the cooperation is manifest and groups in which cooperation is neither readily apparent nor the most important feature of the practice. A church congregation often will be a cooperative practice, for example, but the congregants' shared faith should be more important to their conception of the practice than its cooperative nature. Cooperative practices also may be in conflict with one another, so that someone may find what she owes as fair play to the members of her sports team to be incompatible with what she owes to her business partners. It is also likely that some cooperative practices will fit or nest within others, as in the earlier example of the volleyball players who are also members of a group that cooperates to maintain the park in which they play. Because cooperative practices are multiform in these ways, the degree to which we think of them as cooperative, competitive, coercive, or something else will vary significantly from one practice to another. In the case of a tennis tournament, competition is the dominant factor even though the tournament cannot proceed without a significant degree of cooperation among the players, officials, and organizers. In the marketplace, we tend to see cooperation as being more important within firms and competition as more important between or among them. Nor is this way of

[25] Ibid., p. 91.

thinking unreasonable. But it is also necessary to understand that the economic competition is itself nested within the framework of a legal system that makes fair competition possible. That legal system, I contend, should itself be regarded as a cooperative practice.

My second point concerns the mutually beneficial nature of cooperative endeavors. It is indeed hard to see how all parties benefit from economic competition when one drives another out of business, as Horton points out. But the difficulty of seeing the mutual benefit does not mean that it is not there. Athletes can enjoy neither the prospect nor the triumph of victories and championships— nor the intrinsic pleasure of playing the game—unless they are participating in one of Hart's joint enterprises according to rules. As for professional athletes, their salaries and endorsement contracts are benefits they could not receive but for the cooperative nature of their sports leagues and associations. At worst, moreover, cooperative practices produce mutual benefits in the lesser-of-evils sense I alluded to earlier. Being driven out of business is no doubt painful, but it is better to be driven out of business in fair competition than by force or fraud. It is certainly better to try to make a go of a business when the rule of law is in force than when it is not. These points may be hard to grasp when the law seems to be primarily coercive, but that coercive threat is itself necessary to make fair competition possible. And that coercive threat, under the rule of law, is itself grounded in law as a cooperative, and mutually beneficial, practice.

The third and final point concerns the critical, aspirational element of fair-play theory. The theory neither claims that all joint enterprises according to rules are perfect embodiments of cooperation nor that they must be. That is because cooperative practice—like city, plumber, and many others—is a threshold concept. Someone who picks up a musical instrument must be able to play more than a few simple tunes before she has a claim to being a musician, but she can be worthy of that designation even if she falls far short of virtuosity. In the same way a scheme needs to be something more than a Hobbesian state of nature or free-for-all before we can call it a cooperative practice, but it need not achieve the ideal of altruistic devotion or selfless commitment to the common good. In those circumstances, after all, there would be no work for the principle of fair play to do. Once there is sufficient cooperation to take it across a vague and contestable threshold, however, we may reasonably think of a scheme or endeavor as a cooperative practice. But we may also think of it as a cooperative practice that stands in need of improvement because it falls short of what it could and should be. That is the critical, aspirational element of the idea of a cooperative practice.

Whether the cooperative threshold has been crossed is, as I have said, contestable. Critics of capitalism will no doubt complain that talk of fair competition in the marketplace is misplaced, and they will object even more strenuously to the claim that capitalist competition is grounded in a cooperative, mutually beneficial practice. They will have to make their case, however, in light of the ideal of a cooperative practice, as will those who defend capitalism. The same point holds with regard to war. To the extent that people continue to believe that all is fair in love and war, it makes no sense to think of war as a cooperative practice. To the extent, however, that states can reach and maintain agreement on conventions and rules for the instigation and conduct of wars, to that extent we are working toward, and may even be engaged in, a cooperative practice. The problem with war in this respect, of course, is that a cooperative practice successfully governing warfare would seem to lead to its elimination—to the elimination of warfare, that is, and thus to the elimination of the practice governing it. But that is a problem to be welcomed, if the opportunity ever arises. A more realistic standard of success, in my view, is a cooperative practice governing warfare as effectively as a legal system that keeps crime to a minimum even if it can never eradicate it. For now, though, the key point is to recognize that there may be important elements of a cooperative practice—elements worth cultivating— even with regard to warfare.

Once we start to speak of the critical, aspirational aspect of cooperative practices, we are not far from a consideration of the role of justice within them. As it happens, justice is also the second concern Horton raises in his criticism of fair-play theory's reliance on schemes of social cooperation. It is appropriate, then, to turn to that subject now.

Cooperation, Justice, and Fair Play

As Horton observes, those who advocate the fair-play account of political obligation typically insist that obligations of fair play only obtain when the cooperative practice in question is fair in the sense of being just, or at least nearly or reasonably just. To be sure, that qualification does not appear in Hart's formulation, but it does in Rawls's supposition of a "mutually beneficial and just scheme of social cooperation."[26] Qualifying the principle in this way appears to forestall some objections, such as the complaint that some cooperative practices may themselves be unjust. This is the potential embarrassment I referred to earlier in connection with Shirley Jackson's "The Lottery." Some joint enterprises according to rules may be corrupt or wicked enterprises, and we must confront the possibility that playing fair with one's fellow participants in such circumstances could require one to contribute to the evil or injustice the enterprise does. That is one reason for insisting that the principle of fair play only

---

[26] Rawls, "Legal Obligation and the Duty of Fair Play," p. 9.

applies to reasonably fair or just schemes of cooperation. Another is to make it clear that the benefits and burdens of cooperation must be distributed not only in a way that benefits all of the cooperators but that benefits them justly. If ten people work together to provide a good, and work equally hard and well, then something is likely to be amiss if four of them take more of its benefits than the remaining six. All benefit, that is, but the disparity in how much they benefit seems unfair. If it is wrong for free riders to enjoy benefits without contributing, it must also be wrong for the benefits and burdens of the scheme to be out of balance among the cooperators. Hence the insistence that the principle of fair play pertains only to *just* schemes of cooperation.

The "potentially rather large problem" with this qualification, according to Horton, "is that what is fair [or just] is itself highly controversial and contestable."[27] This is, he admits, not "a conclusive argument against the fair-play theory," but he is right to regard it as a serious problem.[28] For it requires the fair-play theorist to defend an already controversial principle by taking on the daunting challenge of devising or defending a fully developed theory of justice—a theory that will almost certainly prove to be at least as controversial as the fair-play account of political obligation itself.

How should the fair-play theorist respond to this "potentially rather large problem"? One way would be to accept the challenge and set about developing a theory of justice within which to embed the fair-play account of political obligation. Rawls may have had something of this sort in mind, Horton notes;[29] in any case, it is clear that Rawls's conception of "justice as fairness" is deeply connected to "the idea of society as a system of fair cooperation over time, from one generation to the next."[30] But it is also clear that any effort in this direction is sure to be controversial, as Horton says, if not altogether futile. In any case, it is not a challenge I shall take up in this book.

---

[27] Horton, *Political Obligation*, p. 92.

[28] Ibid., p. 93.

[29] Ibid., p. 92.

[30] John Rawls, *Political Liberalism*, expanded ed. (New York: Columbia University Press, 2005), §3.1, p. 15. Strictly speaking, as George Klosko has reminded me, Rawls says that "the guiding idea" of justice as fairness "is that the principles of justice for the basic structure of society are the object of the original agreement"—that is, principles chosen under fair conditions. See Rawls, *A Theory of Justice*, p. 10. The connection of this procedural understanding of justice as fairness to a substantive idea of society as a fair system of cooperation becomes prominent, however, in Rawls's later work. On this point, see Frederick Neuhouser, "Rousseau's Critique of Economic Inequality," *Philosophy and Public Affairs* 41 (Summer 2013), p. 217: "It is difficult to overemphasize the importance that the idea of society as a system of mutually advantageous cooperation plays in Rawls's theory of justice." See also my "Citizenship as Fairness: John Rawls's Conception of Civic Virtue," in *A Companion to Rawls*, ed. Jon Mandle and David Reidy (Chichester: Wiley-Blackwell, 2014), pp. 297–311.

A second possible response is to backtrack a bit and deny that fair-play obligations only come into force in cooperative practices that are just or reasonably just. Faced with the objection that considerations of fair play may place us under an obligation to a corrupt or wicked practice, in other words, the fair-play theorist could simply agree. Nor is this an altogether implausible response. To return to the example of Tessie Hutchinson in "The Lottery," there does seem to be a sense in which her apparently uncomplaining participation in the lottery throughout her life places her under a duty of fair play to be the victim of the stoning when her name is drawn, fair and square, from the lottery box. If that seems unpalatable, one need only remember that the obligation in question is *prima facie* or *pro tanto*, and thus subject to being overridden or limited by more important moral considerations, such as the duty not to take an innocent life. The fair-play duty in this case may also be in conflict with a duty to follow the rules of a larger practice within which it is nested—in particular, the obligation to obey the laws of a polity. There is also the question of whether the lottery is truly a mutually beneficial scheme. Aside from the difficulty of seeing how it benefits the annual victim, there is the question of whether it provides any benefit at all to the village. The villagers must believe that the ritual stoning somehow contributes to the well-being of their community, but Jackson makes it clear that some have begun to doubt whether it does, and all are aware that other villages have abandoned the practice. Perhaps, in light of these reasons, it would be best simply to drop the qualification that the principle of fair play applies only to *just* schemes of social cooperation.

There is a third way, however, to respond to Horton's "potentially rather large problem," and it is the one I think best. In brief, the response is to accept the justice qualification while maintaining that the ingredients for a modest but suitable conception of justice lie within the idea of a cooperative practice itself. Rather than situate cooperative practices within a fully developed theory of justice, in other words, we should try to extract enough substance from the ideas of fair play and cooperation to provide the basis for both procedural and substantive justice.

The point is perhaps more evident with regard to procedural justice. Fair play is largely a matter of adhering to rules, formal or informal, including the previously mentioned ideas of taking turns, reciprocity, and equal standing as a participant in a joint enterprise according to rules. In the case of political obligation, as I shall explain in Chapter 5, this is largely a matter of adhering to the procedural requirements of the rule of law. As the reference to equal standing indicates, however, there is also a concern for substantive justice built into cooperative practices. To enjoy equal standing need not mean that one must play an equal part in producing the benefits of a practice or receive an equal share of them. The fact that baseball stars and umpires are not paid the same salaries, for example, does not prove that professional baseball is an unjust enterprise. In a dispute between a star and an umpire, though, the umpire must receive an equal hearing. Whether justice requires more than that—higher salaries for umpires, say—is open to debate. But the idea of substantive justice as equal standing is contained in the idea of a cooperative practice itself. What exactly counts as equal standing will be controversial at times, but it is a consideration of fairness within the practice that cannot be ignored without an injustice being done.

Two examples should help to clarify this point. The first, slavery, poses a challenge to fair-play theory because there is a sense in which it seems to involve a cooperative practice within an unjust enterprise. In the American South before the Civil War, for instance, there is evidence that slave owners understood themselves to be engaged with one another in a cooperative practice, working together to prop up slavery by proscribing abolitionist literature, denying education to slaves, and various other measures. One could thus conclude that slave owners were engaged in a mutually beneficial enterprise, slave owning, that entailed duties of fair play to one another despite the injustice of slavery itself. But this conclusion would be both hasty and wrong. To be a slave owner, one must own slaves, which is to say that slave owning is not a discrete practice independent of the institution of slavery. Nor is it reasonable to regard slavery itself as a cooperative practice, for it obviously is not mutually beneficial to all involved, once we take the participation of the slaves into account; nor does it grant anything approaching equal standing to all who are caught up in the practice. Without slaves there would be neither slave owners nor benefits for them to enjoy *qua* slave owners. Slave owning, then, is no more a cooperative endeavor than slavery itself. Once the equal standing of the slaves is recognized, the institution may begin to be transformed into a cooperative practice, but only with the abolition of slavery and slave owning.

The second example concerns immigration into an existing practice. As I noted earlier in the case of volleyball players, the principle of fair play does not by itself tell us whether outsiders should be admitted into a cooperative practice. Unless there is reason to believe that the one who wants to join the game is already a co-participant in some larger cooperative practice, considerations other than fair play will have to be invoked to determine whether she should be admitted into the game. Fair play neither can nor should try to cover everything. When people are admitted, however, it must be with the intent to grant them the opportunity for full membership in the cooperative practice. In informal volleyball this happens almost immediately, but it can take more time in an organized sport—imagine admitting someone who knows nothing more about volleyball than that it appears to be an enjoyable form of exercise—and in many other cooperative practices, including political societies. Once they have established themselves inside the practice and contributed to the production of its benefits, immigrants have a claim to full membership, and equal standing, in political society. The claim does not entail an automatic grant of citizenship, but it is a claim to a place in the process that leads to that status. Fair play requires that the immigrants' contributions be recognized in this way.

As these examples indicate, there is enough substance within the ideas of cooperative practices and fair play to generate a modest conception of justice. This conception will not be powerful enough to answer every question one may raise about justice, but it is strong enough, I believe, to deflect the "potentially rather large problem" that Horton identifies. To underscore this point, we should consider the problem of incompetents. Fair play, as I noted earlier, presupposes that the participants in a cooperative practice have certain abilities, including the ability to follow rules, make choices, and understand the point of reciprocity. We simply cannot engage in fair play with those, human or non-human, who lack these capacities. In addition, particular cooperative practices require special abilities of those who engage in them—athletic skill, musical talents, and so on. Occasionally cases will arise that test exactly what those abilities must be, or how far they must extend, as in the previously mentioned case of the professional golfer, Casey Martin, who petitioned to be allowed to ride in a golf cart during tournaments. In those cases, I argued, considerations of *fairness* may help us to decide whether a person should be part of the practice even though appeals to fair play will not. There are other cases, though, in which the lack of competence excludes people from a cooperative practice—and even from cooperative activities altogether. Those who are severely limited, especially in their mental capacities, will simply lack the competence required to take part in a joint enterprise according to rules. With such people, considerations of fair play cannot apply; nor is it easy to see how broader considerations of fairness, or justice understood as fairness, can guide us in our responses to them. That is why Rawls's conception of "justice as fairness" proceeds from the assumption that "persons as citizens have all the capacities that enable them to be cooperating members of society."[31]

Where incompetents are concerned, in short, there is no way to squeeze enough substance from the ideas of fair play and cooperative practices to help us know how to treat them. If our proper responses to them are a matter of justice—rather than charity, say, or simple humanity—it is a different kind of justice from that involved in cooperative endeavors. To acknowledge this limitation of cooperation and fair play, however, is only to acknowledge that these considerations are not all-encompassing. But there is no reason they should be.

---

[31] Rawls, *Political Liberalism*, I§3.4, p. 20.

The Polity as Cooperative Practice

To this point the discussion in this chapter has involved fair play and cooperative practices in general, with only scattered remarks about political and legal systems as instances of such practices or the duties of fair play involved in them. I have noted, however, that the most formidable objection to the fair-play account of political obligation may well be the complaint that it simply strains credulity to conceive of political society as a cooperative practice. My response to that complaint, both specifically and in general terms, comprises the next two chapters of this book. At the conclusion of this chapter, though, it will be useful to lay the groundwork for this twofold response by explaining how political societies under law have a claim to be counted as cooperative endeavors, albeit of a special kind.

To think of the political system or polity as one of Hart's joint enterprises according to rules is to think of it as an enterprise according to the rule of law. Other characteristic features of states, governments, or polities might be added—Klosko identifies "seven important functions," most of which take more than one form[32]—but the rule of law is of special significance, in my view, and sufficient for present purposes. Among other things, this form of rule includes a clear connection between cooperation and the need for coercion.[33] On this point, it is worth quoting Hart at length:

> The facts that make rules respecting persons, property, and promises necessary in social life are simple and their mutual benefits are obvious. Most men are capable of seeing them and of sacrificing the immediate short-term interests which conformity to such rules demands. ... On the other hand, neither understanding of long-term interests, nor the strength or goodness of will, upon which the efficacy of these different motives towards obedience depends, are shared by all men alike. All are tempted at times to prefer their own immediate interests and, in the absence of a special organization for their detection and punishment, many would succumb to the temptation. ... [E]xcept in very small closely-knit societies, submission to the system of restraints would be folly if there were no organization for the coercion of those who would then try to obtain the advantages of the system without submitting to its obligations. 'Sanctions' are therefore required not as the normal motive

---

[32] Klosko, *Political Obligations*, pp. 22–23.

[33] The remainder of this section draws on my "Republicanism and the Foundations of Criminal Law," in *Philosophical Foundations of Criminal Law*, ed. R. A. Duff and S. P. Green (Oxford: Oxford University Press, 2011), pp. 60–63.

for obedience, but as a *guarantee* that those who would voluntarily obey shall not be sacrificed to those who would not. To obey, without this, would be to risk going to the wall. Given this standing danger, what reason demands is *voluntary* co-operation in a *coercive* system.[34]

What Hart calls "a special organization for [the] detection and punishment" of those who break the rules that protect "persons, property, and promises" is usually called the state or government; or, if the emphasis is on the word 'special', some branch(es) of the state or government. Those terms will suffice, but 'polity,' as I noted in Chapter 1, is more likely to convey the cooperative aspect of the organization Hart has in mind.

To say, in any case, that a system of laws is a cooperative practice is to indicate, first, that no system of laws can rely entirely on coercion. Even the most thorough-going dictatorship, in which the dictator's every wish is an enforced command, cannot rest entirely on coercion. Anyone who thinks that *laws* cannot be reduced to the commands of the powerful will have all the more reason to believe that a system of laws must depend upon the general cooperation of those to whom the laws apply. For these people, as Hart argues in *The Concept of Law*, the law will have the *internal aspect* characteristic of social rules, so that "some at least must look upon the behavior in question as a general standard to be followed by the group as a whole."[35] In the case of a system of laws, the "behavior in question" will consist in taking the laws as rules by which members of the group may enjoy the benefits of the rule of law, benefits that would be unavailable to them if there were not sufficient cooperation in the form of obedience to the law.

Obeying the law is sometimes burdensome, however, which points to the second respect in which a legal system is a cooperative practice. Cooperation often entails restraint or sacrifice, and the temptation to avoid doing one's part is sometimes quite strong—for some people, it seems, frequently so. Coercion and the threat of coercion are thus necessary to discourage shirking and free riding, and to ensure, as Hart says, that "those who would voluntarily obey will not be sacrificed to those who would not."[36] In some circumstances, such as the small and close-knit societies Hart mentions, the sense of solidarity will be powerful enough to make the threat of sanctions for noncooperation almost unnecessary. But those circumstances are rare, and probably growing rarer; and even when they do obtain, the threat of coercion must still be present.

---

[34] Hart, *The Concept of Law*, 2nd ed. (Oxford: Oxford University Press, 1994), pp. 197–98; emphasis in original.
[35] Ibid., p. 56.
[36] Ibid., p. 198.

These points should be familiar enough to require no further elaboration here. There is a sense, however, in which the rule of law is a distinctive kind of practice, and something needs to be said on that point. To put it succinctly, a system of laws is a *super-* or *meta-*cooperative practice, or a meta-practice for short. That is, the legal order is not only a cooperative practice; it is a cooperative practice that enables people to engage in other cooperative practices. The members of a carpool, for example, are engaged in a cooperative practice that provides them with benefits that they produce for themselves by taking in turns the burdens of picking up and driving those who are sharing the ride. But in order to produce these benefits for themselves, they must also be able to take advantage of benefits provided by the legal order, such as the traffic laws that make it possible for them to drive in relative safety to the workplace, school, playgroup, or other destinations. Unless they live in a libertarian utopia, wherein every inch of their journey takes place on privately owned roads governed by the owners' regulations, they must rely indirectly on the law as a meta-practice if their carpool is to be the joint venture for mutual benefit they want it to be.

A further implication of this way of thinking about a system of laws is that such a system is necessarily *political.* As a meta-practice, the legal system must establish laws that make it possible for people to engage in other cooperative practices and to go about their individual lives. Laws by themselves are not sufficient, however. The members of the carpool need not only traffic laws but traffic signals and roads on which to drive, and these require the collection and expenditure of funds. They also require that decisions be made as to where roads are to be built, what kinds of roads they should be, and where the signals should be placed, among other things. What is necessary, in short, is a political order operating through the rule of law.

In a political order of this kind, the polity itself will be a cooperative practice—or, more properly, a cooperative meta-practice. The laws in such an order will be the terms of fair cooperation, or of what the members take to be the terms of fair cooperation. Laws will thus need to be promulgated, and cooperation will need to be encouraged, but the laws themselves will become matters of debate and the products of public decisions. "What laws do we need?" thus becomes a vital question, as do the related questions of who should make these laws, who should enforce them, and who should apply and interpret them. There is also, finally, the question of how to hold those who make, enforce, and apply the laws accountable to the public—that is, to those who have not only duties but rights as members of the cooperative meta-practice that is the political order.

Conclusion

Conceiving of the legal order as a cooperative practice, in Hartian fashion, thus has a number of significant implications. One is that the legal order is also a political order, with the further implication that the philosophy of law, including the criminal law, is entangled with political philosophy. Other things being equal, those who commit crimes threaten the rule of law, and it is necessary to find ways to prevent them from doing anything more than merely posing a threat, and then to punish them on those occasions when the preventive efforts fail. What kinds of actions really do threaten the meta-practice, and should therefore count as crimes, and how best to respond to these actions, are questions I address in Part II of this book. For the present, it will be enough to note that decisions affecting the members of the polity have to be made in these cases, which is to say that crime and punishment are necessarily public or political concerns.

Another implication of conceiving of the legal *cum* political order as a cooperative practice is that the reasons for preferring 'polity' to 'state' or 'government' become clearer. To the extent that the latter terms imply that faceless, nameless functionaries are the ones who make, enforce, and apply the laws, these terms are less satisfactory than 'polity,' or even the more old-fashioned terms 'commonwealth' or 'republic.' The latter all convey that law is a matter of public concern, a crucial part of the public's business. Such must be the case if the legal *cum* political order is a meta-practice, for then the terms of fair cooperation will be of vital importance to the government of their lives. That means both the ability to govern their individual lives, free from interference when possible, and the ability to govern their lives collectively through the making of laws, whether directly or indirectly through the election of legislators.

A final implication is that the conception of the legal *cum* political order as a meta-practice helps to clarify the communicative aspect of the law, and especially the criminal law. This too is a subject to which I shall return in Part II, in which I set out and defend the fair-play theory of punishment. At this point it is enough to note that prominent legal philosophers regard punishment as, among other things, an attempt to communicate to those who break the law the wrongfulness of their actions, with the aim of bringing them into the fold or restoring them to the community whose standards they have violated.[37] But what gives some of us the right or authority to communicate our standards in this way? We may grant that punishment of lawbreakers is a way of communicating the society's, community's, or polity's displeasure with them, but punishment is typically a harsh and unpleasant form of communication. As such, it requires more of a justification than, say, a remonstrance or reprimand. Such a justification may be found, though, in the offender's violation of the laws giving substance to the

---

[37] For perhaps the most prominent example of this approach, see R. A. Duff, *Punishment, Communication, and Community* (Oxford: Oxford University Press, 2001).

meta-practice that, *ceteris paribus*, supplies him with benefits through the cooperative restraint of others. As part of that practice, we give some of our members, as Hart said, the authority to detect and punish those who do not respect the "persons, property, and promises" of the other members of the practice—that is, the other members of the polity. That is why the polity is justified in communicating its censure to the offender by means of punishment.

What I have said in the last parts of this chapter concerns the ideal of the polity as a meta-practice. Critics of the fair-play approach, however, are quick to note the discrepancy between the ideal and the actual states, governments, and citizens of the modern world. They have good reason to do so, of course, and I shall respond further to this observation in subsequent chapters. But it is important first to make the ideal clear—to show that it makes sense to grant the polity an initial claim to being a cooperative practice, as Hart and Rawls and others have believed. Beyond that, it is important to grasp that it is, or can be, a distinctive kind of cooperative practice—that is, a meta-practice. With this and the other fundamental elements of the fair-play account established, or at least set out, it is now possible to turn to the elaboration and defense of the fair-play account of political obligation. The elaboration begins in the next chapter with a critical analysis of rival theories that should further define the features, and strengths, of the fair-play account.

3

Fair Play and Its Rivals

With the notable exception of Robert Nozick's comprehensive rejection in *Anarchy, State, and Utopia*, critics of the fair-play theory of political obligation typically raise no objections to the principle of fair play itself. Fair play is a significant moral principle, they acknowledge, within its limited range of applicability. They insist, however, that political obligation falls well outside that range. In the standard examples of cooperative schemes—games, musical groups, working with others to dig a well, put out fires, or provide local security—the need for cooperation is usually obvious; so too is the point of praising those who bear their fair share of the burdens of cooperation and chastising those who do not. But these conditions are not characteristic of political societies, and especially not of modern polities with sprawling territories and millions of highly mobile inhabitants. To apply the principle of fair play to such a society, the critics say, is to stretch it farther than it can reasonably go.

This is an objection that proponents of the fair-play theory of political obligation cannot ignore. An effective response, however, requires a sharper delineation of the principle of fair play, and particularly its application to the problem of political obligation, than I have thus far offered. Part of that delineation will occur in Chapter 5, which responds directly to criticisms of the fair-play account of political obligation. But it will be helpful to consider first some of the other accounts on offer, with an eye to defining the fair-play approach in contrast to them. The aim, as I stated in the introductory chapter, is not to provide a comprehensive survey of theories of political obligation. That is why arguments from necessity, utility, gratitude, and other proposed grounding principles will receive little or no attention here. There are some theories, though, that provide important points of contrast with the fair-play account, and these theories—grounded respectively in consent, association, and natural duty—are the subjects of this chapter.

Political Obligation, Fair Play, and Three Rivals

As the discussion in Chapter 2 indicates, some features are common to all theories of political obligation. They all reject anarchism, of course, in both its political and its philosophical forms, and they all agree on the need for some kind of political authority. Without such authority, only the smallest and most tradition-bound societies would find it possible to provide even a modicum of security and overcome the various problems of coordination and collective action that confront them. All theories of political obligation also agree that this obligation is a moral requirement, or duty, even though they may disagree on its force or extent.[1] What supplies the foundation of this duty, however, is the subject of considerable contention. Indeed, their disagreement on this point is what gives each theory its name—consent theory, gratitude theory, samaritanism, and so on. In the case of fair-play theory, political obligation is a particular form of the obligation or duty to do one's fair share when one is involved in any "joint enterprise according to rules," in H. L. A. Hart's terms, or in any "mutually beneficial and just scheme of social cooperation," in John Rawls's.[2] For someone to have a political obligation, according to this theory, there must be good reason to conceive of her polity as a cooperative enterprise or practice. If there is, then this person has a general obligation, grounded in the principle of fair play, to obey the laws of the polity.

Other theories look to other grounding principles, three of which I shall examine here. The first, consent theory, will receive the least attention despite its popularity over the centuries with both social-contract theorists and ordinary citizens. This relative neglect follows largely from my sense that the well-known objections to consent theory have made it a less plausible rival to the fair-play account than the other two. But it also follows from the need to provide more

---

[1] Margaret Gilbert's "actual contract" theory is a possible exception, for Gilbert holds (as noted in Chapter 2) that political obligations are "obligations of joint commitment" that need not be moral requirements (Gilbert, *A Theory of Political Obligation* [Oxford: Oxford University Press, 2006], p. 293, and p. 56 for her brief account of actual contract theory). I am inclined to discount this exception for two reasons. First, whether Gilbert's "obligations of joint commitment" are really devoid of moral content is open to question; as she says, these obligations "trump one's inclinations and self-interest as such" (ibid.). Second, if Gilbert does indeed divorce political obligation from moral duty, then her theory seems to lose its point. As John Horton remarks, "if all moral content were evacuated from the idea [of political obligation], then the dispute between the defenders and critics of [political] obligations would become largely nugatory" (Horton, *Political Obligation*, 2nd ed. [Basingstoke: Palgrave Macmillan, 2010], p. 156). But cf. Gilbert's further defense of her position in *Joint Commitment: How We Make the Social World* (Oxford: Oxford University Press, 2013), chap. 16.

[2] Hart, "Are There Any Natural Rights?," *Philosophical Review* 64 (1955): 85; Rawls, "Legal Obligation and the Duty of Fair Play," in *Law and Philosophy*, ed. Sidney Hook (New York: New York University Press, 1964), pp. 9–10.

detailed accounts of the other two rivals in order to make clear how fair play differs from—and is superior to—the associative and natural-duty theories of political obligation.

Consent Theory

If we are told that someone has an obligation to do something, then we should be able to identify something she has done—some promise, vow, oath, contract, or other indication of consent—that indicates how she has placed herself under that obligation. That is the straightforward premise on which *consent theory* rests. Obligations arise from consent, according to this theory, and that is as true of political obligations as of any other. Where there has been no consent, there is no obligation.

The intuitive power of this idea is, I take it, obvious. It lies behind not only affirmations of various obligations—you must do X because you consented to do it—but also their denials. Nozick's rejection of fair-play obligations is an example of the latter sort, for it rests on the belief that one only has obligations when one has agreed to undertake them.[3] Nevertheless, consent theory is beset with difficulties. One of them, as the advocates of both the associative and natural-duty theories of political obligation maintain, is the impossibility of construing all important obligations as the results of voluntary choices. Unless we draw a strict and implausible distinction between obligations and duties, they say, we must acknowledge that many important obligations—those we owe to family members, for example, or to people in distress—are simply not grounded in consent.

Nor do the problems of consent theory vanish if we take a strictly voluntarist position with regard to obligations. In that case, the most obvious problem is that relatively few people seem to have consented to place themselves under the laws of the government that claims authority over them—or to any other government, for that matter. That in turn makes it hard to see how consent can provide the basis for a general obligation to obey the law. This difficulty has led Hobbes, Locke, and others to invoke the distinction between express consent to government, which relatively few have given, and tacit consent, which virtually everyone has. As Locke notoriously argues in §119 of his *Second Treatise of Government*, people tacitly consent to "obedience to the laws" in so many ways that, "in effect, it [i.e., tacit consent] reaches as far as the very being of any one within the territories of that government." But such a broad interpretation of

---

[3] Nozick, *Anarchy, State, and Utopia* (New York: Basic Books, 1974), pp. 90–95.

consent simply robs the idea of any value, as astute critics from David Hume to John Simmons have made clear.[4] For how can we attribute political obligation to consent when it seems that we tacitly consent whether or not we mean to do so?

The difficulties do not disappear, moreover, even if we grant for the sake of argument that almost everyone has somehow consented, expressly or tacitly, to obey the law. Granting that point simply leads to further questions: How long does one's consent remain in effect? What exactly has one consented to do? What if the character of the regime in power changes from, say, rule by the virtuous and wise to rule by the ignorant and corrupt? When pressed on these points, consent theorists have to acknowledge that there are limits to the obligations one can undertake by way of consent. In Locke's case, this means that an expansive notion of tacit consent is joined to a limited notion of what one may consent to do: "for no rational creature," he declares, "can be supposed to change his condition with an intention to be worse."[5] But this is tantamount to saying that consent, the supposed foundation of obligations, is itself limited by some other, and presumably more fundamental, consideration or set of considerations. What, then, is the point of a theory of political obligation grounded in *consent*?

This question is especially important for the fair-play theory of political obligation, which may seem to be a kind of consent theory in disguise. After all, games and other cooperative activities frequently involve something that seems to be a kind of tacit consent on the part of their participants, who typically do not participate against their wills. According to the theory, however, the obligation one has to the other participants in a cooperative practice is not grounded in consent but in the principle of fair play. As Simmons puts the point, "a man *can* accept benefits from a scheme, and be a participant in that sense, without giving his consent to the scheme."[6] Suppose, he says, that Jones openly and adamantly refuses to join in a cooperative scheme to dig and maintain a public well in his neighborhood. Suppose further that, once the well is providing water, Jones takes water from the well under cover of darkness, knowing that his neighbors will not miss what he has taken. Jones is a free rider, in other words, who takes advantage of a public good others have created through their collective efforts. Moreover, he "has made himself a participant in the [cooperative] scheme by accepting its benefits, although he has refused to give his consent."[7] Jones has an

---

[4] Hume, "Of the Original Contract," in *David Hume's Political Essays*, ed. C. W. Hendel (Indianapolis, IN: Bobbs-Merrill, 1953), pp. 43–61; Simmons, *Moral Principles and Political Obligations* (Princeton, NJ: Princeton University Press, 1979), pp. 75–100.

[5] Locke, *Second Treatise of Government*, §131; see also §§23, 137, and 164. For discussion of this point, see Hanna F. Pitkin, "Obligation and Consent I," *American Political Science Review* 59 (December 1965): 995–96.

[6] Simmons, *Moral Principles and Political Obligations*, p. 126; emphasis in original.

[7] Ibid., p. 127.

obligation to the others who participate in the scheme, in short, but it is an obligation grounded in fair play, not in consent (which he has expressly withheld).

As the example shows, considerations of fair play are not simply disguised appeals to tacit consent. On the contrary, fair play can account for obligations even in the absence of consent. Given the difficulties of consent theory, this is a signal advantage of the fair-play account of political obligation.[8]

Associative Theory

Dissatisfaction with consent theory and resistance to philosophical anarchism seem largely responsible for the emergence in recent decades of the *associative* or *membership theory* of political obligation.[9] According to the proponents of this view, the members of a group or association are under an obligation, other things being equal, to comply with the norms governing the group. This obligation holds, moreover, even for groups or associations, such as families and polities, that people typically do not consent to join. Voluntary or not, membership entails obligation. Anyone who acknowledges that he or she is a member of a particular polity must therefore also acknowledge a general obligation to obey its laws.

This argument takes different forms in the hands of its various proponents, but the key idea is that political obligation is a nonvoluntary obligation on a par with familial obligations.[10] Political society, in Ronald Dworkin's phrase, is one of those associations that are "pregnant of obligation":

---

[8] This cursory discussion ignores several recent attempts to bolster consent theory, none of which strikes me as persuasive. Those interested in exploring this theory further should consult the following: Harry Beran, *The Consent Theory of Political Obligation* (London: Croom Helm, 1987); Mark Murphy, "Surrender of Judgment and the Consent Theory of Political Authority," *Law and Philosophy* 16 (1999): 115–43; Peter Steinberger, *The Idea of the State* (Cambridge, UK: Cambridge University Press, 2004), chap. 5; and David Estlund, *Democratic Authority: A Philosophical Framework* (Princeton, NJ: Princeton University Press, 2008), esp. chaps. 7 and 8. Of these, Estlund's "normative consent" theory is the most radical departure from traditional consent theory. His argument at pp. 154–56, however, suggests that "normative consent" is better understood as a version of natural-duty theory, and subject as such to the criticisms I advance under that heading later in this chapter.

[9] The following discussion of the associative theory of political obligation draws on, but amplifies considerably, my "Membership, Fair Play, and Political Obligation," *Political Studies* 48 (March 2000): 105–12.

[10] Margaret Gilbert's theory, which relies on the ideas of both "actual contract" and group membership, once again may be an exception, but Gilbert holds that her theory "is in an important sense 'non-voluntarist'" (Gilbert, *A Theory of Political Obligation*, p. 290). She also states that her theory provides an affirmative answer to the question, "does membership in a political society, in and of itself, involve obligations to uphold that society's political institutions?" (ibid., p. 287). Another possible exception is Yael Tamir, who allows that identification with a group may contain a voluntary element. As she says, "One may have acquired associative membership in a particular social group by

[T]he best defense of political legitimacy—the right of a political community to treat its members as having obligations in virtue of collective community decisions—is to be found not in the hard terrain of contracts or duties of justice or obligations of fair play that might hold among strangers, where philosophers have hoped to find it, but in the more fertile ground of fraternity, community, and their attendant obligations. Political association, like family and friendship and other forms of association more local and intimate, is in itself pregnant of obligation.[11]

The same line of reasoning, with an explicit analogy between family and polity, is at the heart of John Horton's associative account of political obligation:

My claim is that a polity is, like the family, a relationship into which we are mostly born; and that the obligations which are constitutive of the relationship *do not stand in need of moral justification in terms of a set of basic moral principles or some comprehensive moral theory*. Furthermore, both the family and the political community figure prominently in our sense of who we are; our self-identity and our understanding of our place in the world.[12]

As members of families and political communities, on this view, we are subject to what Michael Hardimon calls "noncontractual role obligations"—that is, obligations that simply flow from "roles into which we are born."[13]

---

birth rather than through voluntary choice, but unless one identifies with this membership, it cannot generate obligations. In this restricted sense, we *could* approach associative obligations as voluntarily assumed" (*Liberal Nationalism* [Princeton, NJ: Princeton University Press, 1993], p. 135; emphasis added). Yet another possible exception is Massimo Renzo, who advances a "quasi-voluntarist" theory that gives special weight to the option of repudiating or denying one's membership in an association; see Renzo, "Associative Responsibilities and Political Obligations," *Philosophical Quarterly* 62 (January 2012): 106–27.

[11] Dworkin, *Law's Empire* (Cambridge, MA: Harvard University Press, 1986), p. 206. Dworkin's *Justice for Hedgehogs* (Cambridge, MA: Harvard University Press, 2011), pp. 311–24, elaborates his defense of the associative theory of political obligation without revising it in ways that require attention here.

[12] Horton, *Political Obligation* (Atlantic Highlands, NJ: Humanities Press, 1992), pp. 150–51; emphasis added. This quotation is from the first edition of Horton's book, but nothing he says in the second edition serves to retract what he says in the quoted passage. Horton does provide a richer account of his position in the second edition, though, and a robust response to critics of the associative theory, including me, which I shall attend to below.

[13] Hardimon, "Role Obligations," *The Journal of Philosophy* 91 (July 1994), p. 347. In a footnote to this passage, Hardimon adds that "I am assuming that the roles of family member and citizen exhaust the class of noncontractual social roles."

This account of political obligation has at least three attractive features. The first is the refusal of its proponents to treat 'voluntary' and 'involuntary' as two parts of a dichotomy. Hardimon puts this point especially well. If we hold that only voluntary actions can place us under obligations—"the volunteer principle," in his terms—then the claim that we have "noncontractual role obligations" sounds threatening. "It may sound even more threatening," he observes, "if we look closely at a basic source of [the volunteer principle's] appeal: our horror at the thought of being *impressed*—like the seamen of old—into social roles and burdened with their attendant obligations against our will." But it is a mistake to think that there is no middle ground between volunteering and being impressed. We must recognize, Hardimon says,

> that the metaphor of impressment is particularly ill-suited to the roles associated with the noncontractual role obligations we are inclined to take seriously. It would simply be wrong to say that we are impressed into the roles of sons or daughters, wrong to say that we are impressed into the roles of brothers and sisters, and wrong to say that we are impressed into the role of citizen. We do not, it is true, choose these roles, but we are not impressed into them either. They are roles into which we are born.[14]

Adolescents may find this point hard to accept when they protest that they did not choose to be born into their families; but one sign of maturity is their eventual recognition that they were not exactly impressed into them, either.

A second attraction of the membership account of political obligation is that it accords with a common intuition. A great many people apparently do think of themselves as members of political communities who have an obligation to obey their polities' laws. If a theory's ability to support widespread intuitions counts in its favor, then the argument from membership surely has the advantage of philosophical anarchism.[15]

---

[14] Ibid., p. 347; emphasis added. Dworkin makes the same point in a different way: "If we arrange familiar fraternal communities along a spectrum ranging from full choice to no choice in membership, political communities fall somewhere in the center. Political obligations are *less involuntary* than many obligations of family, because political communities do allow people to emigrate, and though the practical value of this choice is often very small the choice itself is important, as we know when we contemplate tyrannies that deny it" (*Law's Empire*, p. 207; emphasis added).

[15] For evidence bearing on this intuition, see George Klosko, *The Principle of Fairness and Political Obligation*, 2nd ed. (Lanham, MD: Rowman & Littlefield, 2004), Appendix 2, and Klosko, *Political Obligations* (Oxford: Oxford University Press, 2005), chaps. 9 and 10. But cf. Leslie Green, "Who Believes in Political Obligation?," in *For and Against the State*, ed. J. T. Sanders and J. Narveson (Lanham, MD: Rowman & Littlefield, 1996), pp. 1–17.

This intuition also points to the third attractive feature of the associative theory, for the intuition is connected with the *sense of identity* that members of a polity commonly share. According to Horton, "This sense of identity and the corresponding responsibility is part of what it means to be a member of a polity and to recognize one's political obligations."[16] So it should not be surprising, he goes on to remark, that

> some institutional obligations, through their deep-rooted connections with our sense of who we are and our place in the world, have a particularly fundamental role in our moral being. That these kinds of institutional involvement generate moral obligations, and that these obligations rather than standing in need of justification may themselves be justificatory, is only to be expected.[17]

In all three of these respects the argument from association is quite appealing, at least for those who find neither consent theory nor philosophical anarchism compelling. But that is not to say that it provides a satisfactory account of political obligation. I am more sympathetic to the argument from membership than other critics tend to be, but I nevertheless believe that it is plagued by problems.[18] Three of these problems deserve attention here.

Problem One: The Polity as Family

The first problem has to do with the analogy between the polity and the family—or, in Dworkin's broader terms, between political community, on the one hand, and familial and fraternal associations, on the other. For this analogy to have force, families must generate obligations of membership that flow, as Hardimon says, from "roles into which we are born." Perhaps in most families these obligations do follow in this fashion, but it is easy to find troublesome cases. If John's parents abandoned him shortly after his birth and never gave any evidence of caring whether he lived or died, does he ever have an associative obligation to

---

[16] Quoting again from the first edition of Horton, *Political Obligation*, p. 154.

[17] Ibid., p. 157.

[18] For less sympathetic critics, see A. John Simmons, "Associative Political Obligations," *Ethics* 106 (January 1996): 247–73 (reprinted in Simmons, *Justification and Legitimacy: Essays on Rights and Obligations* [Cambridge, UK: Cambridge University Press, 2001]); Christopher Heath Wellman, "Associative Allegiances and Political Obligations," *Social Theory and Practice* 23 (Summer 1997): 181–204; and, focusing on Dworkin's argument, Leslie Green, "Associative Obligations and the State," in *Dworkin and His Critics*, ed. J. Burley (Oxford: Blackwell Publishing, 2004), pp. 267–84; Dworkin responds at pp. 376–80.

them? If he has an obligation instead to the people who adopted and cared for him, does this obligation flow from a role into which he was born?

For present purposes, I shall set such troublesome cases aside and grant that families generate nonvoluntary obligations for their members. The next question, then, is whether the analogy between family and polity is sound. Here the obvious objection is that the members of the modern polity lack the close and intimate relationships with one another that family members typically share.[19] As nation-states grow larger and less national in character, the spirit of fraternity dwindles as people tend to look less familiar to their fellow citizens. The proponents of the membership theory could respond, of course, that obligations of membership obtain in some polities—those that more closely resemble families—and not in others. But such a response would be tantamount to admitting that the theory lacks relevance in precisely the kinds of polities in which questions of political obligation are most likely to arise.

If we agree that polities are sufficiently similar to families for the analogy to be plausible, however, we must then ask whether the analogy proves too much. That is, does accounting for political obligations in this way require us to model the polity on the family in other respects? If it does, the door is open to a thoroughgoing form of paternalism that might have appealed to Sir Robert Filmer in the seventeenth century but is likely to attract few adherents today. To avoid this outcome, membership theorists must find some way to show that the analogy between family and polity holds with regard to political obligation but not to paternalism. They must do this, moreover, without reducing the analogy to a single point of resemblance—that is, the point that both families and polities generate nonvoluntary obligations—for such a move would amount to a thinly disguised assertion that membership in a polity grounds an obligation to it.

There are serious difficulties, then, that confront those who share Dworkin's belief that political association, "like family and friendship... is in itself pregnant of obligation." These difficulties may not prove that the family–polity analogy is misconceived or that political obligations cannot be understood in terms of this analogy, but they surely indicate that it is a shaky foundation for an account of the obligation to obey the law.

Problem Two: Identity and Obligation

The second problem with the associative theory relates to the *sense of identity* or *connection* so important to its argument. This sense is important because it leads people to regard themselves as *belonging*, as being members of a group, and in

---

[19] On this point see Simmons, "Associative Political Obligations," pp. 260 and 272.

this way it fosters their sense of obligation. The problem arises, however, when the argument slides from the *sense* of obligation to the *obligation* itself. Someone may have a sense of obligation, even a powerful sense of obligation, without truly being under the obligation in question. In Charles Dickens's *Martin Chuzzlewit*, for example, Seth Pecksniff's assistant, Tom Pinch, feels an overwhelming obligation to Pecksniff, when all along Pecksniff is selfishly exploiting Tom's innocent good nature. Conversely, someone may be subject to an obligation that he has no sense of at all. A man who does not know that he has fathered a child has an obligation to the child and its mother, *ceteris paribus*, even though he has absolutely no sense of this obligation. From either direction, the difference between the sense of obligation and the obligation itself undercuts the argument from association. The fact that people feel themselves to be under an obligation to their polity does not mean that they are indeed under such an obligation, nor does the fact that they feel no such obligation mean that they are not.

The advocates of the membership theory may reply that this criticism does not give the sense of identity its due. To *identify* with someone or something is not merely to submit passively to a feeling or set of feelings; it is to undertake an active role as an identifier. That, at least, is the burden of Yael Tamir's account of associative obligations. As she sees it, formal membership in a group cannot ground an associative obligation to it unless one identifies oneself as a member of that group: "If someone acquires, by birth, citizenship in a state he despises, his formal membership cannot serve as grounds for generating obligations to that state." Associative obligations

> must therefore be based on some sense of belonging, on an *active* and *conscious* discovery of one's position, and on an *affirmation* of this position. One may have associative membership in a particular social group by birth rather than through voluntary choice, but unless one *identifies* with this membership, it cannot generate obligations.[20]

The "true essence of associative obligations" is that they "are not grounded on consent, reciprocity, or gratitude, but rather on a feeling of belonging or connectedness."[21]

Tamir's conception of identification or connectedness does capture something of value, but that something bears on loyalty or patriotism or, again, the *sense* of obligation rather than obligation itself. As a response to the complaint that the sense of identity cannot ground or generate an obligation, it simply fails

---

[20] Tamir, *Liberal Nationalism*, p. 135; emphasis added throughout.
[21] Ibid., p. 137.

to meet the objection. Tom Pinch undoubtedly identifies himself, in Tamir's active sense, as an associate of Seth Pecksniff; he is grateful to Pecksniff for allowing him to be an associate, and he believes that he has an obligation to Pecksniff doubly rooted in gratitude and association. To Dickens's reader, however, it is clear that Pinch has misunderstood his situation and has no obligation of any sort to continue as Pecksniff's associate *cum* lackey. As long as people can *mis*identify themselves and their situations in this way, neither the sense of identity nor the activity of identifying can be sufficient to ground an obligation.

Setting misperceptions of this sort aside, Tamir's emphasis on active identity is still not enough to rescue the membership theory from the objection that it mistakes the sense of obligation for obligation itself. It simply does not follow that someone who (correctly) identifies herself as a member of a group thereby acquires or assumes an obligation to the other members of the group. Among the groups with which I identify, for instance, is the Janeites, devoted readers of Jane Austen's novels. I feel a kinship with my fellow Janeites; I have rubbed elbows with some of them at the Austen house in Chawton; I identify myself as one of them. But I do not see how this identification by itself imposes an obligation, associational or otherwise, on me.

Perhaps Tamir could respond that I have not truly identified with the Janeites unless I take membership in that group to entail a responsibility to proselytize or otherwise act on behalf of Janeism. That is, the Janeites' devotion to Austen's works must bind them in a common endeavor to bring others to an appreciation of the virtues, literary and moral, of her writings. To fail to do my part in this endeavor is to open myself to the censure of the other participants, who may rightly charge that I have failed to meet my obligations as a Janeite.[22] The problem with this response, however, is that it builds the conclusion into the definition of the key terms. *Identifying with* or *being a member of* a group simply means, according to the response, to have an obligation to the other members of the group; a *group* or an *association* simply is a common endeavor in which the members have an obligation to do their parts. These definitions tell us something that is undoubtedly true of some groups, but certainly not of all the groups with which one may identify—as the example of the Janeites should make clear. Indeed, whatever persuasive power Tamir's argument has rests on her implicit appeal to the ways in which many groups or associations bring people together in a shared or common endeavor. That is an important point, and one that proponents of the fair-play theory of political obligation are happy to accept. But it is not a response

---

[22] For an amusing account of how far some Janeites take their obligations to extend, see Deborah Yaffe, *Among the Janeites: A Journey Through the World of Jane Austen Fandom* (Boston and New York: Houghton Mifflin Harcourt, 2013).

to the objection that the *sense of identity* or even the *activity of identifying with a group* is not enough to ground an obligation to it.

Massimo Renzo has suggested a solution to this problem in the form of a "quasi-voluntarist" version of the membership theory. According to Renzo, membership is indeed a necessary condition for associative obligations, but it is not sufficient to establish them. In his terms, membership *grounds* the obligation, but a further *precondition* of endorsement is also necessary. We start, that is, with the recognition that we have not voluntarily entered into various roles, such as family member or citizen, but we must also recognize that "our occupying the roles is voluntary in the sense that we could have stepped out of them if we had not endorsed them; and in this case we would have stopped having the obligations attached to the roles."[23] In the case of the polity, this means the following:

> none of us ever chose to be born in the polity in which we were born, but this does not change the fact that since we were born in it, we came to occupy a role—the role of citizen—which brings with it specific responsibilities and obligations. However, our occupying this role is conditional on the fact that we endorse our membership. If we do not identify with the polity in which we happen to be, we cannot be said to be members; nor, as a consequence, can we be said to have any of the obligations attached to that membership. In this case, when states treat us as if we had such obligations, they do so unjustifiably.[24]

Like Tamir, Renzo seeks to give 'identify' a more active reading than the mere fact of membership seems to imply. He goes further than Tamir, however, by insisting on the need for the *endorsement* of one's membership as a precondition for the existence of associative obligations. But this insistence prompts the question of whether Renzo's proposed solution is only *quasi*-voluntarist. Endorsement, after all, is usually taken to be a form of consent—even express consent. So how is Renzo's solution to the sense-of-identity problem different from a straightforward acceptance of consent theory, with its attendant problems? For Renzo, the answer is that his solution does not require active endorsement but the withholding of endorsement—that is, a denying or "stepping out" of a certain role in which one finds herself.[25] Someone who repudiates membership in a polity or family, and who does so in a reflective way, no longer identifies with the association, and therefore no longer has any associative obligations with regard

---

[23] Renzo, "Associative Responsibilities and Political Obligations," p. 121.

[24] Ibid., p. 121.

[25] Ibid., pp. 121–23.

to it. One is a member, it seems, and subject to the obligations of membership, so long as one does not actively and reflectively deny one's membership.

A further advantage of this quasi-voluntarist approach, according to Renzo, is that it avoids "the manipulation objection"—that is, the objection that someone may identify with a political community because of indoctrination or manipulation.[26] Renzo allows that someone's sense of identity with a political society may indeed develop in this way, but he denies that such a sense of identity is genuine:

> The identity we end up acquiring when manipulated is not meaningful because it does not reflect who we really are, but rather what our exploiters want us to be. And if we cannot be said to have truly endorsed our identity when manipulated, no genuine obligation will follow from being manipulated into accepting membership in a political community.[27]

Renzo is wise to recognize the possibility of manipulation as a serious problem for associative accounts of political obligation. Indeed, I shall argue below that it is part of a larger set of problems relating to the content or character of groups in which one may be a member. His response to the manipulation objection, though, shares a difficulty with those consent theorists who tell us, as previously noted, that there are some things to which we simply cannot genuinely consent. In the case of Renzo's quasi-voluntarist theory, there are apparently some associations—those that brainwash or otherwise manipulate people into a sense of membership—that we simply cannot endorse no matter how we may try to do so. As he says, any "feeling of identification we might have when we are manipulated into believing ourselves to be members of a political community, no matter how strong, cannot ground genuine obligations any more than a promise that has been extracted with force or obtained by fraud."[28] But if this is so, then obligations must be grounded in something other than overt endorsement or membership or even the combination of the two. In other words, only groups that rest on genuine endorsement, however that is to be determined, can generate associative obligations. It seems, then, that it is the quality of the group that matters rather than membership or endorsement of one's membership. This is, once again, a conclusion that fair-play theorists will welcome, but it does nothing to strengthen the associative account of political obligation.

Renzo's quasi-voluntarist approach also founders on a second and equally serious problem. In this case, however, the problem comes from the opposite

---

[26] Ibid., p. 125.
[27] Ibid., p. 125.
[28] Ibid., p. 125.

direction. Rather than manipulation, the problem here is that some people may reject membership, or refuse to endorse it, when they have no good reason to do so. Perhaps selfishness or short-sightedness or a simple failure to appreciate what it means to be a member will lead someone to renounce his membership in his family or polity. Perhaps Seth Pecksniff, for example, mistakenly concludes that he is an oppressed member of the British polity and proclaims that he is withholding his endorsement of it. Or suppose a philosophical anarchist today issues a similar denial of being under an obligation to obey the laws of her polity. According to Renzo's quasi-voluntarist version of the membership theory, it appears that neither Pecksniff nor the philosophical anarchist will be under a political obligation to their polities once they have rejected membership. They will be free from this obligation, moreover, even if they remain where they were and continue to receive the benefits of the political order they have rejected.

The point, in short, is one I have previously made. Someone's sense of identity may lead him to feel an obligation that he does not truly have, or the lack of a sense of identity may lead him to deny an obligation that he truly does have. To be sure, Renzo is aware of the difficulty here, and he attempts to deflect it by requiring the refusal to endorse membership to be the product of careful reflection. Imagine, he says,

> that I declare that I intend to detach myself from my family, but I still have the kind of meaningful ties to it that are normally associated with membership. Had I thought more carefully about it, I would have realized that I still feel part of that complex web of practices, emotions and beliefs that constitute family relationships. In this case it is less obvious that my choice to detach from my family is morally significant. Indeed, I think most would agree that in spite of my formal rejection of family membership, I still am in an important sense a member of the family, with at least many of the obligations (and the rights) that generally follow from this membership.[29]

Renzo is right to qualify the force of his quasi-voluntarism in this way, but he is right at the expense of quasi-voluntarism. As his example indicates, the obligation to the family persists in this case—and rightly so, in my view—even when one declares one's intention to detach oneself from the family. Once again, the voluntary element is doing no work in what seems to be a strictly associative account of obligation. There will be cases, of course, in which we may well want to concur with those who declare their intentions to detach themselves from

---

[29] Ibid., p. 122.

their families, as I indicated earlier. What makes those cases different from the one in Renzo's example, however, is not the voluntarist element, quasi- or otherwise, but the content or character of the families involved. When someone is viciously and continuously mistreated and abused by her family, she has little reason to feel herself "part of that complex web of practices, emotions and beliefs that constitute family relationships." But this will be true whether she does or does not withhold her endorsement of her membership in the family—or, *mutatis mutandis*, in the polity. Quasi-voluntarism is thus a valiant but failed attempt to rescue the associative account of political obligation.

Problem Three: Group Character and Obligation

Hints of the final problem besetting the membership theory have already appeared in the foregoing discussion. This is the problem of what I shall call *group character*. Tracing political obligation to obligations of association or membership, especially of membership in nonvoluntary or noncontractual associations, presents this problem because membership is not confined to groups or associations that are decent, fair, or morally praiseworthy. Philanthropic groups have members, but so do the Mafia and assorted terrorist groups. All families have members, but some families are so abusive or dysfunctional that some of their members presumably have no obligation to abide by family rules. The same is certainly true of political societies. If the character of a polity is such that some or even many of its "members" are routinely exploited and oppressed, it is difficult to see how those "members" are under an obligation to obey its laws.

The advocates of the membership argument are aware of this problem, and they try in various ways to deal with it. One way is to define 'membership' or 'association,' or both, so as to make it impossible for a person to have obligations of membership within an evil or abusive association. Another is to distinguish between "bare" and "true" communities, as Dworkin does when he states that "not every group established by social practice counts as associative: a bare community must meet the four conditions of a true community *before the responsibilities it declares become genuine.*"[30] Yet another way to try to handle the problem is to

---

[30] Dworkin, *Law's Empire*, p. 204; emphasis added. Dworkin's "four conditions" are as follows (pp. 199–200; emphasis in original): "First, [the members] must regard the group's obligations as *special*, holding distinctly within the group, rather than as general duties its members owe equally to persons outside it.

Second, they must accept that these responsibilities are *personal*: that they run directly from each member to each other member, not just to the group as a whole in some collective sense....

"Third, members must see these responsibilities as following from a more general responsibility each has of *concern* for the well-being of others in the group; ...

acknowledge that one may be a member of an association that is unjust or immoral, either inherently or contingently, but to insist that obligations to comply with injustice or immorality are not real obligations. "Of course," Hardimon says, "we are assuming that role obligations deriving from unjust institutions are void *ab initio*."[31]

If these maneuvers succeed in solving or escaping the problem posed by groups of bad character, they do so by moving beyond the straightforward appeal to associative obligations. In Hardimon's case, nonvoluntary roles place us under obligations, but only so long as the associations in which we play these roles are just. In Dworkin's case, membership in a group counts as "associative" only when the group is a "true community" in which "members must suppose that the group's practices show not only concern but an *equal* concern for all members."[32] In both cases, membership is not in itself sufficient to ground or generate an obligation. Something extra must be added—an appeal to justice or to the nature of a true community—to supply what a straightforward appeal to membership lacks.

These attempts to escape the problem of group character will not avail, then. But neither will Tamir's different response to the problem. Contrary to the other advocates of the associative theory, Tamir holds that associative obligations are

> independent of the normative nature of the association. There is no reason to assume, as Dworkin does, that only membership in morally worthy associations can generate associative obligations. For example, members of the Mafia are bound by associative obligations to their fellow members, meaning that they have an obligation to attend to each other's needs, to support the families of those killed "in action," and the like. These obligations are not ultimate, and there are obviously sound moral reasons that could override them, but we cannot rule out their very existence.[33]

This is in two ways a helpful response to the problem. First, Tamir recognizes that obligations sometimes come into conflict with one another, and when they do we have to find some way to decide which of the two (or more) obligations is overriding. Second, and more important here, Tamir also recognizes that the

---

"Fourth, members must suppose that the group's practices show not only concern but an *equal* concern for all members."

[31] Hardimon, "Role Obligations," p. 350.
[32] Dworkin, *Law's Empire*, p. 200; emphasis in original.
[33] Tamir, *Liberal Nationalism*, pp. 101–102.

attempt to confine associative obligations to "true" or morally sound associations undercuts the argument from membership. As she puts it,

> If only morally valuable communities could generate associative obligations, the latter would become a meaningless concept. Our obligation to sustain just associations is not contingent on our membership in them but rather on the justice of the association's actions. Conversely, our obligation to help fellow members derives from a shared sense of membership rather than from the specific nature of their actions. Hence had we been born in a community of "villains" we might, nevertheless, be bound by associative obligations, although the latter could be overridden by moral obligations.[34]

If membership truly is a ground of obligation, then membership must count in itself; the morality or justice of the association in question cannot do all the work. On that point Tamir is surely correct. But that does not establish that membership truly is a ground of obligation. The Mafiosi and villains in her examples may have obligations to the other members of their associations, but it is not at all clear that those obligations are grounded in membership alone. In the case of the Mafia, the oaths and rituals that characterize popular accounts of Mafia practices suggest that express consent is a condition of membership. If the Mafiosi do indeed have "an obligation to attend to each other's needs, to protect each other, to support the families of those killed 'in action,' and the like," it is apparently because they have agreed to place themselves under these obligations. As for those who are born into Tamir's "community of villains," their putative obligation to help and support their fellow villains seems to rest on gratitude for the protection and nurture they received while growing up, not on their membership *as such* in the community.

The case of the person who is born into a community of villains is also instructive in another way. That is, we may grant that such a person has an obligation to help and support his fellow villains without granting that he has an obligation to follow the rules of villainy. Whether formal or informal, every association has some rules or norms that its members are expected to follow. In the case of a community of villains, one such norm might be to rob and murder "outsiders" whenever possible. Would someone born and raised in this community have an obligation—even an obligation that may be overridden—to follow this norm? Such a person might well *believe* that he has such an obligation, the power of socialization being what it is. But it does not follow that he really does have this

---

[34] Ibid., p. 102.

obligation to rob and murder "outsiders." One can discharge an obligation to help and support others without endorsing or joining in all of their activities. In the case in question, one could even argue that the best way to help and support other members of the community of villains is to try to persuade them, perhaps in the fashion of a biblical prophet, to change their villainous ways.

There is a difference, in other words, between having an obligation to the other members of our communities and having a general obligation to obey the rules, norms, or laws of those communities. Whether we are talking about a community of villains or a nation-state, obligations of membership do not extend to political obligation as it is ordinarily understood—that is, as a general obligation to obey the laws of one's polity. There is no such obligation when the polity in question is sufficiently unjust. Such an obligation does obtain when the polity is reasonably just, but membership or association alone cannot ground the obligation. Tamir's attempt to grasp the nettle and admit that membership by itself cannot distinguish moral from immoral associations is thus no more successful in overcoming the third problem facing the associative theory than the efforts of Dworkin and Hardimon.

Despite its attractions and the thoughtfulness of its supporters, the argument from membership collapses under the weight of the three problems I have noted here. It is simply not robust enough to account for a general obligation to obey the law. Something extra must always be added. Once we see this, we can also see that it is the something extra, and not the mere idea of membership, that accounts for the attractions of the membership theory. To find that something extra, I believe that we must look to the principle of fair play.

Reconsidering the Associative Theory

Before we look to fair play for that something extra, and before we even consider the natural-duty approach to political obligation, we should take note of John Horton's forceful response to criticisms of the associative theory. This response warrants special consideration because Horton speaks directly to my "something extra must be added" complaint, which he takes "to misstate the matter in a way that does a serious disservice to the robustness of the idea of associative obligations."[35] In his response, Horton makes two arguments.

The first argument is that the critics are holding the associative theory to a standard they do not apply to voluntarist theories of obligation. Proponents of the associative theory must admit that not all associations are morally praiseworthy, Horton says, but advocates of voluntarist theories must also admit that

---

[35] Horton, *Political Obligation*, 2nd ed., p. 161.

someone may voluntarily undertake an obligation to do something morally wrong. In the latter case, however, the tendency is to say that the voluntarily incurred obligation is not binding or that it will be overridden by the general obligation not to do wrong; either way, there is no concern that these escape clauses tend to undercut the general claim that voluntary actions generate obligations. But why not grant the same courtesy to associative obligations? As Horton says, it is unclear "why the fact that some associations may not be 'decent, fair or morally praiseworthy' should undermine or trivialize the significance of associative obligations *in general*, any more than it does voluntarily assumed obligations."[36]

This is an effective but limited response, in my view. It is effective because Horton makes a fair point against voluntarist theories, but it is limited because the point does not apply to fair-play and natural-duty theories, which ground political obligation in considerations that include fairness, justice, or some other moral requirement from the outset. Horton could reply that political obligations grounded in fair play or natural duty are still subject to being overridden, and thus in the same position as strictly voluntarist and associative theories, but that is not enough to sustain his *tu quoque* argument. For there is a difference between invalidating a putative obligation from the outset—as happens when we say that there are some things to which one cannot truly consent or some associations in which membership carries no obligations—and overriding a valid obligation. Horton himself hints at the difference when he says, parenthetically, "For the purposes of this argument, although not for all purposes, it does not much matter which of these formulations we adopt," with "the formulations" being cases in which "people will not be regarded as having acquired an obligation," on the one hand, and cases in which "whatever obligation that they have acquired will be overridden by their duty not to do wrong," on the other.[37] Perhaps which formulation we use does not much matter when the target is consent theory, but it surely matters when we bring fair-play and natural-duty theories into the argument.

We may set that concern aside, however, for Horton's *tu quoque* argument at best can do nothing more than demonstrate that other theories suffer from the same weaknesses as the associative theory. Stopping at this point will simply give comfort to those who doubt that there are any genuine political obligations. That is why Horton goes on to his second argument in response to the "something extra must be added" objection to the membership theory. In this case the argument comprises an extended defense—several pages of Chapter 6 of the second edition of *Political Obligation* and all of Chapter 7—of the merits of

---

[36] Ibid., p. 161; emphasis in original. The phrase Horton quotes is from my "Membership, Fair Play, and Political Obligation," p. 110.

[37] Horton, *Political Obligation*, p. 161.

the associative theory. The aim is to show why associative relationships "cannot *simply* be reduced to relations of reciprocity or gratitude, and are also very different from contractual relations."[38]

This positive argument for the associative theory has two aspects. The first, which Horton calls "the Hobbesian argument," recognizes that membership in a polity can entail an obligation to it only if it supplies "the generic good of a polity"—that is, "an effective coercive authority to provide order, security and some measure of social stability."[39] A polity that is too weak, divided, or ineffective to provide this generic good runs the risk of being no polity at all. One that does well enough in this regard, though, will satisfy a necessary but not sufficient condition for associative obligations. That is why the second aspect of the argument must come into play before these obligations are fully in force. This second aspect is the strictly associative, or even "communitarian," part of the argument.[40] Without this element, there will be nothing to attach a person to any particular polity that meets the "generic good" criterion, and thus to satisfy the particularity requirement for political obligation. This attachment must be rooted in one's identification with one's polity, and this attachment in turn will have both an objective and a subjective aspect. Objectively, "membership may be conferred on one by place of birth or through descent. In this sense the political identity that derives from membership of a polity can be understood as a kind of ascribed status; in the contemporary world, typically that of a citizen."[41] Subjectively, one must identify or think of oneself as a member of the polity, even if one sharply disagrees with some of its actions or practices. More important than the endorsement or approval of its practices and values is "the acknowledgement of a common political authority: this is the core content of political obligation." And this acknowledgement "will be embedded in something like a narrative of political identity ... in which the history, actions and future of the polity, in general its fate, are seen as connected in a meaningful way with the member's own."[42]

This defense of the associative theory is both powerful and in many ways appealing. Its emphasis on the subjective aspect of the argument indicates, though, that Horton continues to conflate the sense or feeling of obligation with obligation itself, albeit more openly and subtly than before. Indeed, Horton's position seems to be that we cannot conflate the two, for they are not truly distinct from each other. His aim, he says, is to provide some commonplace reminders

---

[38] Ibid., p. 164; emphasis added.
[39] Ibid., p. 176.
[40] For the connection with communitarianism, see, e.g., ibid., pp. 150 and 180.
[41] Ibid., p. 183.
[42] Ibid., p. 184.

of the importance of the sense of obligation. These reminders "do not 'prove' that we have political obligations (whatever that might mean), ... but they are an important part of any remotely accurate phenomenology of our ethico-political experience: they show how people commonly think, feel and act, at least *as if* being members of a polity were something meaningful."[43] As a matter of phenomenology, I suspect that Horton is right about the common "ethico-political experience" of a great many people. His account certainly tells us something significant about the importance of loyalty, patriotism, and the sense of civic duty in the lives, and deaths, of polities. But there is a price to be paid for eliding the distinction between the sense of obligation and obligation itself.

This price becomes clear when Horton addresses the "one obvious question" that may be asked about his two-dimensional account of associative theory. "When a polity possesses its generic value," he says, "and both objective and subjective aspects of political identity are in place, we have a situation in which all the conditions of political obligation are fully met." But "what happens when they come apart, especially if they radically diverge, as there is no strictly necessary connection between them"?[44] To this question Horton's answer seems to be that various things can happen, from the dissolution of the polity to the reaffirmation of its integrity, much as we would expect from the experience of actual polities. This answer follows, though, brief reflections on three ways in which the objective and subjective aspects of political order can, and do, come apart. First, "people may identify with an actual or potential polity that is distinct from that of which they are 'objectively' taken to be members."[45] Second, "people may identify very weakly if at all with 'their' polity, perhaps having only the most narrowly instrumental attitude towards it." And third, "there is the case of people who identify with a polity that effectively rejects or excludes them." In such a case, Horton says,

> there may not always be a straightforward answer ... as to where this leaves their political obligations; although, if the polity no longer offers them *any* security, it would seem that subjective identification may not be sufficient to support the attribution of political obligations.[46]

For present purposes, cases of the second and third kind are especially significant—and especially troublesome for the membership theory. In cases of the second kind, we may want to know why these people have only a very weak

---

[43] Ibid., p. 171; emphasis in original.
[44] Ibid., p. 187.
[45] Ibid., p. 187, as are the two following quotations.
[46] Ibid., p. 188; emphasis in original.

and instrumental identification with "their" polity. Is it because the polity itself is too weak and ineffective to inspire much by way of identification? If so, then the remedy—easier said than done, to be sure—is to find ways to bring the polity closer to what it should be. Or is it the result of the "apathy, cynicism and political alienation" to which Horton refers, or perhaps the result of subscribing to a misguided theory, such as philosophical anarchism? If that is the problem, then the remedy is to convince the apathetic, cynical, and alienated that their subjective understanding of their political situation is inaccurate, misguided, and dangerous. Being a member of the polity is valuable, in other words, whether they appreciate it or not. Furthermore, their failure to identify properly with the polity will serve only to make it more difficult for the polity to provide the generic good of order and security from which they benefit. Their attitude is self-defeating, in short, and threatening to all those who depend upon the generic good only the polity can provide.

To make this argument, however, Horton must move from the sense of identity as it is to what it ought to be. The latter, moreover, requires that the sense of identity be linked to the purposes of the polity and the vital part that properly conceived membership plays in the achievement of those purposes. That is to say that the emphasis must shift from subjective identity to the proper functioning of the polity—to questions about the content and character of political association, and of what membership entails if the polity is to function as it should. Questions of this kind will prompt considerations of fair play, in other words, as one asks what the activities of the other members mean for him and what he owes them in return.

The third way in which the objective and subjective aspects of political identity can come apart leads to the same conclusion by a different route. In this case the problem is that some people may have a sense of identity with the polity despite its rejection or exclusion of them. Perhaps, I will add, they cling to the sense of their membership even when they are oppressed and exploited by other members. In cases such as these, a kind of false consciousness is at work, for some people will not be genuine members of the polity no matter how much they think they are. What really counts, then, is not subjective identity but true membership in a polity that provides the generic good of order and security. To repeat Horton's conclusion, "it would seem that subjective identification may not be sufficient to support the attribution of political obligations."[47]

The problem with Horton's conclusion is that it does not go far enough. In addition to being insufficient to provide a foundation for political obligations, subjective identity is also not necessary. As I argued earlier, there is a difference

---

[47] Ibid., p. 188.

between having an obligation, political or otherwise, and conceiving of oneself as having that obligation. Someone may be a member of a polity, or a participant in a fair scheme of social cooperation, without perceiving that she is. Indeed, this is a crucial point if the challenge of the anarchists and others who doubt the existence of political obligation is to be met, as the advocates of the associative theory hope to do. If subjective identification with a polity is a necessary condition of having an obligation to obey its laws, then the associative theorist must be prepared to say that those who lack or deny this identification are either caught up in a kind of false consciousness of their own, from which they need to be rescued, or they simply do not have an obligation to obey the laws of the polity that claims them as members. But this is an embarrassing conclusion. On the one hand, it requires membership theorists to explain what it is about membership *as such* that grounds political obligation, even in the absence of the subjective sense of membership; on the other, it confines political obligation to those who possess that subjective sense and releases those who do not from the general obligation to obey the law. The latter alternative cannot provide the basis for a satisfactory theory of political obligation, and the former demands an explanation that the appeal to membership alone seems unable to supply.

Despite Horton's efforts on behalf of the associative theory, in sum, I continue to believe that we must look elsewhere—that is, to the principle of fair play—for an adequate foundation for political obligation. There is, however, one more rival theory to consider first.

Natural-Duty Theory

One of the curious features of the natural-duty approach to political obligation is that it begins with Rawls's reliance in *A Theory of Justice* on a distinction between obligations and duties. As I noted in Chapter 2, Rawls holds that a person must do something to acquire an obligation, such as make a promise or sign a contract, whereas natural duties "apply to us without regard to our voluntary acts."[48] One implication of this distinction, according to Rawls, is that most people have no general obligation to obey the laws of their polity, for they have not *done* what is necessary to incur such an *obligation*. Everyone, however, is subject to the natural duty of justice, which "requires us to support and to comply with just institutions that exist and apply to us."[49] For Rawls, this duty takes the place of political obligation. As he says, "there are several ways in which one may be

---

[48] Rawls, *A Theory of Justice*, rev. ed. (Cambridge, MA: Harvard University Press, 1999), p. 98.
[49] Ibid., p. 99.

bound to political institutions. For the most part the natural duty of justice is the more fundamental, since it binds citizens generally and requires no voluntary acts in order to apply."[50]

To find the Rawlsian natural-duty approach to political obedience (if not obligation) persuasive, one will have to agree that there is a natural duty of justice that entails a duty to support and comply with just institutions that apply to us. Agreeing to that does not require acceptance of the contractual reasoning through which Rawls identifies and defines the natural duties, however, and it is noteworthy that the leading proponents of the natural-duty approach to political obligation have discerned the natural duties in other ways. No matter how the natural duties are discovered, however, a difficult problem remains for anyone who would base political obligation, or political obedience, on such a duty. This is the problem of "the particularity requirement" noted in Chapter 2—a requirement, according to John Simmons, that theories of political obligation must satisfy. As Simmons says, "we are only interested in those moral requirements [including obligations and duties] which bind an individual to one *particular* political community, set of political institutions, etc."[51] We may have a natural duty to support and comply with just institutions, in other words, but that duty does not confine us to supporting and complying with any particular just institution. If I, a citizen of the United States, find that my country and Canada are both just polities, then I have a natural duty to support Canadian institutions that apparently is as strong as my duty to support those of the United States. But in that case there seems to be no special bond between me and the institutions of my country. But it is that kind of special bond, as Simmons points out, that theories of political obligation are supposed to provide.[52]

Advocates of the natural-duty approach have tried to show, in response, that there is something about the relationship between a person and her country that establishes a special political bond—some sense in which its institutions "apply" to her in a way that the institutions of other political societies, no matter how just, fail to do. Thus Jeremy Waldron draws a distinction between "insiders" and "outsiders" that "explains much of the specialness of an individual's relation to the institutions of his own country, at least so far as moral requirement is concerned."[53] A New Zealander, to use Waldron's example, has the special insider

---

[50] Ibid., p. 100. For a perceptive critique of Rawls's attempt to base "moral requirements functionally equivalent to political obligations on the 'natural duties of justice,'" see George Klosko, "Political Obligation and the Natural Duties of Justice," *Philosophy and Public Affairs* 23 (1994): 251–70, at 251.

[51] Simmons, *Moral Principles and Political Obligations*, p. 31; emphasis in original.

[52] Ibid., pp. 155–56.

[53] Waldron, "Special Ties and Natural Duties," *Philosophy and Public Affairs* 22 (1993): 3–30; reprinted in, and quoted from, *The Duty To Obey the Law*, ed. William Edmundson (Lanham, MD: Rowman & Littlefield, 1999), p. 284.

relation to the laws of New Zealand because those laws "have been set up precisely to address the question of the rights and duties of someone in his position vis-à-vis his fellow New Zealanders."[54] Because they "apply" to him in a way they cannot apply to a citizen of another country, Waldron believes that the example shows how the appeal to natural duty can satisfy the particularity requirement.

Christopher Heath Wellman makes a similar move in his attempt to derive political obligation from the duty of "samaritanism." That is, rather than appealing to a natural duty to support just institutions, Wellman grounds his argument on a natural duty to rescue those who are in peril, at least when one can do so without unreasonable risk or cost to oneself. As Wellman says, "virtually no one denies that one would have a moral duty to wade into a shallow pond to save a drowning baby, even if this rescue requires one to get one's shoes and trousers wet."[55] He then goes on to argue that political regimes or states are necessary to the fulfillment of this samaritan duty: "Given that states rescue us all from the perilous circumstances that would inevitably prevail in their absence, and because states rely upon the compliance of their constituents to perform their political functions, it seems to follow that each of us has a samaritan duty to obey the law."[56]

As his use of the phrase *seems to follow* indicates, Wellman recognizes that he cannot move quite so quickly from the duty to rescue to the existence of political obligation. Widespread compliance may be necessary if states are to rescue us from "the perilous circumstances that would prevail in their absence," but that is not to say that my compliance, or yours, or any individual's is necessary. If it is not, then no one has a samaritan duty to obey the law. To overcome this difficulty, Wellman recommends "that we merely import the nonconsequential consideration of fairness" and "understand our political obligations as our fair share of the communal samaritan chore of rescuing others from the perils of the state of nature."[57] Following this recommendation, though, requires Wellman to confront two difficult questions for his theory. First, how does this "samaritan chore" become "communal"? And second, how can a samaritan duty to rescue satisfy the particularity requirement? Why can't I do my samaritan duty, that is, in some way other than by obeying the law? And if complying with the law is required, why can't I do my duty by complying with the laws of some state (or states) other than the one that claims my allegiance?

---

[54] Ibid.

[55] Wellman, "Samaritanism and the Duty to Obey the Law," in C. H. Wellman and A. J. Simmons, *Is There a Duty to Obey the Law?* (Cambridge, UK: Cambridge University Press, 2005), p. 31.

[56] Ibid., p. 31.

[57] Ibid., p. 33.

Wellman's answer to these questions is to point to the "key function of states," which is "to get everyone in the given territory to defer to a single definitive set of rules."[58] Disobeying the law is therefore impermissible—and here Wellman adds not only the usual *ceteris paribus* clause but also the qualification that one has no *prima facie* duty to obey the unjust laws of a legitimate regime—"because legal obedience is required as one's fair share of helping to rescue others from peril."[59] The answer to the first question, then, is that obedience to law is necessary to the performance of one's samaritan duty, if not perhaps sufficient, because of the vital importance of the rule of law, without which we would be living in something resembling an inhospitable state of nature. The rule of law is not something that one can institute by himself, so establishing and maintaining "a single definitive set of rules" is necessarily a communal chore. To the second question, the answer is that obedience to the laws of a particular state is required because that is the only way one can do her "fair share" toward the performance of the "key function of states." A citizen of Sweden, for example, has a responsibility to help maintain the rule of law in that country, and in the ordinary course of events she cannot discharge that responsibility by obeying the laws of Switzerland or Saudi Arabia. The "political chaos" of the state of nature would present a "coordination problem" that only political institutions can solve; and "once one recognizes what is distinctive about political institutions, it is not difficult to appreciate why one must support one's own state and why this support must come in the form of obedience to the government's legal commands."[60]

Wellman's samaritan theory thus responds to the particularity problem in a way that speaks directly to the problem of political obligation. It does so, however, by transforming samaritanism into a form of fair-play theory. This is not a transformation that Wellman intends, for he has elsewhere rejected fair-play theory, as Simmons notes in his rebuttal to Wellman.[61] Nevertheless, Wellman's appeal to "considerations of fairness" and doing one's "fair share" clearly indicates that he is conceiving of political and legal systems as cooperative practices to which the principle of fair play applies. Moreover, Wellman must make this appeal, for he knows that samaritanism itself is a humanitarian rather than a political duty; hence the need to "merely import" considerations of fairness into his theory.

---

[58] Ibid., p. 44.

[59] Ibid., p. 45; and p. 53 for the intent "to show only that there is a prima facie obligation to obey the *just* laws of a *legitimate* regime" (emphasis in original).

[60] Ibid., pp. 41 and 43.

[61] Simmons, "The Duty to Obey and Our Natural Moral Duties," in Wellman and Simmons, *Is There a Duty to Obey the Law?*, p. 186, citing Wellman, "Toward a Liberal Theory of Political Obligation," *Ethics* 111 (2001): 737–38.

Wellman might take this criticism on board, as it were, by arguing that it is the samaritan grounding that is not only the distinctive but the crucial feature of his theory. Without the samaritan duty to rescue others from the perils of the state of nature, he might say, there is no justification for forming political societies and establishing "a single definitive set of rules" in the first place. If that is his point, then I am willing to grant it. Fair-play considerations only apply to ongoing enterprises. They do not give us reasons to launch new ones, except perhaps when introducing a new enterprise is a way of correcting an unfair aspect of an existing practice. This is a point, though, that one may concede without admitting a defect in the fair-play approach to political obligation, as I shall explain at the end of this chapter. The main point here is that samaritanism in itself is inadequate as the basis for political obligation. Wellman's recourse to considerations of fairness is absolutely necessary to his case for a moral duty to obey the law that meets the particularity requirement. Samaritanism may be the distinctive feature of his theory, in short, but it is fair play that is crucial.

Much the same point applies to the natural-duty arguments for political obligation advanced by Waldron and Anna Stilz.[62] Rather than the samaritan duty to rescue, however, Waldron and Stilz follow Rawls in resting their arguments directly on the natural duty to support and comply with just institutions. In fact, both reach beyond Rawls to Immanuel Kant's *The Metaphysics of Morals*, and particularly to Kant's claim that persons living in a lawless state of nature would be duty-bound to create and enter into a law-governed society—the only condition, in Kant's view, in which it is possible to live justly. As Waldron quotes Kant, "'If you are so situated as to be unavoidably side by side with others, you ought to abandon the state of nature and enter, with all others, a juridical state of affairs, that is, a state of distributive legal justice.'"[63] Following Kant, then, Waldron and Stilz take the state to be a necessary institution: "an indispensable means to fulfilling a moral duty by which we are already bound, namely, the duty to respect others' rights."[64]

---

[62] Waldron, "Special Ties and Natural Duties"; Stilz, *Liberal Loyalty: Freedom, Obligation, and the State* (Princeton, NJ: Princeton University Press, 2009); and Stilz, "Why Does the State Matter Morally? Political Obligation and Particularity," in *Varieties of Sovereignty and Citizenship*, ed. S. R. Ben-Porath and R. M. Smith (Philadelphia: University of Pennsylvania Press, 2013).

[63] Waldron, "Special Ties and Natural Duties," p. 280, quoting from John Ladd's translation in Kant, *The Metaphysical Elements of Justice* (Indianapolis: Bobbs-Merrill, 1965), p. 71. In *Liberal Loyalty*, Stilz twice quotes the same passage from §42 of the first part of *The Metaphysics of Morals*, translating the passage as follows: "'When you cannot avoid living side by side with all others, you ought to leave the state of nature and proceed into a rightful condition'" (p. 53 and p. 198, n. 30).

[64] Stilz, "Why Does the State Matter Morally?," p. 256.

This still leaves the particularity problem to be addressed, and Waldron and Stilz each do so by way of the "side by side" aspect of Kant's argument. As Waldron puts the point,

> Since no one can afford to wait until all possible conflicts arise so that all can be definitively settled at once, the Kantian approach implies that I should enter quickly into a form of society with those immediately adjacent to me, those with whose interests my resource use is likely to pose the most frequent and dangerous conflicts.[65]

The upshot, according to Stilz, is that "[m]embers of a state are bound together solely by their territorial situation, a situation that brings them into sustained contact with each other."[66] From this sustained contact the state emerges as a system of laws to settle conflicts and "mediate" some of "our general, coercible duties"—that is, natural duties. According to this "institutional mediation hypothesis"—an hypothesis Stilz believes to be true—"[i]f some of our duties were so mediated, then we might have a general, coercible duty to comply with and support the state's system of law."[67] For both Waldron and Stilz, then, the natural duty to support and comply with just institutions leads quickly to the moral obligation to obey the laws of the body politic that those who live "side by side" are morally required to form.

Waldron's and Stilz's Kantian natural-duty theories thus resemble Wellman's samaritan approach in their ability to meet and overcome the particularity problem. They also resemble Wellman's approach, however, in their implicit reliance on the principle of fair play. Waldron's way of clarifying the distinction between "insiders" and "outsiders" is instructive in this regard:

> In general, a person is an insider in relation to an institution if and only if it is part of the point of that institution to do justice to some claim of his among all the claims with which it deals. So, for example, a New Zealand resident is an insider in relation to the fiscal and welfare institutions of New Zealand, for it is part of the point of those institutions to do justice to his claims to income and assistance along

---

[65] Waldron, "Special Ties and Natural Duties," p. 281.

[66] Stilz, *Liberal Loyalty*, p. 199. Stilz's argument in "Why Does the State Matter Morally?" places greater emphasis on historical factors, such as "a historical practice of political authority" and "a history of participation in this particular state" (p. 261). Her argument there, though, seems to slide toward associative theory, with the problems that follow from appeals to identity and the *sense* of obligation.

[67] Stilz, "Why Does the State Matter Morally?," p. 247.

with all the other claims that they address. The aim of the institutions is to determine *what burdens it is fair to impose, and what benefits it is fair to confer,* on this person and on others in New Zealand in the course of that overall enterprise.[68]

The evidence of an implicit appeal to the principle of fair play is even stronger in Stilz's more fully developed statement of the Kant-inspired natural-duty theory, beginning with her account in *Liberal Loyalty* of democracy as "a shared cooperative venture" and the state as a "joint law-enforcement practice."[69] Stilz goes on, in "Why Does the State Matter Morally?," to argue that "citizens' history of sharing a state together gives rise to new associative obligations among them," but this argument also trades directly, if implicitly, on considerations of fair play.[70] As she says,

> I suggest we look to two shared activities that peoples characteristically undertake together, sustaining the state and producing the law. First, people sustain the institutions that define and enforce their rights. It is their *cooperative activity*, by obeying the law and paying taxes, that creates these institutions.... They recognize certain rules in common and *play by these rules* in their interactions with one another.... The fact that these people participate together in *a rule-governed social practice* gives them *a special relation to their fellow participants* that they don't have to those outside the practice.[71]

Benefits and burdens, fair shares, cooperative activities, playing by the rules—these are all terms from the vocabulary of fair play. Whether the overt appeal is to the samaritan duty to rescue or to the duty to support and comply with just institutions that apply to us, it is the principle of fair play that is doing the real work in these natural-duty theories of political obligation. The question is why the proponents of these theories fail to recognize that point.

The same question could be put to those who trace the obligation to obey the law to some special feature or features of democracy, as Thomas Christiano and David Estlund do.[72] Although neither author explicitly presents his theory

---

[68] Waldron, "Special Ties and Natural Duties," p. 283; emphasis added. Note also the references to "fair shares" on p. 283 and the discussion of cooperation, the need for assurance, and problems of coordination on pp. 288–89.

[69] Stilz, *Liberal Loyalty,* p. 191 for the first quotation and p. 201 for the second.

[70] Stilz, "Why Does the State Matter Morally?," p. 259.

[71] Ibid., pp. 259–60; emphasis added.

[72] Christiano, *The Constitution of Equality: Democratic Authority and Its Limits* (Oxford: Oxford University Press, 2008); Estlund, *Democratic Authority.*

in the terms of the natural-duty approach, and Estlund even frames his as a "normative consent" argument, their similarities to the broadly Kantian–Rawlsian theories of Wellman, Waldron, and Stilz have not gone unnoticed.[73] Moreover, Christiano does invoke the idea of a natural duty at a key point in his justification of the authority of democracy, where he states, "Each human being has a fundamental *and natural duty* to treat other human beings as equals and this implies that each person must try to realize the equal advancement of the interests of other human beings."[74] This natural duty follows from a *principle of public equality* that is, according to Christiano, at the foundation of democracy, and this duty requires every person "to attempt to bring about, *and to conform his actions to,* those institutions that publicly realize the equal advancement of interests"—institutions that notably include those that secure the rule of law.[75] Conforming our actions to institutions that protect and promote public equality thus entails a *pro tanto* obligation to obey the laws of democratic polities.

So stated, however, the democracy-founded obligation seems to run up against the same difficulty that Wellman, Waldron, and Stilz have all confronted—that is, the particularity problem. Even if we grant that the principle of public equality grounds an obligation to obey the laws of democracies, in other words, we still need a reason to believe that the obligation in question binds everyone to obey the laws of the particular democratic polity that claims her as a citizen or member. But Christiano believes he has an appropriate response to this problem. As he says,

> Each has a duty to comply with *their own* democratic institutions since these institutions are necessary to treating *their fellows* publicly as equals. The duty to treat people as equals is not fully discharged by trying to support the construction of democracy in other parts of the world. If one only did this and failed to act in accordance with a reasonably well-constituted democratic order, then one would be treating *one's fellows* publicly as inferiors. And this would be a very weighty violation of equality.[76]

---

[73] See, e.g., A. John Simmons, *Boundaries of Authority* (Oxford: Oxford University Press, 2016), p. 63.

[74] Christiano, *The Constitution of Equality*, p. 249; emphasis added.

[75] Ibid., p. 249; emphasis added. For the importance of the rule of law, see pp. 172–76 and 238. For *public equality*, see p. 2, where Christiano defines it as requiring not only that we treat others as equals but also that "the institutions of society must be structured so that all can see that they are being treated as equals."

[76] Ibid., p. 250; emphasis added throughout.

Whether the above response deals adequately with the particularity requirement, and whether Christiano has proven the case for the democratic provenance of obligations to obey the law, are matters of dispute.[77] My own sense is that Christiano's position is strong, if not impregnable, in both respects. With regard to the particularity requirement, though, the strength of his position is once again the result of an implicit appeal to considerations of fair play. There are numerous passages that support this conclusion, including the references to "fellows" in the preceding quotation, which hints at the idea of the democratic polity as a cooperative practice in which the participants stand, as equals, in a relationship of reciprocity with one another. To be sure, it is possible that Christiano's references to fellowship indicate that he is drawing on the sense of identity and membership involved in associative approaches to obligation rather than cooperative practices and fair play, but nothing else he says supports this conclusion. Other statements, though, do suggest that he is relying implicitly on considerations of fair play, such as his claim that decision-making in a democracy "is a publicly just and *fair* way of making collective decisions in light of conflicts of interests and disagreements about *shared aspects* of social life."[78] Indeed, Christiano invokes a "duty of justice" that seems to be much the same as the duty of fair play: "The reasonably just state is engaged in a morally necessary activity in the sense that someone who fails to comply with the reasonably just state's publicly promulgated rules is normally violating a duty of justice to his fellow citizens." In addition, these fellow citizens require "the kinds of *assurance* that is necessary in a political society where the rights of persons are so deeply determined by the legal system."[79] Put in the terms of fair-play theory, this is to say that one's fellow citizens require the assurance that their law-abiding actions will not simply open them to exploitation at the hands of free riders and double-crossers who would play them for suckers. When confronted with the need to show that the principle of public equality grounds a duty of justice to the particular polity of which one is a member, Christiano finds himself relying on considerations of fair play within a polity conceived as a cooperative practice, or meta-practice, under the rule of law.

Whether this outcome must be the case for any natural-duty theory of political obligation must remain an open question. On the evidence of the four

---

[77] According to Simmons, *Boundaries of Authority*, pp. 80–82, Christiano's solution to the particularity problem rests on the unsupported assumption that the boundaries we share with our "fellows" are truly legitimate boundaries. According to Harrison Frye and George Klosko, Christiano's (and others') arguments for democratic authority justify a requirement to *respect* the law but not an *obligation* to obey it (Frye and Klosko, "Democratic Authority and Respect for Law," *Law and Philosophy* 36 [2017]: 1–23).

[78] Christiano, *The Constitution of Equality*, p. 250; emphasis added throughout.

[79] Ibid., p. 239 for this and the preceding quotation; emphasis added.

theorists considered above, however, the answer to the question seems to be that it does. Perhaps the more pertinent question, once again, is why the proponents of natural-duty theories have failed to recognize where their implicit appeals to fair play have been leading them. That is a question to be considered in concluding this chapter.

Conclusion

Of the three rivals to the fair-play account of political obligation discussed in this chapter, I have attended most closely to the two that seem to be the most serious, and most attractive, rivals. Neither of them is adequate, however. Associative (or membership) theory is attractive because it speaks to the *feeling* or *sense* of obligation to polity or country that a great many people have, but it does not tell us whether people are right or wrong to have that feeling. Beyond the sense of belonging to a polity, there must be something that justifies people in believing that the polity is worthy of their allegiance and its laws of their obedience. Membership by itself cannot supply that justification; the principle of fair play can. For its part, natural-duty theory has the attractive feature of appealing to widespread and firm moral convictions about the duty to rescue people in distress or to support and comply with just institutions. If these appeals to natural duty are to overcome the particularity problem, however, the theory's advocates must find some way to explain how a natural duty can entail an obligation to obey the laws of a certain, specific polity. In doing so, as we have seen, they resort, more or less openly, to the principle of fair play. Why not, then, simply ground political obligation in fair play?

There appear to be two answers to this question. One is the possibility that fair play may be necessary to an adequate theory of political obligation but not sufficient in itself—hence the need to reach beyond fair play to a natural duty of some sort. The other answer is that fair-play theory is unacceptable on its own terms because it suffers from a defect that an appeal to natural duty can either compensate for or correct. With regard to this second possibility, the principal concern is that fair play cannot withstand the objection that it applies only when people have accepted or willingly received the benefits of a cooperative practice. The proper response, however, is to meet this objection directly, not to try to evade it by cloaking what is essentially a fair-play argument in the guise of a natural-duty theory. Meeting that objection is a challenge I take up in the next chapter.

What, then, of the other possible answer? Is there something that a natural-duty account brings to a theory of political obligation that the principle of fair play cannot supply? The obvious candidate here, as I have acknowledged in discussing Wellman's samaritanism, is that the natural-duty approach can tell us why we should form and enter into polities or states. This is indeed something that considerations of fair play cannot do. An otherwise unconnected group of strangers who find themselves thrown together in something akin to a state of nature will no doubt have good reasons, moral and prudential, to form an association under rules, but fair play will not be one of them. That is, there may be reasons to form an association in which playing fair is a praiseworthy virtue, but one cannot have a duty to play fair with the others until the association is an up-and-going cooperative practice. Natural duty can explain why it is morally necessary to form such practices, though, and that is why the appeal to natural duty is the crucial element in a satisfactory theory of political obligation.

There are, I think, two problems with this argument. First, it requires us to take seriously state-of-nature scenarios in which rational, mature, and apparently self-sufficient individuals find themselves contemplating not only the advantages and disadvantages, but also the justice and injustice, of entering into a cooperative practice governed by law. Others may take such scenarios seriously, but anyone who believes, as I do, that human beings are rational animals dependent upon the society of others to attain some degree of rationality, maturity, and self-sufficiency will find such state-of-nature speculation unpersuasive. The second problem is that this argument has little, if anything, to do with political obligation. The point of a theory of political obligation is to determine whether people do or do not have a general obligation to obey the laws of the political bodies in which they find themselves—already existing, ongoing polities, states, and bodies politic. To reach such a determination, there is no need to find reasons for people to form such political associations. It is enough to start where we are, in the midst of such associations, and find a theory that can help us to know whether we are indeed subject to an obligation to obey the law or not. As a foundation for such a theory, the principle of fair play is perfectly adequate. Or so it will be if it can meet the criticisms brought directly against it. To these criticisms I now turn.

4

Political Obligation as Fair Play

Elaboration and Defense

In the two preceding chapters I have tried to establish the groundwork for the fair-play theory of political obligation. In Chapter 2, this effort took the form of an explication of the fundamental idea of a cooperative practice; in Chapter 3, the focus was on the theory's three principal rivals, all of which were found wanting or—in the case of natural-duty theories—to be a kind of fair-play theory in disguise. But what of fair-play theory itself? What have the critics had to say against it, and how might their objections be met? These are the questions I now address. I begin by elaborating the argument from fair play, with particular attention to the idea of the polity as a meta-practice that administers the rule of law. In the second part of the chapter I defend the argument, as elaborated, against the various criticisms raised against it in the fifty years or so since H. L. A. Hart and John Rawls brought considerations of fair play to a point of prominence in political and legal philosophy. I then complete the account by contrasting my understanding of fair-play theory with George Klosko's multiple-principle approach to political obligation—an approach that relies heavily, but not exclusively, on the principle of fairness.

Fair Play Elaborated

According to the principle of fair play, as we have seen, anyone who takes part in and enjoys the benefits of a cooperative practice has a duty to contribute to the production of those benefits, even when her contribution is not necessary to their production. This principle applies to large as well as to small practices, including any body politic that its members may reasonably regard as a cooperative enterprise. Those who are part of such an enterprise have a *pro tanto* or *prima facie* obligation to obey its laws because they owe it to their fellow citizens and other cooperating members of the body politic to do so. This duty has its correlative in the right of every law-abiding member to similar obedience, *ceteris paribus*, on the part of the other members. The obligation, in other words, is owed not to some impersonal force—usually called the state or the government—but to those persons whose cooperative efforts and sacrifices make it possible for others to enjoy the benefits of the political order. If the body politic is not one that it is reasonable to regard as a cooperative practice, then there is neither a general obligation to obey its laws nor a corresponding right to demand obedience of others. There may be moral obligations to obey particular laws in these circumstances—other things being equal, the wickedness of the regime in power neither justifies nor excuses such offenses as murder and reckless driving—but there will be no political obligation as such.

This is to say, in terms I used in Chapter 2, that fair-play theory has a critical, aspirational element. It holds up an ideal of the polity as a cooperative practice—a "mutually beneficial and just scheme of social cooperation," according to Rawls[1]—that no actual polity is likely to realize fully. But it also entails the existence of a threshold that a practice must cross before it qualifies as a cooperative practice. That is the critical aspect of fair-play theory. Because the principle grounds political obligation not in any individual act, such as the expression of consent, but in the character of the body politic itself, those who follow the principle of fair play will need to determine whether it is reasonable to regard the political order that claims authority over them as a cooperative enterprise deserving of their obedience.

These fundamental features of the fair-play theory of political obligation should require no further comment here. There are two other features, though, that serve to forge the connection between *political* obligation and the duty to obey the *law*, and they do require elaboration. Both features are captured in a single sentence: *The polity is a meta-practice responsible for administering the rule of law.*

To say that the polity is a meta-practice, as I explained in Chapter 2, is to say that it shares the features of other cooperative practices while at the same time rising above or superintending them. To return to an earlier example, the members of a carpool are engaged with one another in a cooperative practice, but that practice itself depends upon the existence of roads, traffic signals, and other resources usually provided by the polity. The people who play volleyball regularly in the park, to recur to another example, need the facilities that the park provides to carry on their cooperative practice, and they will also need some way to settle disputes with the members of other cooperative practices—softball or

---

[1] John Rawls, "Legal Obligation and the Duty of Fair Play," in *Law and Philosophy*, ed. Sidney Hook (New York: New York University Press, 1964), pp. 9–10.

football players, perhaps—who want to use the same part of the park for their activities. There may even be cases in which disputes arise among the participants in a cooperative practice that require intervention or settlement by someone who is not part of that practice. Even if a spontaneous practice develops over time into a highly formal and professional organization, there will still be occasions in which the rules of the organization and the officials who enforce them will not be competent to resolve the conflicts that occur. In ice hockey, for example, the question sometimes arises of whether someone's play has become so rough as to constitute not merely a foul within the game but outright assault and battery; in the suburbs of Detroit, Michigan, not long ago, a soccer player faced a murder charge, and was ultimately convicted of involuntary manslaughter, for striking and killing the official who had ejected him, moments before, from a match.[2] In such cases as these, and many others, the need to appeal to an authority outside the practice is obvious. The polity, as a *meta*-practice administering the rule of law, supplies that need.

What exactly constitutes the rule of law is a question that has been evaded as often as answered, and it has been answered in various ways. As one recent commentator observes, the rule of law "stands in the peculiar state of being *the* preeminent legitimating political ideal in the world today, without agreement upon precisely what it means."[3] Even so, that commentator, Brian Tamanaha, finds sufficient agreement to identify three themes that run through the rule-of-law tradition, and these seem both accurate and concise enough to be of service here. They are (1) government limited by law; (2) formal legality; and (3) the classical republican ideal of the rule of law, not of men.[4] The first of these themes reflects the desire to protect people's rights and interests by confining the authority of those who have power over them within established bounds; and the third requires those in power to act not as they please but in accordance with public reasons and recognized procedures. Each of these themes, and certainly the two together, goes some way toward explaining how the rule of law enables a large-scale cooperative practice to be mutually beneficial and just, at least in the sense of protecting those governed by law from arbitrary and unchecked power.

With regard to the second theme, formal legality (or simply *legality*, in the jargon of legal theory), further explanation may be necessary. The point of this theme is that certain conditions must be met before the elements of a legal system are truly lawful. According to Rawls, for instance, one of the key precepts

---

[2] *Detroit Free Press* (March 13, 2015); available as of July 23, 2017, at http://www.freep.com/story/news/local/michigan/wayne/2015/03/13/soccer-referee-sentencing/70258968/.

[3] Brian Tamanaha, *On the Rule of Law: History, Politics, Theory* (Cambridge, UK: Cambridge University Press, 2004), p. 4; emphasis in original.

[4] Ibid., chap. 9.

of the rule of law is that similar cases are to be treated similarly; another is that there is no offense or crime without a law, which itself comprises several formal provisions, such as the requirement that laws be promulgated, that they be defined clearly, and that they be prospective rather than retroactive in their force.[5] Rawls acknowledges the influence of Lon Fuller here, as do many others who trace their conceptions of legality to the eight principles Fuller identifies in *The Morality of Law*.[6] As conveniently condensed by John Finnis, Fuller's principles hold that:

> A legal system exemplifies the Rule of Law to the extent that ... (i) its rules are prospective, not retroactive, and (ii) are not in any other way impossible to comply with; that (iii) its rules are promulgated, (iv) clear, and (v) coherent one with another; that (vi) its rules are sufficiently stable to allow people to be guided by their knowledge of the content of the rules; that (vii) the making of decrees and orders applicable to relatively limited situations is guided by rules that are promulgated, clear, stable, and relatively general; and that (viii) those people who have authority to make, administer, and apply the rules in an official capacity (a) are accountable for their compliance with rules applicable to their performance and (b) do actually administer the law consistently and in accordance with its tenor.[7]

As the phrase "to the extent that" in Finnis's summary indicates, Fuller's notion of legality resembles the idea of a cooperative practice in containing a critical and aspirational element. Fuller himself calls attention to this element when he refers to "the impulse toward legality" in a section of his book entitled "The Aspiration toward Perfection in Legality."[8] Like cooperative practices, the rule of law may be more or less perfectly realized, and some putatively legal systems may fall so far short of the ideal as not to qualify as rule-of-law regimes. Perfection is not to be expected, however, and it would be a mistake to reject a legal system altogether because, say, some of its laws are not completely clear or some of them on occasion conflict with others. These are shortcomings to be corrected, but not reasons to deny that the rule of law is in effect.

Finnis's summary of Fuller's principles also indicates that some take legality to be the sum and substance of the rule of law. Tamanaha acknowledges that point, which is why he refers to three "themes" rather than three criteria or features of

---

[5] Rawls, *A Theory of Justice*, revised ed. (Cambridge, MA: Harvard University Press, 1999), §38.
[6] Fuller, *The Morality of Law*, revised ed. (New Haven, CT: Yale University Press, 1969), chap. 2.
[7] Finnis, *Natural Law and Natural Rights* (Oxford: Oxford University Press, 1980), p. 270.
[8] Fuller, *The Morality of Law*, p. 41.

the rule of law. Each theme, that is, represents what some significant group of thinkers has taken to be the essence of the rule of law. The three are not mutually exclusive, though, and there is good reason to regard them as complementary. It is, after all, but a short step from the desire to limit the powers of government to the conclusion that it will be better to be governed by laws than by the will or whims of particular persons; and if we want to be governed by laws, we will need to have some idea of what the characteristics of law, or legality, are. Whether we take them individually or together, however, the three themes lead back to the conception of the polity as a meta-practice responsible for administering the rule of law. That conception, in turn, enables fair-play theory to overcome two problems often associated with the idea of a cooperative practice. These are the problems of distributive justice and of spillover practices.

Because it involves a balancing of the benefits and burdens of cooperation, critics and advocates of the principle of fair play alike often associate the fair-play argument with considerations of distributive justice. Ideally, benefits and burdens should be in balance, with everyone bearing an equal or otherwise fair share of the burdens while enjoying an equal or otherwise fair share of the benefits. But what constitutes an equal or fair share? An equal share of either benefits or burdens might seem to be easy to identify, but there are well-known difficulties in this regard. Equal protection of the laws is widely recognized as a desirable good that polities should strive to provide, but that does not mean that every law-abiding member of the polity should receive exactly the same amount of protection from the police and the courts. Someone placed in a witness-protection program, or a woman threatened by an abusive spouse, requires more attention and assistance from law enforcement agencies than more fortunate people do if they are to enjoy the same level of protection.[9] The problem is at least as difficult if we look for "fair" rather than "equal" distributions of benefits and burdens. In fact, as I noted in Chapter 2, John Horton takes this to be one of the fundamental difficulties besetting fair-play theories. It is not enough that a practice be mutually beneficial; it must also distribute its benefits and burdens justly. If ten people contribute equally to an ongoing common effort, as a result of which all are better off than before but two have benefited much more than the other eight, it may be obvious that an injustice has been done and obligations of fair play do not apply to the eight who seem to have been slighted. That, however, is an exceptionally straightforward case. More typical are the cases in which it is difficult to determine who has contributed how much to the common effort and what a proper share of the benefits is. Such cases are especially likely to occur

---

[9] See Gregory Vlastos, "Justice and Equality," in *Social Justice*, ed. Richard Brandt (Englewood Cliffs, NJ: Prentice-Hall, 1962), esp. pp. 40–43.

in large-scale practices in which it is often difficult to tell whether someone has contributed at all, let alone contributed effectively, to the cooperative enterprise.

The upshot is that advocates of the fair-play approach seem to face a dilemma. If they do not insist that a practice must be just in order to generate obligations of fair play, then they must hold that people may well have duties of fair play to contribute to cooperative but unjust practices. If they do insist that fair-play obligations arise only within just practices, then they will find themselves entangled in endless controversies about whether a practice is truly just or at least sufficiently just to count as one that generates fair-play obligations. In the case of a practice as large and complex as a polity, the latter task seems hopeless.

There are ways to escape this supposed dilemma, however, some of which I set out in Chapter 2. In particular, I argued there that the ideas of fair play and cooperative practices are substantial enough to produce a modest but satisfactory conception of justice that centers on the need to assure every participant in a practice that she enjoys equal standing within it . Here I can supplement that argument by way of an appeal to the idea of a polity as a meta-practice responsible for administering the rule of law.

To conceive of the polity in this way is to understand it as producing or securing a public good. That is, the rule of law is a good for every member of the relevant public that is neither excludable nor subject to rivalry. Security against retroactive laws, for example, or against laws that are too vague or convoluted to serve as guides to conduct, is not something that can be extended to some members of the polity while being denied to others; nor does one person's enjoyment of these benefits diminish the amount that others may enjoy. Moreover, the burden to be borne in exchange for these benefits is one that, in principle, falls equally on everyone—namely, the burden of obeying the law when one would prefer to disobey.

It is true, of course, as Anatole France long ago remarked, that the majestic equality of the law is less valuable to those who have to beg in the streets, sleep under bridges, and steal bread than it is to those who have homes and relatively secure incomes. But that is not to deny that the rule of law holds value even for the destitute. In addition to freedom from arbitrary and unchecked power, the poor and homeless gain with everyone else the predictability the rule of law provides and the protection it affords their persons and meager possessions. Traffic laws, for example, may seem to be of little use to those who cannot afford a car, but they are nevertheless important to anyone who has to cross busy streets. The problems here, in any case, are not problems with the rule of law but with its weakness or absence—with the failure, that is, to live up to its requirements.[10]

---

[10] On this point, see Elizabeth Anderson, "Outlaws," *The Good Society* 23 (2014), esp. pp. 109–10.

How close is "close enough" will often be a matter of debate, but any polity that comes close enough to the aspiration of securing for its members equal standing under the rule of law is one that the principle of fair play will endorse as a mutually beneficial and just enterprise. With the rule of law as the focal point—indeed, the focal *good*—in a theory of political obligation, there is no need to worry about exactly how everyone's cooperative benefits and burdens compare to those of every other person in the practice.

I will return to this question of distribution twice more in this book: first in the next section of this chapter, when I respond to some specific criticisms of fair-play theory, and again in the second part of the book, when I turn to the problems of punishment. At this point, though, it is necessary to explain how understanding the polity as a meta-practice responsible for administering the rule of law deflects another potential problem for the fair-play account of political obligation. This is what I have called the problem of spillover practices.

This problem arises because the benefits of cooperative practices are not always neatly confined to a definite or distinct group of people. It may happen, for example, that someone who takes regular strolls through the park will count on the aforementioned volleyball players to be there at a certain time on certain evenings so that he can pause for a while to watch a game or two. He is not a member of the cooperative practice, it seems, but he does take pleasure in watching others play and thus derives a benefit from their activity. Is that enough to place him under an obligation of fair play to the volleyball players? In this case, the answer must be no. The entertainment the spectator derives from the volleyball games is a side effect rather than a benefit integral to the activity itself. He is an outsider—a literal bystander—who has no part to play in the cooperative practice, and therefore no duty of fair play toward its participants. Even if the players take pleasure in knowing that someone is watching them play, the game itself in no way depends on the bystander's presence, for they continue to play when he moves on, and they would continue to play even if no one were to stop and watch. Whatever benefits the volleyball playing yields to him, or his watching yields to them, are thus incidental rather than integral to the practice. For that reason, the bystander's watching places him under no obligation of fair play to the players and them under no obligation of fair play to him.

There are other cases, though, in which the distinction between insiders and outsiders is not so easy to maintain, and cases involving political boundaries are prominent among them.[11] One might argue that Canada is in a fortunate position, for example, because it derives significant benefits from the enormous

---

[11] See in this regard David Mapel, "Fairness, Political Obligation, and Benefits Across Borders," *Polity* 37 (2005): 425–42.

sums the United States spends on providing the public good of national defense. These benefits are not the product of altruism on the part of the United States but of the sheer impossibility of confining the good to those who live within its boundaries. Much as those within the United States who manage to evade taxes and military service are able to receive the benefit of national defense without contributing to its production, so too are Canadians able to receive some of these benefits without paying for them. If this argument is plausible, should we say that Canadians are free riders who are failing to do their duty as participants in the cooperative practice of national defense? Or, turning the example around, should we say that the people of the United States are taking unfair advantage of the law-abiding people of Canada, whose low crime rates and cooperative nature make it possible for the United States to leave its northern border virtually undefended?

If we conceive of the polity as a meta-practice that secures and administers the rule of law, the response to these questions will be "no." The United States forms one polity charged with administering the rule of law within its boundaries, on this view, and Canada forms another. Boundary disputes between countries often arise, of course, and even settled boundaries can be quite porous in some respects. Complications involving questions of international law are also likely. Where political obligation is concerned, however, the point—in keeping with the "particularity requirement" discussed in previous chapters—is that one's obligation is to obey the law of one's own country. If the people of one polity enjoy positive or suffer negative side effects from the activities of another, one country or the other may well have grounds for complaint. Complaints of unfairness, as distinct from fair play, may even be warranted. But in the absence of treaties that set up cooperative endeavors across national boundaries, there will be no free riding or duties of fair play involved. Political obligation is a matter of fair play, but it is a matter of playing fair within the rule of law of one's own cooperative meta-practice.

Fair Play Defended

With this elaboration in mind, we can now turn to the major objections raised against the fair-play theory of political obligation. There are six of these to consider, but the last of them comprises two criticisms pertaining in different ways to the complaint that the fair-play account runs afoul of the distributive problem entailed by the need to strike a proper balance between the benefits and burdens of political cooperation. I begin with the most general objection.[12]

---

[12] Parts of the following discussion draw on and extend the arguments of my *Civic Virtues: Rights, Citizenship, and Republican Liberalism* (New York: Oxford University Press, 1997), pp. 69–78.

Fair Play or Imposition?

The most sweeping attack on fair-play theory is Robert Nozick's root-and-branch criticism in *Anarchy, State, and Utopia*, which I touched on in Chapter 2. According to Nozick, the principle of fair play is objectionable not only as the basis for a theory of political obligation but also in itself. For if we accept the principle, we must also allow that others can place us under obligations to them simply by conferring benefits on us, whether we want those benefits or not. As he puts the point, "You may not decide to give me something . . . and then grab money from me to pay for it, even if I have nothing better to spend the money on."[13]

As previously noted, Nozick's point here is both right and irrelevant. It is right because we cannot simply foist obligations onto others; but it is irrelevant because the principle of fair play does not entail that we can. My neighbors may improve my view when they happen to paint their houses in colors I find pleasing, but in the ordinary course of events their painting imposes no obligation of fair play on me. Unless a homeowners' association or some similar body is involved, the choice of colors for houses is not governed by a cooperative practice, and the principle of fair play applies only to people within such practices. That is why the benefit I receive from my house-painting neighbors is simply a positive externality and not the subject of a fair-play duty.[14]

The problem for fair-play theory is that Nozick sees the same problem arising within cooperative practices. This happens, he believes, whenever the benefits of the practice are nonexcludable goods that are impossible to avoid, as they are in Nozick's fanciful example of the neighborhood public address system:

> Suppose some of the people in your neighborhood (there are 364 other adults) have found a public address system and decide to institute a system of public entertainment. They post a list of names, one for each day, yours among them. On his assigned day (one can easily switch days) a person is to run the public address system, play records over it, give news bulletins, tell amusing stories he has heard, and so on. After

---

[13] Nozick, *Anarchy, State, and Utopia* (New York: Basic Books, 1974), p. 95.

[14] But cf. Daniel McDermott, "Fair-Play Obligations," *Political Studies* 52 (2004): 216–32, for the argument that fair-play theory rests on an "artificial and indefensible" distinction between what is owed to individuals and what is owed to cooperative endeavors (quoting p. 232). In my view, McDermott fails to appreciate the vulnerability of such endeavors to free riding, in part because he overestimates their members' ability to identify free riders and impose sanctions on them. See also Stephen D. Parsons, "Fair-Play Obligations: A Critical Note on Free Riding," *Political Studies* 53 (2005): 641–49.

138 days on which each person has done his part, your day arrives. Are you obligated to take your turn?[15]

Nozick's answer to this question is "surely not," but the point of the example is that anyone who follows the principle of fair play would have to answer affirmatively. Even within cooperative practices, he suggests, some people can impose unwanted obligations on others simply by conferring benefits on them. Because that conclusion is plainly unacceptable, so too must be the principle that leads to it.

In response to this criticism, fair-play theorists—and even one prominent critic of fair-play theory, as we shall soon see—have argued along two lines. One of these, developed most fully by George Klosko, holds that the mere receipt of the "open" or nonexcludable benefits of a cooperative practice may indeed place someone under an obligation, but only when the benefits are of sufficient importance, such as "physical security provided by law and order, national defense, and protection from a hostile environment."[16] In contrast to the trivial goods in Nozick's examples, in other words, the cooperative practice in question must produce *presumptive goods* that are both public and indispensable—that is, "necessary for an acceptable life for all members of the community."[17] Such goods will "be (i) worth the recipients' efforts in providing them; (ii) 'presumptively beneficial'; and (iii) have benefits and burdens that are fairly distributed."[18] Nozick's example of the public address system at best meets the third of these criteria, and thus does not tell against the principle of fairness, properly understood.[19]

The second line of response to Nozick's criticism holds that his example of the public address system rests on too loose an understanding of what it means to participate or be engaged in a cooperative practice. Passively receiving the benefits of a practice, especially when one cannot avoid them, is not enough to place one under a duty of fair play to comply with the rules of the practice.[20] There must be some sense in which one *takes part* in the enterprise or leads those who are participating to believe that he is taking part in it—as there is, for example, in the story from Chapter 2 of the volleyball players who take it in turns to buy a round of drinks at a pub after their games. Only in circumstances such

---

[15] Nozick, *Anarchy, State, and Utopia*, p. 93.

[16] Klosko, *The Principle of Fairness and Political Obligation*, 2nd ed. (Lanham, MD: Rowan & Littlefield, 2004), p. 40.

[17] Ibid., p. 39.

[18] Ibid., p. 39.

[19] For a related criticism, see Richard Arneson, "The Principle of Fairness and Free-Rider Problems," *Ethics* 92 (1982): 616–33.

[20] See Nora K. Bell, "Nozick and the Principle of Fairness," *Social Theory and Practice* 5 (1978): 65–73.

as these can we say that someone is obligated to do his part. Indeed, it is only in these circumstances that we can sensibly talk about one's *part* in a practice. Playing a part may fall short of the consent that Nozick takes to be necessary to ground an obligation, but it is not the entirely passive receipt of the benefits of a practice.

This is a point that John Simmons, who is probably the leading critic of fair-play (and other) theories of political obligation, raises against Nozick. According to Simmons, there are occasions in which it is quite reasonable to attribute duties of fair play to someone who accepts the benefits of a cooperative practice even though that person has not consented to be a part of the practice. In fact, Simmons's example of the man who expressly refuses to join a cooperative well-digging scheme but nevertheless takes water from the well once it is dug (an example briefly discussed in Chapter 3, *supra*) is now the standard illustration of this point within the literature on the principle of fair play.[21] As the example shows, and as Simmons observes, there is nothing wrong with the principle itself, despite Nozick's objections; the problem is that its advocates attempt to apply the principle in unsuitable circumstances, such as those that pertain to political obligation. Whether Simmons's argument on that point is as effective as his criticism of Nozick is a question to be considered shortly. That his criticism of Nozick's objection is effective, though, seems well established.

Benefits, Harms, and Fair Play

According to the second objection, which M. B. E. Smith raised in an early statement of philosophical anarchism, "the obligation of fair play governs a man's actions only when some benefit or harm turns on whether he obeys."[22] Unlike Nozick, Smith believes that the principle of fair play is the source of some genuine obligations. He holds, though, that the principle generates an obligation to obey only when the cooperative enterprise in question is small enough to ensure that any participant's failure to obey its rules is likely to harm it, perhaps "by diminishing the confidence of the other members in its probable success and therefore reducing their incentive to work diligently towards it."[23] But this reasoning will not support a *prima facie* political obligation, Smith says, for there

---

[21] A. John Simmons, *Moral Principles and Political Obligations* (Princeton, NJ: Princeton University Press, 1979), pp. 126–27.

[22] Smith, "Is There a Prima Facie Obligation to Obey the Law?," *Yale Law Journal* 82 (1973): 950–76; reprinted in, and quoted from, *The Duty to Obey the Law: Selected Philosophical Readings*, ed. W. A. Edmundson (Lanham, MD: Rowman & Littlefield, 1999), p. 81.

[23] Ibid., p. 82.

are many cases in which someone's disobedience neither deprives anyone of benefits nor harms the political enterprise in any noticeable way.

Smith presents three hypothetical examples to support this claim. In the first, A's compliance with the rules of a practice "will confer on B a benefit roughly equal to those [A] has received from B"; in the second, A's failure to comply will harm the practice and thus harm B indirectly "by threatening the existence or efficient functioning of an institution on which B's vital interests depend."[24] In both cases, Smith says, fairness demands that A abide by the rules. In the third case, however, A is a free rider in a successful cooperative venture; and

> if A's compliance with some particular rules does not benefit B and if his disobedience will not harm the community, it is difficult to see how fairness to B could dictate that A must comply. Surely, the fact that A has benefitted from B's submission does not give B the right to insist that A obey when B's interests are unaffected.

The problem with this argument is that it rests on an unduly narrow conception of fairness that ignores the distinction between *harms* and *wrongs*. As Smith sees it, one person cannot be unfair to another without directly or indirectly affecting the latter's interests. But if we conceive of fairness in this way, we must abandon the criticism that is most often brought against free riders—that is, that they are acting wrongly by refusing to play fair. To be sure, if too many people are trying to ride free, the cooperative venture will fail, thus depriving everyone involved of its benefits. But even in that case, if we follow Smith's conception of fairness, we cannot condemn any individual among them, for no one in particular is responsible for the harm done by the venture's failure. Should the venture prove successful, moreover, there would be no way, on Smith's argument, to justify the cooperating members' sense of grievance at those who have taken advantage of their willingness to bear the burdens of cooperation. Yet it is precisely this grievance that is typically—and justifiably—directed at free riders.

What Smith overlooks here, in addition to the distinction between harm and wrong, is the importance of equal standing to considerations of fairness and fair play. Those who refuse to cooperate in a practice while they accept its benefits are acting unfairly because they are making exceptions of themselves. They want others to cooperate—enough to preserve the practice, at least—but they are not themselves willing to bear the burdens of cooperation if they can shirk them. By according themselves this special standing and exploiting the cooperation

---

[24] Both quotations are from ibid., pp. 80–81, as is the following quotation.

of others, they betray a lack of respect for other persons. In Kantian terms, they are using others as means to their own ends rather than respecting them as equal members in the kingdom of ends. Their actions may not be harmful, in short, but they nevertheless are wrongful and unjust.[25]

The Problem of Scale

Smith could accept this criticism, however, without accepting the fair-play theory of political obligation, for he has a related objection to raise. That is, even if he were to acknowledge that his emphasis on harm is misplaced, he could continue to insist that fair-play arguments cannot overcome the problem of scale. As I have noted, Smith allows that fair play can provide a ground for an obligation to comply with the rules when the cooperative practice in question is a small one. But he also makes the indisputable point that the polity, if it is a cooperative practice at all, will not be the kind of practice in which one person's failure to cooperate necessarily brings harm—and here he might substitute "does wrong" for "brings harm"—to others. Even a relatively small polity will be too large for that to happen. This is a telling point, as Smith sees it, because it shows how the plausibility of fair-play theory "depends on *an unwarranted extrapolation* from what is largely true of our obligations within small, cooperative enterprises to what must always be true of our obligations within legal systems."[26] Simmons makes much the same point. "We must remember," he says,

> that where there is no consciousness of cooperation, no common plan or purpose, no cooperative scheme exists. I do not think that many of us can honestly say that we regard our political lives as a process of working together and making necessary sacrifices for the purpose of improving the common lot. The centrality and apparent independence of governments does not make it natural to think of political life in this way.[27]

---

[25] On this point, but without the Kantian reference, see Edward Song, "Acceptance, Fairness, and Political Obligation," *Legal Theory* 18 (2012): 218: "Such particular judgments, as well as the general notion of fairness, seem to turn on the same idea: it is wrong for a person to give herself preferential treatment because this is to make an exception of oneself, which shows disrespect to others." For much the same point in a different context, see Alan Wertheimer, "Victimless Crimes," *Ethics* 87 (1977): 315–17.

[26] Smith, "Is There a Prima Facie Obligation to Obey the Law?," p. 83; emphasis added.

[27] Simmons, *Moral Principles and Political Obligations*, p. 140. See also Simmons, *Justification and Legitimacy: Essays on Rights and Obligations* (Cambridge, UK: Cambridge University Press, 2001), pp. 38–42.

Simmons goes on to acknowledge that there may be a "loose sense of 'cooperative scheme'" that justifies fair-play theorists—he specifically mentions Hart and Rawls—in thinking of political communities in these terms. But he immediately adds, "whatever intuitive plausibility the principle of fair play has derives from our regarding it as an acceptable moral principle for cooperative schemes in the *strict* sense"—a plausibility that "may in no way be mirrored in the context of 'cooperative schemes' understood in the loose sense mentioned above."[28]

The question, then, is whether fair-play theory rests, as Smith and Simmons charge, on an implausible and unwarranted leap from cooperative practices in the strict sense, which are necessarily small, to larger enterprises such as the polity. The answer is "no," in my view, but a concession should precede the explanation of this answer. The concession is that Simmons is probably right to say that "many of us" do not "regard our political lives as a process of working together and making necessary sacrifices for the purpose of improving the common lot." In the ordinary course of life, many citizens even of reasonably just, democratic polities probably do not think of themselves as engaged in a cooperative practice. The law seems too impersonal and the governing institutions seem too remote for there to be the kind of widespread "consciousness of cooperation" that Simmons takes to be necessary to the existence of a cooperative scheme. Even so, we should not make too much of this concession.

I say this for two reasons. The first is that evidence of the "consciousness of cooperation" is not as hard to find as Simmons seems to think. Anyone who acts out of a sense of civic duty or on the basis of civic friendship is relying in some way on an understanding of the polity as a cooperative practice.[29] For some people, this sense seems to be a part of their everyday lives. For most, perhaps, something that jolts them out of the ordinary course of life seems to be required. The FDNY (for Fire Department of New York) shirts that appeared throughout the United States in the aftermath of the terrorist attacks of September 11, 2001, and the chants of "Boston Strong!" that followed the Boston Marathon bombing of 2013, are symptoms of this awakened sense of the need to play one's part in civic cooperation and to honor those who have clearly done so. But there are also occasions in ordinary life when an underlying sense of the polity as a cooperative practice is aroused, often by the transgressions of those who take unfair advantage of the law-abiding. Drivers who stay in the left-hand lane when it is clear that the traffic ahead is being restricted to the right-hand lane are offenders who often seem to evoke in others this unconscious conviction that the polity is,

---

[28] Simmons, *Moral Principles and Political Obligations*, pp. 140–41; emphasis in original.

[29] See on this point Thomas A. Spragens, Jr., *Civic Liberalism: Reflections on Our Democratic Ideals* (Lanham, MD: Rowman & Littlefield, 1999), esp. chap. 7.

after all, a kind of cooperative practice involving the belief that turnabout is fair play—a practice that the offenders are abusing.

The second reason to believe that Smith and Simmons are wrong to hold that the polity cannot be a genuinely cooperative practice is that its scale is not the obstacle they believe it to be. It is true that the sense or consciousness of cooperation will be more readily apparent in small enterprises than in large ones. When it is clear that everyone involved in a venture must pull together for the venture to succeed, the consciousness of cooperation—or the lack of it—will be strong indeed. But it does not follow that cooperation occurs only when people are aware of it. To return to the traffic example, the fact that someone drives within the speed limit because she wants to avoid fines, or stops at traffic lights because she wants to avoid crashes, does not mean that she is not engaging in a cooperative practice. Whether she is conscious of it or not, she relies on the cooperation of others when she drives, including the cooperation of those who pay taxes that provide for roads and traffic signals even though they do not themselves drive. Moreover, she cooperates herself, whether she is aware of it or not, when she complies with the traffic laws, no matter how grudgingly she does so. After all, cooperation need not be cheerfully or happily given.[30]

To be sure, informal norms enforced directly by the participants will give way to formal rules enforced by established authorities with coercive power as the scale of a practice increases. But that is a way of securing and ensuring cooperation, not of eliminating it. The point here is similar to one I made in Chapter 2 in response to John Horton's objection that it seems unreasonable to regard the polity, with its heavy reliance on coercion, as a cooperative practice. To reinforce and extend what I said there, we should note that cooperative schemes do not fall into a neat division between small-scale schemes, in which the cooperative element is clearly evident, and large-scale schemes, in which cooperation is either much less obvious or, as the critics would have it, nonexistent. The tendency

---

[30] A similar criticism on p. 74 of my *Civic Virtues* drew the following response from Simmons: "Dagger, oddly, seems to believe that consciousness of cooperation *is* necessary to the existence of (and hence to obligations within) *small* cooperative schemes, but not to the existence of large ones. This curious asymmetry is not explained" ("Fair Play and Political Obligation: Twenty Years Later," in Simmons, *Justification and Legitimacy: Essays on Rights and Obligations* [Cambridge: Cambridge University Press, 2001], p. 39; emphasis in original). I hope that the paragraph above makes it clear that I do not hold to the "curious asymmetry" Simmons identifies. My point is that the sense or consciousness of cooperation in a practice is likely to be stronger, or more prevalent, in a small-scale practice than in a large one, which makes it easier to perceive the cooperative nature of the small-scale practice. But that is not to say that this perception is necessary to the existence of a cooperative practice, whether large or small. Someone who acts simply out of habit, or who fails to grasp the concept of cooperation, may still be participating in a cooperative practice even if it involves only a handful of people.

to think in these dichotomous terms obscures the continuity that cooperative practices exhibit across the scale from small to large.

To bring out this continuity, let us return to the example of the volleyball players. In this case, though, let us consider the history and potential future of their cooperation. They began playing volleyball, let us say, on a highly informal, even haphazard basis. Three or four of them went to the park with volleyball in hand one day simply to bat the ball back and forth, but others—friends or strangers—joined in, until they found themselves playing games according to the rules of volleyball. Deliberately or not, enough members of the original group returned to the park in succeeding weeks for an expectation to develop that one would find a volleyball game to join on a certain day of the week around a certain time of day. As more and more people seeking a volleyball game showed up over time, the players hit upon the idea of forming regular teams with a set schedule of matches. These arrangements could collapse, of course, under the weight of various distractions or loss of interest on the part of many of the players. But it is also possible that gradually a volleyball league would emerge, with rules about eligibility to play, forfeiting matches, and qualifying for tournaments—and with officials to enforce those and other rules. It is even possible that the league eventually might become a professional association in which a great many people are involved, competition is fierce, and pride and money seem far more important than the spirit of cooperation. In these circumstances, the league officials—professionals themselves—must exercise coercive authority by imposing penalties to make sure that fair play is preserved. From a small-scale, cooperative practice, in short, a large and formal institution has evolved. In these new circumstances, is it still reasonable to say playing volleyball is a cooperative practice? If not, when and how did it cease to be one?

In my view, volleyball playing remains a cooperative practice throughout the developments sketched in the preceding paragraph. Of course, other features have been added or taken on greater prominence in the course of development, so that the practice has become less purely cooperative, and certainly less obviously so. The foundation in cooperation, however, remains. The same is true, by analogy, of other large-scale cooperative practices, including the practice, or meta-practice, of the polity. Contrary to Smith's claim, in short, the "extrapolation from what is largely true of our obligations within small, cooperative enterprises to what must always be true of our obligations within legal systems" is *not* "unwarranted."[31] Given the continuous nature of cooperation as practices increase in size, but nevertheless involve the sharing of benefits and burdens, it is not even clearly an extrapolation.

---

[31] Smith, "Is There a Prima Facie Obligation to Obey the Law?," p. 83.

A final qualification is necessary, though, before turning to the next objection brought against fair-play theory. This qualification concerns the "always" in the preceding quotation from Smith's essay. There are complications here involving the question of what counts as a "legal system," but if we take Smith to be referring to political systems in general, then it certainly would be wrong to take every one of them to be a mutually beneficial and just cooperative practice. As I have previously acknowledged, some political systems are so oppressive and exploitative that they cannot be reasonably regarded as cooperative practices. But that is not a function of their size. A bully who forces others into aiding and abetting his schemes has not founded a cooperative practice no matter how small the band of people he dominates. Nor is a large group of people necessarily uncooperative simply because it is large. On the contrary, it is both sensible and helpful to conceive of political society—if not always, then surely often—in Rawls's terms: "as a system of fair cooperation over time, from one generation to the next."[32]

Acceptance, Benefits, and Fair Play

Citing Rawls in this connection, however, may simply show that fair-play theory can escape one set of objections only to fall victim to another. As the quotation above from *Political Liberalism* indicates, Rawls never abandoned the conception of political society as a fair system of cooperation over time; but his acceptance in *A Theory of Justice* of Hart's distinction between duties and obligations did lead him to abandon the fair-play argument for political obligation. Obligations must be incurred voluntarily, he concluded, and in the case of the average citizen, "it is not clear what is the requisite binding action [for a political obligation to exist] or who has performed it."[33]

The same problem has led others to dismiss fair-play theory even when they do not follow Hart and Rawls in trying to distinguish obligations from duties. Whether it is an obligation or a duty, the argument goes, the moral requirement to obey the law must rest on something more than the mere receipt of benefits from a political or legal system. There must also be some sense in which the benefits are voluntarily accepted. Otherwise, as Nozick's example of the public address system suggests, people may be placed under obligations against their will. At the least, one must be able to refuse the benefits of a cooperative practice before we can say that she has a duty or obligation of fair play to bear her share

---

[32] John Rawls, *Political Liberalism*, expanded ed. (New York: Columbia University Press, 2005), p. 15.

[33] Rawls, *A Theory of Justice*, rev. ed. (Cambridge, MA: Harvard University Press, 1999), p. 98.

of the burdens of the practice. If, however, the practice produces nonexcludable benefits, as political and legal systems necessarily do, there can be no genuine obligation of fair play. Once again, it seems, the scope of the principle of fair play is limited in a way that denies its application to political obligation.

Simmons advances the most forceful and influential statement of this argument in his *Moral Principles and Political Obligations*. "To have accepted a benefit," he states, "an individual must either 1) have tried to get (and succeeded in getting) the benefit, or 2) have taken the benefit willingly and knowingly."[34] Someone may *receive* a benefit without satisfying either of these conditions, according to Simmons, but no one can *accept* a benefit without satisfying at least one of them. With regard to the benefits provided by the political order—public goods such as the rule of law—it seems clear to Simmons that most people have not accepted them in either of the two ways he states. He does acknowledge that some people may acquire fair-play obligations by enjoying nonexcludable benefits that they take to be "worth the price [they] pay for them," but they must enjoy them in full awareness that "the benefits *are* provided by a cooperative scheme."[35] Few people, he maintains, will satisfy these conditions; for "even in democratic political communities, these benefits are commonly regarded as purchased (with taxes) from a central authority rather than as accepted from the cooperative efforts of our fellow citizens."[36]

Simmons's argument has prompted two kinds of responses from proponents of the fair-play theory. The first, already familiar from the discussion of Nozick's sweeping objection, is to deny that fair-play obligations must be grounded in the voluntary acceptance of benefits. When "presumptive goods" are involved, as Klosko argues, the mere receipt of these benefits is enough to place the recipients under an obligation.[37] The second response, which I advanced in an earlier work, is to say that Simmons has drawn too sharp a distinction between the acceptance and the receipt of benefits. Between the person who passively receives the benefits of a cooperative practice and the one who knowingly and

---

[34] Simmons, *Moral Principles and Political Obligations*, p. 129.

[35] Ibid., p. 132; emphasis in original.

[36] Ibid., p. 139. For a variant of this criticism, see Patrick Durning, "Two Problems with Deriving a Duty to Obey the Law from the Principle of Fairness," *Public Affairs Quarterly* 17 (2003): 255–56.

[37] Klosko, n. 5, *supra*. For a sample of the ensuing debate between Klosko and Simmons on this point, see Simmons, "Fair Play and Political Obligation: Twenty Years Later," in his *Justification and Legitimacy*; Klosko, *Political Obligations* (Oxford: Oxford University Press, 2005), esp. pp. 226–30; and both authors' essays in the Fall 2007 issue of the *American Philosophical Association Newsletter on Philosophy and Law*, 7. See also Klosko's "Fairness Obligations and Non-acceptance of Benefits," *Political Studies* 62 (2014): 159–71, in which he argues that explicit rejection of one or more of the presumptive goods produced by the polity will be enough to exempt someone from the corresponding political obligation only in rare cases.

willingly accepts them is the person—very many people, in fact—who actively participates in the practice without being fully aware, in the ordinary course of life, that he is undertaking an obligation to do his part by participating in a cooperative practice. This is true even of the citizenry of large polities.[38] Like Michael Hardimon and other proponents of the associative theory examined in the previous chapter, those who take this position believe that there is no clear dichotomy between what is fully voluntary and what is altogether involuntary. In the middle ground, they hold, there is room for the voluntary—but not deliberate or completely conscious—acceptance of obligations.

This is the position I find compelling. For most of us, membership in a polity is akin to our relationship with our native tongue. The fact that I speak English far more easily than any other language is owing in part to my lack of diligence in studying other languages and in part to my failure to pursue opportunities to live for an extended time in places where other languages are spoken. More than anything, however, it is the result of growing up among English-speaking people in a country where English is by far the predominant language. Nor was it anyone's conscious intention that I should grow up this way, so far as I am aware, but a simple contingency of when, where, and to whom I was born. Looking back, I might complain that this contingency imposed on me a rather limited way of expressing myself, for I gather that there are ways of speaking—and perhaps even of perceiving and thinking—that are difficult to grasp and express for those of us who have to stumble along with English. Of course, there also seem to be notions that English captures better than other languages, so perhaps I am as well off in this regard as anyone is with his or her native language. In any case, it would be decidedly odd to complain that English was forced or imposed on me, against my will, even though it is true that I did not choose to learn it. But then, how could I have done so? English is something I began to learn before I even knew that I was capable of making choices. I may not speak it voluntarily, in the ordinary course of things, but that is only true, again, if we take 'voluntarily' to mean deliberately or with full consciousness of what one is doing. But

---

[38] Dagger, *Civic Virtues*, pp. 73–78. For the most extensive discussion of this point, including empirical evidence to support it, see Song, "Acceptance, Fairness, and Political Obligation," esp. pp. 219–27. See also Richard Arneson, "Paternalism and the Principle of Fairness," in *Paternalism: Theory and Practice*, ed. C. Coons and M. Weber (Cambridge, UK: Cambridge University Press, 2013), p. 143; Samantha Besson, *The Morality of Conflict: Reasonable Disagreement and the Law* (Oxford: Hart Publishing, 2005), pp. 487–89; Peter Steinberger, *The Idea of the State* (Cambridge, UK: Cambridge University Press, 2004), pp. 219–20; and Dudley Knowles, *Political Obligation: A Critical Introduction* (London and New York: Routledge, 2010), pp. 134–37. Knowles concludes that "the argument from fairness works well in the case of those who actively solicit the benefits that the state makes readily available. Some may fail to understand this implication of their conduct, but they are obtuse, to speak kindly" (p. 137).

if the only options are to say that we either speak our native language voluntarily or involuntarily, then it seems right to opt for the former.

What is true of native tongues is also true, I suggest, of one's relationship to one's polity, at least if it is reasonable to regard it as a meta-practice that administers the rule of law. For most of us the legal status of citizenship is something we are born into, while membership is something we grow into as we receive the benefits that others make possible through their cooperative efforts. Neither legal citizenship nor citizenship in a richer, more active sense of the term is something that we native-born citizens choose, but neither are they imposed on us against our wills. We are even likely to have the opportunity to renounce them at some point in our lives. Meanwhile, as we grow out of childhood and begin to learn something about how our polity operates, most of us begin to take advantage of the opportunities the polity presents to pursue our interests. We use the streets and public transportation; we begin to drive a car; we apply for admission to a public university or seek a state-funded scholarship or state-supported loan; we enter into contracts secured by law; we do these and many other things that we can do because the cooperating members of the polity enable us to do them. In these ways, we *accept the benefits* of the political order and undertake an obligation, *ceteris paribus*, to obey its laws. No one of these actions is sufficient to establish our consent to the rules of the cooperative meta-practice. Nevertheless, our continuing acceptance of the benefits that flow from cooperation places us under an obligation of fair play to the cooperating members of the polity. If we fail or refuse to obey, we take unfair advantage of those whose cooperation makes it possible for us to enjoy the benefits of membership.

Rawls's worries and Simmons's criticism notwithstanding, then, we should conclude that the members of a reasonably just polity do accept its benefits, and they do so even if they are not fully or always aware that they are deriving these benefits from a cooperative (meta-)practice. Taking into account the importance of the "presumptive goods" on which Klosko bases his response to the criticism—and especially the good of the rule of law—provides even more reason to adhere to the fair-play theory of political obligation. But there is one more set of objections to overcome, and an intramural challenge to meet, before we can declare the theory to be sound.

Is Fair Play Really Fair?

This set of objections raises doubts about the fairness of the fair-play theory of political obligation. In general, the complaint is that attempts to apply the principle of fair play to the polity in one way or another run afoul of Rawls's early statement of the principle, which confined its application to "mutually beneficial and just scheme[s] of social cooperation."[39] Some of these objections I have already addressed, both in Chapter 2 and earlier in the present chapter, but it will be helpful to provide further responses here, with special attention to the place of the rule of law in fair-play theory. Within this set of objections, there are three particular complaints.

Fairness to Those Who Can Contribute Little or Nothing

One of these complaints is that the principle of fair play is itself unfair, as Dorota Mokrosińska charges, to "those who, due to certain impairments or disabilities, can be expected to contribute far less than most to a cooperative endeavor."[40] Because the principle entails a duty of fair play to those whose obedience to the law or other cooperation makes it possible for us to enjoy the benefits of a cooperative scheme, in other words, it ignores those who have little or nothing to contribute. As a result, Mokrosińska argues, "severely handicapped individuals or young children" will fall outside the bounds of fair play; and in "a political state governed by the principle of fairness, they would be denied citizenship and the corresponding political obligations and rights."[41]

Some of my remarks in Chapter 2, in connection with what I called "the problem of incompetents," anticipated this objection. In addition to what I said there, two further points should be noted. The first is that Mokrosińska's complaint, even if it is correct, is hardly a forceful indictment of fair-play theory. To say that the theory would deny "citizenship and the corresponding political obligations and rights" to "severely handicapped individuals or young children" is, at least on one interpretation of those phrases, simply to say that the theory would treat them as they are typically and without controversy treated in existing political systems. That is, young children do not now have the right to vote or stand for office, and neither they nor the severely handicapped bear the full set of rights and obligations attached to citizenship, such as the duty to serve in the military or on juries. We would have to find this situation deplorable—and I know of no reason to do so—if we were to take this objection seriously.

Perhaps, though, we should give a broader interpretation to the terms Mokrosińska invokes when she refers to "citizenship and the corresponding political obligations and rights." On such an interpretation young children and severely handicapped individuals would be denied citizenship in the sense of *consideration*. That is, when they or their representatives are enacting laws and devising policies, the contributing members of the polity would simply ignore

---

[39] Rawls, "Legal Obligation and the Duty of Fair Play," pp. 9–10.
[40] Mokrosińska, *Rethinking Political Obligation* (Basingstoke: Palgrave Macmillan, 2012), p. 109.
[41] Ibid.

the desires and interests of the children and handicapped who are unable to contribute to the cooperative enterprise. In this way, a fair-play polity would prove unfair indeed to many people.

Taking 'citizenship' in this broad sense, however, is still not enough to constitute a serious objection to fair-play theory. Even on this broad interpretation—and this is my second point in response to the objection—it is simply not true that considerations of fair play rule out people who ought to be taken into account. The touchstone here is the rule of law. With regard to children, no one expects them to play fair or even to grasp what it means when they are very young, but we do expect them to learn the value of fair play and a due respect for the law as they mature. There are the inevitable difficulties of knowing when exactly to hold them fully accountable—when to try someone for a crime as an adult, for instance—but the general point is clear. Where the polity and law are concerned, children will receive some of the benefits of the cooperative metapractice, including the benefits of the rule of law, but they will not be expected to bear its burdens until they are adults, or at least "old enough" to know what is expected of them. Until then, to borrow a distinction from the criminal law, we may have to remind them that their illegal actions are not *justified* even if they may be *excused* as youthful mistakes. Along the way, though, we will certainly take their interests into account, and we will do so in part because we expect them to become contributing members of the cooperative enterprise—or citizens, in the case of the polity—when they are mature enough to take on that role.

This expectation, unfortunately, is not one that we can extend to everyone. As Mokrosińska indicates, there are some people whose impairments or disabilities render them permanently incapable of contributing effectively to a polity or any other cooperative practice. She does not note, though, that this is likely to be a very small group of people. Many impairments and disabilities do not prevent people from contributing to cooperative enterprises, or even from contributing in highly effective ways, as examples ranging from blind musicians to handicapped athletes to people as profoundly impaired as Helen Keller and Stephen Hawking amply attest. In the case of the polity, moreover, the primary question is whether someone can contribute to the maintenance of the rule of law, which has both a positive and negative aspect. On the positive side, the question is whether someone is able to form judgments and engage in discussions about law and policy; on the negative side, the question is whether someone is sufficiently competent to be held accountable for infringements of the law. Most people who suffer from serious impairments or disabilities are nevertheless capable, I believe, of contributing to the polity in these ways—by obeying the law, at least, rather than violating it. To be sure, those who are truly incompetent in these respects are, as I argued in Chapter 2, beyond the bounds of the principle of fair play. But this is a small group indeed, and it is growing smaller with advances in medical treatment and communications technology. The people within this group, moreover, also will be those who are incapable of consent, of identifying with a polity, and of recognizing the existence of natural duties—people who are beyond the reach, in short, of any theory of political obligation. The failure of fair-play theory to find a place for them is not, therefore, a serious objection to that theory.

Fairness to Those Who Dislike the Status Quo

A related but very different criticism is that the principle of fair play is biased in a conservative direction. The problem, according to Calvin Normore, is this:

> If a group of us can create obligations in others by setting up an institution marginally better than the status quo and that thereby preempt[s] much better ones that the others might well have set up had we not preempted them, then the Principle of Fairness becomes not a way of avoiding unfairness but a powerfully conservative principle.[42]

Put in terms of the balance or distribution of benefits and burdens, in other words, the problem with the principle is that it fails to take account of potential benefits, or benefits forgone, because it directs our attention entirely to the benefits and burdens of existing practices.

Although he does not draw the comparison himself, Normore's complaint is similar to one often brought against the Pareto principle, which states that a move from one condition to another is efficient if the move improves someone's position while worsening no one's; and if it becomes impossible to improve someone's position without worsening some other person's, the arrangement then is Pareto optimal. The principle seems unobjectionable at first glance, but reflection soon reveals that it can do little or nothing to correct an untenable or unpalatable starting position. If a handful of people control the great bulk of a society's wealth, for example, and any attempt to increase the wealth of others will worsen even slightly the position of the handful, then the Pareto principle will rule out the attempt. In much the same way, according to Normore, the principle of fair play holds us bound to obey the rules of a practice that provides us with modest benefits even when we would much rather participate in a considerably more beneficial practice. This obligation may even block us from considering other practices that could have been established, and perhaps still could be

---

[42] Normore, "Consent and the Principle of Fairness," in *Essays on Philosophy, Politics, and Economics: Integration and Common Research Projects,* ed. C. Favor, G. Gaus, and J. Lamont (Stanford, CA: Stanford University Press), p. 231.

established, rather than the ones in which we now find ourselves. Fair play is thus an objectionably conservative principle.

Normore is right to say that the principle of fair play requires us to start from where we are and not from where we might have been—in some state of nature, perhaps—or from where we might be if cooperative practices had not developed as they did. But this aspect of fair play is, to my mind, a strong point of the approach. Political obligation is not a problem for people who are completely detached from political and legal systems, and therefore free to create *ex nihilo* the practices in which they will live. It is, instead, a problem for people who find themselves living under some kind of rule and must determine what their moral duties are, if any, toward the rules and rulers. We can set that point aside, however, and focus on a straightforward reason to reject Normore's criticism.

Put simply, the problem is that Normore treats obligation as if it were optimality. Because it defines the optimal situation as one in which it is impossible to make someone better off without making someone else worse off, the Pareto principle will have the objectionably conservative effect of entrenching a highly unjust status quo. The principle of fair play, however, says nothing about optimality. It does say that those who participate in a mutually beneficial and just cooperative practice have *prima facie* or *pro tanto* obligations to obey the rules of the practice, but it in no way precludes the members of the practice from taking steps to transform it. If someone thinks that the practice has developed in a less advantageous way than it might have done, or that new possibilities hold the promise for better outcomes within the practice, there is nothing within the principle to dissuade her from trying to improve it. For that matter, the principle of fair play does not even foreclose the possibility of abandoning a cooperative practice altogether. It requires only that the participants meet their obligations to one another as long as the practice exists.

To put the point the other way around—that is, from the standpoint of obligation rather than optimality—the fair-play approach is no more conservative than ordinary understandings of promises or contracts. Other things being equal, your promise to take me to a concert places you under an obligation to me regardless of whether you could have, given better opportunities, found a more pleasant companion. In the same way, my contract to buy a car from one agency remains binding even when I subsequently happen upon a better price or a better car at another agency. There may be ways to extract ourselves from promises and contracts, of course, including ways that are beneficial to all concerned. Nevertheless, the obligations are in force until we make such arrangements. The same is true, for the reasons set out above, of obligations that follow from the principle of fair play. One could call that a conservative bias of the principle—and of promises and contracts—but it is better to say that holding ourselves accountable to standards of fair play and reliability is necessary if we are to meet the reasonable expectations of others who are counting on us, *ceteris paribus*, to do our duty.

Fairness to Those Who Shun the Benefits of Cooperation

The remaining complaint within this set of objections concerns the possibility that the fair-play approach is itself unfair to those who are willing to forgo or forswear the benefits of political cooperation. I say "forgo or forswear" because the benefits in question here are typically public goods, such as national defense and clean (or clean*er*) air, and such goods are nonexcludable. The person who does not want such goods will receive them notwithstanding how fiercely she protests that she does not regard them as genuine benefits or that the costs of doing her part in producing them outweigh any benefit she receives. Someone who cannot *forgo* the benefits may thus *forswear* them, and her forswearing is likely to be accompanied by complaints of unfair treatment. To tell her that fair play requires her to do her part in a cooperative practice that produces benefits she forswears is likely to strike her as either hypocritical or, at best, confused.

At worst, however, the complaint here demonstrates only that following the principle of fair play will not guarantee outcomes that everyone involved will regard as fair. In the case of the provision of clean(er) air, for instance, those who suffer from respiratory problems may think that the resistance of those who do not want to contribute to pollution-reducing efforts is unfair to the sufferers, and especially so if the resisters carry the day. Supposing that the sufferers succeed, moreover, and the air they breathe does become significantly cleaner, they are still likely to bring the charge of unfair play against those who try to avoid contributing to the (unwanted) benefit of clean air. Wanted or not, the argument goes, the resisters are still benefiting from cleaner air, and it is only fair that they do their part in the endeavor to cleanse it. Such a charge will be pressed with special vigor if there is reason to suspect that those who forswear the benefit in question are simply seeking an opportunity to ride free on the efforts of others. Complaining of unfair treatment, in short, is not an option available only to those who shun the benefits of cooperation.

Even so, acknowledging that considerations of fair and unfair play may arise from both sides in cases such as these is not sufficient to settle the case against those who want to stand apart from cooperative practices and their benefits. We must look for ways of evaluating the claims of each side in such cases, and such evaluations often turn on the question of how important the contested benefits are. Nozick's well-known example of the neighborhood public address scheme is a case in point. In the case of political obligation, however, the benefits in question are clearly more important than those of listening occasionally to whatever entertainment one's neighbors may provide through their broadcasting. Such benefits are even likely to be, in Klosko's phrase, *presumptive goods* in that they are "necessary for an acceptable life for all members of the community."[43] When someone denies that he wants to receive the benefits of national defense or clean air, then, we should be prepared at least to challenge the reasonableness of his denial.

This is the path that Klosko and Massimo Renzo have taken in their recent responses to the problem posed by those who claim to reject the benefits of cooperative practices that produce presumptive goods.[44] Both admit that someone may be sincere in rejecting these benefits, but each points out various reasons for being suspicious of such rejections. There is, again, the possibility that the person who rejects the benefit(s) in question is simply trying to be a free rider. More troublesome are cases involving complex psychological phenomena, such as adaptive preference formation, that may lead people to deceive themselves into denying that they really want something that presumably is beneficial to everyone. Such people, according to Renzo, "have developed the motivationally-biased mistaken belief that they do not need the benefits provided by the state," with the motivation being the desire "to receive those benefits without having to contribute to their production." To allow them to do this, he contends, would be unfair to the contributors, and in such cases "recipients do have duties of fairness to the state that provides them with those benefits."[45]

It seems, then, that the challenge is to find a way to uncover the biases and self-deceptions that lead people to believe that some apparent or even presumptive good is not truly beneficial to them, or not beneficial enough to outweigh its costs, when it truly is beneficial and definitely worth the cost. In different ways, Klosko and Renzo devote considerable ingenuity to meeting this challenge. In the end, though, both acknowledge that some people who shun the benefits of the polity may be acting not only sincerely but without irrationality or self-deception. In such rare cases, both conclude, we must resort to a pluralistic approach to political obligation. Fair-play considerations on their own, in other words, cannot establish that those who shun one or more of the benefits of the polity are failing to meet their obligations, so it will be necessary to supplement fair play with some other approach or approaches to political obligation.[46]

---

[43] Klosko, *The Principle of Fairness and Political Obligation*, p. 40.

[44] Klosko, "Fairness Obligations and Non-acceptance of Benefits," *Political Studies* 62 (2014): 159–71; Renzo, "Fairness, Self-Deception, and Political Obligation," *Philosophical Studies* 169 (2014): 467–88.

[45] Renzo, "Fairness, Self-Deception, and Political Obligation," p. 469.

[46] See Klosko, "Fairness Obligations and Non-acceptance of Benefits," p. 170; Renzo, "Fairness, Self-Deception, and Political Obligation," p. 487. To be sure, Klosko says that "considerations other

This resort to pluralism is, in my view, neither necessary nor desirable. I will have more to say on this general point in the next section of this chapter, but for the moment we need only consider how the fair-play approach can handle, on its own, the problem presented by those who straightforwardly and sincerely would shun the benefits of the polity. Here it may help to consider an example John Simmons employs in a different but related context—that is, in the course of his defense of a Lockean theory of territorial rights. In this example, a man protests against "wrongful subjection" to the polity that claims authority over him for reasons apposite to the present discussion. As Simmons portrays him, the man is "an individual, living in isolation from other persons (such as an idealized version of Henry David Thoreau), who develops a conception of the good that is both firmly opposed to membership in any political organization and revolves crucially around his relationship to the particular land on which he resides."[47] Were he to be told that he owes a duty of fair play to the members of the surrounding polity, we may imagine this idealized version of Thoreau responding that he wants no part of the polity, that he would forgo its benefits if he could, and that he wants only to be left alone on his land. What he wants and what he can achieve through his solitary efforts, though, are quite different matters. Much as he might want to be left alone on his land, he will have reason to worry that others will want to deprive him of that land or some part of what he produces on it. Some of the people who would do these things are likely to care little about rights, justice, or any other reasons in support of his desire to be left alone, and that disdain will make it even more important that he have protection against them—and more protection, surely, then he can provide for himself. Others may even deny that the land, in whole or in part, is truly *his*, and among them will be some who care as much about rights, justice, and good reasons as he does. How is he to persuade them that the property truly is his, or that his way of drawing the boundary line is right and theirs is wrong? Even this idealized version of Thoreau, in short, is almost certain to find that he needs the benefits of the rule of law if he is to overcome what Locke called the "inconveniencies" of the state of nature; and he will need them despite his own efforts to live as if he were occupying a small state of nature in the midst of a political society.

But let us suppose that our idealized version of Thoreau remains convinced that he can best fulfill his conception of the good by remaining free of the polity's entanglements no matter how beneficial the rule of law is. The proper response to his stubbornness, other than persisting in the attempt to persuade him that

---

than receipt of benefits *could* justify obligations on other grounds" (idem., emphasis added), but elsewhere he has advocated a pluralistic approach to political obligation, as we shall see shortly.

[47] Simmons, *Boundaries of Authority* (Oxford: Oxford University Press, 2016), p. 138.

he is wrong, is to maintain that he nevertheless owes a duty of fair play to the cooperating members of the polity. After all, our idealized version of Thoreau is not living in a state of nature, no more than Thoreau himself was. He has grown up among people who have been enjoying the benefits of the rule of law throughout the course of their lives, and he has been sharing in those benefits. If he has decided, as a mature adult, that these benefits are not worth the costs he must bear in the payment of taxes and other burdensome forms of obedience, then he should be free to act on his convictions by leaving the polity and its co-operative duties in hopes of finding a less demanding residence elsewhere. He should be free also to try to talk the rest of us into dissolving the polity so that all of us individually may enjoy the freedom of living anarchically. In the meanwhile, though, he cannot be free from the obligation to obey the law. He has a duty to the cooperating members of the polity to ensure that he treats them fairly, in boundary disputes and other matters, by contributing his fair share toward the maintenance of the rule of law as long as he lives among them. Perhaps the rest of us should grant him exemptions in certain respects, as we now do with conscientious objectors to military service, but the fundamental point is that we are not treating him unfairly when we require him to bear a share of the burdens imposed on those who benefit from the cooperative meta-practice of the polity—not, that is, as long as he remains among us and the polity remains in existence.

The proper conclusion, then, is that the fair-play theory of political obligation is not itself guilty in some way of being unfair, whether it is through a bias in favor of the status quo, through neglect of those who are unable to contribute to the cooperative practice, or through a refusal to allow those who would shun its benefits to be free from the obligation to obey the law. Nor is it vulnerable to the other objections I have examined in this and previous chapters. There is a further challenge to be met, however, and it comes not from an opponent but from the foremost proponent of fair-play theory, George Klosko. In this case the challenge takes the form of a two-fold revision to the fair-play approach that I believe to be misguided. Whether I am right or wrong on that point, it is necessary at least to distinguish my understanding of fair-play theory from Klosko's.

Fair Play Revised?

In the last decade or so Professor Klosko has departed from the standard fair-play or fairness approach to political obligation in two ways. First, he now argues that the principle is not in itself sufficient to account for political obligations. The principle has a crucial part to play in such an account, he maintains, by covering the "central public goods" that states provide; but it "establishes political obligations that are general but not comprehensive."[48] To provide a comprehensive theory—that is, one that will not only ground obligations for virtually all citizens (i.e., generality) but also "support a full range of governmental functions"[49]—it is necessary to supplement fairness with appeals to natural duties and the common good. The result is a pluralistic or multiple-principle theory of political obligation in which the principle of fairness has the leading role.[50] Such a theory may be less tidy than one that rests entirely on considerations of fair play, but the only alternative to the multiple-principle approach, Klosko says, appears to be "no satisfactory theory at all."[51]

Klosko's second departure from standard fair-play arguments consists in his rejection of the prevailing view that political obligations are *content-independent* obligations—that is, obligations to obey the law as such, simply because it is the law, regardless of what the law in question prescribes or proscribes. In fact, as I noted in Chapter 2, virtually everyone who writes about political or legal obligation, critics and defenders alike, takes these to be content-independent obligations. When Klosko argues that such obligations depend on the content of the laws in question, then, his arguments have implications that extend beyond fair-play theory. As he says, rather

> than *creating* moral reasons why subjects should obey, through legislation, state authorities determine or specify the content of subjects' already existing moral requirements.... [T]his view turns on "content dependent" reasons to obey the law. On such a view, the fact that L is a law carries no independent moral force.[52]

I shall set these broader implications aside, however, to concentrate on their bearing on fair-play theory. In this case, as in the first, I believe that Klosko's departure from standard versions of the theory is neither necessary nor helpful.

In the article in which he makes his case for the content *dependence* of political obligations, Klosko provides a statement that connects the two ways in which he proposes to revise fair-play theory. As he says there, a content-dependent theory of obligation

---

[48] Klosko, *Political Obligations*, p. 102.

[49] Ibid., p. 100.

[50] For other pluralistic approaches to political obligation, see Jonathan Wolff, "Political Obligation: A Pluralistic Approach," in *Pluralism: The Philosophy and Politics of Diversity*, ed. M. Baghamrian and A. Ingram (London: Routledge, 2000), and Knowles, *Political Obligation*.

[51] Klosko, *Political Obligations*, p. 101, n. 8.

[52] Klosko, "Are Political Obligations Content Independent?," *Political Theory* 39 (2011): 499; emphasis in original, but an abbreviation omitted. For similar views, see Harrison Frye and George Klosko, "Democratic Authority and Respect for Law," *Law and Philosophy* 36 (2017): 1–23.

> will work from the ground up, establishing reasons to behave in accordance with individual laws or different classes of laws.... The key idea is that, as long as laws serve valid public purposes, identifying reasons to behave as they say one should will not be overly difficult. This position will not rely on a single moral principle but will employ multiple and overlapping moral reasons bearing on each law it aims to justify. Central to this approach, as it seems to me, is the principle of fairness (or fair play). If individuals receive important benefits from the burdensome cooperative activities of their fellow citizens, they incur moral requirements to bear like burdens themselves.... [T]his principle establishes general moral requirements to comply with all laws through which central public goods are provided.... [T]he moral force of this requirement is clearly [to] do [one's] fair share in providing the public goods because of [one's] own need for defense and obligations of fairness owed to [one's] fellow citizens, with the moral force of the latter *passing through* to the laws in question.[53]

As this passage indicates, Klosko's worries have led him to adopt a piecemeal or patchwork approach to the problem of political obligation. In contrast to the traditional conception of political obligation as a general obligation to obey the law as a whole, Klosko aims to provide a theory that will piece together discrete obligations to various laws or classes of laws in a way that will comprehensively cover, like a patchwork quilt, virtually all laws. This approach preserves the standard account of political obligation as a moral duty, to be sure, but it takes the moral force of this duty to be something grounded in the content of the law rather than the authority from which it issues. That is why he talks about the moral force of political obligations *passing through* to the laws in question. In the case of fair play, this means that there is a moral duty to obey laws that are necessary to secure the provision of "central public goods," but the moral force of these laws derives entirely from the demands of fairness rather than from political authority or law itself. Law has no independent moral force, as Klosko says, and any obligations to obey it must therefore be content dependent. If a specific law lacks moral content, no moral force will pass through it, and there will be no moral obligation to obey it. Moral force will pass through most laws, however, with one or more of three principles—fairness, mutual aid, or the common good—supplying the moral content and accounting for political obligations that together prove to be comprehensive. But there is no way to justify content-independent obligations to obey the law as such.

---

[53] Klosko, "Are Political Obligations Content Independent?," pp. 516–17; emphasis added.

From the standpoint of fair-play theory as I understand it, the chief problem with Klosko's two-fold revision is that it fails to give the rule of law its due. Indeed, his own arguments seem to lead, albeit inadvertently, to the conclusion that fair play is the foundation of an obligation to obey the laws of the polity, with the polity understood as the agency responsible for administering the rule of law. As Klosko says, the principle of fairness accounts for the obligation to obey the law when central public goods are involved, such as law enforcement and national defense; and it also covers other goods, such as transportation and communication facilities, that are necessary to the provision of the central or indispensable goods. But he holds that fairness cannot underpin all of the dispensable or discretionary public goods that governments provide—parks, libraries, and wilderness areas, for example—nor can it account for social-welfare programs, which cannot be justified in terms of a fair sharing of benefits and burdens. That is why fairness requires the supplementary principles of mutual aid, in the case of social welfare, and the common good. According to this last principle, "the mechanism in place in society X to provide indispensable and other necessary public goods and to aid the unfortunate can also take reasonable measures to promote the common good in other ways"—measures that include "regulating the economy to keep inflation and unemployment in check, supporting public education, museums, symphonies, and national parks."[54] This common-good principle, in other words, apparently requires the existence of a state or government— "a standing mechanism to take measures for the common good."[55] "Arguably," Klosko goes on to say, "such a mechanism is itself indispensable."[56] But that, regrettably, is an argument he does not pursue. If he did, it would lead him back to a theory of political obligation grounded solely in fair play.

Klosko has a reason, as we shall soon see, for not pursuing this kind of argument. Before considering that reason, though, it is important to notice that his appeal to the supplementary principle of the common good is troubling in two ways. First, it seems to be entirely *ad hoc*.[57] The two other principles he invokes, fairness and the natural-duty principle of mutual aid, both have a provenance outside his theory, but the common-good principle does not. It is, in fact, a principle that Klosko seems to have discovered himself while looking for a way to render his multiple-principle theory comprehensive in its coverage. Its *ad hoc* nature even seems evident in his formulation of the common-good principle:

---

[54] Both quotations are from Klosko, *Political Obligations*, p. 111.
[55] Ibid.
[56] Ibid.
[57] As Simmons has been quick to note: A. John Simmons, "The Particularity Problem," *APA Newsletter on Philosophy and Law* 7 (2007): 26–27, n. 17.

> The government of society X, which provides indispensable (and necessary discretionary) public goods and basic social welfare services, may take reasonable measures to promote the common good in additional ways, with citizens required to do their fair shares to support its efforts.[58]

Aside from its uncomfortably *ad hoc* appearance, the second way in which Klosko's common-good principle is troubling is its obvious appeal to considerations of fair play. If citizens are "required to do their fair shares" to support their government's efforts to promote the common good, then why is it necessary to invoke the previously unnoticed common-good principle? Klosko's answer is that the new principle adds the element of consequentialism to that of fairness. This combination is necessary, he argues, because

> the principle of fairness is able to justify obligations only in regard to cooperative efforts that benefit the obligee himself. The CG principle grounds wider obligations to support efforts *that are beneficial to society* . . . . in accordance with consequentialist requirements to promote the public good.[59]

Not only does this limitation of fair-play theory make it necessary to call on the natural-duty principle of mutual aid, in short, but so also does it require the consequentialist element embodied in the common-good principle.

Combining appeals to fair play and consequences in this way does nothing to overcome worries about the *ad hoc* appearance of the common-good principle, but what of the second concern? Does it overcome the objection, which Klosko anticipates, that "the CG principle might appear to be an extension of fairness rather than a separate moral principle"?[60] I do not see how. In order to meet the particularity requirement, Klosko must show how the public good to be promoted is the public good of one's own society. Meeting this requirement leads him into the following argument:

> Community is constituted by joint production and consumption of indispensable public goods. Because people require these for acceptable lives, . . . they are "naturally" members of the community and have requirements to support the community's effort to promote the common good, as the community sees this.[61]

---

[58] Klosko, *Political Obligations*, p. 111.
[59] Ibid., p. 113, emphasis added.
[60] Ibid., p. 113.
[61] Ibid., p. 115.

As the language of "joint production and consumption" suggests, however, Klosko is once again speaking in terms of cooperative practices and fair play. The common-good principle, consequently, does indeed seem to be merely an extension of fairness.

More to the point, it is an altogether unnecessary extension. What Klosko hopes to achieve by means of the common-good principle is something the principle of fair play already does, taking that principle to apply to the meta-practice of the polity and its administration of the rule of law. Understood in this way, the principle clearly meets Klosko's requirements. It does this, first, because it constitutes community, in accordance with his conception of community, by making possible the joint production and consumption of perhaps the most indispensable of public goods: the rule of law. Second, it includes a consequentialist element, for the polity as an ongoing practice must aim at maintaining the rule of law into the future. Finally, it overcomes the limitation that so concerns Klosko. That is, considered as a cooperative practice, as I have previously argued, the polity administering the rule of law provides benefits to everyone subject to it. If such a polity establishes social-welfare programs and wilderness areas— benefits that may mean nothing to me as an individual person—I still have an obligation to obey under the fair-play duty to uphold the rule of law. This stance, moreover, is in keeping with Klosko's belief that members of a community "have requirements to support the community's effort to promote the common good, *as the community sees this*."[62] There no doubt will be debate and dissension regarding the proper scope and direction of this effort, but these disagreements are to be settled within the rule of law. That, indeed, is why we need the rule of law: not only to establish coordination points and to solve collective-action problems, but to provide ways of resolving and controlling disputes about what the polity should and should not be doing.

Why, then, does Klosko not pursue the argument that the meta-practice of the polity is itself an indispensable public good that gives rise to a comprehensive obligation of fair play? He answers this question, in the course of a long footnote, in the following way:

> On an alternative construal, the law as a whole is viewed as a cooperative enterprise from which citizens benefit and so should support. The problem with this construal is that it depicts the law as a "seamless web," with all parts thoroughly implicated in one another. Given the breadth of the legal systems of modern countries, I believe this view does not correspond to the facts.[63]

[62] Ibid., p. 115; emphasis added.
[63] Ibid., p. 101, n. 8.

The question, then, is whether the "alternative construal" to which Klosko refers is as flawed as he thinks.

Proponents of this construal—that is, of the position I have elaborated and defended in this chapter—will say that it is not, of course, and there are two ways in which they can support that response. One is to defend the seamless-web conception of the law. I shall not pursue that argument here, however, in part because it is not clear what counts as a seamless web in this context. The second way is to deny that law must be a seamless web, however that term is understood, in order to be a cooperative practice that generates obligations of fair play. If it is a web at all, it is a web that is constantly under construction—expanding in some directions, contracting in others, and undergoing repair and renovation in various places. There may even be instances in which the workers in one part of the web are at cross-purposes with the workers in another. Indeed, it would be surprising if there were not, especially in countries where the law has both a common-law and a statutory basis. Add to that the complicating factor of a federal system of government and it will be almost a matter of course that a country's laws will form a ragged web-in-the-making. But none of these complications and irregularities prevent the *rule of law* from operating as a cooperative practice.

To see why, it may help to reconsider the three themes Tamanaha associates with the rule of law: limited government, formal legality, and a government of laws rather than of persons. None of these themes requires a legal system to be a seamless web, perfectly coherent and free from internal tension. This point is especially clear with regard to formal legality, which openly acknowledges that the ideal of a completely clear and harmonious set of laws is something toward which we should strive rather than something we can expect to achieve. To be sure, we cannot honestly declare a society to be under the rule of law when the rulers change the laws willy-nilly, with no attempt to make the so-called laws clear, consistent, or general, or even to make them known to the people subject to them. But neither should we hold that the rule of law is absent when some laws are unclear or in conflict with one another. Like the idea of a cooperative practice, as I have argued, the rule of law has a critical, aspirational element, and there is a threshold below which a polity cannot fall without losing its claim to administering the rule of law. But that does not mean that its legal system must be a seamless web.

Klosko is right, in sum, to give the principle of fairness (or fair play) the central part in his multiple-principle theory of political obligation, but I believe he is wrong to confine it to this role. His revision of fair-play theory is neither necessary nor helpful, as I see it, for the principle of fair play is capable on its own of grounding a general and comprehensive obligation to obey the law of a polity that administers the rule of law.

Conclusion

This chapter completes the account of the fair-play theory of political obligation begun two chapters ago. In addition to filling out that account in this chapter, I have defended it against objections raised by those who would either reject the theory or, in one case, revise it in ways I believe to be mistaken. The result, I hope, is a coherent and compelling justification of a general obligation to obey the law, at least when the law in question is the law of a polity that qualifies as a cooperative (meta-)practice.

There remains, however, a final worry to address before proceeding from political obligation to the fair-play justification of punishment. This worry concerns the longstanding problem of the moral status of law itself. The problem arises here because of the emphasis I have placed on the importance of the rule of law to the fair-play approach to political obligation. In this context the problem takes the form: What if the rule of law does not guarantee a just or morally valuable polity? What if it is true, as one skeptic insists, that "the rule of law is not an inherently moral ideal"?[64] Is it possible (as this same skeptic, Matthew Kramer, maintains) that "the co-ordination-enhancing and security-providing effects of law can be wholly derivative of its role as a vehicle for wicked oppression"?[65]

For what it is worth, my inclination is to resist such conclusions.[66] Fortunately, though, there is no need to explain, defend, or rely upon this inclination here. In the fair-play theory of political obligation as I have elaborated it, the polity is the meta-practice responsible for administering the rule of law. That means, once again, that the polity must qualify as a cooperative practice that honors the equal standing of all of its members. Even if we concede, then, that a wicked regime of slaveholders, Nazis, or other tyrants may operate within the framework of law, it still would not follow that such a regime is a cooperative practice, for the reasons set out in Chapter 2. As long as a regime of this kind denies equal standing to a significant number of those whose labor and other contributions sustain the regime, it is not the subject of general obligations of fair play, no matter that it (apparently) operates within the rule of law. Again, my own view is that the rule of law is necessarily a cooperative practice that generates duties of fair play. To develop and defend that point, however, would take us into depths that need not be plumbed in this book.

---

[64] Matthew Kramer, *In Defense of Legal Positivism: Law Without Trimmings* (Oxford: Oxford University Press, 1999), p. 96.

[65] Ibid., pp. 259–60; parenthesis omitted.

[66] For reasons akin to those set out in Nigel Simmonds, *Law as a Moral Idea* (Oxford: Oxford University Press, 2007), esp. pp. 77–85.

There are other challenges to face, however, in the form of political and legal theorists who have sought a kind of middle ground between philosophical anarchism, on the one hand, and commitment to a traditional theory of political obligation, on the other. These challenges are best postponed, however, until we have established the case for fair play as the proper justification of punishment.

PART II

PUNISHMENT AS FAIR PLAY

5

Justifying Punishment

Concepts and Challenges

Perhaps the most curious feature of the extensive literature on the fair-play approach to punishment is that it seldom connects to the corresponding literature on political obligation. Other than a common ancestry in seminal essays by H. L. A. Hart and John Rawls, in fact, there is almost no overlap between the two. Why this should be so is not clear. Both bodies of literature rely on the same moral principle, fair play, and the idea of a cooperative practice is also fundamental to both. Given what seems to be an obvious connection between the two, the paucity of attempts to develop a unified fair-play theory of political obligation and punishment is something of a mystery.[1]

My aim in this and the following chapters, however, is not to solve this mystery but to dispel it. To do so will require the forging of a fair-play theory that accounts for both the obligation to obey the law and the justification of punishment under law. There will be complications to untangle and challenges to confront, of course, and this and the two succeeding chapters will undertake those tasks. Nevertheless, the basic argument is straightforward. If the members of a polity have good reason to regard it as a cooperative meta-practice that administers the rule of law, then they have a *pro tanto* obligation to obey its laws. This obligation is one that they owe, following the principle of fair play, to one another as citizens—that is, as members of the meta-practice of the polity. These points I take to be established by the arguments of the preceding chapters. The next step is to acknowledge that those who fail in this obligation by breaking

---

[1] As noted in the introductory chapter, I know of only one other attempt to treat punishment and political obligation together from the standpoint of fair play: Zachary Hoskins, "Fair Play, Political Obligation, and Punishment," *Criminal Law and Philosophy* 5 (2011): 53–71. Göran Duus-Otterström, however, does call attention to the connection in "Fairness-Based Retributivism Reconsidered," *Criminal Law and Philosophy* 11 (2017): 481–98.

the law pose a risk to the practice and act wrongfully toward the law-abiding members. In order to secure the practice and right the wrong, the authorities are justified in punishing the offenders.

As it was with the discussion of political obligation, so it is necessary to begin the elaboration and defense of this argument by clarifying key terms and confronting fundamental challenges to the enterprise of justifying punishment itself. Those preliminary matters are the principal concerns of this chapter. I will also take advantage, though, of occasional opportunities to fill out the fair-play account of punishment sketched above. Specific objections to the fair-play theory of punishment are reserved, for the most part, for discussion and response in Chapter 6.

Justifying Punishment: Conceptual Concerns

In historical terms, the concept of legal punishment appears to be prior to that of political obligation. Indeed, more than a millennium before Sophocles wrote *Antigone* and Plato recounted Socrates' trial and death, the Code of Hammurabi had already prescribed the kind of retaliation that later came to be known as *lex talionis*. Prescription is not the same as justification, of course, and the question of whether *lex talionis* or any other approach to punishment is itself appropriate or justified has long been the subject of vigorous debate—and never more so, it seems, than in recent years.[2] Conceptual disputes have figured in these debates too, including disputes regarding the concept of punishment itself. I begin, then, with a brief exploration of that concept before turning to the aims and justification of punishment.

What Is Punishment?

Our concern here is with punishment under law, or *legal* punishment. This will be similar in most respects to other kinds of punishment—of children by parents, for instance, or students by teachers—but different from those cases in which 'punishment' means something on the order of 'forceful' or 'brutal,' as it does when someone says that a prize fighter delivered a "punishing blow" or that the soldiers marched under a "punishing sun." Except for an occasional reminder, however, I will follow common practice and use the term 'punishment' as shorthand for 'legal punishment.'

---

[2] Note in this regard Michael Davis, "Punishment Theory's Golden Half Century: A Survey of Developments from (About) 1957–2007," *Journal of Ethics* 13 (2009): 73–100.

When subjected to the scrutiny of lawyers and philosophers, punishment proves to be one of those familiar concepts that are surprisingly difficult to define. For present purposes, fortunately, we can rely on the efforts of those who have already confronted these difficulties. One such scholar is Antony Duff, who provides a succinct and broadly acceptable definition that requires only a little elaboration here. According to Duff, legal punishment typically "is something intended to be burdensome or painful, imposed on a (supposed) offender for a (supposed) offense by someone with (supposedly) the authority to do so; and ... intended to express or communicate censure."[3]

So defined, there are two peculiar forms of what is sometimes called punishment that are ruled out of bounds and two others that are ruled in. In the excluded category are *vicarious* and *natural* punishments. The former could consist either of scapegoating—that is, "punishing" someone selected more or less at random—or of inflicting suffering on the innocent family or associates of the supposed offender. The second excluded form, natural punishment, supposedly occurs when an offender suffers a calamity of some extra-legal kind during or following the commission of his offense. The offender who suffers a crippling stroke moments before the guilty sentence is pronounced might be taken as an example of such "natural punishment." Duff's definition rules out both vicarious and natural punishments, however, by stipulating, in the first case, that punishment must be "imposed on a (supposed) offender," and in the second, that it must be imposed "by someone with (supposedly) the authority to do so."

The other side of this coin is that Duff's definition does allow the inclusion of two kinds of punishment that are conceptually troublesome. One of these is *welcome* punishment. This can take the form either of someone who finds her intended punishment enjoyable—someone who takes pleasure in the structure and confinement of prison life, perhaps—or of someone who believes that her punishment, unpleasant as it may be, is nevertheless what is best for her at this low point in her life. Such cases seem to defy the widespread sentiment that punishment is not truly punishment unless it is harsh, painful, and something that the offender strives to escape. On that view, "welcome punishment" is an oxymoron, and some way must be found to make the offender suffer the pain of genuine punishment. On Duff's definition, though, all that is necessary is that we *intend* to impose something burdensome or painful on the offender, not that we succeed in doing so by tailoring every sentence to the peculiar situation and inclinations of every offender.

---

[3] R. A. Duff, *Punishment, Communication, and Community* (Oxford: Oxford University Press, 2001), pp. xiv–xv.

The other troublesome form of punishment the definition allows is the mistaken punishment of the innocent. The trouble in this case is that it is paradoxical, and perhaps oxymoronic, to speak of punishing someone for an offense he did not commit. Even so, people sometimes do complain that they are being "punished" for something they did not do. Duff's way of handling the paradox is to say that punishment is "imposed on a (supposed) offender," and his inclusion of 'supposed' seems both appropriate and conventional in theoretical discussions of punishment. Including 'supposed,' moreover, preserves the exclusion of vicarious punishment, on the one hand, while recognizing, on the other, that innocent persons sometimes suffer the injustice of being subjected to punishment under law.

Duff's definition is also noteworthy for its final clause, which states that legal punishment typically is "intended to express or communicate censure." Were it not for this clause, Duff's definition would be simply a compressed version of the earlier and widely cited definitions of A. G. N. Flew, S. I. Benn, and H. L. A. Hart.[4] By adding the clause, Duff captures not only an important feature of his own communicative theory of punishment but also an important theme in analyses of punishment since at least the publication, in 1965, of Joel Feinberg's "The Expressive Function of Punishment."[5] That theme is especially significant here because of the place it occupies in the fair-play theory of punishment—a place I shall return to later in this chapter, when I elaborate the fair-play account in light of Jean Hampton's "expressive theory of retribution."[6] What makes the theme important to the understanding of punishment in general, though, is that it complicates and thickens the relationship between the punisher and the punished. Without the final clause, punishment appears to be a straightforward matter of society, through its agents, imposing unpleasant treatment on someone who has broken its laws. With the final clause added, other possibilities arise. One is the possibility that offenders can and should learn something from the expression of society's censure; another is that punishment can convey valuable

---

[4] Flew, "The Justification of Punishment," *Philosophy* 29 (1954): 291–95; Benn, "An Approach to the Problems of Punishment," *Philosophy* 33 (1958): 325–26; and Hart, "Prolegomenon to the Principles of Punishment," in Hart, *Punishment and Responsibility: Essays in the Philosophy of Law* (Oxford: Oxford University Press, 1968), pp. 4–5. According to Leo Zaibert, "the so-called 'standard' definition of punishment found in the literature" is "also known as the Flew-Benn-Hart definition of (legal) punishment." Zaibert, "Punishment, Restitution, and the Marvelous Method of Directing the Intention," *Criminal Justice Ethics* 29 (2010): 41–53 at p. 46.

[5] Feinberg, "The Expressive Function of Punishment," *The Monist* 49 (1965): 397–423; reprinted in Feinberg, *Doing and Deserving: Essays in the Theory of Responsibility* (Princeton, NJ: Princeton University Press, 1970).

[6] Hampton, "An Expressive Theory of Retribution," in *Retributivism and Its Critics*, ed. Wesley Cragg (Stuttgart: F. Steiner, Verlag, 1992).

messages not only to offenders but also to law-abiding members of society, who find assurance and affirmation in the enforcement of the law.

Is Punishment Harmful?

One further feature of Duff's definition—the absence of the term 'harm'—requires attention at this point. Duff's definition agrees with those of Flew, Benn, and Hart on this point, for they speak variously of "evil," "unpleasantness," "burdensome," and "painful" when defining punishment, but not of harm or damage. In this respect, their definitions differ from several others. Deirdre Golash provides a notable example of the contrary tendency when she begins her case against punishment by declaring, "Punishment, at its core, is the deliberate infliction of harm in response to wrongdoing."[7] She reinforces the point—again, on the first page of her book—by referring to "the harm we do in punishing: the deprivation of life, liberty, or property, or the infliction of physical pain." The question, then, is whether Duff's silence on this point is acceptable. Should the deliberate or intentional imposition of harm count, as Golash and others insist, as a defining feature of punishment?

Again, I think it better to adhere to Duff's definition. If we take the term seriously, to harm someone is to do him lasting damage or to worsen his condition in some global sense. If that is what we mean by 'harm,' then holding "the deliberate infliction of harm" to be necessary to punishment will have the effect of excluding from consideration such well-known approaches to punishment as the rehabilitative aim and moral education, both of which hold that suffering punishment can and should serve to promote the interests of those who are punished. It would also render the names of "penitentiary" and "correctional facility" utterly euphemistic. Such names and approaches may indeed prove to be unacceptable or inadequate, but they should not be ruled out of consideration simply by means of a contestable definition of punishment.

The alternative, for those who insist that harm is integral to punishment, is to loosen the definition of harm. In Golash's terms, for example, this loosening means that depriving someone of "liberty, or property, or the infliction of physical pain," all count as harmful. Conceiving of harm in this relaxed way thus would allow us to say that someone may be better off as a result of his punishment even though the punishment did him harm, or perhaps that his punishment, harmful though it was, did him no lasting or on-balance harm. Such a

---

[7] Golash, *The Case against Punishment* (New York: New York University Press, 2005), p. 1. See also David Boonin, *The Problem of Punishment* (Cambridge, UK: Cambridge University Press, 2008), p. 25: "legal punishment is authorized intentional reprobative retributive harm"; and Michael Zimmerman, *The Immorality of Punishment* (Peterborough, Ontario: Broadview Press, 2011), p. 20.

conception of 'harm' strikes me as strained, unhelpful, and—for reasons to be discussed below, in connection with the justification of punishment—possibly tendentious. Given the other words available, such as those Duff and others have taken to be defining features of punishment—'an evil,' 'painful,' 'burdensome,' or 'unpleasant'—there is neither need nor good reason to include 'harm' in the definition. What matters is that punishment involves suffering of some sort, not that it be the kind of suffering that proves harmful.

David Boonin, in *The Problem of Punishment*, disagrees on this point. As he sees it, defining punishment in terms of harm avoids the deficiencies that plague these other terms.[8] The problem with defining punishment in terms of *pain*, he argues, is that someone subjected to capital punishment could be executed painlessly; and much the same problem arises if we insist that punishment is a matter of subjecting people to *unpleasant* experiences, for we can always envision a punishment that some idiosyncratic person will regard as pleasant. In the case of *evil*, the difficulty is that we would be using a negative word in connection with something, punishment, toward which we ought to be neutral, at least at the outset. That is why it is better, according to Boonin, to define punishment in terms of harm, "where harming someone means making her worse off in some way, which includes inflicting something bad on her or depriving her of something good."[9]

These arguments are not persuasive. To begin with, Boonin's notion of pain is unduly narrow, focused as it seems to be on physical pain. There are surely other kinds of pain, including emotional pain—for instance, "the pain of loss." We also speak of someone being held accountable "on pain of death," and such a locution could apply even to someone whose death conceivably could be, in physical terms, painless. With regard to evil, there is no need to worry that invoking that term will prejudice anyone's judgment of punishment itself. For one thing, many people agree with Jeremy Bentham's proclamation that "all punishment in itself is evil"; but they also agree with Bentham in concluding that punishment is justified as a necessary evil—that is, "in as far as it promises to exclude some greater evil."[10] More to the point, the evil in question here is not the evil of punishment itself but something that is evil from the offender's point of view—the evil of a treatment that she would much rather avoid. So

---

[8] Boonin, *The Problem of Punishment*, p. 6.

[9] Ibid., p. 7.

[10] Bentham, *Introduction to the Principles of Morals and Legislation* (New York: Hafner Publishing, 1948), p. 170. Note also Zaibert's comment in "Punishment, Restitution, and the Marvelous Method of Directing the Intention," p. 47: "If anything, I find the term 'harmful' to be *less* neutral, and to be normatively thicker, than 'painful': my dentist may cause me pain, but she does not, I would hope, harm me."

understood, there is no need to worry about attaching a pejorative term to the practice of punishment. Contrary to what Boonin suggests, in fact, calling punishment an evil in this sense does not "beg the question" against those who maintain that the offender's punishment "is not merely allowable but a positive good," no matter how great an evil it may seem to the offender.[11] Finally, in the case of the term 'unpleasant,' Boonin's position seems to be that defining punishment as imposing something unpleasant on the offender fails in the face of so-called welcome punishment. But Duff's harm-free definition deals with this problem, as I have pointed out, by stipulating that the punishment need only be *intended* to be painful or burdensome. Besides, Boonin himself responds to much the same objection—he calls it "The Masochist Objection"—by holding that an "offender who is forced to do something she would otherwise not do [even if she subsequently finds it enjoyable] is thereby harmed; for this reason, such offenders [as the masochist] fail to serve as counterexamples to the harm requirement."[12] But we could respond to the masochist or welcome-punishment objection equally effectively if we were to substitute forms of 'pain' or 'evil' or 'unpleasant' or 'burden' for 'harmed' and 'harm' in Boonin's response. To wit: "An offender who is forced to do something she would otherwise not do is thereby made to endure an *evil*; for this reason, such offenders fail to serve as counterexamples to the *enduring-evil* requirement."

We should also note, once again, that Boonin's response leaves open the paradoxical possibility that the same punishment both harms and does not harm the offender. By forcing her to do something that she does not want to do, as Boonin would have it, we harm her. But if it happens that she finds herself enjoying what she is forced to do, or if she profits from the experience in some way that provides her with a net benefit, then it seems we have *not* harmed her. Boonin seems willing to accept this paradox, as does Golash. We can easily avoid it, however, by following the example of Duff and the others who leave 'harm' out of the definition of punishment. My own preference is to speak of punishment as something that typically involves *suffering*—something we usually regard as painful, unpleasant, burdensome, and an evil to be avoided, even if it proves to be, in the end, not harmful. Everyone will agree, I take it, that a person may suffer harm without suffering punishment; and everyone ought to agree that a person may also suffer punishment without suffering harm. If punishment and harm are too often linked in practice, that is not a matter of conceptual entailment but an indication that our punitive practices stand in need of reform.

---

[11] Boonin, *The Problem of Punishment*, p. 6.
[12] Ibid., p. 12.

Justifying Punishment: Challenges

Whether 'harm' is essential to the definition of legal punishment or not, there is no doubt that the pain, burden, evil, unpleasantness, and/or suffering involved in punishment pose the most fundamental challenge to its justification. If it is true, as Bentham says, that "all punishment in itself is evil," then the challenge is to find a way of demonstrating that it is sometimes right to visit that evil upon people in the name of law and justice. That challenge I shall return to shortly. First, though, it is necessary to take account of a complication arising from the various ways in which one may try to justify punishment. As with any social practice or institution, the justification of punishment requires us to establish that punishment does what it is supposed to do; but establishing its efficacy in turn requires agreement on the point or purpose of the practice. In the case of punishment, that agreement has proved elusive.

The Aims of Punishment

A large part of the problem is that those who try to identify the aims of punishment tend to look in two different directions. On one side are Bentham and many others who maintain that punishment is an essentially forward-looking practice to be assessed in terms of the consequences it produces. Opposing the consequentialists are those—Michael Moore is a prominent recent example[13]— who insist that punishment is an essentially backward-looking enterprise that aims to exact retribution from criminals by paying them back for the wrong they have done. To be sure, there are many others who believe that punishment, like Janus, can and should be both forward- and backward-looking. Benn, for example, has argued that attempts to justify punishment must address two distinct questions: first, what justifies punishment as a social practice? and second, what justifies punishing particular persons?[14] Following this distinction has led Benn and Hart, among others, to advocate a mixed or two-level justification of punishment that answers the first question in consequentialist terms and the second on the basis of largely retributive considerations—in other words, punishment is justified *qua* practice because it produces desirable consequences, but justifying

---

[13] Moore, *Placing Blame: A Theory of Criminal Law* (Oxford: Oxford University Press, 1997), esp. p. 153: "[R]etributivism is the view that we ought to punish offenders because and only because they deserve to be punished."

[14] Benn, "An Approach to the Problems of Punishment," *passim*.

the punishment of any particular person must begin with the conviction of his guilt.[15]

The problem with this and other mixed or hybrid approaches is that they seem to be unstable. At some point, that is, we are likely to face a situation in which consequentialist considerations pull in one direction and retributivist sentiments in another; and at that point, the justification we offer of punishment will prove to be not a hybrid of the two but fundamentally one or the other.[16] That is why other philosophers have tried to combine consequentialist and retributive considerations in more unified justifications, some of which I will touch on below. Indeed, the principle of fair play itself offers such a unified or unitary justification. Before turning to justifications of this kind, however, there is a bit more to say about the nature, and complications, of consequentialism and retributivism.

In general, consequentialism is the doctrine that an act or institution is right, just, or proper if it produces consequences better than, or at least as good as, those that any other act or institution could produce in the same circumstances. In the case of punishment, as I have said, consequentialists thus believe that it can be justified, if it can, only because of its ability to produce desirable consequences. Consequentialists differ among themselves, however, in a number of significant ways. Some, such as Benn and Hart, want to impose limits on the aspects of punishment to which the consequentialist test is to apply, while others would apply it without limit or exception. To take perhaps the most notorious example, J. J. C. Smart even holds that a guilty person should go free if no good will come of punishing him and, conversely, that an innocent person should be punished if doing so will serve the greater good.[17] Consequentialists also disagree as to the kinds of consequences they would like to achieve and avoid. There is general agreement that deterring and preventing crime are desirable consequences, but why exactly these are desirable is a matter of dispute. For Bentham and the

---

[15] Ibid., and, for Hart's views, "Prolegomenon to the Principles of Punishment." See also John Rawls, "Two Concepts of Rules," *Philosophical Review* 64 (1955): 3–32, for a much-discussed attempt to develop a two-level approach to punishment within a rule-utilitarian framework.

[16] John Gardner puts the point in this way: "As students of criminal law, we have all been brought up on the idea that the various arguments for having such an institution [as criminal law and punishment] are rivals, each of which takes the wind out of the others' sails." Gardner rejects this "received wisdom," however, in favor of the view that the criminal law, and "its punitive side . . ., patently needs all the justificatory help it can get." Gardner, "Crime: In Proportion and in Perspective," in his *Offences and Defences: Selected Essays in the Philosophy of Criminal Law* (Oxford: Oxford University Press, 2007), p. 214. For a useful survey of the arguments for and against pluralist approaches, see David Wood, "Punishment: Consequentialism," *Philosophy Compass* 5/6 (2010): 464–67.

[17] Smart, "An Outline of a System of Utilitarian Ethics," in Smart and Bernard Williams, *Utilitarianism: For and Against* (Cambridge, UK: Cambridge University Press, 1973).

classical utilitarians, deterring crime is good because it serves the ultimate aim of maximizing happiness or pleasure. For others, the justification of punishment rests on its ability to promote some other good: perhaps the rehabilitation of offenders and their reintegration into society; or perhaps the moral education of offenders and, indirectly, of society in general; or perhaps, in John Braithwaite and Philip Pettit's republican theory of criminal justice, the "dominion" of everyone whose person, property, and province are rendered insecure by crime.[18] This last theory is also notable for Braithwaite and Pettit's claim to embrace retributive considerations within their consequentialist approach. They can do this, they argue, because dominion combines an aggregative element—that is, it can be maximized across society—with a distributive concern for assuring everyone of equal standing as a dominion-bearing citizen. Whether they are right or wrong on this point, they are clearly aiming for a unitary theory of punishment that is fundamentally consequentialist.

Retributivism, by contrast, is a backward-looking approach that is concerned with doing what is right or just rather than with promoting any kind of good. How to determine what is right or just—and how much concern, if any, to devote to promoting the good—are problems that have given rise to many varieties of retributivism. Retributivists often appeal to desert, for example, but not all do; and what they mean by 'desert' also varies considerably. In 1979, in fact, John Cottingham identified nine different, if occasionally overlapping, varieties of retributivism.[19] Since then, other species have been added to the genus, including "negative," "positive," and "permissive" retributivism, to use John Mackie's terms, and what Jeffrie Murphy has called "grievance" and "character" retributivism.[20] There is, however, no need to sort through these varieties and untangle their complexities here. Instead, I shall illustrate the characteristic concerns of retributivism by examining at some length one philosopher's attempt to provide a fundamentally retributive justification of punishment.

The attempt I refer to is Jean Hampton's expressive retributivism. In addition to its own merits, Hampton's theory is worthy of attention here for three reasons. First, although it is indeed fundamentally retributivist, Hampton's theory makes

---

[18] Braithwaite and Pettit, *Not Just Deserts: A Republican Theory of Criminal Justice* (Oxford: Oxford University Press, 1990). For further discussion of their theory, see my "Republican Punishment: Consequentialist or Retributivist?," in Cécile LaBorde and John Maynor, eds., *Republicanism and Political Theory* (Oxford: Blackwell Publishing, 2008).

[19] Cottingham, "Varieties of Retribution," *Philosophical Quarterly* 29 (1979): 238–46.

[20] Mackie, "Morality and the Retributive Emotions," in Mackie, *Persons and Values: Selected Papers*, vol. II (Oxford: Oxford University Press, 1985); Murphy, "Repentance, Punishment, and Mercy," in Murphy, *Character, Liberty, and Law: Kantian Essays in Theory and Practice* (New York: Kluwer Academic Publishers, 1998).

room for consequentialist considerations—so much so that she considered it to provide a "pluralist" justification of punishment. Second, the expressive or communicative function of punishment is integral to Hampton's retributivism. In this respect, Hampton's theoretical project is closely akin to my argument for the fair-play approach to punishment. Hampton, however, explicitly rejected the fair-play approach, and the need to understand why she rejected it provides the third reason to examine her theory here. Once we grasp the basis of her dissatisfaction and the nature of her response, we will find that her theory is not as distant from the fair-play account as she took it to be.

Expressive Retributivism and the Argument from Fair Play

Hampton's commitment to expressive retributivism arose from her dissatisfaction not only with the fair-play approach but also with her own early advocacy of the moral-education theory. Indeed, at one point she advanced the consequentialist claim that "punishment should not be justified as a deserved evil, but rather as an attempt, by someone who cares, to improve a wayward person."[21] She even proclaimed that moral education affords the "full and complete justification" of legal punishment.[22] Soon, though, she came to perceive important defects in the moral-education approach. One of them, as she said in acknowledging Joel Feinberg's criticism, is that there are "too many criminals on whom such a [morally educative] message would be completely lost; for example, amoral risk-takers, revolutionary zealots, sociopathic personalities."[23] If moral education provides the "full and complete justification" for punishment that she once sought, then it would seem that there is no good reason to punish such people, no matter how heinous the crimes they committed. A second defect Hampton came to appreciate is that the moral-education approach neglects the victims of crime. By focusing on the "wayward person" who is to be improved through punishment, in other words, moral education deflects attention from those who suffered at the hands of the wrongdoer. As she admitted in the course of her exchanges with Jeffrie Murphy in their co-authored book, *Forgiveness and Mercy*, there is a sense in which criminals seek to lower, demean, or degrade their victims, and the law ought to do something in response to reaffirm the victims' human worth. She proposed, accordingly, that

---

[21] Hampton, "The Moral Education Theory of Punishment," *Philosophy and Public Affairs* 13 (1984): 237. The following pages draw extensively on my "Jean Hampton's Theory of Punishment: A Critical Appreciation," *American Philosophical Association Newsletter on Philosophy and Law* 10 (2011): 6–11.

[22] Hampton, "The Moral Education Theory of Punishment," p. 209.

[23] Hampton, "An Expressive Theory of Retribution," p. 21.

retributive punishment is the defeat of the wrongdoer at the hands of the victim (either directly or indirectly through an agent of the victim's, e.g., the state) that symbolizes the correct relative value of the wrongdoer and victim. It is a symbol that is conceptually required to reaffirm a victim's equal worth in the face of a challenge to it.[24]

In contrast to moral education, "retribution isn't about making a criminal better; it is about denying a false claim of relative value."[25] Retribution, she concluded, is thus to be understood not only as a way of paying back the offender for the wrong he has done but also as an expression of society's refusal to accept the wrongdoer's implicit claim to be more important or valuable—of greater worth—than his victims. Hence Hampton's theory of *expressive retributivism*.

In developing her theory, Hampton found it necessary to distinguish it from the fair-play approach. Her focus in this case was on Herbert Morris's highly influential essay, "Persons and Punishment."[26] According to Morris, there is a direct connection between the fair distribution of benefits and burdens in a rule-governed activity, on the one hand, and the justification of legal punishment, on the other. Someone who violates the rules, Morris reasoned,

> has something others have—the benefits of the system—but by renouncing what others have assumed, the burdens of self-restraint, he has acquired an unfair advantage. Matters are not even until this advantage is in some way erased. ... [H]e owes something to others, for he has something that does not rightfully belong to him. Justice—that is, punishing such individuals—restores the equilibrium of benefits and burdens by taking from the individual what he owes, that is, exacting the debt.[27]

This argument is at the heart of the fair-play theory of punishment. It has inspired at least as much criticism as emulation, however, and Hampton was certainly among the critics. She must have found something attractive in Morris's reasoning, though, for she deemed "Persons and Punishment" one of the two "most persuasive brief presentations of retributive thinking" she had encountered, and

---

[24] Murphy and Hampton, *Forgiveness and Mercy* (Cambridge, UK: Cambridge University Press, 1988), pp. 125–26.

[25] Ibid., p. 133.

[26] Morris, "Persons and Punishment," *The Monist* 52 (1968): 475–501.

[27] Ibid., p. 478.

she returned to it repeatedly in her writings on punishment.[28] The attraction apparently resides in two features of Morris's theory: first, that it is retributive; and second, that it is at least potentially expressive or communicative. For if criminals deserve to be paid back for the wrong they have done in taking unfair advantage of the law-abiding members of society, as Morris argued, then society has a right to express its disapproval of the lawbreakers' unjust conduct as it punishes them.[29] In this respect, considerations of fair play are more powerful than those of moral education.

Hampton, though, finds Morris's position deficient in two ways. First, she argues that Morris's theory is insufficiently retributive. That is, Morris's reliance on the idea that punishment is a way of restoring the equilibrium between benefits and burdens upset by criminal wrongdoing leads him, and those who have followed him, to a theory that "essentially makes retributive justice a species of distributive justice."[30] On such a view, punishment is nothing more than a matter of depriving people of undeserved advantages so as to return the benefits and burdens of social cooperation to their proper balance. Morris's theory is headed in the right direction, Hampton says, in that it attempts to provide an account "of what it is that makes an action wrong"; but the attempt fails because Morris's account "is simply incorrect."[31]

This charge of incorrectness follows from Hampton's second line of criticism, which she shares with other critics of fair-play theory. Morris's account of the wrongfulness of criminal actions is mistaken, she argues, because it requires us to take an "odd, even disturbing view of crime"—a view in which rape, robbery, murder, and other heinous acts are nothing more than ways of gaining an unfair advantage.[32] Moreover, this is an advantage that we would presumably wish to enjoy ourselves. Such a view is not only incorrect but "repulsive," for "those who value right relationships with others do not find laws against extortion or rape or theft burdensome constraints that they would willingly throw off if only such constraints weren't collectively rational."[33] The wrongfulness of crime must

---

[28] Murphy and Hampton, *Forgiveness and Mercy*, p. 95. The other essay to which Hampton refers here is P. F. Strawson, "Freedom and Resentment," in Strawson, *Freedom and Resentment, and Other Essays* (London: Methuen, 1974).

[29] Morris's commitment to the expressive or, in his words, "communicative component" of punishment is explicit in another essay of his that Hampton frequently cited, "A Paternalistic Theory of Punishment," *American Philosophical Quarterly* 18 (1981): 263–71.

[30] Hampton, "Righting Wrongs: The Goal of Retribution," in Hampton, *The Intrinsic Worth of Persons*, ed. Daniel Farnham (Cambridge, UK: Cambridge University Press, 2007), p. 109.

[31] Hampton, "A New Theory of Retribution," in *Liability and Responsibility*, ed. R. G. Frey and C. W. Morris (Cambridge, UK: Cambridge University Press, 1991), p. 5; see also "Righting Wrongs," p. 110.

[32] Hampton, "A New Theory of Retribution," p. 4.

[33] Ibid., p. 4.

reside elsewhere, and on Hampton's account, it resides in criminals' attempts to degrade or demean their victims.

These are cogent criticisms, but I believe them to be mistaken. To begin with Hampton's complaint that Morris reduces retribution to the mere distribution of benefits and burdens, the response is that there is more to Morris's argument—and more that is helpful to Hampton's retributivism—than she acknowledges. As Hampton concedes, Morris's approach more readily accounts for the wrongfulness of some crimes than her own theory does. It is much easier, for example, to conceive of tax evasion, shoplifting, and speeding as taking advantage of the cooperative efforts of others than it is to see them as attempts to demean or degrade other people. Even so, Hampton tries to turn this difficulty into an advantage of her theory in the following way: "it is not so much the free-riding as what the free-riding symbolizes about the worth of the victim that makes the tax evasion wrong."[34] In saying this, I take it, she means that tax evaders and other free-riding criminals are doing something more, and worse, than simply seeking an advantage for themselves. They are also acting on the belief that they are of greater value or worth than those nameless, faceless people whose law-abiding cooperation makes it possible for them to enjoy the benefits of the legal order without bearing their fair share of its burdens. These criminals are not only free riders, in other words; they are wrongdoers who must be defeated in order to deny the false claims their actions imply about the relative value of the wrongdoers and their victims.

This position is, I believe, substantially correct. But it is also, contrary to what Hampton says, substantially the same as Morris's. The two appear to be different only because Hampton's account of Morris's position is misleading. "Morris," she states, "thought that we objected to free riders merely because they got something for nothing and we did not. I am arguing that this situation bothers us in a morally significant way because of how it represents them as superior to us—with entitlements to goods and services we cannot claim."[35] To characterize Morris's argument in this way, however, is unfair.

If Hampton were right, then Morris would be saying that criminals are on a par with the person who is simply lucky enough to enjoy a windfall, for both get something for nothing. But Morris says nothing of the kind. One need only look to the passage from "Persons and Punishment" quoted above to see that he takes the rule-breaker to be "*renouncing* what others have assumed, the burdens of self-restraint" (emphasis added). Moreover, the rule-breaker must *act* to take unfair advantage of others, thereby *acquiring* something that does not "*rightfully* belong

---

[34] Ibid., p. 24, n. 11.
[35] Hampton, "Righting Wrongs," p. 130.

to him" (emphasis added). Other passages from "Persons and Punishment" make the point even more clearly, beginning with Morris's striking claim that "we have a right to punishment" that "derives from a fundamental human right to be treated as a person."[36] This claim Morris develops by way of a contrast between punishment and therapy, with the former being the appropriate treatment for a *person* who violates "the core rules of our criminal law"—rules "that prohibit violence and deception and compliance with which provides benefits for all persons."[37] But these benefits, as we have seen, are possible only because enough people bear the burden of exercising self-restraint "over inclinations that would, if satisfied, directly interfere or create a substantial risk of interference with others in proscribed ways."[38] The lawbreaker does not simply *happen* to enjoy an advantage over others, in short: he takes steps to gain this advantage without regard to the rights that others have, as persons, to fair treatment. That is why the punishment of lawbreakers is "associated with resentment, for the guilty are those who have done what they had no right to do by failing to exercise restraint when they might have and where others have."[39] It is also why we try to make the punishment fit the crime by aiming at "some equivalence between the advantage gained by the wrongdoer—partly based upon the seriousness of the interest invaded, *partly on the state of mind with which the wrongful act was performed*—and the punishment meted out."[40] On Morris's account, in sum, the rule-breaker is not merely someone who, in Hampton's words, "got something for nothing and we did not." For Morris, as for Hampton, the rule-breaker is morally wrong, and deserving of punishment, because his actions reveal that he holds himself to be superior to, or more important than, those whose cooperation he is exploiting and whose value he is demeaning.

Hampton is wrong, then, when she charges that Morris's theory is insufficiently retributive. She could concede this point, however, while continuing to insist that her expressive retributivism is superior to the fair-play theory of punishment. After all, Morris and other advocates of the fair-play theory are still in the embarrassing position of reducing rape, murder, assault, and other terrible crimes to the status of free-rider offenses such as tax evasion and littering public property. But are they? That is a question that I shall address more fully in the next chapter. For now, though, two brief comments are in order.

The first is that Hampton's attempt to indicate how her expressive retributivism can account for tax evasion and other crimes of free riding is a

---

[36] Morris, "Persons and Punishment," p. 476.
[37] Ibid., p. 477.
[38] Ibid., p. 477.
[39] Ibid., p. 483.
[40] Ibid., pp. 483–84; emphasis added.

kind of philosophical two-way street. That is, if she can appeal to "what the free-riding symbolizes about the worth of the victim" to explain how the free riding is wrong, as I have noted, then Morris and the advocates of the fair-play theory can appeal to similar considerations when they apply their theory to murder, rape, and other crimes that are more than simply matters of free riding and unfair play. If free riding expresses a kind of contempt or disrespect for others, then it differs only in degree from the egregious crimes that bespeak, according to Hampton, a false claim about the relative value of victim and wrongdoer.

My second comment bears on the question of who is to do the punishing. As we have seen, Hampton holds that "retributive punishment is the defeat of the wrongdoer at the hands of the victim (either directly or indirectly through an agent of the victim's, e.g., the state) that symbolizes the correct relative value of wrongdoer and victim."[41] But what is it that makes the state the victim's agent? To answer this question we shall need a theory of legal authority; and that is something Morris's approach can supply by reference to the state as the agency—or cooperative meta-practice—that maintains the cooperative, rule-governed practice that we call the rule of law. By broadening the category of victim to all who suffer at the hands of criminals, furthermore, we can even conceive of the polity—the cooperative meta-practice as a whole—as both victim and as agent charged with righting the wrong through its legal system.

In my view, then, Hampton's criticism of Morris's theory rests on a misunderstanding of his enterprise—an enterprise grounded, like hers, in the idea of the equal worth of persons. Playing fair is in large part a matter of respecting the equal worth of others, and punishment is justified, for Morris as for Hampton, as a way of denying the wrongdoer's implicit claim to superior standing. Hampton's theory would be stronger, therefore, if she had built on Morris's insights rather than rejected them. I shall try to substantiate this claim shortly, but first it is necessary to take note of a second mistake in her writings on punishment.

This mistake occurs in the course of Hampton's shift from the moral-education theory of punishment to expressive retributivism. She was wise to move in this direction, as I have said, but I believe that she erred in adopting a pluralistic approach to punishment along the way. In "The Moral Education Theory of Punishment" Hampton not only argued that moral education "can provide a full and complete justification" for punishment; she also criticized "patchwork" approaches that draw on more than one justificatory reason.[42] When she later concluded that moral education cannot provide the "full and complete justification" she was seeking, however, she apparently decided that

---

[41] Murphy and Hampton, *Forgiveness and Mercy*, p. 125.

[42] Hampton, "The Moral Education Theory of Punishment," pp. 208–209, and p. 209, n. 2.

no unitary justification is possible. Retribution thus came to be the "primary justification" of punishment in a theory that also includes deterrence and moral education as "moral obligations of states"—obligations that "can affect, *and sometimes override*, the obligation to inflict retributive punishment."[43]

The problem here is not that Hampton tried to find room for deterrence and moral education in her theory; the problem is that she did not try to integrate them into the kind of unitary or unifying approach she had previously endorsed. As a result, her theory offers no clear way of accommodating the sometimes conflicting demands of retribution, moral education, and deterrence. Hampton has not been the only philosopher to adopt a pluralist approach, of course, and it may be that some kind of awkward, *ad hoc* juggling is the best we can do when these considerations seem to be at odds with one another. Relying on juggling of this kind is not the most elegant or desirable theoretical posture, however, and Hampton would have done well to look for a way to provide greater unity to her theory. Had she not died at the age of 41, I suspect that she would have done so. But she had already dismissed the theory that offers the most promise of bringing retribution, deterrence, and moral education into harmony—that is, the theory of fair play.

The fair-play approach is the most promising because it incorporates both forward- and backward-looking elements. That is, fair-play punishment is fundamentally backward-looking, or retributive, in that it is to be imposed only on those who have committed a criminal offense; no other consideration, such as deterrence, is a sufficient warrant. But punishment on the fair-play account is also forward-looking in two respects. First, it aims to deter the commission of crimes, thereby providing a measure of assurance to those who are willing to obey the law that others will not take unfair advantage of them. Second, fair-play punishment looks to the future by aiming at the reform or moral education of those who break the law. To be sure, this is not the kind of moral education that will aim at turning a criminal into a paragon of virtue, for its focus will be on promoting the virtues associated specifically with cooperation and fair play. In this respect, though, one of the purposes of punishment will be to support the cooperative enterprise by encouraging those who have not played fair to see the error of their ways. By doing so, punishment can help to secure the cooperative enterprise as it pays back wrongdoers for actions that, in one way or another, to lesser and greater extents, have failed to respect the equal standing of other members of the enterprise.

Such an approach to punishment will not eliminate the occasional tensions that arise when considerations of retribution, deterrence, and moral education

---

[43] Hampton, "Righting Wrongs," p. 149; emphasis added.

pull in different directions. Fair play is not a unitary theory in the sense that classical utilitarianism is, with a single, supposedly simple principle supplying the standard according to which all judgments and decisions are to be made. But neither is it a theory that requires independent and rival considerations to be patched together, case by case; nor does it provide a "primary justification" for punishment that other considerations may "sometimes override," as Hampton's expressive retributivism does. When tensions do arise among retribution, deterrence, and moral education—and perhaps other considerations—the fair-play theorist will have resources for reconciling those tensions. In the case of the desire to enhance the deterrent or educative effect of punishment, fair-play theory requires us to look for ways in which greater deterrence or better moral education can strengthen the cooperative enterprise by bringing the benefits and burdens of the enterprise closer to equilibrium. Perhaps stricter sentences will reduce the number of certain offenses, for example, and thus provide greater assurance to law-abiding people that their cooperation is not in vain; or perhaps efforts to promote reparation and reintegration will contribute to this assurance by leading to a decline in recidivism and a rise in the number of law-abiding members of the polity. Cooperative enterprises are not static; they require adjustments and adaptation. But if investigation reveals that enhanced deterrence or improved moral education is only to be achieved at the expense of the fairness of the enterprise, then those demands must be rejected. Whether they should or should not be rejected will not always be easy to determine. Judgments will differ, and debate may persist. Nevertheless, fair-play theory offers valuable guidance in these matters by setting the terms of the debate. In this respect, it is clearly superior to a patchwork approach to the justification of punishment.

I conclude, then, that Hampton's theory of punishment is doubly mistaken: first, in its rejection of the fundamental insight of Morris's "Persons and Punishment"; and second, in its rejection of a unitary approach in favor of a pluralistic one. That said, I believe that Hampton is right both in her retributivism and in the emphasis she places on the expressive possibilities of punishment. To support this contention—and to indicate how Hampton's theory could and should be grounded in fair play—I turn to an essay published in 1998, two years after her death.

This essay is a product of the invitation Hampton received in 1995 to testify as an expert witness in a case in Canada.[44] The case involved the Canadian practice of suspending voting rights for prisoners serving sentences of two years or more—a practice that some prisoners challenged as a violation of their rights under the Canadian Charter of Rights and Freedoms adopted in 1982. Hampton

---

[44] Hampton, "Punishment, Feminism, and Political Identity: A Case Study in the Expressive Meaning of Law," *Canadian Journal of Law and Jurisprudence* 11 (1998): 23–45.

testified on behalf of the government, and she subsequently elaborated her reasons for doing so in this essay.

These reasons, not surprisingly, are drawn from her theory of expressive retributivism, with nods to deterrence and moral education. In particular, she argues that Canada is justified in denying voting rights to serious offenders during their prison terms as a form of expressive punitive response. The response is justified because those who commit crimes that damage their victims' ability to live as free and equal members of the polity are in a sense attacking the core political values of a democratic society. It is fitting, then, that society respond with an expression of its refusal to countenance such actions by, among other things, temporarily disenfranchising these offenders. As Hampton puts the point,

> When we vote, we do something. . . . Our hands are on the levers of political power. Now we would not give that lever to an enemy of our state—someone who would want to destroy it, or who wants to undermine the values animating it. We would not do such a thing because it would be a betrayal both of our country and of the values we believe it stands for, especially the values of freedom and equality.[45]

Because serious offenders have acted in ways that "undermine the values animating" the democratic state, it is entirely proper that their punishment include disenfranchisement while they are imprisoned.

Hampton also appeals to moral education and deterrence to support this conclusion. In the former case, her claim is that "[e]xpressive punitive responses, such as the suspension of voting rights, have the potential for provoking thought that can bring about a change in the wrongdoer's way of thinking about himself and his society."[46] Moreover, the policy has the salutary effect of telling not only offenders but every member of the society that "this law links the exercise of freedom with responsibility for its effects,"[47] thereby extending its value as a form of moral education to the entire population. With regard to deterrence, Hampton acknowledges that the standard arguments are not likely to apply, for there is no reason to believe that the prospect of losing one's right to vote will be enough to deter anyone from committing the kind of serious offense that leads to a sentence of two years or more in prison. Still, she argues, the policy of disenfranchisement

> hopes to achieve an *educative deterrent effect*, based upon its ability to make us think. Whether or not prisoners in penitentiaries reflect on

---

[45] Ibid., p. 41.
[46] Ibid., p. 43.
[47] Ibid., p. 43.

what this law means, perhaps the rest of us will, reaching conclusions about what society expects of us in our conduct and attitudes toward others that will make us better citizens.[48]

In addition to her appeals to retribution, moral education, and deterrence, Hampton also bases her case on two other considerations important enough to feature in the title of her essay: feminism and political identity. Feminism is important to her position here largely as a means of countering an argument advanced by expert witnesses who testified on behalf of the plaintiffs in the case—that is, on behalf of the convicted offenders who were seeking to have their voting rights restored while serving their sentences. According to Hampton's account, these witnesses maintained that the offenders were themselves typically the victims of oppression and abuse, so that suspending their voting rights simply added insult to the injuries they had already received. In response, Hampton argues that serious offenders are overwhelmingly male and many of their offenses have been directed against women. In these cases, their crimes are

> forms of hate crimes—ways not only of hurting particular women but also of subordinating women as a whole. To hand the levers of political power over to someone whose behavior manifests an intention to accomplish the subordination of women to men undermines not only the democratic value of equality but the status and safety of women in that society.[49]

She thus links feminism to "political identity," and particularly the identity of a polity committed to democratic values, which "not only helps to hold the pluralist society together but also helps people to have a sense of themselves as members of that political community."[50]

Is Hampton right to defend laws that suspend the voting rights of serious offenders? I believe so. But I believe that the position she defends would be stronger were it couched in the terms of the fair-play theory of punishment. For one thing, as I have previously suggested, these terms would provide her with a more coherent basis for her arguments than the various considerations she invokes. For another, fair-play theory points to a second conclusion about voting rights that I am confident Hampton would want to endorse—that is, the conclusion that these offenders should regain the vote when their sentences

---

[48] Ibid., pp. 43–44; emphasis added.
[49] Ibid., pp. 41–42.
[50] Ibid., p. 23.

come to an end. Once the debt to society has been discharged, it is only fair that the ex-offender be restored to full membership in society; or so I shall argue in Chapter 7. Finally, fair-play theory provides a firmer basis for Hampton's position than does her appeal to "political identity." Law, as she says, can be "a significant expressive force" in a community by "symbolizing the community's sense of its values and (what I will call) its 'political personality.'"[51] This appeal to political identity or personality, however, will produce the results Hampton wants only when the values of the community are democratic values that respect everyone as a free and equal citizen. In a thoroughly hierarchical and highly traditional society, Hampton's attempt to link concerns about the domination and oppression of women to the society's "political personality" would be a nonstarter. What she needs, and what she seems to be presuming, is a conception of the political and legal order grounded not in identity or personality but in the conviction that the properly functioning order is a cooperative enterprise in which the members enjoy rights and incur duties to one another as free and equal citizens. Such a conception is the foundation of the fair-play theory of punishment.

In the next chapter I will address the concerns of other philosophers who have raised objections to attempts to ground legal punishment in the principle of fair play. My response will vary with the details of their objections, of course, but in general I shall be arguing along the same lines as I have argued with regard to Hampton's critique. That is, I will argue that the objections to the fair-play approach to punishment are in one way or another misguided and that the critics' own theories—when they advance them—would be stronger were they cast in terms of fair play. Before responding to these objections, however, it is necessary first to attend to those who flatly deny that punishment is ever justified.

The Abolitionist Challenge

Those who pose this fundamental challenge to punishment are in many ways a disparate lot. Some of them clearly take the abolition of punishment to be part of a sweeping transformation of the modern state that they would like to see; others focus more narrowly on doing away with punishment. Within the former group, moreover, there are sharp differences between those of a libertarian bent, who focus on material restitution to the victims of crime, and those of a broadly communitarian inclination, who want to take power away from bureaucrats and penal professionals in order to return it to local communities and neighborhoods.[52]

---

[51] Ibid., p. 23.

[52] In the first category, see Randy Barnett, "Restitution: A New Paradigm of Criminal Justice," *Ethics* 87 (1977): 279–301; and Mane Hajdin, "Criminals as Gamblers: A Modified Theory of

Within the narrowly focused group of abolitionists, there are some who hope to see more rather than less professionalism within the penal system, with the treatment of offenders left primarily to professional therapists. Others seem to have no problem with professionalism or the modern state, but simply see no good reasons for imposing intentional harm or suffering on those who have broken the law. Despite their differences, however, all of these abolitionists believe that neither consequentialist nor retributivist considerations can justify legal punishment. Punishment, they all agree, produces more harm than good and fails to treat offenders as they ought to be treated.

For expository purposes, I shall divide the abolitionists into three groups: the therapists, the political abolitionists, and the philosophical abolitionists. This last group raises the most important concerns for my attempt to justify punishment in terms of fair play, but the other two also require attention.

Therapeutic Abolitionism

The leading idea of those in the first group is that crime is a kind of disease, or perhaps the symptom of underlying disease. In either case, the proper response is to treat the offender therapeutically rather than punitively. This idea is at least as old as Samuel Butler's satirical novel *Erewhon* (1872), which portrays a fictitious society that prescribes medical treatment for those who commit crimes while subjecting those who are physically ill to harsh punishment. By the middle of the twentieth century, however, satire was no longer in evidence as Karl Menninger, Barbara Wootton, and others argued on putatively scientific grounds for therapy, and against punishment, as the sensible response to criminal conduct.[53] In place of "the frightened vengeance of the old penology," Menninger urges the adoption of "a quiet, dignified, therapeutic program for the rehabilitation of the disorganized one [i.e., offender], if possible, the protection of society during his treatment period, and his guided return to useful

---

Pure Restitution," *Dialogue* 26 (1987): 77–86. In the second category, examples include Nils Christie, "Conflicts as Property," *British Journal of Criminology* 17 (1977): 1–15; Herman Bianchi, "Abolition: Assensus and Sanctuary," in *A Reader on Punishment*, ed. R. A. Duff and D. Garland (Oxford: Oxford University Press, 1994); and David Scott, "Visualising an Abolitionist Real Utopia: Principles, Policy, and Praxis," in *Crime, Critique, and Utopia*, ed. M. Malloch and B. Munro (Basingstoke, UK: Palgrave Macmillan, 2013).

[53] Menninger, *The Crime of Punishment* (New York: Viking Press, 1968); Wootton, *Crime and the Criminal Law* (London: Stevens, 1963). For a recent argument in favor of a therapeutic approach that stops short of calling for the abolition of punishment, see Adam Benforado, *Unfair: The New Science of Criminal Injustice* (New York: Broadway Books, 2015), esp. pp. 280–84.

citizenship, as soon as this can be effected."[54] There is, to be sure, an important insight here; many crimes are the effects of alcoholism and other forms of substance abuse, which in turn seem to be related to illnesses of one kind or another, and may even be illnesses themselves. In such cases, therapy may well be more fitting, both in terms of consequences and just treatment of the offender, than traditional punishment. Nevertheless, the idea that therapy should supplant rather than supplement punishment has not won widespread support, not even among the other abolitionists. Nor should it.

I say this for three reasons.[55] The first is that the therapists' reduction of crime to disease is simply not persuasive. There are undoubtedly some important points of connection between the two, as I have conceded, but hardly enough to warrant the dissolution of one category, crimes, into the other, diseases. There is considerable difference, for example, between the pyromaniac who burns down a building and the man who does the same thing in hopes of collecting the insurance money. Someone who takes the therapeutic position perhaps could say that a kind of compulsion is at work in both cases, but taking that position would require her to demonstrate both that compulsion is involved in the second case and that this kind of compulsion should count as an illness. Furthermore, there are numerous cases in which crimes seem to be rational responses to the circumstances in which one happens to find oneself. This is true of free-rider offenses such as tax evasion, for example, and of virtually all crimes in which the risk of being caught is low and the projected gain is high. That being so, the challenge for the advocates of therapeutic abolitionism is to show that rational action is somehow the product of mental illness or other disease. Failing that, the therapist could insist that there is a difference between acting rationally and acting morally—or acting in a pro-social manner, to use what seems to be a more neutral term than 'morally.' On this view, the therapist could still hold that the rational criminal was nonetheless caused to break the law by some anti-social impulse. To take this step, though, is to assume that society's legal and moral code is not only correct—a highly contestable assumption in itself—but also the standard of good health. Such a stance leaves no room for civil disobedience or, for that matter, for those who *feel compelled* to work within the law for significant change in their societies.

Similar considerations arise in connection with the second reason for rejecting the therapists' case for abolishing punishment. As Morris points out in

---

[54] Menninger, "Therapy, Not Punishment," in *Punishment and the Death Penalty: The Current Debate*, ed. R. M. Baird and S. E. Rosenbaum (Amherst, NY: Prometheus Books, 1995), p. 49.

[55] For a different but overlapping set of responses, see Jeffrie Murphy, "Criminal Punishment and Psychiatric Fallacies," in Murphy, *Retribution, Justice, and Therapy* (Dordrecht, Holland: D. Reidel Publishing, 1979).

"Persons and Punishment," the system of punishment treats the wrongdoer as a *person* but the system of therapy does not.[56] This difference has many important implications, including implications for how we think about rights. If we conceive of offenders as persons rather than patients, according to Morris, we will acknowledge that they have, among other rights, a right to be punished for their wrongdoing and a right to present a reasoned justification for their acts. "In a system of punishment," Morris says, "a person who has committed a crime may argue that what he did was right. We make him pay the price and we respect his right to retain the judgment he has made. A conception of pathology precludes this form of respect."[57] From the standpoint of criminal law, moreover, following the therapeutic approach would also render reference to *mens rea* pointless, as it would with appeals to insanity, incapacity, and other *excuses* for apparently criminal conduct. However unpalatable or even abhorrent these may seem, though, they are implications Menninger is happy to accept. In his words,

> We psychiatrists don't want *anyone* excused. In fact, psychiatrists are much more concerned about the protection of the public than are the lawyers. I repeat; psychiatrists don't want anyone excused, certainly not anyone who shows antisocial tendencies. We consider them all responsible, which lawyers do not.[58]

It is a curious kind of "responsibility," however, that leaves no room for excuses. Indeed, Menninger seems to have in mind here nothing more than causal connection of the simplest kind—the kind of "responsibility" that one billiard ball may have for causing another to move, or the "responsibility" of a bird that spreads avian flu. It is not the kind of responsibility that we associate with persons, and certainly not the kind that exercises those who take pains to develop theories of criminal responsibility.

Responsibility is a daunting topic, and no less so in the case of crime than in other contexts. We may set such considerations aside, however, and still face another controversial implication of the therapists' position—and a third reason to reject it. The problem in this case is that the therapeutic approach has no way to accommodate the widely shared conviction that the response to someone's offense ought to be in some way proportionate to the offense itself. This is the position that retributivists take, even though they often struggle with the question of how to make the punishment fit the crime. Consequentialists have even more difficulty in this respect, for the severity of the punishment

---

[56] Morris, "Persons and Punishment," p. 490.

[57] Ibid., p. 488.

[58] Menninger, "Therapy, Not Punishment," p. 46; emphasis in original.

required to deter people from committing crimes does not always match common notions of how serious various crimes are. Even so, consequentialists generally hold that the gravest offenses are those that should be liable to the most severe punishment. In both cases, however, whether consequentialist or retributivist, punishment theorists believe that some limits must be set to punishment. If the punishment is to be a life sentence or even the death penalty, it must be attached to the most grave and heinous offenses.

Where therapy is concerned, there are no such limits. In fact, in the name of public safety, those who take the therapeutic approach are willing to countenance indefinite confinement. Menninger is explicit on this point: "If we were to follow scientific methods, the convicted offender would be *detained indefinitely* pending a decision as to whether and how and when to reintroduce him successfully into society." Then, three paragraphs later, he adds the following: "And if the *prisoner* . . . cannot be changed by genuine efforts to rehabilitate him, we must look *our* failure in the face, and provide for his indefinitely continued confinement, regardless of the technical reasons for it. This we owe society for its protection."[59] Such an approach places tremendous discretionary power in the hands of the therapists who decide "whether and how and when" to release convicted offenders from their confinement, which surely shows a misplaced confidence in how much "scientific methods" are even close to accomplishing in the treatment of wrongdoers. It gives therapists this power, furthermore, without even a nod in the direction of the belief that the treatment should be proportionate to the offense. If the therapists decide that someone found guilty of vandalism is more likely to be a repeat offender than someone who commits murder, they may well detain the vandal far longer than the murderer.

For these reasons, we should not accept proposals to replace punishment under law with a system of therapy. But that is a conclusion most abolitionists themselves will accept. We need to turn, then, to the political and philosophical abolitionists to see how their arguments fare before concluding that we should reject abolitionism altogether.

Political Abolitionism

This category comprises various writers and activists who tend to see abolition as part of a broader effort to transform political society. As previously noted, however, they are divided in their visions of the direction this transformation should take. Some are libertarians who want to free individuals to go their own way with as little restraint as possible from the state or society; others also want

---

[59] Ibid, p. 44 (emphasis added) and p. 45 (emphasis in original).

to cut the state down to size—or even eradicate it—but they would do so by returning or transferring power to people in neighborhoods, work groups, and local communities. Political abolitionists of both sorts would move toward converting what are now typically regarded as crimes into torts, but they differ again on the manner in which their preferred legal system would dispose of these crimes *qua* torts. Those in the libertarian category would apparently maintain a formal, legalistic system of trials and settlements, but those of a communitarian bent would prefer to treat crimes as "conflicts" to be handled as informally as possible in face-to-face meetings between the offender, the victim(s), and other members of their community. Such conflicts, on this view, are a kind of property that has been commandeered by the agents of the state—not only judges, prosecutors, and police officers, but defense attorneys, expert witnesses, and all of the other professionals involved in the criminal law. According to these communitarian abolitionists, such conflicts really belong to the individuals in conflict, including those in the neighborhood where the events in question took place. They are not the property of the state, in other words, but these conflicts are nevertheless *public* property. In Nils Christie's words,

> one of the major ideas behind the formulation "Conflicts as Property" is that it is neighbourhood-property. It is not private.... It is intended as a vitaliser for neighbourhoods. The more fainting the neighbourhood is, the more we need neighbourhood courts as one of the main functions any social system needs for not dying through lack of challenge.[60]

Such a view is at odds with that of the libertarian abolitionists, who regard crime as an offense by one person against another. While explaining his theory of "pure restitution," for instance, Randy Barnett gives this account of the transformation he hopes to promote: "Where we once saw an offense against society, we now see an offense against an individual victim. In a way, it is a common sense view of crime. *The armed robber did not rob society; he robbed the victim.*"[61] Whether this truly is "a common sense view of crime" is a point that Christie and others in the communitarian branch of political abolitionism would surely dispute. Be that as it may, I shall set aside Barnett and the libertarians here, reserving discussion of their argument for pure restitution until Chapter 8, where I maintain that requiring criminals to make restitution to their victims, broadly construed, fits neatly within the fair-play approach to punishment. For the present, the focus is on the communitarian abolitionists.

---

[60] Christie, "Conflicts as Property," p. 12.
[61] Barnett, "Restitution," p. 219; emphasis in original.

A thorough assessment of this form of abolitionism would address the questions of whether the kind of legal and political transformation its proponents seek is either feasible or desirable. Rather than attempt such an assessment here, however, I shall concentrate on the narrower question of whether the communitarians make a good case for the abolition of punishment. There are three reasons to think that they do not. First, what they propose to do is dangerous; second, it would be a mistake to abandon the condemnatory force of punishment; and third, it is by no means clear that adopting their proposals truly would lead to the abolition of punishment.

To substantiate the charge that communitarian abolitionism is dangerous, and too much so to be acceptable, it will help to begin by noting a similarity between those who take this position and those who would replace punishment with therapy. Both groups recognize the need for some form of compulsory confinement of violent offenders, and both justify this detention by appealing to concerns for public health and safety. For the communitarian abolitionist, detention will not be imprisonment but a form of *quarantine*.[62] Unlike a prison sentence, furthermore, the quarantine will last until the threat to public safety is gone. The result, despite their hostility to the therapists' embrace of penal professionalism, is that the communitarians join the therapeutic abolitionists in endorsing open-ended confinement. In their case, however, the danger is the result of their weakening of the formal safeguards associated with the rule of law.

To be sure, the rule of law is at best a mixed blessing from the point of view of these abolitionists. To some of them, the rule of law is really nothing more than the artfully disguised rule of well-placed persons who have the power to determine what the law is.[63] Whether these abolitionists are truly condemning the rule of law, however, or only various perversions of the rule of law, is a question as old as Socrates' interrogation of Thrasymachus' definition of justice in Plato's *Republic*. From the standpoint of fair-play theory, and of other theories of law and punishment, the failure to live up to the ideal of the rule of law is no reason to conclude that the ideal is either illusory or nothing more than an ideological tool of the powerful. To the contrary, the fact that some political and legal systems come much closer to the ideal than do others, and evidently reduce oppression and domination as they do, lends strength to the belief that the rule of law is a worthy ideal. Such a view, certainly, is in keeping with the critical, aspirational aspect of fair-play theory.

---

[62] Bianchi, "Abolition: Assensus and Sanctuary," p. 342.

[63] According to a pre-publication reviewer more sympathetic to political abolitionism than I am, in fact, "Most abolitionists see law as a 'confidence game' in which insiders—and those with the social or professional or economic resources to have access to insiders—have significant advantages."

For some abolitionists, though, there is a further problem with the rule of law that remains even if we discount or dismiss its ideological function. In this case the objection is that it promotes rigidity and bureaucratic hierarchy while stealing conflicts from the individuals and neighborhoods to which they properly belong. For these reasons, communitarian abolitionists advocate a more local, informal, and directly political response to those accused of crimes. The problem with this approach is that the communitarian abolitionists would also eliminate procedural safeguards protecting individual rights and liberties. There is perhaps much to be said in favor of a political system that gives people at the local level a greater and more effective voice in their government, but there are also well-known reasons to worry about the possibility of "oppressive and unrestrained responses" within neighborhoods and communities to crimes and apparent crimes.[64] There are also reasons to be grateful, as John Gardner notes, that the criminal law has displaced private feuds and vendettas to a considerable extent, thus taking "the heat out of the situation and remov[ing] some of the temptation to retaliate, eliminating in the process some of the basis for excusing those who do so."[65] Whether the communitarian abolitionists' alternatives to trial and punishment can achieve the same success in removing or dampening the temptation to retaliate is a risk we should not be willing to take. In view of the possibility, furthermore, of maintaining trials, punishment, and other features of the rule of law while taking steps to promote more local and informal settling of some conflicts, the call for the abolition of punishment seems as hasty as it is risky.

A second objection is that the communitarian-abolitionist approach will do away with the condemnatory force of punishment. This may not be a necessary consequence of abolitionism, as we shall see when we turn to what I have called its philosophical variant, but it seems to be the intent of those who take the communitarian approach. Here is how one of them, Herman Bianchi, makes the point:

> In the abolitionist perspective a 'criminal', or a 'delinquent', is a person who has committed a liability-creating act, as a result of which he is in a difficult, and not always enviable, but certainly not hopeless, position in which he has to participate in a discussion on the harm he has done, and how it can be *repaired*. He is thus no longer an evil-minded man or woman, but simply a debtor, a liable person whose human duty is to take responsibility for his or her acts, and to assume the duty of repair.[66]

---

[64] See the editors' comments in Duff and Garland, *A Reader on Punishment*, p. 334.

[65] Gardner, "Crime: In Proportion and in Perspective," p. 214. But cf. Bianchi, "Abolition: Assensus and Sanctuary," p. 347.

[66] Bianchi, "Abolition: Assensus and Sanctuary," p. 340; emphasis in original.

As his language suggests, Bianchi's aim is to treat crimes as torts and criminals as "debtors" and "liable persons." The offender is not an "evil-minded" person to be condemned, but someone who is to engage in a discussion that aims to make him aware of the harm he has done and to find a way for him to go about repairing the damage.

This is in some ways an attractive picture, and especially so in an overly punitive time and place, such as the United States has been in recent decades. But it is important to notice that public condemnation or censure is altogether missing from the picture. However wrong it is to brand all offenders as vile and "evil-minded," it is no less wrong to treat all of them as if their conduct has been no worse than that of someone who has inadvertently damaged a neighbor's property. People who willfully harm others or display a wanton disregard for the rights and well-being of others deserve both retribution and denunciation. That is the whole point of expressive or communicative theories of punishment, such as Hampton's, Duff's, and Morris's.[67]

This point, moreover, has three distinct aspects to it. The first, as in Morris's theory, places the emphasis on the offender as a *person* with a right to be held accountable for what she has done. If she has really done nothing for which she can be held accountable—if mental illness has caused her to break the law, for instance— then therapy is probably the appropriate treatment. If she is responsible for accidental damage to another person's interests, she should be called to account under the law of torts. If she acted with malice aforethought, however, then she has, as Morris argues, a right to be treated as a person responsible for her wrongdoing. To be treated in this way, in these circumstances, is to be punished, which means, among other things, that "wrongdoers are generally made aware that the deprivation [they suffer] is imposed because of the wrongdoing."[68] The communicative element is thus integral both to the punishment and to respect for the wrongdoer as a moral being.

Hampton brings out a second distinctive aspect of the expressive or communicative nature of punishment by insisting that punishment has at least as much to do with the moral standing of the victim as of the offender. Prompted by Murphy's qualified defense of what he called "retributive hatred," Hampton

---

[67] To these three should be added Christopher Bennett's "Apologetic Ritual" theory of punishment, according to which "the main purpose of punishment is condemnation of the offender for a 'public wrong.'" Bennett, *The Apology Ritual: A Philosophical Theory of Punishment* (Cambridge, UK: Cambridge University Press, 2008), p. 152.

[68] Morris, "A Paternalistic Theory of Punishment," as reprinted in *A Reader on Punishment*, ed. Duff and Garland, p. 97.

went on to develop her theory of expressive retributivism.[69] As we have seen, this theory holds that punishment aims to defeat the wrongdoer's implicit claim to superiority and to reaffirm the victim's equal worth as a person. Punishment is thus both retributive—aiming to pay back the offender for the wrong she has done—and an expression of society's condemnation of the offender's demeaning treatment of her victim(s). For Hampton, then, an essential aim of punishment is to communicate to victims an appreciation of their worth as free and equal persons.

The third aspect of the communicative element of punishment, at least when punishment is properly conceived and administered within a reasonably just polity, is that every member of the polity—offender, victim, and those not directly involved in the crime—is equally subject to its laws. In Duff's communicative theory of punishment, the point is that proper punishment both grows out of and reinforces the values of a liberal political community. As he conceives it, punishment

> is consistent with, indeed expressive of, the defining values of a liberal political community. It addresses offenders not as outlaws who have forfeited their standing as citizens, but as full members of the normative political community; it is inclusionary rather than exclusionary.... It holds them answerable, as responsible moral agents, for the public wrongs they commit.[70]

When criminals *answer for* their crimes, in other words, they are *answering through* their punishment and *answering to* both their victims and the members of society who uphold "the central liberal values of autonomy, freedom, and privacy."[71] When society condemns or censures their misdeeds, the offenders are not being cast out; they are being called to account by the society their actions threaten. The law-abiding citizens, at the same time, should take from the wrongdoer's punishment the reassurance, in Hart's words, that "those who would voluntarily obey shall not be sacrificed to those who would not."[72]

---

[69] For Murphy's remarks on "retributive hatred," see Murphy and Hampton, *Forgiveness and Mercy*, pp. 90–110; for Hampton's reconsideration of her position in light of Murphy's remarks, see chap. 4 of the same volume.

[70] Duff, *Punishment, Communication, and Community*, pp. 129–30. For a similar emphasis on punishment as the appropriate response to public wrongs, see Bennett, *The Apology Ritual*, esp. chaps. 6 and 7.

[71] Duff, *Punishment, Communication, and Community*, p. 230. See also Duff, *Answering for Crime* (Oxford: Hart Publishing, 2007), pp. 15–18 and 51–56.

[72] Hart, *The Concept of Law*, 2nd ed. (Oxford: Oxford University Press, 1994), p. 198.

There is, in short, a communicative aspect to punishment that ought to hold some appeal even for communitarian abolitionists. By attempting to replace punishment with a response that carries no expression of condemnation or censure, and that collapses the distinction between criminals and tortfeasors, these abolitionists would surrender this appealing aspect of punishment. They would also surrender the opportunity to communicate to criminals and their victims what punishment is capable of communicating.

We ought to reject political abolitionism, then, because abolishing punishment would endanger individual rights and deprive society of an important means of communicating with victims, offenders, and citizens in general. There is also, finally, a third reason to reject political abolitionism. In this case, the problem is that following the prescriptions of these abolitionists would not, despite their intentions, really bring an end to legal punishment. Like the therapeutic abolitionists, as we have seen, they would continue to subject offenders they deem dangerous to compulsory confinement, even though they would refer to it as "quarantine" rather than imprisonment. Indeed, their position at times seems to consist in arguing for a change in attitude and language rather than in actual practice. "The new system," as Bianchi envisions it, "would no longer be called criminal law but *reparative law*"; even "the word trial as such must be abolished."[73] Regardless of the altered vocabulary, though, the abolitionists will be continuing the practice of compelling many offenders to do what they do not want to do, such as returning what they have stolen, making good their victims' other losses, apologizing to those they have wronged, and suffering the loss of freedom while they are forcibly confined. In fact, the only difference seems to be the lack of the stigma that attaches to words such as 'crime' and 'punishment'; and whether the stigma would disappear along with those words is far from certain.

In the end, the principal difference between the punishment of offenders and the treatment to which political abolitionists would subject them is a matter of intent. Following Duff's definition, again, legal punishment typically is *intended* to be burdensome or painful, and that intent is no part of the political abolitionists' program, however necessary it may be to treat offenders in ways that they consider burdensome or painful. There is a difference, that is, between foresight and intent in this respect—a difference that I shall return to shortly in the discussion of philosophical abolitionism. Even if we grant this point, however, we must also grant that the political abolitionists will be giving up the communicative dimension of punishment when they forsake the intent to punish; and they will be left with the dangerous prospect of the indefinite detention that follows from their

---

[73] Bianchi, "Abolition: Assensus and Sanctuary," p. 340, emphasis in original; and p. 343.

approach to the settlement of conflicts. These are reasons enough to reject the appeals of the political abolitionists.

Philosophical Abolitionism

By applying the designation *philosophical* to the third group of abolitionists, I am drawing an analogy between them and the philosophical anarchists discussed in connection with political obligation. This analogy forms part of a larger parallel relationship between two of the three forms of abolitionism, on the one hand, and the two groups, on the other, that deny the existence of a general obligation to obey the laws of even a just society—that is, the political and the philosophical anarchists. On both sides there is a set of people whose specific objection, whether to political obligation or punishment, is part of a larger program for social, political, and legal transformation; and in both cases there is a set of people—a set of philosophers, in fact—who seem more concerned, to borrow the terms of Marx's Theses on Feurbach, to interpret the world than to change it. Thus the philosophical anarchists find themselves maintaining, as I noted in Chapter 1, that widespread acceptance of their position would lead neither to rampant lawbreaking nor to anarchy in the political sense of the word. Radical transformation of liberal-democratic political and legal systems is simply not one of their aims.

The same is true of those I am calling the philosophical abolitionists. The analogy, however, is not perfect. Even though the philosophical abolitionists appear to have no fundamental quarrel with the rule of law or the political institutions characteristic of liberal democracies, they are nevertheless calling for the *abolition* of a fundamental component of all existing legal systems. In that sense, they are clearly seeking more than the adoption of an attitude toward the law that will call, in the fashion of the philosophical anarchists, for nothing in the way of organization or concerted action. Of the principal advocates of philosophical abolitionism, though, only one has given much attention to the changes that ought to attend the abolition of punishment. I refer to Deirdre Golash, whose *The Case against Punishment* includes a chapter that sketches the measures that could take the place of punishment.[74] But these measures—among them, crime prevention through social and economic reform, communicating wrongness through trials and symbolic condemnation, providing compensation for victims of crime—are all reforms that could find advocates within the ranks of the staunchest defenders of punishment. To speak only of the three

---

[74] Golash, *The Case against Punishment*, chap. 8, "What If Punishment Is Not Justified?" But see also the less detailed discussion in Zimmerman, *The Immorality of Punishment*, pp. 165–76.

defenders who have received significant attention in this chapter, neither Duff nor Hampton nor Morris would have much difficulty, I suspect, with any of the measures Golash suggests; but neither would they have to give up on punishment to accept those measures.

Other advocates of philosophical abolitionism, such as David Boonin, Geoffrey Sayre-McCord, and Michael Zimmerman, resemble Golash in devoting far more attention to the criticism of arguments that seek to justify punishment than to explaining what they would put in its place. In response to the "what if" question, though, they have less to say than Golash does. To be sure, Boonin argues in the final chapter of his book that a system of pure restitution could take the place of a system of punishment. Whether there is a meaningful distinction between *pure* and *punitive* restitution is a topic that, as previously promised, I shall return to in Chapter 8. For the moment, the important point is that Boonin stops short of advocating the abandonment of punishment in favor of pure restitution. His aim in this regard, he says, is twofold: first, to demonstrate that "there is no reason to reject the theory [of pure restitution] that is not also a reason to reject punishment"; and second, to show that "there is at least one acceptable way to do without punishment."[75] His abolitionism, in short, is *philosophical* in a way that seems clearly analogous to philosophical anarchism.

That point applies even more clearly to Sayre-McCord's philosophical abolitionism. As he sees it, punishment should give way to a system of "legal reparations" that aims "not at inflicting pain (or harm) but at enforcing efforts at making amends for the offense."[76] Nor do these "efforts at making amends" amount to the same thing as making restitution to the victims of one's crimes. The difference, according to Sayre-McCord, is that his legal-reparations approach takes account not only of the victim's losses but also of the offender's "assault on the victim's rights"—an assault that requires the offender to make amends. In this way, he distinguishes his position from that of the advocates of pure restitution while preserving the distinction between criminal and civil actions that they call into question. Indeed, Sayre-McCord would preserve so much of the contemporary practice of criminal law and punishment—a practice that some think imposes "on the offender a duty to make amends"[77]—that his abolitionism proves to be as thin as the anarchism of the philosophical anarchist. In the end, his position is analogous to that of the *a posteriori* version of philosophical anarchism, for his argument is not "that punishment is unjustified but that the

---

[75] Boonin, *The Problem of Punishment*, p. 274.

[76] Sayre-McCord, "Criminal Justice and Legal Reparations as an Alternative to Punishment," *Philosophical Issues* 11 (2001): 504.

[77] Bennett, *The Apology Ritual*, p. 171. Rather than taking it to be an abolitionist alternative, Bennett takes "making amends" to be a fundamental element of an adequate theory of punishment.

various considerations that might successfully justify punishment recommend the alternative offered by a system of legal reparations."[78]

Sayre-McCord's position also differs from those of Golash, Boonin, and Zimmerman with regard to the definition of punishment. Unlike the others, Sayre-McCord takes punishment to be "at its core *the intentional infliction of pain or harm*."[79] As the disjunctive "or" indicates, harm is not at all necessary to punishment as he understands it: "a response to an offense or violation counts *as punishment* only if it involves the intentional infliction of pain (or other unpleasantness)."[80] This is both an advantage and a disadvantage of his approach. The disadvantage is that defining punishment as he does makes it more difficult to distinguish his position from one that is punitive. But it is an advantage because it keeps him free from the difficulties of a tendentious definition. As I have already argued, there is no compelling reason to believe that punishment must be harmful. It may be true, as Plato's Socrates concludes in Book I of his *Republic*, that "it is never just to harm anyone," but it does not follow that punishment is necessarily unjust.[81] Nor do defenders of punishment—Morris, Hampton, and Duff again prove apposite—necessarily intend harm to the wrongdoers they believe are properly subject to punishment. On the contrary, each argues that condign punishment shows respect for the wrongdoer as a person—a moral being—and also holds some promise of improvement in his condition. Insofar as philosophical abolitionists rely on a definition that takes punishment to be intentionally harmful, to that extent is their argument suspect. Sayre-McCord at least escapes that suspicion.

I refer to "extent" here because Golash and Boonin do not always adhere to their stated definitions of punishment as the intentional infliction of harm. In the course of their discussions, moreover, both occasionally indicate that 'harm' includes pains, deprivation, burdens, and suffering that need not do lasting or net damage to someone. This relaxed conception of harm places them effectively in the same position as Sayre-McCord, with all three taking punishment to involve the intentional imposition of pain *or* harm. For all of them, it seems, the key feature of punishment ultimately is the *intent* to make the wrongdoer suffer. As Sayre-McCord says, in words that both Boonin and Golash would surely

---

[78] Sayre-McCord, "Criminal Justice and Legal Reparations," p. 510.
[79] Ibid., p. 504; emphasis in original.
[80] Ibid., p. 504; emphasis in original.
[81] Plato, *Republic*, 335e; trans. C. D. C. Reeve (Indianapolis, IN: Hackett Publishing, 2004), p. 12. It is worth noting that Boonin himself invokes the distinction between "being hurt and being harmed" when responding to an objection to the theory of pure restitution (*The Problem of Punishment*, p. 239). Why he does not recognize the importance of the distinction when he defines punishment as intentional harm is something of a mystery.

endorse, "Punishment is in place only when the infliction of pain is part of the point of the practice."[82]

To support this position, all three of these philosophical abolitionists appeal to the doctrine of double effect.[83] So too does Zimmerman, albeit with qualifications.[84] They all acknowledge, for instance, that even a society that has abolished punishment will sometimes find it necessary to force wrongdoers into confinement, and they admit that those wrongdoers are likely to find their confinement unpleasant, burdensome, or painful. Nevertheless, they argue that, as long as the suffering is not *intended* but only *foreseen*, the wrongdoers' confinement is not a form of punishment. To abolish punishment is thus to forswear the intention to impose suffering on those who have broken the law; the fact that we cannot eliminate their suffering may be regrettable, but it is beside the point where the argument for abolition is concerned.

Whatever its merits in other contexts, the distinction between intended and foreseen suffering is not free from problems. From the offenders' standpoint, in fact, it may seem to be a distinction without a difference. We may grant the value of the distinction, however, without conceding the argument over the justification of punishment to the philosophical abolitionists. For if punishment is the intentional imposition of suffering on wrongdoers, and if the intentional imposition of suffering on wrongdoers is justified, then the punishment of those wrongdoers is justified. The question, then, is whether the intentional imposition of suffering is justified. The philosophical abolitionists insist that it is not, but the defenders of punishment maintain, with good reason, that it is.

Put simply, the reason is that intentionally imposing suffering is in some cases the appropriate response to wrongdoing. For some, the appropriateness of this suffering is a straightforward matter of desert; the offender brought suffering on his victim(s), and it is only right that he suffer in return.[85] For Duff, imposed suffering is integral to the "secular penance" he hopes to bring about through punishment, with punishment understood as "a burden imposed on an offender for his crime, through which, it is hoped, he will come to repent his crime, to begin to reform himself, and thus reconcile himself with those he has wronged."[86]

---

[82] Sayre-McCord, "Criminal Justice and Legal Reparations," p. 507.

[83] Golash and Sayre-McCord do so explicitly: see *The Case against Punishment*, p. 45; and "Criminal Justice and Legal Reparations," p. 507. Boonin seems not to refer to the doctrine as such, but he directly invokes its core distinction between effects that are intended and effects that are merely foreseen (e.g., *The Problem of Punishment*, p. 233).

[84] Zimmerman, *The Immorality of Punishment*, pp. 159–64.

[85] See, e.g., Moore, *Placing Blame*, p. 91.

[86] Duff, *Punishment, Communication, and Community*, p. 106.

For Hampton, the intentional imposition of pain on wrongdoers has both a deterrent and an affirmative aspect:

> pain, or more generally, a humbling defeat which prideful wrongdoers will intensely dislike, can deter the commission of a crime against someone (or even something) having value; and the victim can come to see the value which the humbling defeat is meant to protect as symbolically expressed through the protection.[87]

For these reasons, the pain, deprivation, or defeat that the offender suffers is not merely a foreseen but regrettable accompaniment of the corrective response to her offense; it is integral to the response itself. It conveys a message about the worth of the victim and society's commitment to the integrity of its members that is not simply the "vindictive satisfaction" the abolitionist may take it to be.[88] That is why the intentional imposition of suffering on wrongdoers—that is, punishment—is sometimes justified.

As a partial response to this argument, the philosophical abolitionists argue that punishment is not the only way to convey messages to wrongdoers. Golash points out, for example, that the law communicates its disapproval to someone who loses a civil suit arising from breach of contract; and Boonin notes that court-ordered restitution conveys social disapproval of the offender's act.[89] In the first case, however, it is important to remember that the agents of the law adjudicate civil suits, but they do not initiate them. The fact that crimes are considered public wrongs that the agents of the law are responsible for prosecuting conveys a message that no civil judgment can convey. There is a marked difference, that is, between *Jones v. Smith*, on the one hand, and *The Commonwealth of Virginia v. Smith*, on the other. It is also important to keep in mind that civil judgments and court-ordered restitution are supported by the threat of punishment. For those who do not comply with the judgment or order, the possibility of intentionally imposed suffering looms in the background. Whatever communicative or expressive value such orders and judgments carry with them, in short, is owing in large part to the potential punishment of those who would ignore the message.

---

[87] Murphy and Hampton, *Forgiveness and Resentment*, p. 143.
[88] Sayre-McCord," "Criminal Justice and Legal Reparations," p. 522.
[89] Golash, *The Case against Punishment*, p. 56; Boonin, *The Problem of Punishment*, p. 268, n. 47. In that note, Boonin cites an earlier work of mine in support of his claim. I will return to this point in chap. 8, but here it is worth noting that I was defending *punitive* restitution in the earlier essay ("Restitution: Pure or Punitive?," *Criminal Justice Ethics* 10 [1991]: 29–39.

Conclusion

None of the abolitionists, in sum, have made their case against punishment. Properly understood—that is, taking punishment to involve the intentional imposition of suffering rather than harm on wrongdoers—there is no reason to believe that punishment is an altogether unjustifiable practice. To stop there, however, would not be to give the abolitionists their due. Their arguments against punishment and their attempts to find a substitute for it may not be convincing, but their complaints about the way punishment has and continues to operate in modern legal systems are often well founded. Overzealous though they may be, the therapeutic abolitionists are surely right to emphasize the role that therapy can play in the treatment of many offenders, including many chronic offenders. There is also something to be said for the political abolitionists' efforts to return the resolution of crime-related conflict to neighborhoods and local communities. There is also, finally, much truth to the philosophical abolitionists' objections to the severity and unreflective harshness of what too often passes for appropriate punishment, and much good sense in their desire to promote crime prevention and restitution to the victims of crime. The important point, though, is that we can give the abolitionists their due in these regards without abolishing punishment. In the end, their arguments lead in the direction of reform, not abolition.

In the chapters that follow, and in Chapter 7 in particular, I will give some indication of how reforms of these kinds can find a place within a theory of punishment grounded in the principle of fair play. Such an effort presupposes, though, that the fair-play theory of punishment is itself adequate, and that claim is much too controversial simply to presuppose. Indeed, I have noted in this chapter that one of the leading advocates of retributive punishment, Jean Hampton, has dismissed fair-play theory as an inadequate foundation for punishment. In response, I have argued that Hampton is not only wrong on this point but that her own theory of expressive retributivism is itself best understood, and defended, as a form of the fair-play approach to punishment. Hampton is not the only critic, however, and the others will require careful attention before I can take up the task of developing the fair-play account with an eye to its implications for punitive practices.

6

Playing Fair with Punishment

Elaboration and Defense

Appeals to fairness and complaints of unfairness have long been central to debates about crime and punishment. Such considerations only began to take a systematic form, however, with the publication of Herbert Morris's influential "Persons and Punishment" in 1968.[1] Even then, Morris's primary purpose was not to develop a justification of punishment grounded in considerations of fairness but to refute those who proposed to replace punishment with therapy. In fact, his essay includes no references to H. L. A. Hart's or John Rawls's seminal essays on the duty of fair play, nor does it make explicit reference to the principle of fair play.[2] Nevertheless, the principle is clearly fundamental to Morris's argument in "Persons and Punishment," as his synopsis of a "just system of punishment" attests:

> To summarize, then: first, there is a group of rules guiding the behavior of individuals in the community which establish spheres of interest immune from interference by others; second, provision is made for what is generally regarded as a deprivation of something of value if the rules are violated; third, the deprivations visited upon any person are justified by that person's having violated the rules; fourth, the deprivation, in this just system of punishment, is linked to rules that fairly distribute benefits and burdens and to procedures that strike some balance between not punishing the guilty and punishing the innocent, a class defined as those who have not voluntarily done acts violative of the law,

---

[1] Morris, "Persons and Punishment," *The Monist* 52 (1968): 475–501.
[2] Hart, "Are There Any Natural Rights," *Philosophical Review* 64 (1955): 175–91; Rawls, "Legal Obligation and the Duty of Fair Play," in *Law and Philosophy*, ed. Sidney Hook (New York: New York University Press, 1964).

in which it is evident that the evil of punishing the innocent is regarded as greater than the nonpunishment of the guilty.[3]

One need not look long or hard, I take it, to find the principle of fair play at work between the lines of Morris's brief summary. Nor is it difficult to discern an implicit reliance on a related theory of political obligation here and elsewhere in his essay. Without authorities responsible for enacting and enforcing laws that citizens are obligated to obey, there could be no "provision" for visiting "a deprivation" on one who violates the rules that establish "spheres of influence immune from interference by others." That implicit reliance required elaboration and defense, however, in the form of an explicit theory of political obligation grounded in considerations of fair play. Such a theory I have set out in Part I of this book. Now, in this chapter, the task is to provide a corresponding elaboration and defense of the fair-play theory of punishment. In doing so, I shall be relying once again on the notion of the polity as a meta-practice responsible for administering the rule of law.

Before proceeding with this elaboration and defense, I should note a general concern that seems to underpin some of the specific objections to be considered later in this chapter. Jeffrie Murphy, who had been one of the early advocates of the fair-play account of punishment, expressed this concern when he observed that

> the moral balance theory at least flirts with explaining the obvious in terms of the controversial. If someone asks me why a murderer deserves to be punished, I would be far more inclined to answer . . . by saying with emphasis "because he is a *murderer*," rather than by saying, "because he is a free rider."[4]

Murphy's concern is easy to understand, for there is indeed something odd about condemning a murderer for upsetting the moral balance of benefits and burdens in society and taking unfair advantage of others. Not all wrongdoings are as obviously deserving of punishment as murder, however; nor is it obvious to those who would abolish punishment altogether that *anyone* ought *ever* to be punished—not even murderers. Moreover, those who do believe that punishment is justified often begin their reflections with the "morally troubling" question of how it can possibly be right to inflict deliberate suffering or

---

[3] Morris, "Persons and Punishment," pp. 479–80.
[4] Murphy, "Legal Moralism and Retribution Revisited," in Murphy, *Punishment and the Moral Emotions* (New York: Oxford University Press, 2012), p. 81; emphasis in original.

deprivation, to use Morris's word, on anyone.[5] Punishment stands in need of justification, in short, even if that justification is nothing more than the straightforward retributivist principle that those who culpably cause suffering deserve to suffer in return. We should notice, though, the hint of an appeal to the conviction that "turnabout is fair play" even in that straightforward statement of retributivism. This hint, in my view, is reason enough to believe that looking to the principle of fair play for a justification of punishment is more likely to reveal and clarify the important issues than to complicate and obscure them. But the point remains controversial, as Murphy says, and it will be necessary to make a case for the plausibility of the fair-play account of punishment if the controversy is to be dispelled.

Punishment as Fair Play: Elaboration

As Morris's brief summary and my response to Jean Hampton's criticism of his theory in the previous chapter indicate, the fair-play justification of punishment relies on the understanding of a legal system as a cooperative practice. The core idea is that cooperative activities provide benefits to the participants, with the benefits ranging from the simple pleasure of playing a game to those of sharing the profits of a commercial enterprise or of enjoying the protection afforded by a system of mutual defense. These benefits are not without costs, however, and those who participate in the activity are expected to bear a fair share of its burdens. Punishment enters the picture because cooperative endeavors usually produce the desired benefits even when some of the participants shirk their responsibilities. To prevent these potential free riders from taking advantage of the cooperative efforts of others, the participants invoke the threat of punishment. When the threat is not successful, then actual punishment is justified as the proper response to those who have violated the principle of fair play.

For this account of fair play to provide a plausible theory of legal punishment, we must be able to conceive of a legal system as a cooperative enterprise—in Rawls's words, as "a fair system of cooperation over time, from one generation to the next."[6] Such a conception I have developed and defended in Part I of this book, with special emphasis on the way in which a polity is a cooperative metapractice responsible for administering the rule of law. Following this conception, we can hold that—to the extent the rule of law is in force—a country's people

---

[5] See, e.g., Daniel McDermott, "The Permissibility of Punishment," *Law and Philosophy* 20 (2001): 403–32, quoting "morally troubling" from p. 403.

[6] Rawls, *Political Liberalism*, expanded ed. (New York: Columbia University Press, 2005), p. 15.

are receiving the benefits of a cooperative enterprise and owe it to their fellow citizens to bear a fair share of the burdens of the enterprise by obeying the law. Everyone will find that obedience is at least occasionally burdensome, but good citizens will not leave it to others to shoulder this burden while they ride free. To assure these citizens that their cooperative efforts will not be in vain, those who break the law must be subject to punishment.

A Misguided Analogy?

In this respect, fair play in a polity is much the same as fair play in the contexts in which it is most familiar, such as fair play within a game. Whether that is a reasonable way to think of crime and punishment within a legal system, however, is a controversial matter, as Murphy has observed. If someone playing ice hockey stabs an opponent with a knife, he has certainly failed to play fair; but we will not be content with sending him to the penalty box or even expelling him from the match. Justice requires a legal response in this case, not one governed by the rules of hockey. Moreover, the paradigm cases of crime—assault, robbery, rape, murder—are not merely violations of the rules or failures of fair play. To think of them as analogous to cheating in a game, the critic will say, is to misunderstand them altogether.

These are serious objections. The second of them will receive considerable attention later in this chapter; the first I shall address here by pointing to five ways in which the analogy between a game and a polity, or legal system, is not only accurate but illuminating.

The first of the five is that respect for the rules is vital to both the play of a game and the survival of a polity. Some flouting or surreptitious breaking of the rules is tolerable, of course, but there comes a point at which such violations make the play of a game or the preservation of a polity impossible. There may be political and legal systems in which brute force seems to be the prevailing cause of obedience, but even tyrants rely on some degree of respect for their authority. More to the point, respect for the rules themselves is necessary in any system that professes to follow the rule of law. Laws need not be regarded as sacred or immutable, but neither should the citizens dismiss them out of hand as nothing more than arbitrary commands or meaningless regulations. When laws encourage that kind of attitude, they stand in need of reform or replacement.

A second strength of the analogy between games and legal systems is that the communicative aspect of rules and rule enforcement is essential to both. Both laws and the rules of a game are guides to conduct, and they cannot serve that purpose if they are not communicated to the people whose conduct they are supposed to guide. That is why St. Thomas Aquinas, centuries ago, included *promulgation* among the defining features of law.[7] Rules and laws thus are matters of public concern, taking "public" to encompass all those who are participating in the cooperative practice. Punishment, too, serves a communicative function, as I noted in the previous chapter and will elaborate below. So much is as true of punishment within polities as it is of the punishment of those who violate the rules of games. Those who participate in a game or belong to a polity must have a chance to know what the rules and the penalties for violating them will be. Without this knowledge, it will be impossible for the participants to play at all, let alone to play fair.

A third point of analogy is that both games and legal systems rely on the ideal of equality. That is not to say that we always expect the competitors in a game to be evenly matched, but we do want them to have an equal chance to display their talents, as the familiar metaphor of the "level playing field" attests. The same is true within legal systems, where the ideal is for everyone to be equal before, or "in the eyes of," the law. In neither games nor legal systems is the ideal always achieved, to be sure, and in some cases the actuality is a travesty of the ideal. But we can only recognize it as a travesty if we have the ideal to animate and inspire us. To play fair is to treat participants as equally worthy of respect *qua* participants in a cooperative, rule-governed enterprise.

If all goes well within a game, then, there will be a high degree of respect for the rules, which are communicated clearly to the participants and under which everyone is treated equally. Even in these circumstances, however, some means of enforcing the rules will be necessary, even if they are highly informal or simply a matter of self-policing on the part of the players. As games become more competitive and the stakes become greater, the need to codify the rules and to establish an impartial agent or agency to enforce them becomes manifest. The same is true of political and legal systems. Some form of coercive authority charged with maintaining fair play under the rules is thus the fourth point of analogy between games and polities.

In all four of these respects, there does indeed appear to be a close analogy between games and legal systems. Before turning to the final point of analogy, though, it will be helpful to take stock of where we stand with regard to the two objections to the analogy introduced at the beginning of this section. The short answer, for now, is that the analogy may not be exact, but it does not have to be in order to support the fair-play theory of punishment. In the case of the first objection, this means that there is no need to deny that the political or legal system is larger and more encompassing than any of the games that take place

---

[7] According to Aquinas, law is "an order of reason for the common good by one who has the care of the community, and promulgated" (*On Law, Morality, and Politics*, trans. R. J. Regan, 2nd ed. [Indianapolis, IN: Hackett, 2002], p. 15).

within its boundaries. But that admission means only that we need to regard the polity, once again, as a special kind of game—that is, as a *super-* or *meta-*game that encompasses and governs other games and activities.[8] It is also true, as the second objection holds, that fair play does not capture the full wrongfulness of murder, rape, robbery, and assault; but again, it need not do so. What fair play does is to justify the punishment *of* those who break the rules or laws *by* those who have the authority, within the game or the polity, to impose punishment. The offenders, moreover, not only injure their specific victims but also threaten the cooperative order in general; and that is why punishment is in the hands of "the authorities."

These remarks, finally, point to the fifth respect in which the analogy between games and polities is both accurate and illuminating. In both cases, considerations of fair play can also help us to understand how some failures to play by the rules are more serious than others. The distinctions among more and less serious offenses may be marked within the law by establishing different orders of crime, such as felonies, misdemeanors, and infractions; within a game, the difference between a foul, an intentional foul, and a flagrant foul will denote a similar set of distinctions. The basketball player who inadvertently fouls an opponent is supposed to incur a penalty; the player who intentionally fouls should incur a more severe penalty; and the one who flagrantly fouls should incur one that is still more severe. There is a violation of fair play in each instance, but the violation is progressively more serious in the latter two instances because of the offender's intention and the consequences of his foul. In the case of a flagrant foul, not only did the offender intend to violate the rules; his foul could also physically harm one or more of his opponents, thus making it difficult or impossible for them to participate in the game on an equal footing. Specific opponents have been put at risk or harmed, in other words, and the fair play of the game itself has come under threat.

But what of the player who draws a knife or gun on an opponent in the course of play? Surely he deserves not only an extremely harsh penalty from the game's officials but also punishment under the laws of the polity—and surely, the critic will say, fair play has nothing to do with it. To this objection, the proper response is that the player who draws a weapon does indeed deserve punishment under the laws of the meta-practice of the polity, and he deserves it in addition to whatever punishment the basketball authorities will impose. Contrary to the critic's claim, however, punishment under law in this case does indeed have something to do with considerations of fair play; for the basketball player who

---

[8] Avihay Dorman and Alon Harel make a similar point when they refer to government as an "integrative practice" in "The Case Against Privatization," *Philosophy and Public Affairs* 41 (Winter 2013): 67–102, at p. 84.

threatens an opponent with a weapon—or worse still, uses the weapon against his opponent—is making it difficult or even impossible for his opponent to continue to participate not only in the basketball game but also in the life of the polity. The flagrant foul spills from one cooperative practice, as it were, into another, as it becomes not only a foul but a crime.

In view of this and the other four points of resemblance between fair play in a game and in a polity, it is reasonable to conclude that the analogy between them is far from misguided. To the contrary, the analogy with games provides valuable guidance when confronting problems of crime and punishment, as I shall try to demonstrate in the next chapter. For now, though, we may simply conclude that the analogy is sound. If fair play does not tell us everything we need to know about an offense, it tells us enough to justify legal punishment and to supply some sense of why some crimes are worse than others.

Fair Play as a Theory of Punishment

In the previous chapter, principally in the course of discussing Hampton's theory of expressive retributivism, I sketched an account of the fair-play approach to punishment that called attention to its forward-looking, backward-looking, and communicative aspects. Now it is time to fill in that sketch and, in so doing, to advance the case for fair play as the true justification of a system of legal punishment. When the sketch is complete, we shall have a general compliance theory of fair play that is fundamentally retributive in character while also giving due attention to the consequences of punishment and its communicative element.

That fair-play theory supports a retributive response to crime is widely recognized. In *The Problem of Punishment*, David Boonin even refers to the theory as "fairness-based retributivism."[9] Such a classification is not surprising, especially in view of the fair-play theorists' emphasis on desert. In Morris's "Persons and Punishment," moreover, punishment is clearly a matter of "paying back" those who take unfair advantage of others in cooperative schemes. As Morris writes, the criminal "owes something to others, for he has something that does not rightfully belong to him. Justice—that is, punishing such individuals—restores the equilibrium of benefits and burdens by taking from the individual *what he owes, that is, exacting the debt*."[10]

The criminal deserves punishment, in effect, because he has not treated the cooperating members of the practice—in this case, the law-abiding members

---

[9] Boonin, *The Problem of Punishment* (Cambridge, UK: Cambridge University Press, 2008), pp. 119–43. See also Göran Duus-Otterström, "Fairness-Based Retributivism Reconsidered," *Criminal Law and Philosophy* 11 (2017): 481–98.

[10] Morris, "Persons and Punishment," p. 478; emphasis added.

of society—as they deserve to be treated. Instead, he has taken unfair advantage of their cooperation by failing to bear his share of the cooperative burdens—in this case, obeying the law when its burden has fallen on him. In this fundamental respect, the fair-play theory of punishment is certainly a form of retributivism.

Beyond this point, no further venture into the intricacies of retributivism seems necessary. There are many varieties of retributive theory, as I noted in the previous chapter, but the commitment to fairness-based retributivism does not entail a commitment to any particular one of them. In the case of positive and negative retributivism, for example, the distinction turns on the question of whether *only those* who are culpable of an offense should be punished or whether *all of those* who are culpable should be punished. On the first view, retributivism is essentially negative because it takes culpability to be a necessary but not dispositive condition for punishment; but on the second, positive view, culpability is both necessary and dispositive. My own inclination is toward negative retributivism, but there seems to be nothing in the fair-play approach that precludes adoption of the positive position, or of other particular varieties of retributivism.

Fair play is a fundamentally retributive theory, then, which is to say that it is a backward-looking or desert-based theory. But that does not mean that it forecloses forward-looking considerations. To the contrary, fair-play theorists will have an eye to the security of the cooperative practice in which the transgression has occurred, and therefore will be mindful of the need to assure the law-abiding members of the polity that their cooperative attitudes and efforts will not simply make them vulnerable to crime. Sanctions, as Hart says, are "required not as the normal motive for obedience, but as a *guarantee* that those who would voluntarily obey shall not be sacrificed to those who would not.... Given this standing danger, what reason demands is *voluntary* cooperation in a *coercive* system."[11]

To be sure, fair-play theorists will insist that the sanctions must be deserved; but they will also recognize the need to assure those who cooperate that the cooperative practice remains healthy and their cooperation is not in vain. Fair-play theory thus includes a forward-looking concern for the well-being of the practice—in this case, the cooperative meta-practice of administering the rule of law—that will have implications for the practical problems of punishment, such as how severely to punish and what forms punishment should and should not take. Tracing some of these implications will be the concern of the next chapter.

---

[11] H. L. A. Hart, *The Concept of Law*, 2nd ed. (Oxford: Oxford University Press, 1994), p. 198; emphasis in original.

In both its forward- and backward-looking aspects, the fair-play approach to punishment also incorporates the communicative aim that many philosophers take to be essential to punishment. How it does this is a point I have already touched on in defending the analogy between games and legal systems. Those who live under a system of laws must have a chance of knowing what the law requires of them and what the penalties for transgressions are. Such communication is not only a matter of fairness to those who are called to account; it is also necessary to the accomplishment of "the *'three Rs'* of punishment"—repentance, reform, and reconciliation—that R. A. Duff has identified as the appropriate goals of punishment.[12] The polity may express its condemnation of criminal offenders, in other words, but it must communicate to them the reasons for its condemnation if there is to be any hope of repentance and reform on the offenders' part and of their eventual reconciliation with the polity. The key point to note here is that this communicative element is not merely a feature of punishment that the fair-play approach accommodates; it is *integral* to such an approach. Because it rests on the conception of the polity or legal system as a cooperative practice, the goals of repentance, reform, and reconciliation are all elements of the larger goal of ensuring the flourishing of the practice. For an offender to repent, he must come to understand that his actions wronged the law-abiding members of the polity; for him to reform, he must aim to do his part in maintaining the rule of law as a cooperative meta-practice; and for there to be reconciliation, the polity must indicate its willingness to welcome him back into the cooperative enterprise. Both communication and fair play are thus central to this enterprise. But we should also note that communication and fair play both have an inclusive aspect. In this context, that means that the polity should be encouraging cooperation by helping those involved in it to conceive of themselves as members of the practice with an important part to play rather than as outsiders or outcasts. This is a point I shall return to in the next chapter.

A final feature of the fair-play theory of punishment turns on the question of whether the balance of benefits and burdens is to be assessed in general or specific terms. Should we say, in other words, that a burglar owes a debt of fair play that requires his punishment because he refused to bear the burdens of a particular law—in this case, against burglary—that provides benefits to him *qua* homeowner or renter? If so, then we are treating fair-play theory as a *partial compliance* theory. Such a view, however, is incompatible with the position I have developed regarding political obligation, according to which the obligation to obey the law is a systemic obligation. That is, the obligation is not to obey this law and

---

[12] Duff, *Punishment, Communication, and Community* (Oxford: Oxford University Press, 2001), p. 106ff. For a similar set of Rs—recognition, recompense, and reassurance—see Philip Pettit, "Republican Theory and Criminal Punishment," *Utilitas* 9 (1997), pp. 75–77.

that law and other laws severally; it is an obligation to obey all of the laws, *ceteris paribus*, of one's polity. Put in terms of punishment, this means that the burglar has acted unfairly by breaking the law *simpliciter*, and thus by failing to bear a full share of the burdens required to provide the benefits of the legal order. Hence the fair-play theory of punishment, as I understand it, falls into the category of a *general compliance* theory. In addition to its harmony with the fair-play account of political obligation developed earlier in this book, conceiving of fair-play in terms of general rather than partial compliance provides a ready response to an important objection to fair-play accounts of punishment.

According to this objection, the problem with the principle of fair play is that it offers no coherent or plausible account of benefits and burdens on which to base punishment. In many cases, in fact, the analysis of a crime as an unfair distribution of benefits and burdens simply makes no sense. As Duff and others have observed, it is easy enough to see how the would-be rapist or murderer will find compliance with the laws against rape or murder burdensome; but those who are never tempted to commit these crimes will not feel the restrictions of these laws at all.[13] What, moreover, are we to say of laws such as those proscribing cruelty to animals? How does the person who wants to engage in such cruelty benefit from these laws, and how does his compliance amount to a balancing of burdens and benefits?[14] There are, it seems, laws that provide no benefit to some people and laws that impose no burden on some people, which means that it is impossible to balance benefits and burdens in these cases. Therefore, the fair-play approach to punishment cannot possibly be adequate. Indeed, such an approach leads, according to Jean Hampton's indictment, to the "odd, even disturbing view of crime" that takes rape, assault, murder, and other vicious acts as nothing more than ways of gaining an unfair advantage.[15]

This criticism is effective, however, only if we take the benefits and burdens in question to be those provided and imposed by obedience to particular laws—that is, only if we take fair play to be the basis of a *partial compliance* theory. But this is not what the principle of fair play requires. On the *general compliance* view I have been developing, the benefits and burdens in question are those that follow from obedience to the laws of a cooperative practice—in this case, the rule of law in a polity.[16] In these circumstances, everyone engaged in the cooperative practice (or

---

[13] R. A. Duff, *Trials and Punishments* (Cambridge, UK: Cambridge University Press, 1986), p. 213.

[14] Richard Burgh, "Do the Guilty Deserve Punishment?," *Journal of Philosophy* 79 (1982): 193–213, at p. 205.

[15] Hampton, "A New Theory of Retribution," in *Liability and Responsibility*, ed. R. G. Frey and C. W. Morris (Cambridge, UK: Cambridge University Press, 1991), p. 5. The following discussion is in part an elaboration of my response in the previous chapter to Hampton's criticism of fair-play theory.

[16] Burgh acknowledges this point, but he argues that this "retreat to a second-order set of benefits, viz., those received from obedience to law in general" must fail because it entails "that all

meta-practice) is free to act and to enjoy her rights with a security that would otherwise be impossible. This is a benefit everyone within the polity shares. But everyone also shares the burden of self-restraint under law. Everyone thus receives the same general benefits—freedom and security under law—and bears the same general burden—obedience to the law, even when obedience is disagreeable. Rights and obligations are thus in balance, for every person in the practice has a right to the cooperation of the others and an obligation to cooperate in turn.

This balance is upset when someone breaks the law—not this law or that law but *the* law. In some cases the lawbreaker may have good, even public-spirited reasons for disobedience, as noted in my discussion of political obligation. In most cases, however, the lawbreaker seeks a double benefit for himself: he seeks, that is, to enjoy the benefits of freedom under law while enjoying freedom from the burden of obedience as well. If he succeeds, the lawbreaker achieves an excess of freedom over the law-abiding members of society.[17] In this way he enjoys the benefits of cooperation without bearing his share of its burdens; and by doing so, he upsets the balance of benefits and burdens. The offender achieves this aim, furthermore, by doing what he cannot want everyone else to do. This is the Kantian aspect of the reciprocity that Jeffrie Murphy once emphasized.[18] By taking advantage of the obedience of others in order to enjoy benefits for himself, he treats the law-abiding citizens as means to his own ends. And he does this whether the particular law in question does or does not provide him with benefits or impose on him any burden other than the general requirement to obey the law.

Properly understood, then, the fair-play theory of punishment is a general compliance theory capable of withstanding at least this one important objection. There are other objections, however, and even another version of the foregoing objection—I shall call it *the irrelevance objection*—that seem to bear on the fair-play account even when it takes the form of a general compliance theory. To these criticisms I now turn.

Punishment as Fair Play: Defense

By now it should be clear that the attempt to ground punishment in fair play has been subjected to serious criticism by a number of philosophers. Their criticisms

---

offenders are, regardless of the offense they committed, deserving of the same punishment" ("Do the Guilty Deserve Punishment?," p. 206). I respond to this charge below in the context of the "false equivalence" objection.

[17] Here I follow George Sher, *Desert* (Princeton, NJ: Princeton University Press, 1987), pp. 78–80.

[18] See esp. Murphy, "Kant's Theory of Criminal Punishment," in his *Retribution, Justice, and Therapy* (Dordrecht, Holland: D. Reidel Publishing, 1979).

often overlap with one another, and the critics sometimes criticize one another's criticisms,[19] but it is possible to distinguish five principal objections in addition to the one rebutted in the preceding section of this chapter and those discussed in the context of Hampton's criticism of the fair-play approach in Chapter 6. These I shall refer to as (1) the misses-the-point objection; (2) the false-equivalency objection; (3) the irrelevance objection; (4) the lacks-integration objection; and (5) the self-subverting objection. There is a further objection to the supposed narrowness of the fair-play account that I shall take up in the concluding section of this chapter.

First Objection: Fair Play Misses the Point

The first complaint is that the principle of fair play in two ways misses the point, for it can justify neither prohibiting criminal actions nor punishing those who engage in them. Considerations of fair play do give us reasons to require offenders to restore the losses of their victims, according to this argument, but not to *punish* them. After all, as Morris elaborates it, the principle of fair play requires only that a just balance be maintained between the benefits and burdens of social cooperation. Lawbreakers upset this balance by taking benefits that do not belong to them and shirking burdens that do. To restore the proper balance, the authorities must remove the extra benefit from the offender while imposing again the burdens of social cooperation—that is, of obeying the law. Doing so, however, does not require that the offender be *punished*. An abolitionist might take this to be a point in favor of the fair-play approach, but anyone who believes punishment is a justifiable practice must find this approach unacceptable.

According to Herbert Fingarette's statement of this objection, restoring the balance and punishing the offender are quite different matters. As Fingarette says, with reference to Morris's "Persons and Punishment,"

> On [Morris's] view, provided the books are ultimately balanced, I would seem to have two equally legitimate options—paying my debts earlier in cash, or paying later in punishment. But surely that's not the intent of the law *prohibiting* stealing. The intent is precisely to *deny* us a legitimate alternative to paying the storekeeper for what we take. And even if I restore the balance by returning the stolen goods, and by paying back any incidental losses incurred by the storekeeper, it still remains

---

[19] For a critic of fair play who criticizes others' criticisms, see Burgh, "Do the Guilty Deserve Punishment."

intelligible and important—not only in principle but in the practice of the law—to ask whether I should *also* be punished. So Morris' kind of view . . . fails to account for law as prohibition, and . . . to make intelligible the question of punishment as something over and above the equitable distribution of burdens and benefits.[20]

If correct, this would be a devastating criticism of the fair-play theory of punishment. The criticism, however, rests on a misconception of the relationship between reciprocity and punishment. To be sure, Fingarette is right to call attention to the difference between restoring the balance and punishing offenders. If a payroll clerk mistakenly pays an employee more than he is supposed to do, the clerk may have to retrieve the money from the overpaid employee, or take the surplus amount out of the employee's next paycheck, or make good the loss to the company in some other way in order to balance the books. These ways of restoring the balance need not involve punishment, either of the clerk or the other employee. But balancing the books in this case does not require a balance of benefits and burdens of the kind that Morris has in mind. The clerk and the overpaid employee do not stand in the same relation to each other as the law-abiding citizen (the storekeeper in Fingarette's example) and the lawbreaker (the thief). The clerk in my example makes an innocent mistake; the thief in Fingarette's example exhibits the *mens rea*, or guilty mind, usually associated with the commission of a crime. In the terms of fair play, the thief intends to take advantage of a law-abiding member of society. To restore the balance between the storekeeper and the thief thus requires not only restitution for what the thief stole but also restoring the balance between the benefits and burdens of cooperation under the rule of law. Indeed, when the thief steals from the storekeeper, he upsets the balance with regard not only to her but to all law-abiding citizens.[21]

The benefit that the thief gains, in other words, is not simply whatever he steals from the storekeeper. That can be repaid, as Fingarette says, without punishment. Instead, the benefit is to be understood as the double advantage of not obeying the law when it suits one's purposes while also enjoying the advantages of the rule of law made possible by the cooperation of the law-abiding citizens. This benefit cannot be repaid simply by forcing the thief to make good

---

[20] Fingarette, "Punishment and Suffering," *Proceedings and Addresses of the American Philosophical Association* 50 (1977): 502; emphases in original.

[21] This response also applies to a similar objection to fair-play theory that Richard Wasserstrom raises in his *Philosophy and Social Issues* (Notre Dame, IN: University of Notre Dame Press, 1980), pp. 143–46. Wasserstrom's distinction between restitution and compensation, on one hand, and punishment, on the other, is a topic I return to in the next chapter in the course of a defense of punitive restitution.

the storekeeper's loss, for that would leave the "books" unbalanced. To restore the balance, the lawbreaker must be punished. The whole point of the principle, then, is to secure a cooperative practice—in this case, the meta-practice of administering the rule of law—by prohibiting actions that will undermine the practice and by punishing those who nevertheless commit such offenses. The first criticism simply misses this point.[22] Indeed, it is the first objection that is beside the point, not the fair-play theory of punishment.

Second Objection: Fair Play as False Equivalency

The second criticism is that fair-play theory, at least in the general compliance form, establishes a false equivalency among the various criminal offenses and thus fails to account for differing kinds and degrees of crime. As Boonin puts the point, the general compliance version of fairness-based retributivism entails not only that "all offenders are free riders"; it "also entails that all offenders are *equally* free riders."[23] That being so, fair-play theory fails to justify "aiming more punishment at the murderer than at the tax evader."[24] In an earlier essay, I had addressed this concern by arguing that the murderer is in effect guilty of two offenses—that is, the crime of unfairness and an offense against (at least) the person he has murdered—while the tax evader is guilty only of one. On this argument, the principle of fair play explains why the polity is justified in punishing lawbreakers, but it leaves open the possibility that considerations other than fair play may be invoked when determining how, and how severely, to punish offenders—considerations that may appeal to the value of deterring would-be offenders or reforming those who have offended, for example.[25]

Boonin finds this argument unsatisfactory. If the deterrence value of punishing a murderer is not sufficient to justify punishing him in the first place, Boonin objects, then

> the fact that punishing a murderer more than a tax evader will deter others from committing these offenses cannot justify punishing the murderer more than the tax evader. If the only thing that gives the state the right to punish is the state's right to prevent offenders from enjoying an unfair benefit, after all, then the state can punish a particular offender only up to the point at which that offender's unfair benefit has been

---

[22] See Burgh, "Do the Guilty Deserve Punishment?," p. 203, n. 18, for a related criticism of Fingarette's argument.

[23] Boonin, *The Problem of Punishment*, p. 124.

[24] Ibid., p. 125.

[25] Here I refer to my "Playing Fair with Punishment," *Ethics* 103 (1993): 473–88, but esp. p. 484.

removed. If, by the general compliance response, the unfair benefit that every offender enjoys is precisely the same, then the state only has the right to punish every offender to the same degree. Punishing the murderer more than the tax evader would therefore be positively unfair.[26]

In response to this false-equivalence objection to fair-play theory as a general compliance theory, there are three points to make. The first is to recall and reinforce the distinction between justifying punishment and determining how to punish. It is, after all, not uncommon to face a situation in which we are convinced that someone did wrong and deserves punishment, yet we are not at all sure of what his punishment should be. Even when there are reasonably clear guidelines for the punishment this kind of offense typically warrants, there may well be special or individual circumstances that call into question the fairness of such "typical" treatment. In such cases, the desire to play fair does not lead directly to a certain sentence. The second point to note here bears on the backward- *and* forward-looking elements of fair-play theory. As we have seen, only those who play foul by breaking the law are to be punished. That said, however, they are to be punished in ways consistent with maintaining the cooperative practice of the rule of law. Punishing fairly thus requires us to punish with an eye to maintaining fair play under the rule of law, which in turn requires us to consider how serious a threat a particular offense poses to that rule. Thus we can hold that a murderer and a tax evader are both guilty of foul play—that is, of refusing to play fair—while we also hold that the former has committed a more serious violation of the meta-practice than the latter. Finally, the third point is that there is an important difference between *equivalent* and *identical* treatment. This distinction is familiar from discussions of what is involved in providing equal protection of the law to differently situated people. Providing such protection to a woman with a physically abusive spouse requires greater expenditure of public resources than providing equivalent protection to a more fortunate woman, for example, and providing the same level of protection to someone who is testifying against vicious criminals will require an even greater expenditure.[27] Everyone is to be treated as an equal participant according to fair-play theory, however, and thus deserves equivalent, if not identical, protection. Conversely, those who threaten fair play under the rule of law by their assaults on other members of the practice

---

[26] Boonin, *The Problem of Punishment*, p. 126. See also Matt Matravers, *Justice as Punishment: The Rationale of Coercion* (Oxford: Oxford University Press, 2000), p. 62, for the complaint that "fair play theory risks reducing all criminal actions to the same act: the non-mediation of one's self interest by the duty of fair play."

[27] See, e.g., Gregory Vlastos' "Murder, Inc." scenario in "Justice and Equality," in *Social Justice*, ed. R. B. Brandt (Englewood Cliffs, NJ: Prentice-Hall, 1962), pp. 41–42.

will deserve more severe punishment than those whose threats are less egregious than those of the murderer, rapist, and robber. If equivalency is a feature of the fair-play account of punishment, in sum, it is not a *false* equivalency.

This reply is enough, I believe, to meet the false-equivalency objection to general compliance versions of fair-play theory. There is, however, another reply directly rooted in the notion of fair play itself that also supports general compliance. Because that reply bears even more directly on the irrelevance objection, I take it up under that heading.

Third Objection: Fair Play Is Irrelevant

The most common objection to the fair-play approach to punishment, and perhaps the most forceful one, is that it fails to bear on the most serious breaches of the criminal law. The problem, in Duff's succinct statement, is that fair-play theory simply fails to capture "the punishment-deserving character of crime."[28] Indeed, as Duff elsewhere remarks, attributing the wrongfulness of crimes such as rape to a failure of fair play is not only irrelevant but "perverse: what is wrong with rape is that it attacks another person's interests and integrity, not that it takes unfair advantage of the law-abiding."[29] To be sure, the critics usually concede the relevance of fair play to *malum prohibitum* offenses, "which covers a wide range of white collar and other regulatory offenses that typically govern the conduct of activities that are not inherently immoral, perhaps the paradigmatic example being tax evasion."[30] But tax evasion, as we have seen, is quite different from murder, rape, robbery, and assault, and the critic may grant that tax evasion is a crime of unfairness without reaching the same judgment about these acts of violence. In cases such as these, they insist, fair play is simply irrelevant.

I have two arguments in response to this charge, the first of which is the direct response promised at the end of the preceding section. This direct argument rests on the conception of the political order as a meta-practice responsible for administering the rule of law—a meta-practice in which all of the participants should enjoy an equal standing. On the fair-play account, those who disobey the

---

[28] Duff, *Punishment, Communication, and Community*, p. 22.

[29] Duff, *Trials and Punishment*, p. 212. This complaint also figures in Hampton's rejection of fair-play theory, as discussed in the previous chapter. Others who have advanced this objection include Boonin, *The Problem of Punishment*, pp. 123–24; Matravers, *Justice as Punishment*, pp. 64–66; and Philip Montague, *Punishment as Societal-Defense* (Lanham, MD: Rowman and Littlefield, 1995), p. 85.

[30] Samuel T. Morison, "The Politics of Grace: On the Moral Justification of Executive Clemency," *Buffalo Criminal Law Review* 9 (2005): 1–138, at p. 90, n. 160. But cf. Douglas Husak, *Overcriminalization: The Limits of the Criminal Law* (Oxford: Oxford University Press, 2008), pp. 116–19, for the argument that some *mala prohibita* fall outside the scope of fair play.

law take unfair advantage, *ceteris paribus,* of the law-abiding participants. Their unfair advantage disturbs "the equilibrium of benefits and burdens," to return to Morris's formulation, and matters are "not even" until that advantage is "erased," as punishing the lawbreakers aims to do. That is why all crimes are crimes of unfairness. But considerations of unfairness can also justify the conclusion that some offenses are more serious violations of equal standing and fair play than others. The tax evader takes unfair advantage of many people, but her offense typically does not make it difficult for them to continue doing their part in the cooperative practice. With the rapist, the murderer, and the batterer, however, the offender has done something that makes it difficult or even impossible for his victim to contribute further to the ongoing cooperative endeavor. He has offended against the interests and integrity of his victim(s), to be sure, but he has also offended against the requirements of a society based on fair play, and his offense is thus a more serious crime of unfairness than the tax evader's. Fair-play theory, in short, does not make the mistake of treating more and less serious offenses as equivalent to one another, nor does it lack relevance to those serious offenses that we tend to regard as the paradigmatic crimes.

If this direct response seems unpersuasive or *ad hoc,* it may help to consider again simple cases of unfairness in a sport. In baseball, for instance, there are many ways in which a player may "bend" the rules in order to gain an unfair advantage, as when a pitcher applies a substance to the baseball that makes it more difficult for the batter to hit the pitched ball. But there are other violations of fair play in the game that directly threaten the health and well-being of other players, as when the pitcher throws the ball at the batter with the intention of intimidating or even injuring him. In both cases the pitcher violates fair play, but one violation is considerably more serious—and warrants a more severe punishment—than the other. The first offense is analogous to a *malum prohibitum* crime—there is, after all, nothing inherently wrong with rubbing a baseball with a greasy substance—while the second is an instance of the attacks on someone's interests and integrity, in Duff's words, that we associate with *mala in se.* Within the context of the game, however, the two are alike in being instances of foul play, even if one is admittedly less serious than the other. The same is true, I contend, of *mala prohibita* and *mala in se* in the context of the polity.[31]

It is one thing, though, to demonstrate that some instances of unfairness are more serious than others, and quite another to conclude that this demonstration disposes of the irrelevance objection. For the critic may still insist that some crimes are simply not crimes of unfairness—especially not those we usually

---

[31] In this way the direct response provides an answer to Matravers' complaint that "in focusing [as fair-play theory does] on the restoration of some state of affairs the important retributive connection between the act of the offender and that offender's punishment is threatened" (Matravers, *Justice and*

regard as the most serious. To return to the baseball example, the critic may point out that a pitcher who throws a live grenade at the batter is doing something more heinous than one who throws a baseball at him—something that simply is not captured by reference to degrees of unfairness.[32] What I am calling the direct response to the irrelevance objection is therefore unsatisfactory.

It is no doubt true that the direct response, with its reference to degrees of unfairness, does not capture everything we want to know about the nature of crime and the kinds of punishment that ought to be assigned to different crimes. Nevertheless, the direct response tells us something of value about these matters. That it does so is evident in the case of two American figure skaters, Nancy Kerrigan and Tonya Harding, who were competing for a place on the US Olympic team in 1994. Harding entered into a conspiracy to remove Kerrigan from the competition by attacking her and injuring one of her legs. Insofar as competitive figure skating may be considered a cooperative enterprise conducted according to rules, it seems that Harding was guilty of a violation of fair play, and a much more serious violation than, say, making distracting noises while Kerrigan was skating. As such, she deserved a more serious punishment, such as the lifelong ban from competition subsequently imposed on Harding. The critic of the fair-play theory may agree but quickly point out that the lifelong ban is not the same as the punishment imposed on Harding and her coconspirators for their *criminal* assault on Kerrigan. They will be right, of course, but not in a way that overturns the analogy between fair play in a sport and fair play in the political and legal order. Just as everyone is entitled to equal consideration as a participant in a sporting competition, so every member of a polity is entitled to equal consideration—that is, to equal standing under law. Every criminal offense is a crime of unfairness, or an affront to this equal standing, but some are more grievous—and some much more so—than others. Those offenses that would render someone less capable or even incapable of being a fully cooperating member of a cooperative political order are *in that respect* more serious affronts to the sense of fair play than are lighter, less grievous offenses. That point may not be enough to give us a complete explanation of why some crimes are more *heinous* than others, but it provides a significant part of the explanation.

Punishment, pp. 60–61). As I see it, restoring the proper state of affairs—a state of fair play—*requires* that the offender's act be connected to his punishment.

[32] Readers more familiar with cricket than with baseball will appreciate Antony Duff's way of stating the example: "if I bowl a live grenade rather than a ball at an opposing batsman, my wrongdoing is more heinous than that of someone who bowls a beamer, or who cheats—but I don't think that's a matter of unfairness." I have borrowed this example to respond to an objection Duff raised at a conference at the University of Stirling to an earlier version of this argument.

There is, in any case, a second response to the irrelevance objection, one that appeals *indirectly* to the idea of fair play. In this case, the central point is that the members of the political order want to be treated fairly under the rule of law, and the rule of law requires not only law obeying but also lawmaking, law enforcing, and law interpreting. That is, the members want a legal system that will sustain their cooperative practice and respect their equal standing as participants. Such a legal system will include the punishment of offenders as one of its features. But neither the lawmakers nor the people to whom they are accountable will be required to hold that all offenses are crimes of unfairness and nothing more. To the contrary, we should expect that the lawmakers and the people alike will insist that offenses must be graded according to the public's view of their gravity. If all offenses are treated in the identical way—with a fine of 100 Euros for the murderer and the traffic offender alike, for example, or lifetime imprisonment for both of them—then those subject to the law are likely to lose their regard for the law and for the cooperative practice it underpins. Indirectly, then, the desire to maintain a cooperative practice grounded in fair play requires that some crimes be treated as much more grave than others, even if their offensiveness is not entirely or even mainly a matter of their unfairness.

For both of these reasons, I believe that the fair-play theorist is entitled to hold that her theory *does* capture, contrary to Duff's charge, "the punishment-deserving character of crime." Fair play does this either directly, by showing how some offenses are more serious violations of fair play than others, or indirectly, by allowing that the members of a cooperative political order will believe that grading offenses and punishments will enable them both to secure their order and to communicate their sense of the wrongfulness of various offenses.

As I indicated earlier, this response to the irrelevance objection also bears on Boonin's false-equivalence criticism of my general compliance argument. Because all crimes of unfairness are *equally* crimes of unfairness, he says, the fair-play theory provides no way to justify punishing some offenders more severely than others. There is, to be sure, a sense in which all crimes of unfairness are equal, but I believe I have shown above that the fair-play theory has the resources to justify different punishments for, say, the murderer and the tax evader. All crimes are crimes of unfairness, but some are more than that, and some are worse *qua* crimes of unfairness than others.

Fourth Objection: Fair Play Lacks Integration

This response is also helpful in dealing with the further objection that fair-play theory *lacks integration*. In this case, the complaint is that fair-play theory, as I have developed it elsewhere, creates an unfortunate fissure by separating the justification of punishment as an institution from the justification of punishing particular offenders. As Matt Matravers states this objection:

> Dagger's suggestion is that the maintenance of the social order explains the general justifying aim of punishment, but the question, "Whom to Punish?" is correctly addressed by the fair play theory . . . . [T]he maintenance of the social order explains why we punish; the argument from fair play explains what makes it morally permissible for us to do so (Morris, also, seems to have a similar division in mind). However, this leaves far too many questions unanswered, not least those concerning how the two parts of the theory are to be integrated. . . . Fair play theory, as it stands, does not have the resources to deliver priority rules [i.e., rules justifying differential punishment, thus avoiding the false-equivalency objection] or to integrate an assurance-based explanation of "why the system of punishment?" and a "benefit and burden" based account of individual punishment.[33]

Once again, there seem to be two lines of response to the objection. One is to deny that an integrated theory of punishment is either necessary or desirable, and the other is to deny that the fair-play approach truly lacks integration. I shall forgo the first line of response, however, even though some philosophers have argued in favor of mixed or blended theories of punishment—theories, as noted in the previous chapter, that usually appeal to forward-looking considerations of deterrence to justify punishment as an institution, yet rely on backward-looking considerations of retribution to justify punishing particular offenders. In forswearing this response, furthermore, I acknowledge that it is reasonable to count my earlier statement of the fair-play account of punishment as one of those mixed theories. I therefore concede Matravers' point about the desirability of a univocal or integrated theory both for the sake of argument and in recognition of the superior elegance of an unmixed justification of punishment.

What I do not concede, though, is that fair-play theory properly understood lacks the necessary integration. To be sure, exactly how much integration is necessary or even desirable in a theory of punishment is a difficult point to establish. We certainly do not want a theory fractured by its reliance on contradictory considerations; but does that mean that we must insist on a theory that takes one and only one consideration into account? Assuming that the answer is no, let us say that a theory must rest on one primary consideration if it is to be coherent, with others taking a secondary or subsidiary role. That is the position I took, in

---

[33] Matravers, *Justice as Punishment*, p. 69, n. 41.

fact, in my criticism of Jean Hampton's pluralistic account of punishment in the preceding chapter. If a theory grounded in a primary consideration will be coherent enough to achieve the necessary degree of integration, then I believe that I have already made the case for the coherence of punishment as fair play. It is true, as Matravers notes, that my earlier account makes "maintenance of the social order" the justification for punishment *qua* institution. In this book, however, I have developed a richer and emphatically political account of the legal order, and this account should make it clear that it is not just any social order that is to be maintained. Instead, it is the polity understood as a cooperative enterprise secured by the rule of law—the kind of enterprise in which considerations of fair play are at home. That account is enough, I think, to warrant the claim that fair play is the primary and integrating feature of this theory, bearing as it does the major burden in explaining both why the institution of legal punishment is justified and why particular offenders ought to be punished.

To say this is not to say that other considerations have no place in a fair-play account of punishment. If those who bear the responsibility for making the laws of a cooperative political order have reasons to believe that one way of writing a law is more likely to prevent crime than others, then they should take that reason into account when writing the law, even if it is not dispositive. If they have reason to think that changing the ways in which criminals are punished will lead to the offenders' reform and the reparation of cooperative relationships, then they probably have sufficient reason to make those changes. As these abstract examples indicate, considerations such as deterrence and reparation are not necessarily hostile to a theory based on fair play. Insofar as they strengthen cooperative relationships and help to guarantee that "those who would voluntarily obey shall not be sacrificed to those who would not," we may even say that they are considerations internal to the fair-play theory of punishment.[34] That is enough, I believe, to overcome the lacks-integration objection.

Fifth Objection: Fair Play Is Self-Subverting

A final major objection to the fair-play account of punishment is that the account dooms itself to failure by demanding more than it can deliver. As Andrew von Hirsch states the objection, fair-play theories

> require a heroic belief in the justice of the underlying social arrangements. Unless it is in fact true that our social and political systems have succeeded in providing for mutual benefits for all members

---

[34] Hart, *The Concept of Law* (Oxford: Oxford University Press, 1960), p. 198.

including any criminal offender, then the offender has not necessarily gained from others' law-abiding behavior.[35]

If, however, the facts about our social and political systems do not warrant such "a heroic belief," then fair-play theory is incapable of justifying the punishment of criminals within those systems—which is to say, within any existing social and political system. As an ideal theory aimed at justifying punishment within legal systems *as they should be*, the fair-play account of punishment may well be compelling; but as a justification of punishment in the non-ideal legal systems in which we live, the fair-play account simply leads to the self-subverting conclusion that we have no justification for punishing criminals.

One response to this objection is simply to grasp the nettle. That is, one may agree that fair-play theory sets a high standard for its application but deny that this is a weakness of the theory. As Duff has observed, any normative theory of punishment—indeed, any "normative theory of a human practice"—will offer "a critical standard against which we must judge our existing practice, an ideal account of what that practice ought to be, towards which we can aspire, but in whose light we must recognize the (perhaps radical) deficiencies in our actual practice."[36] Fair-play theory, as I have developed it here, certainly has these qualities. Its employment as a means of calling attention to "deficiencies in our actual practice" is perhaps most evident in Jeffrie Murphy's oft-cited "Marxism and Retribution," in which Murphy concludes,

> if we are morally sensitive enough to want to be sure that we have the moral right to punish before we inflict it, then we had better first make sure that we have restructured society in such a way that criminals genuinely do correspond to the only model that will render punishment permissible—i.e., make sure that they are autonomous and that they do benefit in the requisite sense.[37]

If our institutions fall short of what our best theory requires, in short, we should conclude that the fault lies not with the theory but with the institutions. If fair-play theory enables us to perceive the defects of our punitive practices and

---

[35] Von Hirsch, *Past or Future Crimes: Deservedness and Dangerousness in the Sentencing of Criminals* (New Brunswick, NJ: Rutgers University Press, 1985), p. 58.

[36] Duff, *Punishment, Communication, and Community*, p. 175.

[37] Murphy, "Marxism and Retribution," *Philosophy and Public Affairs* 2 (1973): 217–43; reprinted in Murphy, *Retribution, Justice, and Therapy*, where the quoted passage appears on p. 110. For Murphy's subsequent doubts about the fair-play theory of punishment, see his "Retributivism, Moral Education, and the Liberal State," *Criminal Justice Ethics* 4 (1985): 3–11, esp. p. 7 and n. 11; and "Legal Moralism and Retribution Revisited," pp. 79–81.

inspires us to try to correct them, then its grounding in fair play counts as a virtue of a theory that is far from self-defeating.

The problem with this response is that it still leaves a troubling gap between the ideal and the actual. Even if we grant that fair-play theory is properly critical of existing arrangements and properly aspirational about when and how punishment is justified, it will not count as an adequate justification of punishment if it cannot justify any punishment whatsoever—not even punishment of the most vicious murderers and rapists—within legal systems that fall short of its ideal of a cooperative practice. To say that the fair-play account of punishment is only critical and aspirational, in other words, is to admit that it is self-subverting, for it denies itself the ability to do what a satisfactory theory of punishment must do.

But does it? There are two further lines of response open to fair-play theorists on this point, both of which deny that the gap between the ideal and the actual is as troublesome as the objection holds. According to the first, the self-subverting objection rests on an assertion—that is, that fair-play theory requires an heroic but obviously incorrect belief in the justice of existing social arrangements—but this assertion itself presumes that fair-play theory can apply only within societies that are perfectly fair in their distribution of the benefits and burdens of social cooperation. Such a presumption is itself unfair to fair-play theory. If we think of a legal system as a cooperative practice, or meta-practice, then we must recognize, as I argued in Chapter 2, that such practices are not all-or-nothing affairs. There must be, of course, some degree of cooperation among people—some cooperative threshold they must have crossed—before we can properly deem them to be engaged in a cooperative practice, but it need not be complete and unfailing cooperation. Indeed, if such a level of unanimous cooperation were ever attained, there would be little need for the principle of fair play. Between the cooperative threshold at one end, however, and complete cooperation at the other, there will be ample room for the principle of fair play to do its critical and aspirational work, with much more to be done in some times and places than in others.

Here again the analogy with games is helpful. If everyone who joined in a game always played fair, they would have no need for umpires, referees, or other officials charged with enforcing the rules—interpreting and applying, perhaps, but not enforcing. When there is reason to worry about cheating, though, there is likely to be need for officials to ensure fair play. Moreover, considerations of fair play continue to apply even when the officials cannot ensure that no violations of fair play occur or go unpunished. To be sure, there may be a point at which disregard for the rules of the game is so widespread that we have to throw up our hands and admit that fair play no longer applies—but we would also have to say, in such a case, that the "players" are no longer playing the game. They have fallen below the cooperative threshold, to put the point more broadly, and are no longer engaged in a cooperative practice—or not, at least, the cooperative practice of baseball, cricket, badminton, chess, Monopoly, or whatever game they ostensibly were playing.

To move from games and cooperative practices in general back to legal systems, we must acknowledge that some legal systems come closer to the ideals of justice and fairness than others. In our time, Norway is closer to the ideal, in my view, than is the United States or the United Kingdom, particularly in its emphasis on forms of punishment that aim to reintegrate offenders into the polity—a point I shall return to in the next chapter. In that respect, at least, the United States and the United Kingdom deserve greater criticism and require greater reform than does Norway. Nevertheless, all three count as cooperative practices pursuing the rule of law. Of course, if some subjects of a political or legal system are so thoroughly ignored or exploited as to be denied any significant benefit from that system, then the practice falls below the cooperative threshold, as I argued in Chapter 2, and neither the exploited subjects nor their exploiters will have a general obligation to obey its laws as such. In cases of this kind, moreover, those who are the agents of the exploitative system are not justified in punishing the exploited lawbreakers. Short of such an extreme situation, though, fair play can justify the punishment of those who break the law in an imperfect but reasonably just legal system.

Use of the term "reasonably just" takes us to the second line of response to the complaint that fair-play theory is a self-subverting theory of punishment. In fact, the complaint applies not only to fair-play theory but to any theory that links retributive justice to social justice more generally. In developing his communicative, penitential theory, for instance, Duff acknowledges that his version of retributivism poses a "serious challenge to the legitimacy of punishing those who have been unjustly excluded (to the possibility of doing penal justice in an unjust society)."[38] In response, Matravers argues that this challenge does not warrant sweeping conclusions about the lack of justification for punishing those who break the law. As Matravers notes, a government that loses its standing in one way—by lying about its reasons for invading another country, to use his example—does not thereby lose its standing in other respects, such as its standing to judge cases of insurance fraud. More broadly, he observes, we will always need to determine

> whether the crime for which the defendant is charged is directly related to the value that the polity has failed to respect in relation to the defendant; whether the state of the polity is so parlous that "all bets

[38] Duff, *Punishment, Communication, and Community*, p. 184.

are off" or whether we are in an unjust situation short of the state of nature.[39]

Even if it is true, then, that Jones has been in many ways denied justice by the legal system, it does not follow that the agents of that system act unjustly when they arrest, prosecute, and punish him for raping some other member of the society.

What, though, of the possibility that fair-play theory is particularly susceptible to the self-subverting objection because of the way it requires a benefit of balances and burdens? In this case, we can look to a response from Michael Davis, whose argument is similar to Matravers' but with specific reference to fair play. Davis begins by acknowledging a "principle of excuse" that would bar punishment of people such as starving parents who steal food to feed their families. But this principle, he insists,

> would *not* excuse the poor robber whose victims are poor people. Such a criminal does not bring a just society closer. Nor would the principle excuse the poor robber who uses force when he could simply shoplift. He has violated the moral rights of others more than necessary to make the distribution of benefits and burdens more just. The principle would also not excuse the shoplifter who could instead have applied for welfare or taken a low-paying job. Such a criminal has also violated the moral rights of others more than was necessary. He cannot excuse his conduct by appeal to the injustice he has suffered because he has not simply engaged in self-help against that injustice. He has helped himself by taking an advantage he could not happily allow everyone else to take. He has, in other words, taken unfair advantage.[40]

By taking unfair advantage in these ways, furthermore, the lawbreakers in these cases open themselves to justified punishment. Even granting that they bear too many of the burdens of social cooperation and receive too few of its benefits, it does not follow that they cannot themselves take unfair advantage of others, nor that it is unfair to punish them for doing so.

These are considerations we must keep in mind while trying to identify the conceptual threshold beyond which we may adjudge a society or legal system to be a genuinely cooperative meta-practice, or one that is *reasonably* just. Here our

---

[39] Matravers, "Who's Still Standing? A Comment on Duff's Preconditions of Criminal Liability," *Journal of Moral Philosophy* 3 (2006): 320–30 at p. 326 (for the invasion example) and pp. 329–30.

[40] Davis, *To Make the Punishment Fit the Crime: Essays in the Theory of Criminal Justice* (Boulder, CO: Westview Press, 1992), pp. 220–21; emphasis in original.

best guide, I suspect, is T. H. Green's observation, in lectures delivered in 1879–80, that the justice of punishment depends "not merely on . . . maintaining this or that particular right which the crime punished violates, but on the question whether the social organization in which a criminal has lived and acted is one that has given him a fair chance of not being a criminal."[41] To accept this standard is to acknowledge that there may be, in exceptionally deplorable circumstances, some people so burdened and brutalized that there can be no justification for punishing them no matter what they have done, however necessary it may be to restrain or confine them. More commonly, embracing Green's standard will lead us to conclude, with Davis, that someone who has not received a fair chance of not committing some crimes, such as the theft of food, will still have a fair chance of not committing other crimes, such as rape and murder. As long as that is true, the fair-play theory of punishment will not be vulnerable to the charge that it is self-subverting.[42]

Conclusion

As the foregoing discussion should make clear, the fair-play approach to the justification of punishment has been the subject of serious and varied criticism. But it also should be clear that fair-play theory contains the resources to rebut these criticisms. Whether the rebuttals fully establish that fair-play theory can withstand the objections raised against it is a question that readers will decide for themselves. Even so, I believe that this chapter's elaboration and defense of fair-play theory prove it to be a plausible theory that anyone interested in the justification of punishment must take seriously.

There is, though, one remaining objection to be considered before concluding this chapter. I take it up here for two reasons. First, this objection concedes more to fair-play theory than the others have done. Second, responding to this objection points the way to considerations I explore in subsequent chapters. The

---

[41] Green, *Lectures on the Principles of Political Obligation*, §189 (Ann Arbor, MI: University of Michigan Press, 1967), p. 190.

[42] For a valuable discussion of how "a proper analysis of the relationship between retributive and socio-economic justice should proceed on a case-by-case basis," see Stuart P. Green, "Just Deserts in Unjust Societies: A Case-Specific Approach," in *Philosophical Foundations of Criminal Law*, ed. R. A. Duff and Stuart P. Green (Oxford: Oxford University Press, 2011). According to Green, we should consider three factors in each case before deciding whether punishment is justified: (1) "the specific offence with which the offender is charged"; (2) "the precise form that the offender's disadvantage takes"; and (3) the "economic and social circumstances of the crime victim (assuming there is an identifiable victim.)" All quotations are from p. 353 of Green's essay.

objection, in effect, is that fair-play theory is too narrow; it is sound and valuable as far as it goes, but it simply does not go far enough.

Christopher Bennett raises this objection in *The Apology Ritual* in the course of advancing his own theory of punishment. Bennett's theory is, he says, both retributive and restorative: that is, "aimed at expressing proportionate condemnation of wrongdoing," on the one hand, and "based in the idea of restoring relationships damaged by crime," on the other.[43] Bennett also grounds his theory in a commitment to the central moral values of liberal society, including, perhaps most notably, the value of self-government. To take such a view, as he sees it, is to share in many respects the connection between political theory and punishment evident in the fair-play approach, based as it is in "the guiding moral idea ... of society as a fair system of social cooperation."[44] But we must nevertheless recognize, he says, that the fair-play approach falls short of his Apology Ritual account, which "rejects the narrow view of the political community as merely a fair system of social cooperation."[45] Important as it is, fair play cannot accommodate all of the "relationships in which we cooperate in furthering some intrinsically valuable activity—such as friendships, educational institutions, and so on."[46] Hence the unsatisfactory narrowness of the fair-play approach to punishment.

The problem with Bennett's objection is that it is subject to table-turning. In other words, fair-play theory appears to be unduly narrow only because Bennett has a narrow conception of what the theory involves. That much should be evident not only from the elaboration of the theory set out in this chapter but also in the discussion of cooperative practices and fair play in the chapters concerned with political obligation. On the basis of that elaboration and discussion, it should be obvious that considerations of fair play have much to contribute to the understanding and appreciation of friendships and educational institutions, especially in view of the connection between fair play and equality of standing and respect.[47] Moreover, the fair-play approach produces a justification of punishment that is, like Bennett's, simultaneously retributive and restorative in its aims. Nor does it ignore what Bennett calls the "collective self-government conception" of liberal society, according to which the members of such a society

---

[43] Bennett, *The Apology Ritual: A Philosophical Theory of Punishment* (Cambridge, UK: Cambridge University Press, 2008), p. 175.

[44] Ibid., p. 185.

[45] Ibid., p. 186.

[46] Ibid., p. 184.

[47] Note in this regard Bennett's discussion of "substandard" neighbors and teachers in chaps. 4 and 5, discussions that are both illuminating and laden with references to "collective enterprise," "cooperative endeavor," "cooperative common project," and "members of a common enterprise" (e.g., p. 96 and pp. 104–105).

share a responsibility for its—and thereby their own—direction.[48] On the contrary, as I argued in Chapter 4, with regard to fair play and the rule of law, a polity that realizes the conception of a cooperative meta-practice must be one in which its members will be lawmakers as well as law-abiders. That is a point, however, to be developed further in the next chapter, in connection with the relationship between fair play and democracy, and yet again in the final chapter of this book.

---

[48] Bennett, *The Apology Ritual*, p. 186.

7

Punishing Fairly

As both the title and content of David Boonin's *The Problem of Punishment* indicate, philosophers of law often take the justification of punishment to be *the* problem of punishment.[1] Such a view, though, is hasty at best. Justification may be the fundamental or first problem of legal punishment, but it is hardly the only one. Of course, there is a sense in which other punishment-related problems will vanish if we follow the lead of Boonin and others who advocate the abolition or abandonment of legal punishment; for if we cease to punish, we will cease to confront *problems* of punishment. If the arguments of the previous chapter are correct, however, legal punishment is a fully justified practice that ought not to be abandoned. Even so, settling the problem of punishment's justification in general does not tell us what we need to know about when and how punishment is justified in particular cases, or whether some other response to lawbreaking is preferable or complementary to punishment. Those who believe that punishment is justified must also conclude, then, that punishment presents more than one problem for political and legal philosophy.

In this chapter I explore four of these problems of punishment from the standpoint of fair-play theory. Two of these—the problems of mass incarceration and voting rights for felons—are matters of topical interest, especially in the United States. But these and the other two problems—whether recidivists deserve harsher treatment than first-time offenders and what role restitution should play in the sentencing of criminals—are all matters of both practical and philosophical interest, in the United States and elsewhere. By addressing them here, I hope to fill out the account of the fair-play approach developed in previous chapters and to provide some deeper sense of the value of this approach.

---

[1] Boonin, *The Problem of Punishment* (Cambridge, UK: Cambridge University Press, 2008).

The Problem of Excessive Incarceration

Perhaps the most striking development in the treatment of criminals in recent decades has been the explosive growth of prison populations in the United States—a development so striking that even self-professed conservatives have begun to decry it. As one widely published conservative columnist observed in 2013, the rate of imprisonment in the United States had risen from about 100 per 100,000 in the 1970s to 700 per 100,000 at the time he wrote. "America," as George Will noted with alarm, "has nearly 5% of the world's population but almost 25% of its prisoners." Furthermore, he observed, "African-Americans are 13% of the nation's population but 37% of the prison population, and one in three African-American men may spend time incarcerated."[2] Conservatives were not the first to notice this explosive growth, nor the first to call attention to the dramatic racial disparities among the imprisoned. But when those who see themselves as the champions of law and order join the ranks of those who deplore what they take to be excessive imprisonment, it seems clear that something is amiss.[3]

To be sure, it is conceivable that the prison population of the United States has been just where it ought to be, or perhaps even too low, in recent years. These are possibilities, though, that the statistics cited above and the wide-ranging concern about excessive incarceration make easy to discount. Taking it for granted, then, that mass imprisonment presents a serious problem of punishment, I shall sketch a fair-play approach to this problem, beginning with an analysis of the problem itself.

Analyzing Excessive Incarceration

From a purely analytical point of view, there seem to be four possible reasons for excessive incarceration:

---

[2] Will, "Seeking Sense on Sentencing," *Richmond Times-Dispatch* (June 7, 2013), p. A11; also at the opinion section of Washingtonpost.com for June 5, 2013. Will's unattributed data are consistent with those published in the *Sourcebook of Criminal Justice Statistics* (http://www.albany.edu/sourcebook/pdf/t6132011.pdf).

[3] Even Stephanos Bibas's "conservative" response to the "liberal" claim that racism and enforcement of misguided drug laws caused the explosion in imprisonment includes the following injunction: "Conservatives cannot reflexively jump from critiquing the Left's preferred narrative to defending our astronomic incarceration rate and permanent second-class status for ex-cons." Bibas, "The Truth about Mass Incarceration," *National Review* 67 (September 21, 2015): 27–30, at 28. For a concise account of "racialized mass incarceration" from a distinctly non-conservative point of view, see Tommie Shelby, *Dark Ghettos: Injustice, Dissent, and Reform* (Cambridge, MA: Harvard University Press, 2016), pp. 209–12.

1. Too many people are committing crimes.
2. Too many activities count as criminal.
3. Too many criminals are imprisoned.
4. Too many prisoners are imprisoned for too long.

Any one of these reasons, or any combination of them, could account for over-imprisonment, as a brief elaboration should make clear.

First, there is a sense in which the statement "too many people are committing crimes" is self-evidently true: even one crime is a crime too many. If we proceed from some sense of what a normal or tolerable level of crime is, however, we can make realistic judgments of whether we have reason to worry that too many people are committing crimes. If such judgments are warranted, we then need to ask why so many are engaging in criminal activity, and one possibility is some kind of social failure. This could be a failure of prevention in the straightforward sense of not putting enough police on the streets, for example, or not training them properly. Or it could be a failure to cultivate the appropriate attitudes of respect for law and other persons through family discipline, civic education, and other forms of socialization. Or it could be a failure to provide sufficient opportunities for people to live a decent life without resorting to crime. In any or all of these ways, a society may unwittingly contribute to the high crime rates that lead to high rates of incarceration.

The second analytical possibility—and probably the one scholars most frequently cite—is that too many activities are classified as criminal. The leading example of this tendency "to criminalize too much and to punish too many," as Douglas Husak contends, is "the crime of illicit drug possession."[4] "Nearly one of every five prisoners in America," he notes, "is behind bars for a nonviolent drug offense."[5] Simply repealing the laws that make the possession of various drugs illicit would apparently lead to a significant drop in the rate of incarceration. But repealing such laws is not a simple matter. In addition to the problem of persuading legislators to take steps that may make them appear to be "soft on crime," there is the difficulty of determining exactly what the law ought and ought not to proscribe. This is a difficulty, though, that anyone who attributes mass incarceration to excessive criminalization must face. At the least, fair-play theorists should not be the only ones to acknowledge that justice cannot countenance much harsher sentences for the possession of a relatively inexpensive drug, such as "crack" cocaine, than for its possession in purer and more expensive forms.

---

[4] Husak, *Overcriminalization: The Limits of the Criminal Law* (Oxford and New York: Oxford University Press, 2008), p. 16.
[5] Ibid.

Conviction of a criminal offense, of course, need not entail a prison sentence. There are alternatives, such as probation, electronic monitoring, community service, restitution to the offender's victims, or some form of therapy. That is why the third possible reason for excessive incarceration is that too many criminals are imprisoned. Instead of locking up so many of them, perhaps we would do better to punish offenders in another way—or even to refrain from punishing them at all. Here, though, we face the difficulty of determining what kinds of crimes warrant what kinds of punitive responses—of how to make the punishment fit the crime, in the standard phrase.[6] Hardly anyone would say that supervised community service is proper punishment for a serial killer or that a prison term is fitting for someone who steals an apple from a store (setting aside possible "three strikes and you're out" complications).[7] There are plenty of hard cases between these extremes, however, and some principled means of sorting them out will be required if we are to reduce incarceration.

Similar considerations bear on the fourth possibility. If we believe that excessive incarceration is largely the result of too many prisoners being imprisoned for too long, then we will need to find some way to determine the proper length of the sentences that attach to the various crimes warranting imprisonment. We will also need reasons for deciding whether determinate sentencing or mandatory-minimum sentences or "three strikes and you're out" laws, all of which may boost the length of prison terms, are justified. We will need, in short, a theory of criminal law and punishment.

Such a theory will not provide clear-cut answers to every practical question that arises with regard to mass incarceration. No theory can tell us exactly how many days, months, or years is condign punishment for a particular criminal. Theories do provide necessary guidance, however, perhaps most notably by focusing our attention on a certain consideration, such as one or the other of those venerable rivals, deterrence or retribution, or by promising a harmonious blend of the two. My claim is that the fair-play theory is the most satisfactory in this respect because the principle of fair play provides such guidance. In particular, I shall try to show how it provides useful guidance with regard to the four analytical considerations involved in the problem of excessive incarceration. In doing so, I shall draw once more on the analogy between games and sports, on the one

---

[6] For the purposes of this discussion I take it that my arguments in chap. 5 have settled the case against penal abolitionists who would eliminate legal punishment altogether in favor of some other treatment of criminals. I do, though, argue for *punitive* and against *pure* restitution in the third part of the present chapter.

[7] It is also important to recognize that not all forms of incarceration are equivalent—for example, a year in solitary confinement in a "SuperMax" prison is hardly the same as a year in a minimum-security prison. The difference will not bear on the rate of incarceration, however, unless it turns out that some forms of imprisonment are more likely to encourage or discourage recidivism than others.

hand, and political and legal systems, on the other, that I defended in the previous chapter.

Playing Fair with Imprisonment

With regard to the first consideration—that is, the possibility that too many crimes are being committed—the straightforward application of the principle of fair play suggests that crimes are like violations of the rules of a game. If the play of the game is suffering because too many players are in the penalty box, or suspended, or outright expelled from the sport, then we may want to know why so many are opening themselves to sanctions—and perhaps jeopardizing the sport as a whole—by violating the rules. If it seems that they are simply cheating in order to gain an unfair advantage by free riding on the cooperative efforts of others, then we will need to take the kinds of preventive steps I mentioned earlier—that is, stepped-up policing of the game and/or efforts to cultivate the sense of sportsmanship or fair play on which the game depends.[8] But we should also consider whether there may be something wrong with the rules themselves. There may be a rule, for example, that works systematically to the advantage of some players or teams and the disadvantage of others without being important to the game itself. A case in point could be a game in which the players must equip themselves and only the wealthy can afford the most advanced equipment, thus giving them a significant advantage while playing. If we find that violations of the rules increase because less affluent players or teams are trying to compensate for their disadvantage, a change in the rules regarding equipment may be in order. Fair play is largely a matter of respecting the rules, to be sure, but we should not overlook the possibility that one or more of the rules somehow discourages fair play.

In the case of the second analytical consideration, we may think of the possibility that too many activities are counted as criminal by way of an analogy with a sport that imposes too many rules on its players. Sports leagues and associations typically regulate the kind of clothing and gear players may wear, for example, and they do so in some cases for reasons closely related to the play of the game itself—not allowing football players to wear clothing studded with metal spikes or baseball pitchers to wear mirrors that reflect light into the batters' eyes—and in other cases for reasons that have little or no bearing on its play. Some clothing regulations aim at ensuring that players project what the league officials think is the proper image; others ban clothing that advertises a product

---

[8] Strictly speaking, those who seek an unfair advantage in competitive circumstances may be *parasites* rather than free riders. See chap. 3, n. 22, on this distinction.

not approved by, or contributing to the coffers of, the league. Players who break these rules have been penalized in various ways for their activities, even though the activities seem to have no bearing on the play of the game. Is this fair? Are the nonconformists taking unfair advantage of the players who conform to the regulations? Or would the sport benefit if rules not truly helpful to the play of the game were eliminated? Is it possible that an excess of rules—especially rules that seem petty, trivial, or pointless—will in fact undermine the sport by leading players to lose respect for the rules of the game? If the answer to these last two questions is "yes," then the rules in question should be abolished or altered.[9]

What of the third analytical consideration—that is, the possibility that too many criminals are being imprisoned? In this case the analogy with a game raises questions about the severity of offenses and penalties. There are many offenses that occur inadvertently in the course of play, usually called "fouls," and in some cases players are allowed to accumulate fouls until they reach a set number, at which point they have "fouled out" and are expelled from the game. But some fouls are considered worse than others, such as intentional fouls, and some intentional fouls—flagrant fouls, in particular—may be cause for immediate ejection from the game and perhaps suspension from future games. There are also offenses against the referees, umpires, and officials whose job is to ensure that the rules are followed—offenses that can pose a direct threat to fair play. It is no surprise, then, that those who govern sports leagues and associations devote considerable attention to determining the appropriate penalties for the various offenses that arise in the course of play. Nor is it surprising that the gauge they typically employ is the tendency of the penalty to ensure the fair play of the game.

This same point carries over to the final consideration, which is that too many prisoners may be imprisoned for too long. In the case of sports, the question is not only whether some rule breakers are treated unfairly but also whether they are punished too severely for the good of the sport itself. Gambling presents a case in point. Both players and spectators need to believe in the fair play of the game, and it is difficult to sustain that belief when there are reasonable suspicions of "point shaving" or attempts to "throw"—that is, deliberately lose—a game or match in exchange for gamblers' payments. As a result, sports organizations typically have rules that limit the gambling of those involved in the sport or even prohibit contact with gamblers. Violations of these rules have led to suspensions for lengthy periods, even to the point of banishment for life. The result may be to promote confidence in the fair play of the game, but there also may be reason to question the justice of the sanctions imposed on people who possibly failed

---

[9] There will be cases, of course, in which clear answers to these questions will be hard to find, such as the one that led to the US Supreme Court's ruling in favor of Casey Martin in *PGA Tour, Inc. v. Martin* (2000)—a case I discuss briefly in chap. 2.

to understand or appreciate what they were doing—as in the case of "Shoeless Joe" Jackson of baseball's Chicago "Black Sox" Scandal of 1919. There are also reasons to question the wisdom, and fairness, of penalties that remove excellent players from competition. Surely those who grievously violate the rules deserve punishment; that is the retributive aspect of fair play. But they should be punished in a way, and to an extent, that holds the promise of restoring the offenders, when possible, to the status of full participants in the game. That aim is part of the forward-looking and communicative aspects of fair play.

This last point suggests a direct connection to one controversial question about what constitutes fair or unfair treatment of criminal offenders. I refer here to the question of whether convicted felons should lose their voting rights while serving their sentences, and perhaps even longer. Fair-play theorists may differ on the justice of disenfranchising felons while they are in prison, but they will hold that fairness requires the restoration of voting rights to those who have served their time. Again, this is in keeping with the forward-looking and communicative aspects of fair-play theory. Those who have paid their debts to society—and presumably learned to appreciate the importance of respecting the rule of law—should be restored to full citizenship in the polity. I return to this point in Part 4 of this chapter.

This one example, however, is not typical of what the fair-play approach to the four analytical considerations reveals. In most cases, the principle of fair play does not supply a precise answer to the questions that follow from these considerations. But it does provide a unified approach to these questions that concentrates on the need to establish and enforce rules, and punish those who break them, in order to secure the fair play of the game. This leaves us, though, with the question of whether this approach has any real bearing on law and punishment in the world beyond the sports arena.

Fair Play, the Polity, and Imprisonment

What, in particular, does this talk of games and fair play have to do with the problem of excessive incarceration? One answer is that fair-play considerations help to explain why we are right to worry about the rates of imprisonment in the United States, and perhaps elsewhere, these days.[10] When rates of incarceration are as high as they have become in the last four decades, we must ask how

---

[10] In 2006, according to Nicola Lacey, incarceration rates "across the developed world ... ranged from 36 per 100,000 (in Iceland) to 737 in the USA, with England and Wales, at a rate of 148, ... having one of the highest incarceration rates in the EU." Lacey, *The Prisoner's Dilemma: Political Economy and Punishment in Contemporary Democracies* (Cambridge, UK: Cambridge University Press, 2008), p. 27.

reasonable it is to regard the United States as a cooperative practice. We should be troubled also by the dangerous and degrading conditions in which those who are confined to overcrowded prisons are sometimes forced to live. To return to a point already made more than once in this book, fair-play theory contains critical and aspirational elements that point toward an ideal of a fully fair practice and demand attention to the ways in which a practice, including the meta-practice of the polity, falls short of that ideal. Mass incarceration is evidence that there is much to criticize in the practice of criminal law in the United States.

Such criticism should lead us back to the four analytical possibilities I raised earlier. My claim is that fair play can help us to formulate responses to the problems that arise in all four cases. Are too many crimes being committed? Yes, certainly, but it is far from clear that spending more money on policing is the only answer. More needs to be done to encourage potential offenders to play fair by obeying the law and to provide them with opportunities to participate more fully, and fairly, in their society. Here, as in the preceding chapter, T. H. Green's remark is apposite: before we punish someone, we should be sure that "the social organization in which a criminal has lived and acted is one that has given him a fair chance of not being a criminal."[11] Among other things, steps should be taken to reduce recidivism; for if it is true that too many crimes are being committed, it is also true that the same people are committing many of them. From the standpoint of fair-play theory, a particularly promising effort to reduce recidivism is the "social enterprise approach" sponsored in the United Kingdom by the Royal Society for the Arts, which aims to engage prisoners in paid work for social enterprises while they are in custody, then to continue their employment in a supervised Transition Zone before their full release into society.[12] But I shall have more to say shortly about fair play and the problem of recidivism.

What of the other analytical considerations? Are too many activities classified as criminal? Yes, certainly, to the point where the criminalization of activities that do not amount to violations of fair play is probably undermining respect for law. Laws against gambling are a case in point, and especially so when they exist alongside state-sponsored lotteries. If we want to discourage people from risking their money on wagers, we should rely on education rather than coercion—and avoid the hypocrisy of encouraging them to take their chances in public lotteries all the while. Hypocrisy and unfairness also come quickly to mind with regard to drug laws, and their highly unequal enforcement, in the United States.[13]

[11] Green, *Lectures on the Principles of Political Obligation*, §189 (Ann Arbor, MI: University of Michigan Press, 1967 [1882]), p. 190.

[12] See Rachel O'Brien, *RSA Transitions: A Social Enterprise Approach to Prison and Rehabilitation* (November 2011); available at http://www.thersa.org.

[13] As noted, e.g., in Ekow N. Yankah, "Legal Vices and Civic Virtue: Vice Crimes, Republicanism, and the Corruption of Lawfulness," *Criminal Law and Philosophy* 7 (2013): 80–81.

Are too many convicted criminals imprisoned, as the third consideration asks? Yes, because there are other forms of punishment that are likely to do more to help criminals comprehend the cooperative nature of society and their duties of fair play. Community service is especially worthy of consideration, as is service that can provide some restitution to the particular victim(s) of an offender's crime(s)—points that I return to in Part 3 of this chapter. Finally, in response to the fourth consideration, should we conclude that too many prisoners are imprisoned for too long? Yes again, because of mandatory-minimum sentences and laws such as "three strikes" that do little or nothing to restore criminals to the status of law-abiding citizens—and less than nothing to promote fairness in the form of keeping the punishment in proportion to the offense. There is more, obviously, to be said to clarify and defend every one of these responses, but the point for now is that fair play provides the orientation we need as we work toward the answers.

Fair Play Versus Penal Populism

One question that arises in this connection is whether fair-play theory contributes to or offers a means of counteracting what is sometimes called "penal populism"—that is, the tendency of elected officials to enact "tough on crime" laws and policies in response to the attempt to win votes. Worries about penal populism have some basis in fact, in my view, but only to the extent that a polity is democratic in a simplistic and perhaps corrupt way. On the simplistic view, democracy is merely a matter of majority rule, no matter how majority opinion is formed or what course it takes. Taking this view to its extreme, today's majority could vote to deny the franchise henceforward to those in today's minority, or even to enslave them. No democratic theorist endorses this simplistic view, however, because it fails to respect the fundamental democratic commitment to equality, here understood as a right to the equal consideration of everyone's interests.[14] If the problem of mass incarceration is in large part the result of penal populism, it is because those who make the laws are playing to, and perhaps provoking, an audience that is insufficiently concerned with equal consideration—and therefore with playing fair. In these circumstances, it is reasonable to speak of the corruption of the polity.

A well-functioning polity, I have maintained, is a cooperative enterprise. It must have rules, and it must have means of dealing with those who break the rules, including punishment. But the rules must be fair and so must the

---

[14] For the link between democracy and the "principle of intrinsic equality," see Robert Dahl, *On Democracy* (New Haven, CT: Yale University Press, 1998), esp. chap. 6.

punishment. One sign of their fairness is that they must aim to do only what is necessary to secure and strengthen the cooperative enterprise. That means, among other things, that punishment must proceed in a manner that promises to restore offenders to full participation in the polity. Those who have paid their debts to society by undergoing punishment that communicates to them and their fellow citizens the importance of abiding by the laws of a cooperative society ought to be able to regain the status of full citizenship. Mass incarceration and high rates of recidivism are signs that democracy in the United States is not proceeding in this manner—and is not, therefore, the cooperative practice it ought to be.

There is, of course, a sense in which democracy is largely a matter of electoral competition; and in such competition, even if everyone plays fair according to the electoral rules, there may well be a pressure toward penal populism. To conceive of the polity as a cooperative venture in pursuit of a common good, however, is to resist that pressure. On this conception, democracy is less a matter of eliciting personal preferences than of evoking civic judgments. Everyone's interests are to be accorded equal consideration, and every member of the polity should have opportunities to express her preferences. But the cooperative-venture conception also holds that citizens should look beyond their personal preferences to what is good or best for the polity as a whole. This conception thus accords with the belief that every citizen stands, as John Stuart Mill put the point, in a position of public trust.[15]

Democracy does indeed require electoral competition, then, and that competition must proceed in accordance with regulations that ensure the fair conduct of elections. However, the cooperative-venture conception does not stop at this point; for competition itself must be understood as an element of what is a fundamentally cooperative enterprise. We may be tempted to think of competition in the marketplace or the sporting arena as a matter of winning at all costs, but it is nevertheless true that unbounded competition will lead to the destruction of both the market and the sport. If all that matters is winning, then there is no reason not to cheat and steal at every opportunity, and even to assault or dismiss those whose office is to protect personal property or to uphold the rules of the game. In such cases, though, property rights will count for nothing and the game will no longer be recognizable as baseball, cricket, football, or whatever it is supposed to be. In such cases, both markets and sports will degenerate

---

[15] Note in this regard Mill's claim that the citizen's vote "has no more to do with his personal wishes than the verdict of a juryman." Indeed, Mill went so far as to oppose the secret ballot on the ground that every citizen should stand ready to take public responsibility for how he or she voted. Mill, *Considerations on Representative Government*, in Mill, *On Liberty and Other Essays* (Oxford: Oxford University Press, 1991), pp. 353–55 (p. 354 for the quoted passage).

into something resembling Hobbes's state of nature. To avoid this outcome, the participants must find ways to underpin their competition with a cooperative commitment to playing fair—a commitment that includes the appointment and security of officials whose duty is to elaborate and enforce the rules of fair play.

This cooperative commitment also includes a commitment to regard the other participants as contributors to a common enterprise to whom we owe a duty of fair play—and from whom we should expect reciprocity. In a democracy, according to the cooperative-venture conception, there is a corresponding duty to regard every member of the polity as a potential contributor to the cooperative enterprise of self-government. There is also a duty to encourage reciprocity and to promote the virtues of citizenship among the members. In John Rawls's terms, this is "a natural duty of civility," which requires citizens, among other things, "not to invoke the faults of social arrangements as a too ready excuse for not complying with them, nor to exploit inevitable loopholes in the rules to advance our interests."[16] In order to sustain the cooperative enterprise, in other words, we must play fair even when personal advantage would have us do otherwise. Because we cannot count on everyone always to play fair, we need the police and judges and other officials to provide the security necessary to assure those who are willing to abide by the rules that their cooperative efforts will not be wasted. But we also need to do what we can to promote Rawls's "natural duty of civility." Other things being equal, willing cooperation is better than coerced.

Another implication of the cooperative-venture conception of the polity has to do with the rules that govern the enterprise. In a democracy, these rules are themselves a matter of public determination, and the duty of civility extends to the framing of these rules. Before we enact a law, then, we must try to ensure that it does not impose an unfair burden on other members of the polity. In the present context, this means that we must determine what is to count as a crime in this light. The answer is clear enough in the standard cases of assault, murder, rape, and robbery, for we do not impose unfair burdens on our fellow citizens when we proscribe those actions. Indeed, the unfair burdens would fall on the victims of those crimes, whose suffering would make it difficult, at best, to continue to play the part of the cooperative citizen. There are many other activities, however, that democratically elected legislatures have outlawed even though these activities fall outside the standard cases. Whether such activities should or should not be outlawed is a matter to decide in the light of their bearing on fair play and civility. Some of these cases should be easy to settle. Suborning

---

[16] Rawls, *A Theory of Justice*, rev. ed. (Cambridge, MA: Harvard University Press, 1999), p. 312. For development of this and related points, see my "Citizenship as Fairness: John Rawls's Conception of Civic Virtue," in *A Companion to Rawls*, ed. J. Mandle and D. Reidy (New York: J. Wiley, 2014), pp. 297–311.

witnesses and threatening judges are actions that strike directly at the rule of law, and any burden that anyone suffers as a result of their proscription is hardly an unfair burden. *Mala prohibita* offenses, such as those involving traffic and environmental regulations, are likely to be justified as a means of ensuring cooperation in a collective enterprise; but if it becomes clear that the proscription in question places an unfair burden on some members of the polity, then either the proscription should be altered or the activity in question should be allowed.

From the standpoint of the cooperative-venture conception, in short, the question is not whether the aggregated preferences of the people, either directly or through their elected representatives, should or should not designate a certain activity as criminal. The question, instead, is whether the activity in question inhibits the fair play of the democratic game.[17] If it does, then the question becomes one of efficacy—in other words, whether the criminal sanction is the best way to deal with those actions that interfere with fair play or whether there are better alternatives. If the activity in question poses no threat to fair play, then it should not be proscribed. In some cases this approach leads to straightforward decisions. For instance, anyone who proposes to make a crime of some form of sexual activity between consenting adults would have to show that the activity in question poses a serious threat to the polity as a cooperative venture, which will be a difficult case to make. In many cases, though, the decision will not be at all straightforward. One could argue, for instance, that the production and/or consumption of any drug that renders people incapable of fair play or of carrying out their duties of civility should be a crime. Couched in those terms, the proposal is perfectly acceptable under the cooperative-venture conception of the polity. But those who are charged with determining what is to count as a crime would then have to make an informed judgment as to which drugs, if any, do in fact have those propensities. Once they have identified such drugs, if any, they would then have to make the further determination of whether the criminal sanction is the appropriate way to deal with the problem and, if it is, whether a blanket prohibition or a more limited response is better. In the case of alcohol, there is little doubt that its consumption at some point inhibits civility and the sense of fair play. Laws against public drunkenness and enhanced punishment for those who harm or endanger others while drunk, though, seem likely to address the

---

[17] For a similar conclusion from a perspective somewhat different from that of the fair-play approach, see Christopher Bennett, *The Apology Ritual: A Philosophical Theory of Punishment* (Cambridge, UK: Cambridge University Press, 2008), esp. p. 164: "the sorts of things that *should* be put into law are only those things that are aspects of our responsibility to one another as participants in the common project. When the law seeks to legislate on matters that go beyond the common project then it oversteps its bounds.... [T]he overall task of the law is to make determinate and adjudicable the responsibilities (and rights) that we have by virtue of our status as participants in the common project"; emphasis in original.

problem more effectively than outright prohibition of the production, sale, and/or consumption of alcohol. Nor would such laws place an unfair burden on anyone, such as those who consume alcohol without endangering others or otherwise threatening fair play within the polity. Extending this reasoning to drugs that are widely proscribed at present would almost certainly result in a dramatic reduction of drug crimes and a similar reduction in the prison population. Such a change by itself would not solve the problem of mass incarceration in the United States, but it surely would be a major step in that direction.

In this way the fair-play conception of the polity as a cooperative practice, or meta-practice, reinforces my earlier point about the connection between fair play and the reduction of the number of actions and activities that should be designated as criminal. The conception also speaks to the concern that too many criminals are being imprisoned and too many are being imprisoned for too long. If the polity is a cooperative venture, then it is perfectly reasonable to discourage its members from engaging in actions that harm those whose law-abiding conduct sustains the venture or that threaten in some other way to undermine it. It is also reasonable to punish those who have, despite this discouragement, committed such acts. Except in extraordinary cases, however, the aim should be to restore the offenders to full participation in the cooperative practice, not to banish them forever. Again, there will be difficult judgments to make about whether imprisonment is the proper sentence for certain offenses and, if it is, how long the term should be. Even so, there is little doubt that the lengthy sentences that have contributed to the explosion of the prison population in the United States cannot be justified as the consequences of fair play. Such sentences unfairly burden those on whom they are imposed—and on those who are close to and dependent on them—while doing nothing to restore the offender to a place in society as a full participant in the polity.

Fair play is not compatible with penal populism, in sum, but it is quite congenial to democratic self-government. It must be self-government, though, in the sense that the people *govern* themselves—that is, exercise self-restraint—in a thoughtful, prudent manner. In this context, self-restraint, or self-government, is largely a matter of respecting the rule of law—laws that are to be made publicly, to serve the public good—and the principle of fair play. But that is not to say that self-government is a kind of altruism. Every citizen has a right to care for her own interests and to demand equal consideration of those interests from her fellows. But equality of consideration requires her to extend this same consideration to all of the others. When she votes or otherwise contributes to the making of laws and policies, then, the citizen is to do so in a way that accords this equal respect to all citizens. She must act on the principle of fair play by bearing her share of the burdens of social cooperation and imposing no more than a fair share on others.

Citizenship, on this view, is a kind of public office, and failure to play fair with one's fellow citizens should count as an abuse of public power. A properly democratic polity is one that will look to its political, legal, and educational institutions—to these and other *civic* institutions—to foster a citizenry that is vigilant in maintaining fair play within the polity. In particular, citizens must "be vigilant to the possibility that their laws are unfairly burdening some over others, that their laws are exclusionary or discriminatory."[18] Their laws, that is, and the forms of punishment that support and follow from them, must respect the principle of fair play, and the citizenry must be self-policing in this regard. A polity of this kind will not tolerate the levels of incarceration that the United States has imposed in recent years.

Playing Fair with Recidivists

A second problem for both the theory and practice of criminal justice is recidivism. As a practical matter, persistent offenders threaten public safety and strain public resources. First-time offenders pose their own challenges, of course, but it is those who have been caught and convicted more than once who crowd the prisons and other "correctional facilities."[19] From the perspective of theory, the problem is to determine whether there is any justification for *the recidivist premium*. The public seems to think it obvious that repeat offenders are in some sense guiltier, or deserving of harsher punishment, than those found guilty of a first offense.[20] In some jurisdictions, this sentiment has found expression in laws that require harsher sentences for recidivists, most famously in the "three strikes and you're out" laws in California and many other parts of the United States. But are legislatures justified in passing such laws? Is public sentiment perhaps out of step with what justice itself demands?

These questions are particularly pressing for those who take, as fair-play theorists do, a broadly retributive approach to the punishment of criminals. For most consequentialists, the challenge is only to show whether harsher penalties for recidivists do or do not serve to deter crime. If, however, the point of punishment is in some sense to pay back the offender for the wrong he has done,

---

[18] Albert Dzur, *Punishment, Participatory Democracy, and the Jury* (New York: Oxford University Press, 2012), p. 87.

[19] For supporting evidence, see Julian V. Roberts, *Punishing Persistent Offenders: Exploring Community and Offender Perspectives* (Oxford: Oxford University Press, 2008), pp. 95–96.

[20] See ibid., chap. 8, which concludes: "Public support for the recidivist sentencing premium rests principally on three branches: first, repeat offenders are perceived as being more culpable; second, crime by recidivists is perceived as being more serious than the same offending by novice offenders; and third, repeat offenders are seen as being more likely to reoffend" (p. 183).

or to mete out punishment according to just desert, then it is not at all obvious that someone should be punished more severely for his second offense than for his first, more severely for the third than for the second, and so on. If the offense is virtually the same in every case—say, the theft of an inexpensive used car—then it would seem that retributive justice demands the same punishment in every case.

Fair-play theorists and other retributivists thus face a difficult challenge. Either we must go against the popular grain, and perhaps our own intuitions, by insisting that a criminal offense carry the same penalty or punishment no matter how many previous convictions an offender has accrued, or we must find a way to justify the recidivist premium. From the standpoint of fair-play theory, the second route is appropriate, for recidivism represents a special failure to play fair with the law-abiding members of the polity. This conclusion follows in part from Youngjae Lee's insightful analysis of "recidivism as omission."[21] Lee's analysis is not grounded in considerations of fair play, however, and my claim is that such grounding is necessary to the success of his argument.

Recidivism as Omission

To justify the recidivist premium, Lee argues, we must regard the recidivist not only as someone who has broken the law *again* but as someone who has failed to take seriously the lessons of his previous punishment. Recidivism is thus as much a matter of omission as of commission. According to Lee's summary statement,

> The culpable omission that justifies the recidivist premium is the repeat offender's failure, after conviction, to arrange his life in a way that ensures a life free of further criminality. Although how individuals conduct their lives as a general matter is not properly the business of the state, once offenders are convicted of a crime, they enter into a thick relationship with the state, and that relationship gives rise to an obligation for the offenders to rearrange their lives in order to steer clear of criminal wrongdoing. [O]bligations between the state and offenders run in both directions, and ... we should recognize the ways in which the state may be a responsible actor that should share the blame for a recidivists' reoffending.[22]

---

[21] Youngjae Lee, "Recidivism as Omission: A Relational Account," *Texas Law Review* 87(3) (2009): 571–622. For a more concise statement of the position, see Lee's "Repeat Offenders and the Question of Desert," in *Previous Convictions at Sentencing: Theoretical and Applied Perspectives*, ed. Julian Roberts and Andreas von Hirsch (Oxford: Hart Publishing, 2010).

[22] Lee, "Recidivism as Omission," p. 621.

In developing this argument, Lee takes pains to show how it avoids the problems that beset other retributivist attempts to justify harsher punishment for recidivists. In the case of the "bad character" argument, as Lee acknowledges, it may well be true that recidivism is an indication of bad character traits. It does not follow, however, that we should punish the recidivist both for the new offense he has committed and for the character flaws that led him to commit it. To return to the example of the car thief, the bad-character argument would have us impose on the repeat offender the same punishment he received for his previous conviction for car theft *plus* the premium of extra punishment for the bad character manifested in his repeated offending. But to do this, as Lee points out, is in effect to punish a person not for breaking the law but for displaying certain character traits. Such punishment might be appropriate if those character traits always and necessarily manifest themselves in criminal behavior, but it is not at all obvious that they do, or even that such necessarily criminal traits exist. On the contrary, the character flaws typically associated with criminal conduct—malice, callousness, and insensitivity to others' interests, for example—are often evident in conduct that is unquestionably legal, if not admirable.[23]

The attempt to ground the recidivist premium on the repeat offender's defiant attitude or disrespect for law is also unsatisfactory. As Lee notes, there are well-established legal offenses, such as contempt of court and resisting arrest, that do indeed apply to persons whose defiance would obstruct the course of justice and directly interfere with the rule of law.[24] The question, though, is whether a general proscription of a defiant attitude toward the law is warranted. In polities that encourage people to subject their governing officials to scrutiny, and occasionally even celebrate those who engage in civil disobedience, the answer seems to be no. That being the case, it is difficult to see how defiance or disrespect in itself can justify enhanced punishment for the recidivist.

Lee's solution to the problem of the recidivist premium, as previously noted, is to hold persistent offenders accountable not for their bad characters or defiant attitudes but for their failure to conduct themselves, after conviction, "in a way that ensures a life free of further criminality."[25] On his account, in other words, the recidivist is guilty of two new offenses: first, of committing the crime(s) that

---

[23] Lee lists the following as "some possibilities" for character traits that would warrant extra punishment according to the bad-character argument: "cruelty, malice, abusiveness, arrogance (manifesting in the belief that rules of the society do not apply to them [the recidivists]), callousness, dishonesty (if the crimes involve fraud), greed, hatred (if the crimes are motivated by hateful feelings), indifference (to human suffering), lack of discipline (if the crimes result from an inability to stick to a law-abiding path), weakness of will (if the crimes result from an inability to resist temptations), insensitivity, irresponsibility, or ruthlessness" (ibid., p. 586).

[24] Ibid., pp. 599–600.

[25] Ibid., p. 621.

make him a repeat offender; and second, of omitting to conduct himself in a lawful manner, as his earlier punishment(s) should have taught him to do. For committing the crime the recidivist should receive the same punishment he would receive were he a first-time offender; for the omission—that is, the failure to act on the lessons of his earlier punishment(s)—he deserves the extra punishment that we call the recidivist premium.

As the subtitle of his essay indicates, it is also important to note that Lee's approach to recidivism is "a relational account." The state and the offender, to use his terms, have a "thick relationship" with each other that begins with the offender's first conviction, and the state's right to impose harsher punishment on recidivists than on first-time offenders grows out of this relationship. Moreover, the relationship is in some sense reciprocal. As Lee says, "obligations between the state and offenders run in both directions, and ... we should recognize the ways in which the state may be a responsible actor that should share the blame for the recidivists' reoffending."[26] Before the agents of the state impose additional punishment on recidivists, they should be sure that they have discharged their responsibility by making it possible for the offender "to arrange his life in a way that ensures a life free of further criminality."[27] If prisons are little more than schoolhouses of crime, and if the convict faces legal barriers to employment, housing, and support when he leaves prison, it will be unfair to hold him accountable for omitting to live a law-abiding life. On Lee's account, then, the recidivist premium is grounded in the relationship between the state and the offender, and the state must take its responsibilities as seriously as the offender must take his.

This account of the recidivist premium is the most plausible to be advanced by a retributivist, in my view, but it is not without its problems. One problem is Lee's characterization of the omission that makes the recidivist liable to additional punishment, and another involves the "relational" aspect of his argument. "The key to understanding the recidivist premium," Lee says, "lies in seeing that a self continues over time, and that the self at t_1 can influence what the self does at t_2. ... The key to the recidivist premium lies not just in evaluating an individual's act of reoffending or bad character traits. Rather, the focus should be on the ongoing *relationship* between the offender and the state."[28]

After his initial conviction, then, the offender is engaged in a "thick relationship" with the state that requires him to conduct himself at $t_1, t_2 ... t_n$ in a way that will keep him from committing another crime. If he fails—if he does commit a new offense—then the state may hold him accountable not only for the offense

---

[26] Ibid., p. 621.
[27] Ibid., p. 621.
[28] Ibid., p. 608; emphasis in original.

but for what he failed to do at, say, t_2, when he renewed his acquaintance with people who had encouraged his earlier crimes, or at t_5, when he gambled away much of the little money he had. Such activities may not be criminal in themselves, but they do represent the kind of omission for which the state may invoke the recidivist premium at t_9, when he stands convicted of another offense.

Suppose, however, that we have two first-time offenders, Sally and Sam, who have served their sentences and are now conducting themselves in ways that are likely to lead them back into criminal activity. That is, Sally and Sam both take up with the kinds of people who are likely to land them in trouble, and Sally and Sam both begin to gamble heavily. But Sally does not commit another crime—perhaps because she wins enough while gambling to remove the apparent need for money—while Sam does. Sam is then caught, convicted, and subjected to the recidivist premium, while Sally, who is equally guilty of omitting to arrange her life to stay free of criminality, goes unpunished. It seems, in short, that Sam's *omission* cannot be what justifies the imposition of the premium in his case, since the unpunished Sally is equally guilty of that offense, so it must be his *commission* of the new offense. Either that or the enhanced punishment is simply unjustified (on retributive grounds).[29] In either case, recidivism *as omission* fails to account for the recidivist premium.

The proper response to this objection is not to give up on Lee's recidivism as omission but to recognize that his argument requires elaboration and clarification. One might hold, for example, that Sally is indeed culpable insofar as she has omitted to conduct herself in a way that will keep her free of criminality. Like Sam, she is in a "thick relationship" with the state, and the state has the right to punish or penalize her for her offense of omission. Such a person will not be subject to the recidivist premium, however, because she is not, strictly speaking, a recidivist. Nevertheless, she will be subject to punishment, penalty, or at least closer supervision on the part of parole or probation officers for her failure to conduct herself in the proper way.

Unfortunately, this attempt at rescuing Lee's account of recidivism as omission leads to the unpalatable conclusion that someone ought to be subject to legal punishment for doing things that are not in themselves illegal. Associating with unsavory characters, drinking too much, and squandering one's money in (legal) gambling are not of themselves crimes, however likely they may be to lead to criminal activity. How, then, can we justify punishing someone like Sally for engaging in them when they do not—or have yet to—lead her to commit actual crimes? One might argue that some conduct that is open to ordinary, law-abiding citizens should be closed to those previously convicted of a criminal

---

[29] I owe this objection to Geoffrey Goddu.

offense, but that position would be hard to square with the belief that those who have served their time, or otherwise met the terms of their sentences, have paid their debts to society. The most we can justify in such cases, it seems, is the stricture that parole or probation officers ought to subject someone like Sally to closer supervision and frequent warnings about the dangers of her conduct, but not attempt to punish her for doing what she may legally do.

There is, however, a more promising way to elaborate Lee's analysis of recidivism as a kind of omission. This approach calls for something akin to the "no harm, no foul" reasoning in some sporting events. That is, we might hold that offenders who keep bad company, gamble (at legal venues), and drink immoderately are cause for concern while also holding that they should not be judged guilty of an offense of omission until they show that they cannot live in this way *and* avoid criminality. If Sally can live in this way without committing another crime, but Sam cannot, then it seems reasonable to say that Sally and Sam are not equally guilty, as we had supposed, of omitting to arrange their lives so that they will remain free from criminality. Sally's conduct may be as misguided as Sam's, but it nevertheless stops short of recidivism. It is the commission of the new offense, then, that justifies the state in looking backward to Sam's omission to conduct himself as he should have—and thus to the imposition of the recidivist premium.

This approach, though, seems to have the unfortunate implication of turning Lee's "recidivism as omission" into a straightforward account of recidivism as commission. That is, if we follow the "no harm, no foul" rule, all that really matters is the foul—the criminal offense—and not the misconduct that puts one on the path to criminality. This becomes clear when we consider what would happen if Sam makes a genuine effort to stay free from criminality but fails, while Sally makes no such effort but somehow stops short of breaking the law. Suppose that Sam, despite his earnest intentions, simply cannot resist breaking the law when he notices one day that someone has left the keys in the ignition of an unlocked car. Sally, meanwhile, intends to steal a car, but is too drunk or distracted to make the effort. Sam is guilty of car theft and Sally is not; but is Sam also guilty of omitting to live in a way that will keep him free from criminality? Is Sally not guilty of that omission, as the "no harm, no foul" approach suggests?

In my view, the answer to both questions is yes. Sam did try to live in a law-abiding manner, but he failed; at the crucial juncture he omitted to act as his prior conviction and punishment should have led him to act. Sally has not learned her lesson, evidently, but she has somehow stayed within the law. Sam therefore deserves punishment, including the recidivist premium, but Sally does not. Nevertheless, this reasoning seems to strain the claim that recidivism is a kind of omission. To reduce the strain, and to strengthen Lee's case for recidivism as omission, we shall need to address the second problem with his analysis.

This second problem is a matter of incompleteness, specifically the incompleteness of the "relational account" Lee offers. Lee is right, I think, to direct our attention to "the ongoing *relationship* between the offender and the state"; and he is also right to hold that "[w]hen a person is convicted and punished for a crime, one thing we can say with confidence is that the relationship between that person and the state has changed in a way that makes that person different from others who have not had that kind of encounter with the state."[30] How this relationship develops, however, and what its nature is, are matters he does not explain. He offers an occasional hint in this direction, but nothing that can satisfy someone who doubts that there is any significant relationship, thick or thin, that connects the recidivist to the state.

Lee's "recidivism as omission," as a result, is a promising but incomplete account of the recidivist premium. For a satisfactorily complete account, Lee's argument for the recidivist premium must be grounded in a theory of retributive punishment that itself is grounded in a conception of the political or legal order that makes sense of Lee's "relational" approach. Such a conception will fill out his account of the relationship between offenders and the state, and it will do so in large part by turning our attention from *the state*—a term that connotes a remote, bureaucratic agency—and toward *the polity*—that is, toward the political or legal order understood as a cooperative practice in which legal punishment is a matter of fair play.

Relations, Recidivism, and Fair Play

Conceiving of the legal order as a cooperative practice has a number of significant implications, as I have tried to demonstrate in earlier chapters. In the case of punishment, I have argued, this conception underpins a general compliance theory of fair play that is fundamentally retributive but gives due attention to both the consequences and the communicative aspect of punishment. In all of these respects, this conception is not only compatible with Lee's relational account of the recidivist premium but necessary, I believe, to its success. Indeed, Lee explicitly embraces the communicative view of punishment in "Recidivism as Omission" when he writes,

> The institution of punishment has a communicative, expressive dimension. When the state punishes, it condemns what the offender has done as blameworthy and it communicates to the offender that what he has done is wrong. Implicit in that message . . . is that the offender is being

---

[30] Lee, "Recidivism as Omission," pp. 608, 611–12; emphasis in original.

punished for what he has done, and after his punishment is complete, he shall not offend again.[31]

But what gives some of us the right or authority to communicate our standards in this way? Lee's answer is that this right, and the offender's correlative duty, grows out of the relationship between the offender and the state. The relationship is initially thin, apparently, but it becomes thick in the course of the first-time offender's punishment—punishment that should communicate to him the wrongfulness of his criminal acts. But *how* does this right and the correlative duty grow out of this relationship between the state and the offender? What is it that gives this relationship its normative significance? The answer, I contend, is found in the fair-play theory elaborated and defended in the previous chapter. Insofar as the offender enjoys the benefits of the cooperative meta-practice of the polity without fully contributing to their provision by bearing his share of the burdens of obeying the law, then the offender in effect justifies the rest of us in punishing him. That is why the polity is justified in communicating its censure to the offender by means of punishment.

Before pursuing this point, we should consider Lee's thin-and-thick account of this relationship between the offender and the state. According to Lee,

> the crucial difference between first-time offenders and repeat offenders is that the repeat offender has gone through *a process* with the state that has created *a relationship* with the state, and the point of that relationship was to ensure that whatever led the offender to the status of being a convict should be avoided in the future. It is *that history* of having had *that relationship* that first-time offenders lack. And once a person enters into a thick relationship with the state through the process of conviction and punishment, it is appropriate for the state to attribute blame to how a person has increased the risks of criminal wrongdoing over time.[32]

This is an important but ambiguous passage. On the one hand, Lee seems to be saying that the relationship between the repeat offender and the state is the product or creation of the process that the offender went through upon his initial conviction and punishment. If so, the implication is that there was no relationship between the offender and the state prior to that first offense. If there were no relationship, however, then difficult questions arise as to the state's authority

---

[31] Ibid., p. 613.
[32] Ibid., p. 614; emphasis in original throughout.

to punish the offender in the first place. But perhaps Lee means, on the other hand, that every citizen or subject of a state is engaged in a relationship with that state, but it is only a *thin* relationship until or unless an individual "enters into a *thick* relationship with the state through the process of conviction and punishment."[33] That thin relationship may be sufficient to justify the state's punitive authority in the first place, with the thick relationship then providing the warrant for the recidivist premium. Whether it is or is not what Lee intended, this second reading of the passage above seems to be the sounder of the two. Even so, it leaves two questions unanswered: What is the nature of that thin relationship? And what is it about the first offender's punishment that transforms it into a thick relationship?

To answer these questions we must ground Lee's "relational account" in the fair-play justification for legal punishment. Setting aside the "thin" and "thick" terminology, the justification for the recidivist premium thus takes the following form. Everyone who is a member of a polity—that is, of a political order reasonably regarded as a cooperative practice under the rule of law—is involved in a reciprocal relationship with the other members of that polity. The relationship is reciprocal because all members have an obligation of fair play to the others to bear their share of the burdens of maintaining the practice by obeying, *ceteris paribus*, the law. Those who break the law make themselves liable to penalty or punishment, which is to say that their relationship to the law-abiding members of the polity undergoes a significant change. The offenders continue to be members of the polity, but they are not, so to speak, members in good standing; they are, instead, free riders of a more or less vicious kind. If they are sentenced to punishment, their sentence will communicate to them the law-abiding members' disapproval and condemnation of their criminal deeds; but it should also convey the expectation that the offenders will have the chance to restore themselves to full membership. If they fail to take advantage of this opportunity—if they become repeat offenders—they will in effect be offending doubly against the cooperating members of the polity: first by committing another crime; and second by omitting to live in a way that will keep them free of criminal trespasses against the other members.

Lee's "recidivism as omission" makes sense, then, but only as part of a theory of punishment grounded in the principle of fair play. The recidivist is in effect guilty of a serial failure to play fair—once for the first offense, again for the second, and so on for each new offense. After the first offense, however, each succeeding offense represents a double failure to play fair. That is, each new

---

[33] Ibid., p. 614; emphasis added.

offense is a *crime* of unfairness, but it also is a failure to play by the rules that apply to the offender as someone who has been previously convicted of a crime. To return to the examples of Sam and Sally, Sally is not playing fair with the law-abiding members of the polity when, following her punishment as a first-time offender, she does not act so as to keep herself free of criminality. Fair play requires more of her than that—or it will, at least, when the legal and penal systems give her a fair chance of living such a life. She has not committed another crime, however, and that is what makes her situation different from Sam's, who has. Sam is guilty of a double offense against fair play in that he has omitted to conduct himself in a way that will keep him free of criminality *and* he has committed another crime. This crime may have occurred despite his sincere but weak intention to stay within the law, as in the case of his happening upon an unlocked car with its keys in the ignition, but he is nevertheless guilty of the criminal act and of failing to maintain the fair-play relationship with the other members of the polity. For the criminal act, he deserves the same punishment he would deserve as a first-time offender committing the same crime. He has been given a second chance, however, and his failure to take advantage of that chance to play fair is what justifies the recidivist premium. Should he fail a third or a fourth time, or more, the polity will be justified in increasing the premium for his new and persistent offenses. Whether increasingly severe punishment will be efficacious is a question for criminologists to try to settle; but there is certainly justification for reacting more strongly to someone who persistently refuses to play fair.

What, though, of Sally's failure to play fair? Is it right that she receive no penalty or punishment at all when she omits to conduct herself in a way that will keep her among the law-abiding, even if she should not be punished as severely as Sam, the recidivist? The answer is yes, for much the same reason it is right not to punish someone who forms an intention to commit a crime but never acts on it. As I have developed the example, Sally has remained among the law-abiding members of the polity after her first conviction, even though she has not acted in a way that is likely to keep her in that category. In that respect, she is like someone who plays a game without caring about the rules but somehow commits no intentional or flagrant fouls. Such a person stays within the bounds of fair play without truly playing fair, and those who are playing fair will have good reason to regard her conduct as offensive, to remonstrate with her, and to keep her under closer scrutiny than the average player. In Sally's case, moreover, her lack of respect for the law and the law-abiding likely will lead her to commit another crime. If it does—and assuming that it is equivalent to Sam's crime—then her punishment should be harsher than his; for Sam at least made the effort to play fair that Sally refused to make.

From Theory to Practice

I began this discussion by observing that recidivism presents both practical and theoretical challenges to criminal justice. The discussion itself has concentrated on the theoretical challenge of providing a justification of the recidivist premium on retributivist grounds. That challenge can be met, I have argued, by following Youngjae Lee in conceiving of recidivism as a kind of omission, but with the further step of grounding Lee's theory in the fair-play model of the political or legal order as a cooperative practice. If I am right, then it is fair to say that meeting the theoretical challenge also has practical implications.

To put the point crudely, if we can get the theory right, then we should be able to take steps that will reduce the number of persistent offenders. Getting the theory right means, in this case, that offenders and the polity are engaged in a relationship, as Lee argues, that imposes responsibilities on both parties. On the offender's part, this is a responsibility to "ensure that whatever led [him or her] to the status of being a convict should be avoided in the future"[34]; on the state's part, it is a responsibility not to make it virtually impossible for the offender to live within the law. Getting the theory right means, in other words, that offenders and law-abiding members of the polity have duties of fair play to one another. Failure to carry out these duties on the part of the offenders gives the polity the right to impose extra punishment on recidivists. The polity, however, also has a duty to play fair with the recidivists, and that duty is to arrange their punishment in a way that not only discourages them from becoming repeat offenders but also encourages them to become cooperating, law-abiding members of the polity once again.[35] Playing fair with recidivists in this way offers some hope of reducing recidivism, thereby meeting—or at least addressing—the practical as well as the theoretical challenge of recidivism.

Playing Fair with Restitution

At first glance, programs that require criminals to make restitution to their victims seem to be unproblematic for advocates of the fair-play approach to punishment. There will be practical difficulties involved in securing restitution from offenders to their victims, to be sure, but fairness to both victims and offenders seems to require us to bring about such restitution whenever we can. If the

---

[34] Ibid., p. 614.

[35] For an account of how criminal justice policies and agents often foster recidivism by throwing obstacles in the way of ex-offenders, see Alice Goffman, *On the Run: Fugitive Life in an American City* (Chicago: University of Chicago Press, 2014).

general aim is to restore the balance of benefits and burdens, as Herbert Morris argued in "Persons and Punishment," then it is clearly appropriate not only to take from the offender what he owes—"exacting the debt," in Morris's words—but also to repair as far as possible the damage to the victim(s) to whom he is indebted.[36] Moreover, if fair play aims at the restoration of the offender to membership in good standing in the cooperative practice of the polity, as I argued in the preceding parts of this chapter, then his efforts to make restitution to his victim(s) seem to be promising steps in the right direction.

Indeed, the desirability of restitution seems to be a point on which not only fair-play theorists but virtually everyone concerned with criminal justice can agree. Such programs will seem especially desirable to anyone who believes that the victims of crime are too often neglected and that more should be done to make them whole. Nevertheless, despite its widespread appeal, the prospect of restitution presents two challenges for fair-play theory. The first is the general challenge posed by those who maintain that restitution, properly conceived, is not a form of punishment at all. If they are right, then neither fair play nor any other theory of punishment is compatible with what they call *pure* restitution. If, however, restitution may be joined to punishment in a system of *punitive* restitution, then the second challenge for fair-play theorists is to show that their approach really is compatible with the attempt to secure restitution for the victims of crime. This second challenge is not as serious as the first, in my view, but both require a response here.

The Libertarian Case for Pure Restitution

That criminals should make restitution to their victims is a principle widely accepted among jurists, most of whom regard restitution as either a form of punishment or an important component of a proper scheme of punishment.[37] For the advocates of pure restitution, however, restitution is an alternative to punishment that justice requires us to adopt. That is why both the political and the philosophical abolitionists discussed in Chapter 5 rely on restitution as a vital part of their proposals for the abolition of punishment. The advocates of pure restitution, though, are divided with regard to the question of whether the victims of crime are necessarily individual persons, as libertarian proponents of pure

---

[36] Morris, "Persons and Punishment," *The Monist* 52 (1968): 478.

[37] See, e.g., Stephen Schafer, *Compensation and Restitution to Victims of Crime* (Montclair, NJ: Patterson Smith, 1970), and Patrick McAnany, "Restitution as Idea and Practice: The Retributive Process," in *Offender Restitution in Theory and Action*, ed. Burt Galaway and Joe Hudson (Lexington, MA: Lexington Books, 1978), pp. 15–31.

restitution maintain, or whether there is some sense in which the broader public can be owed restitution as victims of criminal wrongdoing.

The most influential statement of the libertarian case for pure restitution is set out in Randy Barnett's "Restitution: A New Paradigm of Criminal Justice."[38] According to Barnett, we should abandon "the paradigm of punishment" and replace it with a system of criminal justice that takes restitution to victims rather than punishment of criminals as its principal goal. Crime, he claims, is "an offense by one individual against the rights of another. The victim has suffered a loss. Justice consists of the culpable offender making good the loss he has caused."[39] On this view, then, the criminal owes no debt to society. "Where we once saw an offense against society, we now see an offense against an individual victim.... *The armed robber did not rob society; he robbed the victim.* His debt, therefore, is not to society; it is to the victim."[40] If offenders can make good the losses of their victims, they should be allowed—or perhaps forced—to do so; and that should be the end of the matter.

Barnett's arguments have provoked critical responses from writers both more and less sympathetic to libertarianism. In particular, critics who do not share his libertarian orientation have advanced two lines of argument against pure restitution, one concerning crimes in which there clearly is a specific victim and one in which there is not.

If pure restitution has any appeal at all, it should be in the former cases, in which one person clearly harms or violates the rights of another readily identifiable person. But even in such a case the specific victim of a crime is seldom the only person who suffers from it. Others are likely to experience indirect or secondary harm, even if their only connection with the crime is having heard about it.[41] Indeed, someone who never even learns of a particular crime may feel its effects if it fosters a climate of fear and apprehension that leads to suspicion, distrust, or hostility. In such cases restitution to the specific victim cannot do justice to everyone adversely affected by the crime. It may even be impossible to identify everyone injured in this way, especially when people undergo emotional or attitudinal changes, or increased insurance costs, that they cannot trace to a particular event. If criminals incur a debt to their victims, then they are likely to owe a debt to a great many people, including many we cannot identify with any

---

[38] Barnett, "Restitution: A New Paradigm of Criminal Justice," in *Assessing the Criminal*, ed. Randy Barnett and John Hagel III (Cambridge, MA: Ballinger Publishing, 1977), pp. 349–83. A shorter version of this essay appeared under the same title in *Ethics* 87 (1977): 279–301. For similar views, see Murray Rothbard, "Punishment and Proportionality," also in *Assessing the Criminal*, pp. 259–70.

[39] Barnett, "Restitution: A New Paradigm of Criminal Justice," in *Assessing the Criminal*, p. 363.

[40] Ibid.; emphasis in original.

[41] Margaret Holmgren concentrates on this point in "Punishment as Restitution: The Rights of the Community," *Criminal Justice Ethics* 2(1) (1983): 36–49.

precision. This is a debt they cannot discharge fully by making restitution to the specific victims of their crimes.

The second line of argument against pure restitution concerns crimes in which there is not even a single clearly identifiable victim. Here the arguments focus not on controversial cases, such as those involving prostitution, gambling, and other "victimless crimes," but on cases in which there is little controversy about whether the activities in question ought to be outlawed. These fall under three headings: crimes of attempt, of endangerment, and of unfairness. In all three categories, insisting that there is no crime without a specific victim leads to the conclusion that actions or activities widely regarded as criminal ought to be legal. That is, unsuccessful attempts to commit a crime would not be criminal; actions that unintentionally endanger others, such as driving while intoxicated or other kinds of reckless driving, would not be criminal; and successful attempts to corrupt public institutions or take unfair advantage of others, such as violating environmental regulations and evading taxes, would not be criminal.[42]

Taken individually, these are powerful objections to the libertarian version of pure restitution; taken together, they seem to be overwhelming. Libertarians have mounted responses to both lines of criticism, however, that deserve careful consideration.

The Libertarian Defense of Pure Restitution: Crimes with Specific Victims

The first argument against pure restitution rests on the claim that "secondary harm" to the indirect victims of crime makes it impossible for offenders to provide restitution to all of their victims. Barnett seems not to have taken up this challenge, but Mane Hajdin has done so by advancing a "modified theory of pure restitution."[43] His response is two-fold.

First, Hajdin insists that restitution must be *complete*. This means that the criminal must make good all of the losses he has inflicted on the victim, including

---

[42] For elaboration of these critical points, see Franklin Miller, "Restitution and Punishment: A Reply to Barnett," *Ethics* 88 (1978): 358–60, and my "Restitution: Pure or Punitive?," *Criminal Justice Ethics* 10 (1991): 30–31.

[43] Hajdin, "Criminals as Gamblers: A Modified Theory of Pure Restitution," *Dialogue* 26 (1987): 77–86. In *The Structure of Liberty: Justice and the Rule of Law*, 2nd ed. (Oxford: Oxford University Press, 2014 [1998]), Barnett offers no direct response to the critics of his case for pure restitution. Instead, in chap. 11, he makes the case for restitution in two ways: (1) by means of a comparison, grounded in the differences between public and private enforcement of rights, that ostensibly demonstrates the superiority of restitution to punishment (and criminal law more broadly) and (2) by arguing that restitutive schemes are better than punitive ones from the standpoint of deterrence. In chap. 15, he adds a broad attack on retribution (pp. 317–21).

the costs of lost opportunities. Complete restitution may even require recompense for the humiliation the victim suffered "through the very fact that he was a victim of a criminal act."[44] More to the point, complete restitution acknowledges that the criminal may owe something to someone other than his immediate victim: "If someone related to the victim has also suffered losses because of [the victim's] incapacitation, then that person may also be entitled to receive a part of the restitution."[45] Beyond that, Hajdin states that "no restitution is complete without the offender's paying for the costs of apprehending him and establishing his guilt."[46]

Nor does Hajdin regard complete restitution, so defined, as sufficient. As the title of his article indicates, Hajdin believes that we should think of "Criminals as Gamblers" who weigh the probable costs and benefits of their offenses before committing them. If we cannot keep them from playing "the game of criminality," he says, we can at least ensure that the game is fair by calculating in each case

> what the criminal's gain would be if he got away. We can also calculate the probability of his getting away, which then immediately gives us the probability of his being caught. What remains to be done is, then, simply to increase the amount of restitution that he has to pay if he is caught, to an amount that satisfies the requirement of fair gambling.[47]

According to Hajdin, this form of "fair gambling" would lead prospective criminals to consider not only how painful it will be, if they are caught and convicted, to make complete restitution to their victims, but also how much more painful it will be to compensate as well the victims of those criminals who are not brought to justice. Criminals are betting that they will escape capture, in other words, so it is only fair that we compel those who lose this bet to make good the losses of the victims of the criminals who do in fact escape. Hajdin thus proposes that we

> establish the ratio between the total amount of damages that are due to criminal acts of a certain type where the offender was not discovered, and the total amount of restitution that convicted offenders would have to pay on the basis of [complete restitution].... Then we increase the amount that each of the convicted offenders has to pay by that percentage.[48]

---

[44] Hajdin, "Criminals as Gamblers," p. 78.
[45] Ibid., p. 78.
[46] Ibid., p. 78.
[47] Ibid., p. 81.
[48] Ibid., p. 81.

Setting aside the question of whether it is just to force some criminals to pay for the wrongs done by others,[49] Hajdin's scheme certainly has its attractions. It promises both to deter crime and also to compensate the victims of those presumably irrational criminals who would not be deterred, and to do so at the expense of criminals rather than law-abiding taxpayers. To speak to the point at issue, furthermore, this scheme rescues pure restitution from the complaint that it cannot adequately respond to those who suffer indirect or secondary harm.

Or so Hajdin claims. There are, however, at least two problems with his argument. One is the practical problem that troubles all restitutive schemes—that is, how to exact restitution from offenders who are often unable to make good, in any straightforward and timely way, the losses of their victims. For Hajdin's scheme, with its demand for "extra money," this problem will be especially severe. Moreover, even if we grant that his modified version of pure restitution can overcome this difficulty, the second problem poses an inescapable dilemma. That is, Hajdin's scheme will fail in one of two ways to save the libertarian version of pure restitution: either (1) it will not provide restitution for *all* of the victims of crime, or (2) it must proceed on the premise that criminals owe a debt not only to their specific victims but also to a wider public.

With regard to the first point, Hajdin's proposal may address satisfactorily the complaints of those who expect to bear increased insurance costs as a result of crimes from which they do not directly suffer. If his scheme will work, every direct or specific victim will know that she will receive full restitution, even when the person who committed the crime goes free. Insurance companies will also know this, of course, so they will have no reason to raise fees for coverage when the crime rate rises. Nevertheless, there are other kinds of costs that indirect victims bear, notably the attitudinal and avoidance costs borne by people who do not even know the primary victims of particular crimes. To such people, Hajdin's scheme apparently offers nothing but the following query: "Why would it matter to you whether the crime rates in the society are high or low, if the system of justice were set up in such a way that your becoming a victim of a crime could not make you worse-off?"[50]

I would not be alone, I suspect, to respond by saying that I am not going to stop avoiding dangerous areas, or cease to worry about the injuries I or others may suffer, merely because I know that victims will be restored, in some sense, to the condition they enjoyed before they became victims. In some cases, murder

---

[49] This is not a point another libertarian advocate of pure restitution, Joseph Ellin, is willing to concede. As he sees it, the "true difficulty with Hajdin's solution is that it places an unfair burden on the wrongdoer. Why should a wrongdoer be made to compensate people whom he did not injure?" Ellin, "Restitutionism Defended," *Journal of Value Inquiry* 34 (2000): 299–317, at p. 312.

[50] Hajdin, "Criminals as Gamblers," p. 82.

and rape being the most obvious, it is hard to see how a victim could ever be made as well off as she was before the crime. In other cases, such as car theft, it is difficult to believe that the prospect of full compensation—not only for the car, but for inconvenience, opportunity costs, and other losses resulting from the theft—will make potential victims indifferent as to whether or not their cars are stolen. For many burglary victims, it seems that the sense of violation they suffer is something for which there is no completely effective compensation. Other things being equal, people do not want to be victims, and they especially do not want to be the victims of assault. As long as this is true, people will feel the indirect effects of crime, through attitudinal and avoidance costs, in ways for which they cannot be fully compensated.[51]

There is one respect, though, in which Hajdin's proposal could extend restitution to all victims of crime. This appears in his discussion of complete restitution when he says that the criminal must pay for his apprehension and conviction—"to bear a suitable share of the overhead costs of the law-enforcement agency"—because "he is one of those whose activities (unlike the activities of the law-abiding citizen) makes the existence of such agencies necessary."[52] One could argue, then, that all law-abiding citizens are the victims of every crime in the sense that they must pay to maintain police forces and other agencies to try to prevent crime and to punish—or exact restitution from—criminals. On this view, Hajdin's scheme provides restitution to all victims, even if it is not *complete* restitution to everyone, because it relieves the law-abiding citizens of the burden of paying for protection.

To advance this argument, however, is to surrender one of the core notions of the libertarian case for pure restitution—that is, the claim that criminals do not incur a debt to society. If *all* law-abiding citizens feel the secondary or indirect effects of crime, then the criminal owes something to all of them. But what the criminal owes is not a debt to this specific person or that one but to everyone *qua* law-abiding citizen. The criminal's debt is thus a debt to society. Indeed, if it is only fair to require criminals "to bear a suitable share of the overhead costs of the law-enforcement agency," so that they are no longer imposing unfair costs on law-abiding citizens, Hajdin's argument is only steps away from the fair-play theory of punishment.

In one way or another, therefore, Hajdin's scheme fails to save pure restitution from the objection that crimes with specific victims also inflict suffering on

---

[51] According to Ellin, this response to Hajdin "is not to the point; the response is a complaint against monetary damages." It is certainly a complaint against the claim that monetary damages are sufficient compensation, and therefore is, I believe, very much to the point. But cf. Ellin, "Restitutionism Defended," p. 312.

[52] Hajdin, "Criminals as Gamblers," p. 85.

others. But even if it were successful in this regard, the libertarian defense of pure restitution would still confront the challenge posed by crimes without specific victims.

The Libertarian Defense of Pure Restitution: Crimes Without Specific Victims

There are, as previously noted, three general categories of crimes with no specific or obvious victims: those involving unsuccessful attempts, endangerment, and unfairness. Various libertarians have responded to objections concerning all three of these categories, but their responses have not been satisfactory.

Crimes of Attempt

In his original article Barnett anticipated the objection that unsuccessful attempts are crimes even though there is no obvious victim. His response there was to claim that "most unsuccessful attempts worthy of sanction" would still count as crimes in a system of pure restitution because most of these attempts result in actual harm to somebody.[53] Someone who botches an attempt at murder is likely to commit assault and battery in the process, for example, and the culprit should be held liable for the harm he actually inflicted, not for that which he intended to do. If no physical harm is suffered or no property right violated as a consequence of the attempt, it is nevertheless nearly always possible to discover another kind of actual harm, "such as the creation of fear on the part of the intended victim or bystanders," to charge against the offender. All that remains are attempts that are both unsuccessful and undiscovered; and since no one is harmed in these cases, there should be no criminal liability.

This response is unsatisfactory in two ways. First, it effectively takes the *discovery* of an unsuccessful attempt at crime to be what makes the attempt a crime. We can do nothing about a crime that we fail to discover, of course, but that does not mean that no crime has occurred. If a bank clerk transfers money from my account to his, only to have someone else's innocent mistake cancel the transfer, the clerk's attempted theft of my money would be both unsuccessful and undiscovered; but it would be criminal nevertheless. If discovered, it certainly would be treated as such; but we would not say the discovery is what makes a crime of the clerk's attempted theft.

---

[53] Barnett, "Restitution: A New Paradigm of Criminal Justice," in *Assessing the Criminal*, p. 376. This response does not appear in the abbreviated version of his essay published in *Ethics*.

The second problem is that Barnett casts his net wide in order to find victims of attempted crimes, counting not only frightened bystanders but anyone who feels threatened. "Unsuccessful attempts," he states, "may only be sanctionable ... when they are successful threats."[54] At this point, however, Barnett has brought a great many people—all who feel threatened as the result of a criminal attempt—into the category of "victims," and most of them will not be clearly identifiable as the specific victims of the crime. This step may help him to meet the challenge unsuccessful attempts pose to the libertarian theory of pure restitution, but it also seems to be a significant step away from his libertarian claim that criminals owe no debt to society. By casting a wide net, moreover, Barnett invites the question of why not cast it wider still. If we are to count everyone who feels threatened by a criminal attempt as one of its victims, why not also count everyone who suffers insurance and law-enforcement costs as victims? Hajdin effectively concedes that we should do so, and Barnett's effort to turn back the challenge of attempted crimes leads to the same conclusion, unpalatable as it is from the libertarian standpoint. Criminals are indebted to a great many people who suffer indirectly as a result of their misdeeds, and this debt amounts to a debt to society.

To be sure, Hajdin has his own way of trying to rescue pure restitution from the problem of unsuccessful criminal attempts. These attempts should be divided, he says, into three categories:

(a) attempts that cause some actual harm to an identifiable victim,
(b) attempts that are prevented from causing harm by a policeman or other law-enforcement official,
(c) attempts that fail to cause actual harm for some other reason, in particular because they are abandoned by the criminal himself.[55]

Category (a) will include someone who attempts to commit murder but only breaks the victim's leg. Such a person should be punished for assault and battery, but not for attempted murder. As Hajdin notes, this category adds nothing to Barnett's account of criminal attempts. But categories (b) and (c) do bring something new to the discussion.

Cases in category (c) resemble the unsuccessful and undiscovered criminal attempts that should not be considered crimes at all, according to Barnett. Hajdin agrees, adding the observation that "certain kinds of abandoned attempts" are no

---

[54] Barnett, "The Justice of Restitution," *American Journal of Jurisprudence* 25 (1982): 117–32, at p. 131.

[55] Hajdin, "Criminals as Gamblers," p. 85.

longer crimes in some jurisdictions.[56] Cases in category (b), though, truly are crimes, and in these cases, Hajdin says,

> Substantial restitution may be due to the law-enforcement agency itself. In calculating the restitution in these cases we should bear in mind that one of the purposes of having law-enforcement agencies is precisely to prevent completion of attempted offences. This means that a criminal in this category should not merely be "billed" for the costs of the particular law-enforcement operations that were directed at preventing him from completing the particular offence he attempted, but should also be required to bear a suitable share of the overhead costs of the law-enforcement agency. The rationale is that he is one of those whose activities (unlike the activities of law-abiding citizens) make the existence of such agencies necessary.[57]

Hajdin's distinctions are instructive, but they hardly bolster the libertarian case for pure restitution. Category (a), again, simply restates Barnett's position. Category (c) includes the plausible but unhelpful claim that abandoned attempts should not be considered crimes. If I walk into a bank with the intention of robbing it, only to change my mind as I reach the teller's window, I have abandoned an attempt at robbery without committing a crime. If I try to rob the bank but fail, I have unsuccessfully attempted bank robbery and thus committed a crime. To say that abandoned attempts should not be punished, then, is to say nothing about unsuccessful attempts.

Hajdin's category (b) is even less helpful to the pure restitutionist. If my attempt to commit robbery is unsuccessful because the police prevent it, he says, I must make restitution to the law-enforcement agency itself. In doing so, I will make restitution to those law-abiding citizens who must bear the cost of maintaining law-enforcement agencies that protect them from the likes of me. But this claim makes sense only if we hold that criminals have committed an offense against, and owe a debt to, the society or polity that instituted and sustains the law-enforcement agencies—and thus to the cooperative meta-practice these agencies serve. Contrary to Hajdin's intention, in short, the introduction of category (b) undermines the libertarian case for pure restitution.

Crimes of Endangerment

With crimes of endangerment there is neither an apparent nor an intended victim. We typically regard them as crimes, however, and we do not want the

[56] Ibid., p. 85, n. 16.
[57] Ibid., p. 85.

police to wait until a drunken driver smashes into a car or runs down a pedestrian before they make an arrest. But if the drunken driver has the good fortune to injure no one, does he then owe a debt to anyone? Barnett would respond by pointing again to threats, arguing that the threat of harm is itself a kind of injury.[58] But an injury, we may ask, to whom? The answer often is that there is a threat to no particular person but to society or the polity in general. Those who drive while intoxicated endanger all of us either directly, through the threat of damage to our persons and property, or indirectly, through avoidance, insurance, attitudinal, and—as Hajdin reminds us—law-enforcement costs. Only those who fail to take account of these crimes can deny that criminals owe a debt to society.

Hajdin responds to the challenge posed by crimes of endangerment only in a footnote, in which he states:

> Some of these crimes can be dealt with by using the same reasoning . . . [as that] dealing with criminal attempts. In some other cases, the dangerous activity could safely be decriminalized and its regulation left to the realm of contracts (e.g., prohibition of dangerous driving could become part of a contract between a highway owner and a highway user).[59]

Where the highways are public property, of course, this advice is singularly unhelpful. Libertarian advocates of pure restitution may prefer to see roads and other public property converted to private ownership, but they cannot simply assume the existence or the justice of such an arrangement in their attempts to overcome the problem posed for their theory by crimes of endangerment.

Crimes of Unfairness

There is a sense, as I have argued in earlier chapters, in which all crimes are crimes of unfairness, but there is also a narrower category of crimes, including suborning witnesses and tax evasion, to which this term especially applies. Crimes of this sort are particularly important in the present context, for they are most directly connected to the belief that criminals owe a debt to society or the polity. Because pure restitution grows out of the conviction that criminals injure only individuals, not society as a whole, those who champion it must find

---

[58] See his *The Structure of Liberty*, pp. 186–92.
[59] Hajdin, "Criminals as Gamblers," p. 85, n. 17.

a way either to deny that crimes of unfairness should be counted as crimes, or to account for these crimes as offenses against individuals.

Hajdin takes the second tack. As he sees it, "Harm that is done to each honest taxpayer by an individual case of tax evasion is very small but it is nevertheless calculable."[60] The tax evader, then, owes a debt not to society, but to every honest taxpayer who suffered a loss, perhaps without even noticing it, because of his cheating. If the cheater is caught, the penalty he must pay in addition to his original tax bill should be understood as restitution for the law-enforcement costs borne by the honest taxpayers.[61]

Whether tax cheaters do indeed do a calculable amount of harm to each honest taxpayer is doubtful. One person's failure to pay in full will not necessarily increase the costs for others, nor is it likely to force changes in any government program. Even if Hajdin is right on this point, however, it still does not follow that all crimes of unfairness can be reduced to crimes in which one person injures one or more specific persons. There are other cases where there simply is no particular victim because no one is *harmed*. Such may be the case, for instance, when someone dumps waste into a river in violation of antipollution laws. If the water is clean enough and the waste slight enough, the river will be able to absorb the waste with no harm to anyone downstream. Others are *injured*, though, in the literal sense of being treated wrongly. They too might find it convenient to dump waste into the river, but they recognize that restrictions are necessary to keep the river clean. They refrain from dumping, then, and they are wronged when the dumper takes unfair advantage of their cooperation by failing to do his share to prevent pollution of the river.

So far as I am aware, Barnett has not responded to the challenge posed by crimes of unfairness. There is, however, a response available to him, especially in view of his definition of a restitutive theory of justice as "a rights-based approach to criminal sanctions that views crime as an offense by one individual against the rights of another."[62] From this point Barnett could go on to distinguish *rights violations* from *harms*.[63] Doing so would allow him to acknowledge that the

---

[60] Ibid., p. 84.

[61] Boonin makes a similar point (*The Problem of Punishment*, p. 245, n. 31), but not in defense of the *libertarian* case for pure restitution.

[62] Barnett, "The Justice of Restitution," p. 117.

[63] Barnett *could* draw this distinction, but he does not. In "The Justice of Restitution," he links the two when he says "that what was interfered with may have been intangible does not make it any less a 'harm' or rights invasion" (p. 126). In "Pursuing Justice in a Free Society: Part One—Power vs. Liberty" (*Criminal Justice Ethics* 4 [1985]: 65), he states that "an individual-rights approach to decision making requires that we define what is meant by 'harm' to others." He then proceeds to say that the "traditional common law answer is entirely fitting for the Liberty Approach: One is free to do that which he wills with his own resources provided that his use does not *physically interfere with another*

dumper in my example has wronged others by violating their rights to fair play, from which it follows that the dumper should be subject to criminal sanction even though he has done no harm. In this way Barnett could account for crimes of unfairness without surrendering his conviction that all crimes are crimes against individuals.

For Barnett to take this course, though, would be to acknowledge that those who commit crimes of unfairness violate the rights of many individuals who cannot be identified as specific victims. From there, it is but a short step to the conclusion that criminals owe a debt to society. In addition, the distinction between *harm* and *rights violation* raises another serious problem for the libertarian argument for pure restitution—that is, how is the offender to make restitution to those he has not harmed? If the person who dumps waste into the river wrongs me without harming me, what is there for him to repay? On the conditions set out in my example, the dumper's violation of my rights, which I may never discover, does not worsen my situation. How, then, is the dumper to make restitution to me and the others whose rights were violated? One answer is to call for his punishment; but that answer is not available to Barnett, who proposes to replace punishment with restitution.

As with crimes of attempt and crimes of endangerment, in sum, crimes of unfairness reveal serious weaknesses—fatal flaws, I believe—in the theory of pure restitution. Not all of the advocates of pure restitution are libertarians, however, and it may be that the others have taken a position that is not subject to these weaknesses. Let us now consider this possibility.

The Non-Libertarian Case for Pure Restitution

The most extensive argument on behalf of pure restitution from a non-libertarian perspective seems to be the one David Boonin develops in the lengthy final chapter of *The Problem of Punishment*. To be sure, Boonin disclaims any intention of advocating the adoption of a system of pure restitution. Even so, after many pages devoted to rebutting objections to pure restitution, he concludes that a system of pure restitution would afford "at least one acceptable way" of doing without punishment.[64] If Boonin is not an unqualified advocate of pure restitution, his sympathies clearly tend in that direction.

---

person's use and enjoyment of his resources" (emphasis in original). From Barnett's point of view, then, to violate people's rights is to harm them, but harm occurs only when we physically interfere with their use and enjoyment of their resources. The result is not only a conflation of rights violations (or wrongs) and harms, but an unduly narrow conception of both rights and harms.

[64] Boonin, *The Problem of Punishment*, p. 274.

For present purposes, the most notable difference between his position and those of the libertarian advocates of pure restitution is that Boonin openly acknowledges the indirect or secondary victims of crime. As he says, "at least in a good number of cases, individuals other than the offender's immediate victim are also wrongfully harmed by the offense."[65] However, Boonin also holds that acknowledging the existence of debts to society "does nothing to undermine the principle of pure restitution itself"; for it simply follows that we must apply "the theory consistently in light of the assumption that people who break the law often harm society as a whole."[66] There will no doubt be practical difficulties in the way of arranging for offenders to make restitution to society as a whole, but the example of damages assessed against tobacco companies for harming smokers leads Boonin to suggest that the state might compel a robber

> to pay a lump sum to the city, which would use the money to hire an extra patrol officer, or two, or three, depending on how much police power was necessary to restore the community to its previous level of well-being, and which would deploy the new officers in the manner most likely to bring the greatest benefits to those who had suffered the greatest harms as a result of the robbery.[67]

Whether this would be an adequate response to the practical difficulties of an attempt to secure restitution for all the secondary victims of crime is a matter I will not take up here. Indeed, as an advocate of punitive restitution, I am sympathetic to proposals to incorporate restitution within a system of punishment whenever and wherever possible, including restitution of some sort to the polity itself. Practical problems aside, however, there are other reasons to reject Boonin's case for pure restitution as an alternative to punishment.

The first reason arises in response to Boonin's definition of punishment as the intentional imposition of harm on an offender. In Chapter 5 I disputed the adequacy of this definition in part because Boonin's insistence that punishment *harms* the offender rules out rehabilitation or moral education as even potential justifications of punishment. In the context of pure restitution, the problem lies with *intention* rather than harm. According to Boonin's account, restitutive schemes are likely to rely on compulsion to much the same extent as punitive schemes do. As he sees it, offenders who try to evade their responsibilities to make restitution to their victims, including restitution to society or the polity, must be forced to do so, perhaps by imprisoning them while they work off their

---

[65] Ibid., p. 226.
[66] Ibid., p. 228.
[67] Ibid., p. 228.

debts to their victims. When offenders are unable to make sufficient monetary restitution, furthermore, the authorities will have to look for other ways for offenders to restore their victims to the level of safety and security they enjoyed before they became victims. A burglar, to take Boonin's example, could be

> compelled to wear a device by which his location could be monitored by the police at all times. He could be subjected to intensive supervision, such as that accompanying probation in some cases, which often includes a curfew. *He could simply be locked up.* In other cases, an offender might be made to take an anger management course, to undergo therapy, to give up drinking, to stay away from certain areas or certain people or people under a certain age, and so on. If one or more of these impositions are necessary for an offender's victims to be fully restored to their former level of safety and security, then he owes it to them to undergo these impositions, and they could be fully justified by the theory of pure restitution.[68]

At this point, it may appear that there is no significant difference between a system of compulsory pure restitution and a system of punishment, especially when pure restitution may amount to nothing more than simply locking up the offender. Boonin attempts to ward off the objection, however, by invoking the importance of the intention involved in the response to the criminal's offense. "Not every legally imposed restriction on a person's freedom of movement is punishment," he maintains. "It is punishment only if it is done with the aim of making an offender suffer for his offense."[69] We do not punish someone with a highly contagious disease, for example, if we place her in quarantine against her will. But is that correct observation enough to save the distinction between pure restitution and punishment? Critics have lodged two complaints against Boonin's reliance on intentions here. One is that his proposed abolition of legal punishment "turns out to be, fundamentally, a word game" in which "the usual repertoire of legal punishments" undergo "sanitizing... by calling them 'restitution'"—all of which is "possible only by taking at face value unverifiable reports of private mental states [i.e., intentions]" by those who have something at stake in reporting their intentions when they decide how offenders are to be treated.[70]

Boonin might respond by insisting that he is defending only a scheme that rests on sincere intentions to exact restitution rather than punishment from

---

[68] Ibid., p. 232; emphasis added.

[69] Ibid., p. 233. Note that Boonin refers to *suffering* here rather than to *harm*.

[70] Leo Zaibert, "Punishment, Restitution, and the Marvelous Method of Directing the Intention," *Criminal Justice Ethics* 29 (2010): 41–53, at p. 52.

offenders, but that would still leave him facing a second objection. In this case, the complaint centers on Boonin's reliance on the distinction between *intended* and *foreseen* effects. As he sees it, "there is nothing intrinsic to incarceration or intensive supervision that requires that it be done to impose suffering rather than to bring about some other result, with the harms to the person being detained being foreseen rather than intended."[71] Whether the offender's suffering is merely the foreseen but unintended side effect of the compulsion required to exact restitution from him, however, is not a point that everyone is willing to concede. According to one critic, "anyone whose end is to compensate victims for their losses and who recognizes that harming offenders is the indispensable means to achieving that end must rationally endorse harming offenders, and in so acting, intentionally harms the offender."[72] Despite Boonin's intentions, in short, compulsory pure restitution collapses into punishment, with punishment understood to be the intentional imposition of suffering—but not necessarily harm, as I have argued—on criminal wrongdoers.

A third reason to reject Boonin's case for pure restitution turns on another feature of the definition of punishment I have drawn from Antony Duff—that is, that punishment aims at communicating the polity's condemnation or censure of the offender's wrongdoing. Pure restitution cannot provide a satisfactory alternative to punishment because it cannot properly communicate this message. In response, the advocate of pure restitution could concede the point but deny that this is sufficient reason to reject pure restitution. Boonin's response, however, is to maintain that pure restitution can accomplish in this regard what punishment can. In fact, as he points out, some of the critics of pure restitution, including myself, have acknowledged that requiring "restitution does convey social disapproval of the offender's act."[73]

Boonin is correct in this regard, but that is not enough to secure his position. There is, after all, a significant difference between *disapproval*, on the one hand, and *censure* or *condemnation*, on the other. You may disapprove of the way I dress or of my taste in music or my attempts at humor without condemning or censuring me—you may simply shake your head and walk away, for example. In similar fashion, society may express its disapproval of my conduct by requiring me to make restitution to those I have injured without condemning that conduct or censuring me when it does so. To convey such condemnation or

---

[71] Boonin, *The Problem of Punishment*, p. 233.

[72] Michael Cholbi, "Compulsory Victim Restitution Is Punishment: A Reply to Boonin," *Public Reason* 2 (2010): 92. Cholbi presses two more arguments against Boonin's defense of pure restitution, neither of which requires attention here.

[73] Boonin, *The Problem of Punishment*, p. 268, n. 47, citing p. 37 of my "Restitution: Pure or Punitive?"

censure—the terms Duff uses in connection with the communicative aspect of punishment—is to move beyond pure restitution to some form of punishment. Boonin thus faces a choice. He can either hold that the expression of mere disapproval is sufficient, in which case he will not be showing that pure restitution is capable of conveying the communicative message that punishment conveys; or he will have to abandon pure restitution in favor of a form of restitution with an openly punitive aspect.

Another problem for Boonin's defense of pure restitution arises in connection with what appear to be the unacceptable implications of a purely restitutive response to criminals. Would such a response entail, for instance, that wealthy people could escape punishment simply by paying restitution for their vicious acts? And what of the victims of murder and rape? How is restitution to them, or to the secondary and indirect victims of these crimes, even possible? Boonin himself expresses concerns of this kind when he notes that proposals to require compensation to the victims' families, or to force offenders to work for the rest of their lives in prison factories in order to pay restitution, fail "to explain how to handle cases where the victim leaves no survivors (as when an entire family is massacred) or to explain why any murderers would have to be imprisoned if they could earn more money for restitution without being imprisoned."[74] That is why he goes on to defend a form of pure restitution that

> would require far more than a monetary payment from the offender, significant as that burden might be. Something would have to be done to restore the community to its prior level of security, and this would likely involve, at the least, constant monitoring of the offender, if not simply preventive incarceration. Since this is so, there is no reason to believe that a society that abolished punishment could not protect itself from rapists and murderers. We do not punish rapists and murderers who are found to be insane, after all, and this does not prevent us from protecting ourselves from them. There is no reason to think that things should be different in the case of sane offenders. If abolishing punishment meant that the state could never lock up a rapist or murderer to prevent him from attacking others, then perhaps the case of rape or murder would show that punishment is necessary. But it doesn't mean this, and so it doesn't show this.[75]

Boonin's recognition of the importance of secondary victims, including society as a whole, represents an advance, in my view, over the libertarian advocates of

---

[74] Ibid., p. 241, n. 28.
[75] Ibid., pp. 244–45.

pure restitution. Nevertheless, he has not succeeded in rescuing pure restitution from the unacceptable implications noted above. It is not even clear that he has provided the explanations of how to handle cases where the criminal leaves no surviving victims or those in which a murderer could earn more money for restitution without being imprisoned—explanations he himself apparently thinks necessary. To be sure, he does suggest that imprisonment or at least constant monitoring will be necessary to address the "level of subjective anxiety" within society and as a preventive measure. What, though, would Boonin do with a murderer who is capable of making vast sums of money if he is not imprisoned and who is quite unlikely to commit murder again? Suppose that a financial wizard murdered the one and only person he thoroughly detested and then, upon conviction, refused to put his wizardry to work for restitutive purposes unless he were otherwise free to go about his ordinary life. From the standpoint of restitution, it would seem to be a mistake to imprison this person; and from the standpoint of prevention or protection, there would seem to be little point to it. Boonin might accept this conclusion—indeed, it seems he must—but also insist that the murderer should remain under constant monitoring. That might simply push the quandary back a step, for the murderer might also refuse to put his wizardry to work while being monitored; but let us suppose that he would not refuse. In that case, we will be left with a convicted murderer who is free to go on with his life, albeit under surveillance, as long as he continues to make restitution to those who suffered because of his victim's death. That may be the appropriate outcome as far as Boonin and other advocates of pure restitution are concerned, but it will do nothing to assuage the worries of those who believe that offenders may view restitution as simply the cost, which they may be willing to pay, of committing a crime.[76]

The conclusion, then, is that Boonin's case for pure restitution as an alternative to punishment is unsuccessful. We may all agree that, *ceteris paribus*, painless surgery is preferable to painful surgery, but the same is not true with regard to legal responses to criminal wrongdoing. For even if we set aside the suspicion that Boonin is simply "sanitizing" the most common forms of punishment by regarding them as the regrettably painful means necessary to bring about restitution to victims, we must still ask whether justice may sometimes require us to inflict pain or suffering intentionally on criminals. My argument is that it does, both in order to grant the victims, direct and indirect, a measure of what

---

[76] Dennis Klimchuk puts the point nicely: "If we think of punishment as the mere payment of a debt and not (at least also) the punitive condemnation of a wrong, we come close to representing punishment as a kind of tax or fee—the price of doing criminal business—and so to effectively institutionalizing a market in the interests protected by the criminal law." Klimchuk, "Retribution, Restitution, and Revenge," *Law and Philosophy* 20 (2001): 80–101, at p. 101.

Hampton calls expressive retribution, and in order to bring the offender to the kind of "secular penance" that Duff believes will promote his reintegration into society.[77] But that is to say that restitution ought to be regarded, in many cases, as an important part of a punitive response to crime.

Punitive Restitution as Fair Play

Establishing that pure restitution is unsatisfactory in both its libertarian and its less individualist forms does not entail the abandonment of attempts to employ restitution as a criminal sanction. The problem with pure restitution lies not with its emphasis on restitution but with its insistence on purity. The proper response is to regard restitution either as a form of or a supplement to punishment, not as an alternative to it. That said, a case must still be made for punitive restitution, and this case will require answers to two challenging questions: (1) Are restitution and punishment compatible? and (2) Is punitive restitution compatible with the fair-play theory of punishment? The answer in both cases, I shall argue, is yes.

Perhaps the best way to answer the first question is by returning to the Flew-Benn-Hart definition of legal punishment as extended by Duff. Again, that definition states that legal punishment typically "is something intended to be burdensome or painful, imposed on a (supposed) offender for a (supposed) offense by someone with (supposedly) the authority to do so; and ... intended to express or communicate censure."[78] Whether punishment so understood is compatible with restitution will depend entirely on the first and last parts of that definition. As we have seen, the defenders of pure restitution deny that restitution is intended to be burdensome or painful to the offender, even though they concede that it generally will be. There is no reason, however, to believe that an offender cannot make restitution to his victim(s) in a way that gives expression to the intention of imposing some degree of suffering on him—and of subjecting him to censure or condemnation at the same time. We might imagine, for example, a thief whose sentence requires him to earn money to restore the losses of his victim by spending some days in a dunking booth at a local fair, with the words "Dunk the Crook!" emblazoned on the tank of cold water above

---

[77] For those who believe it improper for a polity to try to induce penance, one can substitute the kind of awareness or understanding that will promote the offender's reintegration into society. For reasons to be wary of "secular penance," see Bennett, *The Apology Ritual*, pp. 186–97, and his conclusion (p. 197) that the "type of reconciliation that the state is legitimately interested in" is "the return of that full civic status of which one was deprived because of one's offence."

[78] R. A. Duff, *Punishment, Communication, and Community* (Oxford: Oxford University Press, 2001), pp. xiv–xv.

which he sits. The arrangements will seldom speak as directly to the elements of punishment as they do in this example, but the point will hold even in more common and less direct cases of punitive restitution.

To put the point another way, we can respond to the worry that wrongdoers may find that making restitution to their victims is neither painful nor unpleasant by doing one or more of three things. First, we can try to exact what Hajdin calls "complete restitution" from the offender, which includes not only restitution for *all* of the immediate victim's losses but also the law-enforcement costs of catching and convicting him. Exacting complete restitution assumes that a rough scale of damages can be developed, and there are no doubt difficulties involved in doing so, but all forms of punishment and all attempts to compensate victims, in civil as much as criminal cases, must deal with these difficulties. It seems likely, in any case, that most offenders will find that making complete restitution, or even approaching it, is a highly unpleasant experience. This will be especially true when complete restitution includes *punitive damage*.

If exacting complete restitution is not enough, we can also force offenders to make restitution in ways they ordinarily regard as unpleasant, such as laboring for their victims. Something of this sort is sometimes suggested as a way of exacting restitution from wealthy offenders who might otherwise look upon monetary restitution as the price worth paying for their enjoyment of criminal pleasures.[79] Or, finally, we can simply use restitution as a supplement to forms of punishment that we can expect as well as intend to induce suffering of some kind. No matter which of these tactics we adopt, it is evident that restitution can be made painful, and thereby compatible with punishment.

This conclusion will not satisfy Barnett, however. As he sees it, restitution (or "reparations") and punishment (at least according to retributive theories) try in different ways to correct the imbalance between the victim and the culprit: "A retributive view attempts to lower the criminal to the level at which the victim has been placed as a result of the crime. The restitutive view attempts to force the criminal to raise the victim to the level he or she was at before the crime."[80] Any attempt to make restitution punitive, or to mix it with punishment, will in the end simply convert the restitutive scheme into retributive punishment. "Punitive restitution" is thus a virtual oxymoron.[81]

The problem with Barnett's position is that it applies only to a crude form of retributivism, according to which the point of punishment is to bring the offender low by making him suffer what his victims have suffered. Few retributivists,

---

[79] See, e.g., Roger Pilon, "Criminal Remedies: Restitution, Punishment, or Both?," *Ethics* 88 (1978): 348–57, at 351.

[80] Barnett, "Pursuing Justice," p. 63.

[81] But note the qualification Barnett introduces in *The Structure of Liberty*, pp. 236–37.

however, are so crude. To the contrary, they typically aim to return *both* victim and offender to the positions they occupied *before* the crime insofar as possible. The point is that the crime typically worsens the victim's condition as it improves the offender's, and the criminal must be punished in order to restore the balance that his crime disturbed. In the fair-play view, beginning with Morris's "Persons and Punishment," this amounts to *restoring* the balance of benefits and burdens, not *lowering* the criminal, as Barnett puts it, "to the level at which the victim has been placed as a result of the crime." Even those retributivists who defend resentment and vindictiveness do so largely because of what punishment can offer the victim, such as restored or enhanced self-respect and a willingness to defend one's rights—even, as Jeffrie Murphy argues, a strengthened "respect for the moral order."[82] Moreover, those retributivists who conceive of punishment primarily as *expressive* rather than *communicative*, as Hampton and Christopher Bennett do, also take the legal condemnation of the wrongdoer to be a means of bringing about the offender's reintegration into or reconciliation with the polity. Thus Bennett "sees punishment as aimed at expressing proportionate condemnation of wrongdoing, but [it] is also ... based in the idea of restoring relationships damaged by crime."[83]

In this respect restitution and (retributive) punishment are not at odds, as Barnett maintains, but in harmony with each other. Indeed, restitution is an especially promising way of restoring the balance between victims and criminals in that it offers something more to victims than a strictly punitive scheme can. Other forms of punishment may offer the victim a sense of vindication, but punitive restitution can do both that *and* promise some redress to the victim's material losses, including the prospect of redress to the material losses of the indirect victims of crime. A strictly punitive scheme may allow the victim to pursue a civil suit for the recovery of damages, of course, but this is a private remedy that must be undertaken at the victim's initiative and risk. A scheme of punitive restitution, in contrast, treats the victim as a member of the polity whose right to redress entails a public commitment on her behalf. In this way, punitive restitution is not only a form of punishment but a superior form of it.

A quite different complaint is that restitution lacks the condemnatory or stigmatizing force attached to punishment. The point of punishment, on this view, is not only to restore the balance upset by the criminal but also to express society's conviction that the offender has done something grievously wrong. Contrary to what Boonin argues, in other words, pure restitution does not fulfill the expressive or communicative function of punishment. At most, as I have

---

[82] Jeffrie G. Murphy, "Two Cheers for Vindictiveness," in his *Getting Even: Forgiveness and Its Limits* (New York: Oxford University Press, 2003), p. 19.
[83] Bennett, *The Apology Ritual*, p. 175.

pointed out, pure restitution can convey a sense of disapproval, but that falls short of the condemnation or censure of the culprit's actions. Anyone who holds a view akin to Hampton's—"retributive punishment is the defeat of the wrongdoer at the hands of the victim (either directly or indirectly through... the state) that symbolizes the correct relative value of wrongdoer and victim"[84]—will thus find restitution too weak a response to criminal wrongdoing.

The general response to this complaint is that it overlooks the possibilities of blending punishment with restitution. This blend may be achieved in several ways. First, we can make restitution intentionally painful, so that a stigma is likely to attach to anyone who is required by law to make restitution to his victims. Beyond that, many criminals will have to be imprisoned for at least part of the time in which they are working to make restitution for their crimes, so they should feel social condemnation as much as those now incarcerated do. If punitive restitution is the goal, moreover, the distinction between crimes and torts must be preserved. To do this, the doctrine of *mens rea* will have to be invoked to justify the use of punitive restitution. In such a system the person who accidentally breaks a window will have to make good the loss, but the person who maliciously breaks a window will have to make good the loss of the window and suffer punishment as well. Such punishment could take a number of forms, such as serving time in jail, paying a fine, or wearing a scarlet V (for vandal) for a period of time. The point, in any case, is that punitive restitution will always go beyond restitution to the specific victim(s) of the crime, and in doing so it can incorporate the expression of social condemnation. Punitive restitution thus combines Hampton's emphasis on expressive retribution—that is, of the desire for immediate victims and the polity as a whole to make a statement about those who arrogate to themselves the privileges of the criminal—with Duff's desire to induce "secular penance" within offenders, and thus to promote the possibility of their reintegration into society.

A further point in this connection relates to the previously noted fact that the adverse effects of crime typically spread far beyond its direct victims. If we require criminals to make restitution to *all* of the victims of their crimes, there will be many victims whom we cannot even identify. On the fair-play theory, every law-abiding citizen is in a sense a victim of those who renounce the burdens of self-restraint while continuing to enjoy the benefits of the rule of law. But how is the criminal's debt to society to be exacted if restitution is taken to be a major element in the payment of that debt? One answer is by

---

[84] Jeffrie Murphy and Jean Hampton, *Forgiveness and Mercy* (Cambridge, UK: Cambridge University Press, 1988), p. 125.

way of fines that contribute to the polity's coffers; another is by way of community service of some sort. The latter will not work in all cases, to be sure, but in many it will provide an opportunity for someone who has broken the law to return something of value to the polity. The window-breaking vandal should not only make good the losses of the window's owner, for example, but also help to repair broken windows at a local school or provide some similar service. Community service thus makes restitution to the indirect victims of crime and punishes the offender at the same time. In this respect punitive restitution offers something that neither pure restitution nor traditional forms of punishment can promise.

The answer to the first question, then, is yes, restitution and punishment are indeed compatible with each other. That conclusion, however, does not entail the compatibility of punitive restitution with the fair-play theory of punishment. At first glance, the relationship between the two may seem to be quite close, for the concern with treating everyone fairly, victims and offenders alike, is not only compatible with the desire to make whole the victim but downright congenial to it. If any theory of punishment is hospitable to the inclusion of restitutive schemes, one might think, surely it is the fair-play theory.

The challenge, though, comes from the other direction. As developed by David Hershenov, the complaint here is that fair-play theory may support the demand that criminals make restitution to their victims, but it cannot justify the punishment of criminals. For that justification, Hershenov argues, we must turn to his "atonement/debt theory" of punishment, which "provides a place for vindictiveness in our judicial system."[85] If his criticism is well founded, then we must conclude that—contrary to what I have been arguing—fair play may underpin restitution, but only in its *pure* rather than its *punitive* form.

Hershenov's critique of the fair-play approach proceeds along two lines, one conceptual and general, and the other concentrating on supposed inadequacies in Morris's formulation of fair-play theory in "Persons and Punishment." According to the first line of criticism, the metaphors on which the fair-play approach to punishment relies—"[c]laims about fairness, debt payments, and the restoration of a pre-crime equilibrium"—properly "belong to the vocabulary of restitution and do not cohere very well with the language of retribution. Inevitably, a tension will result because retributivism is concerned with primarily giving the wicked what they deserve, punishing them just because they intentionally did something wrong."[86] But there are two problems with this conceptual point. First, it is not at all clear that the "tension" Hershenov points to is "inevitable." In

---

[85] Hershenov, "Restitution and Revenge," *Journal of Philosophy* 96 (1999): 79–94, at p. 79.
[86] Ibid., p. 80.

fact, Morris and other fair-play theorists will readily agree that it is right to give the wicked what they deserve and to punish them because they intentionally did something wrong. Of course, the fair-play theorist will add, there is more to the story than that. If we are to exact retribution from wrongdoers, we must have some idea of what wrongdoers *deserve* and of what counts as a punishable *wrong*, and the appeal to fair play provides the best explication of those ideas. But that is to say that the relationship of fair-play theory to retributivism is more a matter of "hand in glove" than of inevitable and presumably hostile tension.

The second problem with Hershenov's conceptual argument is that, from an etymological standpoint, his claim is simply false. In English, according to Dennis Klimchuk, retribution originally "meant repayment, and until at least the early nineteenth century, did not necessarily carry the sense of repayment for wrongdoing (though that sense goes back at least as far as Hobbes).... [T]he fact [is] that the idea Hershenov opposes to retributivism has long been closely associated with it."[87] On neither etymological nor more broadly conceptual grounds, then, is there support for the claim that the metaphors invoked by fair-play theorists deny them the possibility of advocating both restitution and punishment—and, therefore, punitive restitution.

Hershenov could concede this point, however, and still press his second line of criticism, according to which the flaws of fair-play theory prevent it from serving as an adequate account of punitive restitution. In this case, the complaint is that the fair-play approach is unsatisfactory from the standpoint of restitution. Here we may distinguish three arguments.

To begin with, Hershenov objects that Morris's emphasis on the fair distribution of benefits and burdens within a legal system cannot provide a sensible account of the compensation owed by offenders to law-abiding citizens. If law-abiding citizens have a duty not to harm innocent persons, why does the person who violates this duty owe anything to the law-abiding citizens he has not harmed? If he is caught, convicted, and punished,

> how does his suffering compensate them for what they have lost out on? ... The answer must be that Morris just believes that since the law abiding have such a strong interest in the fair distribution of burdens, they will just feel better, and thus it could be said that they have been compensated, when someone who dodged his fair share of burdens eventually receives it.[88]

---

[87] Klimchuk, "Retribution, Restitution, and Revenge," pp. 85–86. Note also Klimchuk's two reasons why retributivism "might naturally enough be articulated in the vocabulary of debts, repayment, and the like" (ibid., pp. 86–87).

[88] Hershenov, "Restitution and Revenge," pp. 81–82.

Part of the response to this objection is that we should not be too quick to discount the importance of *feeling better* as a form of compensation. To be sure, the sadistic enjoyment of someone else's suffering ought not to be applauded or endorsed, but that is hardly the only form that feeling better may take. One way in which people often feel better is when they feel more secure; another is when they gain *assurance* that their rights and interests are being protected. Among these rights and interests are those that are intimately connected to the preservation of fair play within a cooperative practice—in this case, the sense that the law-abiding citizen is not simply the prey of those who will free ride, double-cross, and otherwise take advantage of the opportunities and benefits that the cooperative meta-practice of the polity makes possible. If it is not always easy to see how feeling better grounded in assurance serves as *compensation* to the law-abiding citizen, it may help to remember that the aim of punishment (or punitive restitution) on the fair-play approach is to *restore the balance* among the members of the polity—a point that Hershenov notes, as we have seen, when he claims that "the restoration of a pre-crime equilibrium" is one of the metaphors that places Morris's account within the vocabulary of restitution rather than retribution.

Hershenov's second objection is that Morris's benefits-and-burdens justification of punishment overlooks the real victim of unfairness. Punishment may impose on the criminal "a burden that he unfairly avoided by not restraining himself," but "the actual victim of his assault or deceit is still left far worse off than he. She has not received any tangible compensatory payment for the burdens his wrongdoing unfairly placed on her."[89] As a statement about what Morris includes in his formulation of the fair-play theory, what Hershenov says here is correct. But that is not to say that the theory *excludes* the possibility of providing such "tangible compensatory payment" to the "actual" victims of crime. Indeed, the emphasis on fair play and restoring the balance, as I have been arguing, points toward the inclusion of "tangible compensatory payment" to victims who have suffered tangible losses, and thus toward a fair-play theory of punitive restitution.

Hershenov's third objection calls for much the same response. In this case, his claim is that Morris's account of unfairness to law-abiding citizens is misplaced. That is, Morris maintains that criminals take unfair advantage of law-abiding citizens by ignoring the restraints that law imposes and that law-abiding citizens respect. But the "real unfairness," according to Hershenov, is that those who obey the law must bear the tangible costs of protection against criminal wrongdoers in the forms of high taxes that pay for police forces, purchasing

---

[89] Ibid., p. 82.

security systems and insurance, and anxiety. Given these costs, "it would seem that merely bestowing upon any criminal the burdens he avoided provides inadequate compensation."[90] And so it might. Again, however, there is nothing in Morris's formulation of fair-play theory that rules out requiring criminals to make restitution to their victims. One may even argue—as I have been doing—that requiring restitution is a natural extension of the fair-play approach to punishment. Moreover, one may also argue that the kinds of unfair costs Hershenov identifies are themselves specific instances of the general unfairness that Morris says the law-abiding suffer at the hands of criminal offenders. If would-be offenders did restrain themselves, the burdens of obeying the law—and paying taxes for the provision of law enforcement—would be much lighter than they are. The kind of unfairness that Morris identifies, in short, may be more abstract than the kind Hershenov points to, but it is no less "real."

The conclusion, then, is that fair-play theory affords the basis for a system of punitive restitution that does not suffer from the inadequacies Hershenov identifies. On the contrary, it speaks directly, and helpfully, to one of the persistent problems of punishment—that is, the problem of doing justice to the victims of crime.

Felons, Fair Play, and the Franchise

Of the four problems of punishment discussed in this chapter, the final one should require the least attention here. That is not because this problem is less significant or interesting than the others, for it is not. In fact, the question of whether felons and ex-felons should retain their voting rights has attracted considerable attention, scholarly and otherwise, in recent years.[91] The connection to fair play seems more straightforward in this case, however, and the elaboration of fair-play theory associated with the three previous topics—mass incarceration, the recidivist premium, and restitution to the victims of crime—should limit the need for further elaboration here. For these reasons, we may proceed more swiftly with the question of how the fair-play approach to punishment applies to the case of felons and the franchise.

The first point to note in this regard is one already stated in Part 1 of this chapter. Given its fundamental emphasis on fair treatment within a cooperative practice and the related intention of restoring offenders to full membership

---

[90] Ibid., pp. 82–83.

[91] For brief but valuable surveys of the ethical and legal issues involved, see Richard Lippke, "The Disenfranchisement of Felons," *Law and Philosophy* 20 (2001): 553–80; and Mary Sigler, "Defensible Disenfranchisement," *Iowa Law Review* 99 (2014): 1725–44.

within such a practice, fair-play theory cannot condone the policy of depriving ex-felons—that is, citizens who have been convicted of a serious crime and subsequently completed their sentences—of the right to vote. Fair play is a retributivist theory, but it also has its forward-looking and communicative aspects. Those who break the law deserve punishment, *ceteris paribus*, but the terms of punishment should be such as to assure everyone that the cooperative meta-practice of the polity remains intact and that offenders have some chance of regaining full participation in it. From the retributive standpoint, in fact, considerations of fair play enable us to see that what the offender *deserves* is the full restoration of his rights, including voting rights, upon the completion of his sentence. If there are exceptions to this rule, it is only because there may be some offenses so heinous as to require permanent exclusion from the polity, either in the form of capital punishment or of a life sentence. Aside from such possibilities, it is only fair to restore the franchise to anyone who, having lost them while imprisoned, has now completed his sentence.

For fair-play theorists, the more interesting question is whether felons should be deprived of the franchise *while* they are imprisoned. My view is that they should, but there seems to be room for disagreement among fair-play theorists in this regard. Before addressing that disagreement, though, we should attend to the question of whether denying prisoners the vote is a matter of punishing them at all.

This question arises because of a distinction some scholars draw between losing the vote as a result of *disqualification* and losing it as a form of punishment. According to John Deigh, someone who commits a serious crime typically disqualifies himself "from being a legislator or elector," for the crime "shows him to be unfit for assuming the responsibilities of either office, and for this reason he forfeits its essential right [i.e., the vote]."[92] Disqualification, however, differs from punishment because it follows not from wrongdoing but from becoming "unfit or incompetent to meet the responsibilities that go with the right."[93] Mary Sigler also contends that the loss of voting rights is a matter of disqualification that "should not be mistaken for punishment," but regarded instead as "a regulatory counterpart to the institution of criminal punishment."[94] For Sigler, moreover, depriving felons of the right to vote while imprisoned is justified, save for the reference to "disqualification," in terms quite congenial to fair-play theory: "a standard term of disqualification is appropriate to mark the breach of civic trust and to give an offender the chance to reassure the community that he is once

---

[92] Deigh, "On Rights and Responsibilities," *Law and Philosophy* 7 (1988): 147–78, at p. 158.
[93] Ibid., p. 158.
[94] Sigler, "Defensible Disenfranchisement," p. 1737 and p. 1744.

again worthy of its trust."[95] Even Deigh's briefer account, with its emphasis on the offender's becoming "unfit" to vote, is compatible with the claim that those whose lawbreaking counts as a failure to play fair thereby forfeit their voting rights. Why not, then, simply regard the policy of depriving convicted felons of the franchise not as punishment but as a form of regulatory disqualification that complements truly punitive measures?

The answer to this question is that the distinction between disqualification and punishment is neither precise nor powerful enough to rule out denial of the franchise as a form of punishment. That much should be obvious from a consideration of the kinds of regulations that establish voting qualifications, such as age, residency, and citizenship requirements, and the ways in which a qualified voter may become disqualified. The most common cause of disqualification in these respects is likely to be change of residence, for few people renounce or otherwise lose their citizenship at present, and no one is disqualified from voting, so far as I am aware, for being too old. Many people are disqualified from voting in one or more electoral districts, however, when they move from one residence to another. If I were to move from my residence in Virginia to the neighboring state of Maryland, I would lose the right to vote in every election for which I am currently eligible—and there are at least seven of them—except for the presidency of the United States. To be sure, I would gain the right to vote in corresponding elections in Maryland, but I would become, to use Deigh's term, "unfit" to be a voter in Virginia. Barring unusual circumstances, though, no one would regard me as acting in a reprehensible or blameworthy manner were I to move to Maryland. Indeed, the difference between the voter who is disqualified by moving to another state and the one who is disqualified temporarily for committing a serious crime is striking. Both may be "unfit" to vote, but the reasons for their unfitness are remarkably different. So too are the reactions to them, for only one of these two kinds of disqualification is taken to be the result of the kind of unfitness that deserves censure. We may not congratulate people for moving from one state or electoral district to another, but neither do we condemn them as a matter of course; they may, furthermore, surrender the franchise in one district only to take it up in another. For those who are disqualified by their crimes, in contrast, their condemnation is marked in part by the fact that, in addition to losing the vote in their home districts, there are no voting rights for them in the districts in which they are imprisoned.

To put the point succinctly, there is a difference between what we may call *innocent* and *culpable* disqualification. Someone who is disqualified from a sporting league because she is now too old or has graduated from the school that

---

[95] Ibid., p. 1743.

sponsors her team is an example of the first kind; someone who is disqualified because of repeated or egregious cheating is an example of the second. Innocent disqualification may not be a form of punishment, but culpable disqualification certainly is. It is, first, in keeping with the definition of punishment as intentionally imposed suffering, for the person who is banished from a game or series of games or from the league altogether is meant to feel some pain as a result. Culpable disqualification also is in keeping with the communicative aspect of punishment, for it sends a message to both the offender and others of the importance of fair play. If the polity is analogous in this regard to the sports league, as I have argued, then there is every reason to regard culpable disqualification as a form of punishment.

Deigh, though, has a further argument against the claim that the forfeiture of voting rights is a form of punishment. If it were, he says, then those who determine the severity of punishment for a criminal offense would take the loss of the offender's vote into account when deciding upon the proper sentence; but there is no evidence that anyone weighs the loss of the franchise in the balance when punishments are determined. Moreover, a "citizen who commits a crime does not as a rule receive a shorter term in prison or a smaller fine than a resident alien who commits the same crime, which justice would require if forfeiture of voting rights were part of the citizen's punishment."[96] The fact that we do not adjust the citizen's sentence to reflect the punitive value of depriving him of the vote thus indicates that this deprivation is a matter of disqualification rather than punishment.

In response to this argument, I maintain that we are doing justice here by treating the citizen more severely than the resident alien. That is, the citizen may have committed the same crime as the resident alien, but he violated his "civic trust," to use Sigler's term, in a way that the resident alien did not. Therefore, it is fitting to punish him not only with a prison sentence but also with the loss of the vote. As participants in the cooperative meta-practice of the polity who have a claim to be regarded as citizens-in-the-making, resident aliens have a responsibility to play fair with the other members of the polity by obeying the law. Failure to do so makes them subject, on the fair-play account, to punishment just as does a citizen's similar failure. Nevertheless, the citizen holds a civic position that grants her something, the franchise, the resident alien does not (yet) have. For that reason, depriving her of the vote while she is imprisoned is not a departure from justice, or a disqualification in addition to her punishment, but an element of her just punishment.

That being so, the final consideration from the fair-play perspective is whether denying felons the vote during their imprisonment will prove to be efficacious.

---

[96] Deigh, "On Rights and Responsibilities," p. 158, n. 17.

In this case, as I said in Part 1 of this chapter, I do not think that there is a definitive answer. In general, it seems safe to say that the threat of losing one's voting rights is not likely to serve as a significant deterrent to crime, not even the kinds of crime that are coolly and carefully planned. The possibility remains, though, that loss of the franchise may prove efficacious to some extent as a form of condemnation that brings the civic dimension of crime to the attention of offenders and law-abiding citizens alike.[97] It does so, moreover, in a way that keeps open the prospect of restoration to full membership in the polity. Sigler puts the point nicely, albeit with respect to disqualification rather than punishment: "the temporary loss of a citizen's right to vote dramatically conveys the significance of the breach of civic trust that serious crime represents without practically impairing an offender's prospects for rehabilitation."[98] There may even be some reason to think that the prospect of regaining the franchise will encourage some serious offenders to appreciate what they can regain—and should no longer risk losing—at the end of their punishment.

But why wait? If the franchise is important as a sign of one's standing in the polity, why not take advantage of it while the felon is imprisoned? Perhaps what fair play requires is an effort to keep criminal offenders engaged to some extent in the polity while they undergo punishment. Allowing them to vote while they are being punished in other ways may well do more to foster the sense of civic connection and fair play than denying them the vote could do. Indeed, it may be the case that depriving a prisoner of the franchise will have the effect of "symbolically confirming his suspension from society and promoting the idea that society is an other to him that desires separation."[99]

Perhaps it will. All we have here is speculation, however, and there is, so far as I am aware, no way of determining whether depriving felons of the vote will prove more or less efficacious than allowing them to retain it while serving their sentences. My own view is that the communication of civic censure ought to be conveyed as clearly as possible, and denying serious offenders their voting rights is warranted as a proper means of conveying this censure. Still, fair-play theory does not require that felons lose the vote while imprisoned. It only requires that we regard culpable disqualification from voting as a form of punishment that cannot fairly be extended beyond the other terms of the offender's sentence.

---

[97] Consider in this regard the lawsuit, discussed in chap. 5, in which Jean Hampton testified as an expert witness—a suit filed by Canadians who sought to retain their voting rights while imprisoned.

[98] Sigler, "Defensible Disenfranchisement," p. 1744.

[99] Thom Brooks, *Punishment* (New York: Routledge, 2012), p. 214. Brooks reaches this judgment from within his "stakeholder" framework, but the same reasoning could fit within the fair-play approach to punishment.

Conclusion

Nothing I have written in this lengthy chapter constitutes the last word on any of the four problems of punishment examined within it. Nor was it my intention to provide the definitive statement of what political and legal philosophers should think about mass incarceration, the recidivist premium, the relationship between punishment and restitution, or voting rights for felons. Definitive statements are probably impossible to find in any of these contexts, and certainly not four of them in the space of a single chapter. Nor have I attempted to cover all of the important problems of punishment in this chapter. I have not considered the question of whether capital punishment or solitary confinement is justified, for instance, or of how we should try to make the punishment fit the crime more generally. But that is not to say that what this chapter accomplishes is insignificant or hopelessly vague. To the contrary, the chapter provides answers to some important questions—Is it right to deprive felons of their right to vote once they have completed their sentences? Is the recidivist premium justified? Does it make sense to speak of *punitive* restitution?—and valuable guidance in other cases, such as how to approach the problem of mass incarceration. That should be enough to confirm the worth of fair-play theory not only as the proper justification of punishment but also as an approach to other difficult problems of punishment.

PART III

FAIR PLAY AND THE POLITY

8

Authority, Deference, and Fair Play

The preceding chapters present a unified theory of political obligation and punishment grounded in fair play that is, I hope, clear, coherent, and reasonably complete. If I have succeeded, those chapters have accomplished three of the four principal aims of this book. They also go some way, I believe, toward the accomplishment of the fourth and overarching aim, which is to show that the principle of fair play provides the basis for a *compelling* theory of political obligation and legal punishment. Two further challenges remain to be met, however, before that claim can be taken seriously, and meeting them is the aim of this chapter. According to the first of these challenges, a properly revised conception of political and legal authority must lead to the conclusion that there is no general obligation to obey the law; according to the second, what citizens owe to their polity is deference or respect to its laws, but not an obligation to obey them. In responding to these challenges, I shall not only be criticizing the arguments of those who have raised them but also pointing out their deficiencies from the standpoint of a theory that attends to both political obligation and the justification of punishment.

In a sense, these two challenges are themselves responses to the antecedent challenge of philosophical anarchism. In the case of authority, the standard or traditional account has long assumed a straightforward connection between political authority and political obligation. To have such authority is to have a right to rule, on this view, and those who are subject to "the authorities" have an obligation, *pro tanto* or *prima facie*, to obey the directives of those who have the right to rule. This has been the view, moreover, not only of those who believe that there is a general obligation of obedience but also of anarchists who do not. Straightforward anarchists have denied that anyone has an obligation to obey laws, of course, but they have done so because they have rejected all claims to political and legal authority. As we saw in Chapter 1, however, these "political anarchists" have been joined in recent decades by "philosophical anarchists," such as Robert Paul Wolff and John Simmons, who question the legitimacy of political authority and deny the existence of a general obligation to obey the law, but who nevertheless are content to let the state remain in place.[1] In the face of the philosophical anarchists' arguments, a number of philosophers have concluded that the connection between political authority and political obligation is neither as straightforward nor as strong as the standard account has assumed. Properly reconceived, they maintain, claims to the existence of political authority can withstand the criticisms of the philosophical anarchists, but this revised conception is one that entails no correlative obligation, on the part of those subject to authority, to obey its laws.

In the case of those who present the second challenge, the response to philosophical anarchism has been to reconceive the citizen's relationship to the laws of the polity. Confronting Wolff's claim that (1) authority is incompatible with autonomy because it entails an obligation to obey, so that (2) anyone who acknowledges such an obligation is surrendering her moral autonomy, has led such writers as William Edmundson, Ruth Higgins, and Philip Soper to argue that the citizen's duty is to display an attitude of deference or respect to the law, or perhaps to those whose charge is to administer it, rather than a straightforward obligation to obey it.[2] In this way, they seem to say, we can preserve the moral autonomy of the individual, who need not simply surrender her judgment to those who hold authority, without encouraging citizens to dismiss the laws as nothing more than a set of recommendations to consider before deciding how to act.

Neither of these responses to philosophical anarchism is, in my view, satisfactory. The proper response, as I stated in Chapter 1 and have tried to demonstrate in subsequent chapters, is two-fold: first, to rebut philosophical anarchism directly; and second, to elaborate a theory of political obligation, and of punishment, that can overcome the philosophical anarchists' criticisms of such theories. That two-fold response is now largely complete. What remains is to address, in this chapter, the challenges of those who have been lured by the prospect of finding some kind of middle ground between philosophical anarchism, on the one hand, and standard accounts of political obligation and authority, on the other.

---

[1] Wolff, *In Defense of Anarchism*, 3rd ed. (Berkeley and Los Angeles: University of California Press, 1998 [originally published 1970]); Simmons, *Moral Principles and Political Obligations* (Princeton, NJ: Princeton University Press, 1979), and *Justification and Legitimacy: Essays on Rights and Obligations* (Cambridge, UK: Cambridge University Press, 2001), esp. chap. 6, where Simmons draws the distinction between "political" and "philosophical" anarchists.

[2] Edmundson, *Three Anarchical Fallacies: An Essay on Political Authority* (Cambridge, UK: Cambridge University Press, 1998); Higgins, *The Moral Limits of Law: Obedience, Respect, and Legitimacy* (Oxford: Oxford University Press, 2004); and Soper, *The Ethics of Deference: Learning from Law's Morals* (Cambridge, UK: Cambridge University Press, 2002).

Authority, Legitimacy, and Political Obligation

According to those who think it necessary to revise the standard view, there are no good grounds for doubting the possibility and existence of political authority, but that is largely because the connection between authority and obligation is weaker than the traditional account holds or because there is no necessary connection between them at all. In their view, the fact that a group of people hold legitimate political authority does not entail a correlative obligation of obedience on the part of those subject to their rule. Those who are subject to authority may well find themselves under obligation, according to the revisionists, but it will not be an obligation to obey the laws issuing from the authorities simply because they are laws. There is more than one line of argument leading to this conclusion, however, and examining them all would take us too far from the main lines of the fair-play theory of political obligation and punishment. For that reason, I shall concentrate here on Joseph Raz's influential revisionist account of political and legal authority.[3] First, though, there are some conceptual matters to consider.

Conceptual Considerations

Discussions of political and legal authority typically acknowledge the difference between two kinds of authority. On the one hand, there is the kind that someone can *have*; on the other hand, there is the kind that someone can *be*. The two are not unrelated, of course. To *have* or *hold* a position of authority in the Society for American Baseball Research, for example, one almost certainly will need to *be* an authority on baseball. But there is no necessary connection between the position and the expertise, and no reason to think that someone who is *an* authority on a subject will be *in* authority over others. Nor, conversely, is there reason to think that someone who is in a position of authority must be an authority on anything at all. Although there frequently are competency standards that judges, police officers, and others in positions of authority must meet, these need not be so strict as to qualify anyone who meets them as an authority on the subject in question. Moreover, there are some ways of gaining positions of authority— inheritance, election, becoming a parent, and random selection among them— that require little if anything by way of authoritative mastery of a subject.

This distinction is often put in terms of a difference between *theoretical* and *practical* authority, with political authority generally taken to be a form of the

---

[3] I offer a fuller critique of revisionist accounts of authority in a forthcoming essay, "Authority, Legitimacy, and the Obligation to Obey the Law."

latter. There are those, though, who hold that political authority, while clearly practical in its concern for how people are to act, must—or should, at any rate—also partake of a considerable amount of theoretical authority. Plato's apparent argument in *The Republic* for rule by philosophers is a clear example, but so too is David Estlund's recent brief for the epistemic authority of democracy.[4] Even so, few philosophers have been inclined to collapse practical into theoretical authority, for doing so would require us to limit some commonly acknowledged forms of practical authority, such as parental authority, to those who possess the relevant theoretical qualifications.

Another common distinction is that between *de facto* and *de jure* authority. In this case the point is that someone may exercise authority to which he is not entitled or hold title to authority that she is not effectively able to wield. On some accounts *de facto* authority seems to be little more than brute power, but on most accounts it differs from power in that some degree of acceptance on the part of the subjects, rather than their mere acquiescence in the face of threats and violence, must be present. There may even be cases of complete acceptance on the part of the subjects, as when an impostor surreptitiously deposes the rightful ruler and assumes her place, thereby exercising *de facto* an authority to which the impostor has no title. Perhaps the most telling difference between power and *de facto* authority, though, is that the latter necessarily implies an appeal to *de jure* authority. Those who rule by sheer might need not concern themselves with questions of right or title; they can simply rule, as long as they are able, through force and intimidation. But when they lay claim to authority, they are necessarily appealing to some idea of rightful rule, which typically includes the claim that the subjects have a corresponding obligation. As Raz puts the point, "Having *de facto* authority is not just having an ability to influence people. It is coupled with a claim that those people are bound to obey."[5]

The other side of the coin here is that any claim to *de jure* authority also implies some degree of *de facto* authority. That is, no matter how clear a title to authority a group may have, it must be able to *exercise* authority to some extent if it is to retain its authority. If usurpers drive the group in question out of office and into a remote territory, so that no one in the homeland is in a position to follow the directives of those whom they continue to regard as their rightful governors, then the government in exile must either find a way to displace the usurpers or watch its authority dwindle away. Authority

---

[4] Estlund, *Democratic Authority: A Philosophical Framework* (Princeton, NJ: Princeton University Press, 2008).

[5] Raz, *The Morality of Freedom* (Oxford: Oxford University Press, 1986), pp. 27–28. See also A. John Simmons, *Boundaries of Authority* (Oxford: Oxford University Press, 2016), p. 17, n. 10.

must be effective not only to be *de facto*, in other words, but also to be *de jure*.⁶

According to many accounts, the distinction between *de facto* and *de jure* authority is congruent with the distinction between *authority* and *legitimacy*. Some writers do treat these words as virtual synonyms when they equate "those in authority" with "the legitimate government," but doing so makes a redundancy of the widely used phrase "legitimate authority." Other writers try to separate legitimacy from authority, as when Estlund defines authority as "the moral power to require or forbid action" and legitimacy as the morally permitted use of coercion, so that "a state's uses of power are legitimate if and only if they are morally permitted owing to the political process that produced them."⁷ For Estlund, then, legitimate authority combines the right to rule with permission to enforce that right by means of coercion. But that is a point one can agree to without accepting Estlund's distinction. If one takes 'authority' to mean having a moral right to rule, with that right including a right to use coercion, then to talk of "legitimate authority" is simply to reinforce the point that the authority in question is not merely *de facto* but also *de jure*—that is, genuine, real, or true authority. That, anyhow, is the sense in which I will use 'legitimate' and its cognates in this chapter.

Two final points to note with regard to political authority are that its directives are generally taken to be preemptive (or peremptory)⁸ in nature and content-independent. According to the first point, laws preempt or exclude any other reasons for action someone subject to their authority may have. If my parents or employer or church leaders tell me to do something that is contrary to the law, they give me reasons to break the law; but from the law's point of view, its directives preempt the others. That is not to say that people may never have decisive reasons, moral or prudential, for disobeying the law; it is to say that the law does not typically recognize these reasons.⁹ Moreover, the authority of laws, considered individually, does not depend upon their content. Law is binding because it issues from the proper authorities without regard to what its content

---

⁶ When I presented an earlier version of this chapter at a workshop, Bas van der Vossen objected that the existence of *de jure* authority is completely distinct from its effective exercise. The terms *de jure* and *de facto*, I admit, may be conceptually distinct in this way, but as a practical matter, for the reasons set out in the text and supported by the sources in the preceding note, they are not.

⁷ Estlund, *Democratic Authority*, p. 10 and p. 41.

⁸ For the distinction between preemptive and peremptory reasons, see Raz, *The Morality of Freedom*, p. 39. For a discussion that tends to undercut this distinction, see Scott Shapiro, "Authority," in *The Oxford Handbook of Jurisprudence and Philosophy of Law*, ed. Jules Coleman and Scott Shapiro (Oxford: Oxford University Press, 1986), pp. 406–408.

⁹ I say "typically recognize" to allow for the exceptional cases in which the law acknowledges that disobedience is justified or excused, perhaps because of duress or misunderstanding.

may be. There are some limits here associated with the idea of legality, such as strictures against directives that command the impossible or are not made public, but otherwise a law—at least on the standard or traditional account—is binding simply because it is the law. For Joseph Raz, however, matters are more complicated, and the obligation to obey less clear, than they are on the traditional account.

Raz's "Service Conception" of Authority

Raz's conception of authority rests on the belief that authority exists not for its own sake but to serve those who are subject to it. To anyone who asks why he should consider himself subject to some other person's authority, Raz's answer, in effect, is that a genuine authority is more likely than the questioner "to act correctly for the right reasons,"[10] and the questioner would do well to do as the authority says. One attractive feature of this "service conception" is thus the way it brings theoretical and practical authority more closely together. Once we acknowledge, for example, that a licensed physician is more likely to treat our ailments effectively than we can do on our own, we should go on to recognize that her theoretical authority confers practical authority over us within her field of expertise. In addition, as Scott Shapiro points out, Raz's service conception has a response to the two autonomy-based objections anarchists have raised against those who believe in the existence of political authority—that is, Why should I surrender my autonomy, in the sense of thinking and acting for myself, to someone else? And why should I violate the moral duty of autonomy by allowing someone else to think and act for me?[11] The answer, according to Raz's conception, is that you are not really surrendering your autonomy in these cases—not, that is, so long as the authority you are following is a genuine authority more likely "to act correctly for the right reasons" than you are likely to do on your own. Someone can have authority over another "only if there are sufficient reasons for the latter to be subject to duties at the say-so of the former."[12] Acknowledging the sufficiency of these reasons is not the same as surrendering one's autonomy.

Raz's explication of the service conception of authority in *The Morality of Freedom* proceeds by way of three theses, the first of which—the *preemptive*

---

[10] Raz, *The Morality of Freedom*, p. 61.

[11] Shapiro, "Authority," esp. §§ 1 and 3.4; but note that Shapiro refers to "paradoxes" of authority and autonomy rather than "objections."

[12] Raz, "The Problem of Authority: Revisiting the Service Conception," in Raz, *Between Authority and Interpretation: On the Theory of Law and Practical Reason* (Oxford: Oxford University Press, 2009), p. 136.

thesis—rests on the other two. The second is the *dependence thesis*, which states that "*all authoritative directives should be based on reasons which already independently apply to the subjects of the directives and are relevant to their action in the circumstances covered by the directive.*"[13] In subsequent work, Raz replaces this thesis with "the independence condition," but he also indicates that it is the remaining thesis that "provides the key to the justification of authority," so I shall follow common practice by concentrating on this third thesis.[14] According to this *normal justification thesis*,

> the normal way to establish that a person has authority over another person involves showing that the alleged subject is likely better to comply with reasons which apply to him (other than the alleged authoritative directives) if he accepts the directives of the alleged authority as authoritatively binding and tries to follow them, rather than by trying to follow the reasons which apply to him directly.[15]

When applied to specifically political authority, the service conception leads to a highly flexible and discriminating understanding of the scope of authority. "It all depends," as Raz says, "on the person over whom authority is supposed to be exercised: his knowledge, strength of will, his reliability in various aspects of life, and on the government in question."[16] Thus the expertise of those who work for our government's drug-regulation agency will place most of us under its authority, but not those who themselves are expert pharmacologists; the expert pharmacologists will be under the government's authority with regard to the roadworthiness of their cars, but expert mechanics will not; and so on. The result is "a very discriminating approach to the question" of how far the authority of the government may extend: "The government may have only some of the authority it claims, it may have more authority over one person than another."[17] Instead of providing an account of unified political authority,

> the normal justification thesis invites a piecemeal approach to the question of the authority of governments, which yields the conclusion

---

[13] Raz, *The Morality of Freedom*, p. 47; emphasis in original.

[14] Raz, "The Problem of Authority: Revisiting the Service Conception," p. 139.

[15] Raz, *The Morality of Freedom*, p. 53; emphasis in original. In "The Problem of Authority: Revisiting the Service Conception, pp. 136–37, Raz says that the normal justification thesis (or condition) will be met when "the subject would better conform to reasons that apply to him anyway (that is, to reasons other than the directives of the authority) if he intends to be guided by the authority's directives than if he does not...."

[16] Raz, *The Morality of Freedom*, p. 73.

[17] Ibid., p. 74.

that the extent of governmental authority varies from individual to individual, and is more limited than the authority governments claim for themselves in the case of most people.[18]

I shall return to Raz's "piecemeal approach" shortly, but it is important first to note its implications for the relationship of political authority to political obligation. Like the other revisionists, Raz denies that the citizens of even a reasonably just society have a general obligation to obey the law. Even a "qualified recognition of authority" as "the authority of just governments to impose prima facie obligations on their subjects cannot be supported by the argument of the normal justification thesis."[19] To be sure, Raz does acknowledge that there is "probably a common core of cases regarding which the obligation exists and applies equally to all," such as the duty to pay taxes and other duties that follow from the coordinative functions of government.[20] Otherwise, the piecemeal effect of the normal justification thesis blocks the possibility of even a *pro tanto* obligation on the part of every citizen to obey every law in even a reasonably just polity.

Raz's service conception has proved to be both highly influential and highly controversial, with critics claiming that it captures some important aspects of authority but not others. Three criticisms are of particular significance here. The first is that the service conception scants the official—that is, office-holding or institutional—aspect of political authority. As Jeremy Waldron states, taking the normal justification thesis "as a sufficient condition of A's having authority over C ... would imply that millions of people have authority over each one of us." It might even follow that the US Conference of Catholic Bishops, which "produced several powerful and illuminating statements" on welfare reform in the 1980s and 1990s, held authority over the US Congress, which made "disastrously unjust decisions about welfare reform" in that period.[21] Such a conclusion might be acceptable, Waldron says, if we were talking only of *moral* authority, or if we were to say that the Catholic bishops *ought* to have authority over Congress. No doubt there are many who would make such judgments today with regard to the Intergovernmental Panel on Climate Change and the US Congress, but that is quite far from holding that the Conference of Catholic Bishops or the IPCC really does have authority over Congress.

---

[18] Ibid., p. 80.

[19] Ibid., p. 77.

[20] Raz, "The Obligation to Obey: Revision and Tradition," in Raz, *Ethics in the Public Domain* (Oxford: Oxford University Press, 1994), p. 350.

[21] Waldron, "Authority for Officials," in *Rights, Culture, and the Law: Themes from the Legal and Political Philosophy of Joseph Raz*, eds. L. H. Meyer, S. L. Paulson, and T. W. Pogge (Oxford: Oxford University Press, 2003), p. 63. For Raz's response, see pp. 259–64 of the same volume.

The second criticism concerns the piecemeal nature of political authority as the service conception defines it. As we have seen, Raz takes this to be a strength of his conception of political authority, but others regard it as a serious weakness. One critic, Thomas Christiano, argues that "the instrumentalist and piecemeal nature of authority on this account allows it to attribute legitimate authority to ferociously unjust regimes."[22] Another, Christopher Bennett, objects that "the most basic idea of a legitimate authority is that of a governing body whose subjects have a duty to obey it by virtue of its *position* rather than because of the piecemeal helpfulness of following its dictates."[23] To put the point a bit differently, those who hold political authority are supposed to exercise authority over the members of a polity *qua* members, not in their several capacities as pharmacologists, automobile mechanics, computer programmers, plumbers, and so on. To appreciate how the service conception deviates from this systemic understanding of political authority, one need only envision Citizen A explaining to Citizen B why B has a duty to obey a law that A is free to ignore. If that circumstance is not sufficiently embarrassing for proponents of the service conception, we might ask them to explain how their theory of punishment would apply to B and A if both broke the same law. Should both be punished equally even though only one of them was subject to the authority of the law in question? Or should B alone be punished even though A committed the same offense? If punishing only B is the correct answer, is it because he is guilty, unlike A, of the offense of thinking that he is not subject to authority when he really is? These are, at best, awkward questions for the advocates of the service conception.

The third criticism is that the service conception fails to take disagreement and democracy seriously. If we follow the normal justification thesis, the purpose of political authority is not so much to reconcile those who disagree with one another, or to bring order out of conflicting opinions, as it is to find the right answers to questions of practical reason. On this view, Christiano objects, disagreement may simply be taken to indicate "that people's false political views have no direct relation to what they or we have in fact reason to do."[24] Nor is there room for the view, as Shapiro says, that "democratic procedures are capable of possessing legitimate authority because they represent power-sharing arrangements that are fair."[25] If democratic procedures have any value at all in

---

[22] Christiano, *The Constitution of Equality: Democratic Authority and Its Limits* (Oxford: Oxford University Press, 2008), p. 233. See also Christiano's exchange with Steven Wall on this point in *Journal of Political Philosophy* 14 (2006): 85–110.

[23] Bennett, "Expressive Punishment and Political Authority," *Ohio State Journal of Criminal Law* 8 (2011): 296.

[24] Christiano, *The Constitution of Equality*, p. 234.

[25] Shapiro, "Authority," p. 432.

the service conception of authority, it is because they serve practical reason by helping to elucidate the reasons that rightly apply to people who must live together. But there are reasons for thinking that there are features of democracy—features relating to equality, autonomy, and fair play—that not only give it the instrumental value that the service conception recognizes but also endow it with what Christiano calls "*inherent authority*."[26] This, however, is a dimension of authority that the service conception fails to capture.

None of this is to say that Raz has completely misconstrued authority, political or otherwise. On the contrary, the service conception probably does more to clarify the relationship of authority to practical reason than any other conception of authority has done. It also goes far toward explaining why possession of *de facto* authority is necessary to the possession of *de jure* authority. But the service conception has its shortcomings too, as the three criticisms I have called attention to attest. Chief among these is its inability to provide a satisfactory account of the relationship between political authority and the polity itself. Because that account is unsatisfactory, there is also reason to suspect Raz's dismissive conclusions about the possibility of a general obligation to obey the law—an obligation that is at the foundation of the justification of punishment. We should conclude, then, that it is not yet time to give up on the traditional account of their relationship.

Defending the Traditional Account via Fair Play

Pointing out defects in revisionists' accounts of authority is not sufficient, of course, to demonstrate the virtues of the traditional account. Indeed, it is possible that the criticisms above could serve only to encourage the anarchists, philosophical and otherwise, who reject both political authority and obligation. Something more needs to be added to the criticisms, then, if we are to mount a proper defense of the traditional account. But that "something more" is already available in the form of the fair-play theory of political obligation and punishment elaborated and defended in the first two parts of this book. All that seems necessary here is a brief indication of how the fair-play theory of political obligation provides a sturdy foundation for the traditional account.

Fair-play theory adheres to the traditional understanding of the relationship between political authority and obligation in the following way. A reasonably just polity is a cooperative practice that centers on the rule of law, understood as a public good that is not only presumptively beneficial, to use George Klosko's

---

[26] Christiano, *The Constitution of Equality*, p. 241; emphasis in original. See also Shapiro, "Authority," p. 432.

term, but also generally accepted in various ways in the daily lives of members of the polity.[27] For the rule of law to take form and to persist, however, authority is necessary. Those who hold and exercise this authority have the right to rule, subject to the limitations of the rule of law and considerations of fair play, with this being a claim-right that entails a correlative obligation of obedience on the part of those who are subject to their authority. This obligation, in turn, is a defeasible but general obligation to obey the law *as such*.

This obligation, in fair-play theory as in in the traditional account, is a preemptive or content-independent obligation, with morally binding force. How strong that force is will vary from one law to another, and we may occasionally need to examine the content of individual laws to determine whether there are moral reasons that require disobedience rather than obedience. That is why the obligation to obey particular laws is *prima facie* or *pro tanto*. But political obligation is the obligation to obey the law as such of a reasonably just polity, and that obligation is grounded in a single principle: the principle of fair play. This is an obligation, furthermore, that is not owed to the state or government or authorities as such but to the cooperating members of the polity. Nor is it a free-floating duty—that is, a moral requirement "not owed to any agent" that does not "correspond . . . to rights"—of the kind that one revisionist, David Copp, distinguishes from an obligation.[28] Whether we speak of an obligation or a duty to these other entities, it is only as a shorthand way of acknowledging that offices, institutions, and authority are necessary to sustain a cooperative practice under the rule of law—or, more precisely, to sustain the cooperative meta-practice of the polity.

Sustaining the polity, finally, requires securing it from the threats of those who would take its benefits while shirking, when possible, its burdens. That is why the polity gives some of its members the authority to detect, arrest, and punish those who do not respect the persons, property, and promises of the other members of the meta-practice. Insofar as the offender enjoys the benefits of the cooperative meta-practice without fully contributing to their provision by bearing her share of the burdens of obeying the law, then the offender in effect justifies the rest of us in punishing her. In doing so, the polity communicates its censure to the offender by means of punishment and aims at the maintenance of cooperative fair play. How severely to punish, or whether a mere remonstrance will be sufficient, is a judgment that will have to vary with the severity of the crime and other circumstances, as we have seen in previous chapters. But the *authority* to punish rests on the polity's commitment to fair play within the rule of law.

---

[27] Klosko, *The Principle of Fairness and Political Obligation* (Lanham, MD: Rowman & Littlefield, 1992), esp. pp. 39–48.

[28] Copp, "The Idea of a Legitimate State," *Philosophy and Public Affairs* 28 (1999): 10–11.

To tie this discussion of fair-play theory back to Raz's service conception, it may help to consider Shapiro's valuable distinction between two ways in which authorities can serve their subjects. One is by *mediation* between reasons and persons—that is, "by enabling subjects to achieve benefits that they would not have been able to achieve without the [authorities'] directives." The other is by *arbitration* between rival parties—that is, serving subjects "by providing them with a way to resolve their disputes on normative matters."[29] In the end, Shapiro concludes that the arbitration model is the more satisfactory of the two, and he does so for reasons consistent with arguments presented in this chapter in defense of the traditional account of political authority and obligation. Indeed, he draws the following summary contrast between the two models: "In the Mediation Model, obedience itself is instrumentally valuable. In the Arbitration Model, the parties do not benefit through their obedience. Obedience, rather, is the moral *price* that parties must pay in order to secure the compliance of others."[30]

As Shapiro's contrast suggests, and as he explicitly acknowledges on the same page, Shapiro takes fair-play theory to fall under the arbitration model. I believe that he is right to do so. I also think that the connection he goes on to draw between the arbitration model and democracy is correct, insofar as "deference to democratically elected authority under conditions of meaningful freedom is deference to a power-sharing arrangement that is *socially necessary, empowering*, and *fair*."[31] I quarrel, though, with two features of Shapiro's assessment: first, that arbitration must be understood as arbitration between "rival parties"; and second, that "the parties do not benefit through their obedience." According to the fair-play theory, the parties engaged in the cooperative practice are rivals upon occasion, to be sure; if they were not, they would not need laws and authorities to settle their disputes. But their rivalry is within the framework of a cooperative practice in which there will be reason to see one another as fellow participants. Moreover, the parties will benefit through their obedience overall even if they see themselves as paying a *price* from time to time, as Shapiro says. But they should also understand, upon reflection, that they cannot have the long-term benefits of the cooperative practice without bearing its burdens. Suitably modified, in sum, Shapiro's arbitration model is a helpful way to conceive of the traditional account of political authority and obligation that is more than hospitable to the argument from fair play—and a marked improvement over the service conception of authority.

---

[29] Shapiro, "Authority," pp. 432–33.
[30] Ibid., p. 433; emphasis in original.
[31] Ibid., p. 435; emphasis in original.

The Deferential Turn

What, though, of the second challenge to the fair-play theory of political obligation and punishment noted at the beginning of this chapter? Broadly speaking, the writers who have pressed this challenge believe that the best chance of justifying the claim that citizens ought, in general, to obey the law is to take an indirect route. That is, rather than arguing for a direct obligation to obey, these philosophers hold that obedience to the law is justified indirectly by an appeal to respect or deference. Citizens and subjects should obey the law not because they have an obligation to do so, in other words, but because they owe respect or deference to the law, or perhaps to those who administer it. Like the philosophers who have urged a revision of the standard account of political authority, those who have taken the deferential turn have sought a kind of middle ground between philosophical anarchism and political obligation. If it appears, as Wolff has argued, that acknowledging an obligation to obey those who hold authority is to surrender one's moral autonomy, then why not settle for a way to grant political or legal authority its due, in the form of deference or respect, while preserving the autonomous character of the citizen?

My argument in the remainder of this chapter is that this deferential turn leads into a blind alley. Deference and respect are good things in their proper places, to be sure, but they are not sufficient in themselves to provide an answer to the problem of political obligation. Nor is the deferential turn capable of producing a satisfactory middle ground that reconciles the claims of philosophical anarchism with those of legal authority, especially when we recognize that such authority is necessary to the justification of punishment. To sustain these conclusions, I shall examine the arguments for deference and respect advanced in Philip Soper's *The Ethics of Deference* and Ruth C. A. Higgins's *The Moral Limits of Law*. Both books are rich in insight and subtle argument, but neither, I shall try to show, succeeds in establishing the middle ground it seeks.[32]

---

[32] As indicated at the beginning of this chapter, William Edmundson's *Three Anarchical Fallacies* is another example of what I am calling the deferential turn, and it is equally worthy of attention. I have examined Edmundson's arguments at some length, however, in my "Philosophical Anarchism and Its Fallacies," *Law and Philosophy* 19 (2000): 396–403, and for reasons of space will not consider them here. Edmundson's argument in favor of treating the inclination to obey the law as a virtue to be cultivated rather than an obligation to be fulfilled seems to be another form of this deferential turn, albeit one that is fully compatible with a continued belief in the existence of political obligation. See Edmundson, "The Virtue of Law-Abidance," *Philosophers' Imprint* 6 (2006): 1–21.

Soper's Appeal to Deference

Of the two advocates of the deferential turn to be considered here, Soper's position is the closer to traditional defenses of political obligation, for he holds both that political authority entails a right to be obeyed and that those who are subject to legitimate authority have an obligation to obey the law. He departs from the traditional stance, however, by grounding the obligation to obey in deference. As Soper says,

> The question of why I should *defer* to the norms of the state is answered by reminding myself of the point of the state and the sense in which it represents values that I, too, endorse. The state is necessary, and it is the kind of entity that requires some to govern, in good faith, on behalf of all. Thus I, who could do no different were I in charge, have a prima facie reason to do as I would expect others in my situation to do.[33]

By appealing to deference, Soper hopes to resolve the conflict between the claims of the law and those of individual conscience. As individuals, we have both reason and right to think and decide for ourselves; if the law requires us to do what we believe to be wrong, we need not conclude that the law is right. But we are also social beings, and as such we must recognize that we need some agent or agency to settle the disputes that inevitably will arise when individual consciences do not all lead to the same answers or judgments. That is why we need to remind ourselves, in Soper's words, "of the point of the state and the sense in which it represents values that I, too, endorse." Once reminded, though, we need not *surrender* our individual conscience or judgment to the state; we need only *defer* to it. Where the law is concerned, deference consists in obedience, or at least the kind of obedience that recognizes a *prima facie* but defeasible obligation to obey.

This conclusion I find appealing, for it is much the same as the conclusion my account of the fair-play theory of political obligation reaches. The chief difference, of course, is Soper's appeal to deference. The question that must arise, then, is whether deference is really doing any useful work here. There are two reasons to think it is not.

First, there are dangers in the appeal to deference. Deference is no doubt a good thing in some circumstances and relationships, but it also can be taken too far—as it is when citizens become excessively deferential to those in authority. Higgins makes this point when she observes, in a comment on Soper's argument,

---

[33] Soper, *The Ethics of Deference*, p. 167; emphasis in original. Further citations to this book will appear in parentheses in the body of the text.

"We must first ascertain the appropriateness of deference before consistency to it exercises any moral appeal."[34] To be sure, Soper is aware of this danger, which he dubs "the dark side of deference," but he has no remedy for it other than to warn against allowing deference to become unthinking or too easily expected. He even admits, "If one knows that deference is due [to him or her], even if one's view is wrong, the incentive to try in good faith to reach the correct decision may be diminished" (p. 182).

Setting this danger aside, the second problem with the appeal to deference is that it seems, at bottom, simply to restate, perhaps in gentler terms, the traditional position on political obligation. When Soper says, for instance, that the "*duty to respect* the legal norm is a reflection of the duty *to respect* the values I myself acknowledge in recognizing what a legal system is" (p. 164; emphasis added), one could easily substitute the "*obligation to obey* the legal norm is a reflection of the duty *to be faithful* to values I myself acknowledge." Or when he states, on the same page, that the "state's right to deference ... arises not from the subject's voluntary choice about the content of legal norms, but from the acknowledgment of the necessity of an enterprise that requires designated authorities to impose norms, in good faith, on the community at large," one could simply substitute the "state's right to obedience" for the "state's right to deference."

In fairness, it is true that Soper does insist upon a difference that the appeal to deference makes. The ethics of deference, he says,

> shifts the moral focus in deciding what one ought to do from the evaluation of the action in question to a consideration of the interests of the person to whom deference is owed. The primary value that underlies the theory is respect for others; in some cases, as in our argument for political obligation, it is respect for oneself as well and for the implications that follow from one's own understanding and acceptance of the value and nature of law. (p. 181)

Deference thus puts the focus not simply on the individual conscience but also on the relationships between and among individuals; deference even seems to foster "a caring community," whereas "insistence on one's own principles ... fosters competition and antagonism" (p. 157).

Perhaps so, but one may continue to doubt that deference really adds anything new or valuable in this respect to traditional defenses of political obligation. Particularly noteworthy in this regard is Soper's argument that the appeal to deference will strengthen the fair-play theory of obligation—the context in

---

[34] Ruth C. A. Higgins, *The Moral Limits of Law*, p. 93.

which he claims that deference fosters "a caring community." The appeal to fair play in itself presupposes that individuals are involved in a relationship with one another and that persons are to be respected. An excessive or intractable insistence on one's rights may lead sometimes to the "competition and antagonism" that Soper deplores, but such an insistence on rights is not at all a necessary feature of the fair-play approach to political obligation, with its emphasis on doing one's fair share as part of a cooperative practice. To play fair, as I have illustrated in various ways in earlier chapters, is to give others their due and to recognize that one is engaged in a common enterprise with these others—considerations that are as likely to foster caring communities as the ethics of deference. With the appeal to fair play capable of doing this work on its own, what is the need for deference?

That is why I say that the deferential turn with regard to political obligation leads into a blind alley. Or, to adjust the metaphor, it is at best a detour that will take us, in a roundabout manner, where other theories more directly go. But perhaps something more can be said for *respect* as a way of grounding obedience to the law than I have found in the appeal to deference.

Higgins's Case for Respect

Ruth Higgins, as previously noted, believes that it is a mistake to rest the case for obeying the law on deference. She also disagrees with Soper's claim that deference—or any other consideration, for that matter—leads to even a *prima facie* obligation to obey the law. But like Soper and Raz, she believes that the philosophical anarchists go too far with their subversive denials of the legitimacy of political authority. There is no general obligation to obey the law, in her view, but there is a duty to *respect* it; or there is such a duty, at any rate, when the legal system is truly worthy of respect.

In a convenient summary, Higgins states the case for denying "authority's comprehensive claims" while nevertheless viewing "the residual value in both law and community through the prism of respect."[35] As she says in that statement,

> Where law is an instrument presently necessary for, or vital to, preventing harm, and preserving the well-being of members of a community, and is integral in creating opportunities for the realization of human capacity, our duty of respect for persons extends to a duty of respect for law. Respectful behavior towards law, or an attitude of respect,

---

[35] Ibid., p. 244. Further citations to this book will appear within parentheses in the body of the text.

is necessary to respect for persons because, where law functions well, and given its supremacy and comprehensiveness, people organize their expectations around legal directives. *The attitude of respect is necessarily required by the grounds of the duty and is obligatory.* Since it is directed at an instrument, that instrument must first satisfy the demands of (estimation) respect and demonstrate its centrality to the realization of human value. *However, this obligatory respect, given the substantively self-limiting nature of an attitude of (estimation) respect, does not lead to an obligation to obey.* ... When one knowingly undermines law, one knowingly undermines the most comprehensive normative system in a society, and confidence therein. *The requirements of respect are less extensive than an obligation to obey but remain categorical.* We must refrain from damaging or diminishing what is of value. (pp. 244–45; emphasis added)

Her conclusion, Higgins goes on to say, "essentially issues in respect for law conditioned by respect for persons and guided by conscience" (p. 245). As with Soper's case for deference, however, one may wonder whether this appeal to respect really adds anything to the traditional defenses of political obligation, which themselves accord considerable respect to the law. Higgins, of course, believes that her appeal to respect certainly *subtracts* something from the traditional defenses—namely, the claim that there is ever a general obligation to obey the law. But it is by no means clear that she truly has accomplished this subtraction. To be sure, she has done so if the obligation to obey the law must be construed as absolute, unconditional, or indefeasible; but such a construction is one that defenders of political obligation no longer endorse, if ever they did. We might also say that she has accomplished her desired subtraction if she can demonstrate that there is a clear and significant difference between "[r]espectful behavior towards law, or an attitude of respect," on the one hand, and obeying the law, on the other. But it appears that respecting the law consists primarily in obeying it. How else does one undermine the law but by disobeying it? Perhaps we might say that philosophical anarchists undermine the law in their writings, even though their writings are perfectly legal; but it is difficult to believe that Higgins would censor them for failing to fulfill their obligation to respect the law. That being so, what else can respect for the law consist in but obedience to it? Even someone who takes steps to change a law that he derides or decries, but nevertheless obeys, is demonstrating both a measure of respect for that law and for the rule of law in general.[36]

---

[36] Massimo Renzo has observed in correspondence that respecting the law may require more than mere obedience, for someone may hold the law in contempt while obeying it for entirely prudential reasons. The point is well taken, but it does not help Higgins. For one thing, the failure to

To this objection, I suspect that Higgins would respond by insisting that the significant difference between the obligation to obey the law and the obligation to respect it is marked by the fact that one is passive and the other is active. She might say, that is, that obedience is merely passive, but respecting the law requires us to take an active and critical stance toward it and those who make it. This, I take it, is why she refers to respect for law as a kind of "(estimation) respect." In her analysis of respect, Higgins distinguishes "estimation respect" as the particular form that applies to the law, with this kind of respect linked to the idea of measuring or assessing to determine whether something or someone deserves respect—of whether, in other words, it "measures up" to what it should be.[37] "Law," she says, "is a normatively and coercively impressive creature. It must, to some degree, live up to its claims and merit the respect it commands" (p. 54). This is also why she writes, on the last page of her book, of "degrees of legitimacy." Indeed, the book ends with these two sentences:

> No absolute legitimacy may ever be possible, but we will remain sensitive to relative degrees of legitimacy and justification. And law, like the individual, will each day face the challenge of meriting the (estimation) respect it deserves. (p. 248)

Respecting the law must therefore be something different from merely obeying it, for it requires the properly respectful citizen to be alert to the gap between what the law is and what it ought to be—and to be willing, perhaps, to take steps to narrow that gap.

I am suspicious of the idea that there may be degrees of legitimacy, but I shall set that worry aside and grant that respect for law may sometimes require us to take an active and critical stance toward it. Again, though, I do not see how this stance sets Higgins's respect-based theory apart from traditional defenses of political obligation, which typically require the conscientious citizen to subject the political authorities and the laws they enforce to scrutiny. According to fair-play theory, in particular, the obligation to obey the law only obtains when the political society in question may be reasonably taken to be a cooperative enterprise for the mutual benefit of its members. Where cooperation is a sham and the law merely a mask for exploitation and oppression, there is no general obligation

---

respect the law in such cases may well be, on her account, the fault of the person rather than of the law. For another, the duty to respect the law would be even more demanding than the duty to obey it.

[37] On p. 50 Higgins identifies three kinds of respect: "respect for capacities, respect *qua* tolerance, and respect *qua* estimation." She subsequently defines respect *qua* estimation, on the same page, as "an attitude that reacts to that which is distinctive, and on this ground, singles out its object for favourable treatment."

to obey the laws. Whether those conditions do or do not obtain is something that fair-play theory will expect the conscientious citizen to determine before she decides that considerations of fair play do or do not require obedience to the laws to which she is subject. In this sense, respect for the law is already built into the fair-play theory of political obligation. Higgins's approach may serve to highlight the importance of respect, but it does not add it to the already existing theory.

Further Problems for Theories of Deference or Respect

There are, finally, two remaining problems for the foregoing attempts to find a middle ground between philosophical anarchism and traditional accounts of political obligation. The first is that they cannot satisfy what Simmons has called the *particularity* requirement for political obligation, according to which a political obligation is a moral duty to some specific group or entity of which one is a part;[38] and the second is that they are of little help when we turn from political obligation to the justification of punishment.

With regard to the particularity concern, which has arisen in Chapter 1 and subsequent chapters, what Soper and Higgins have to show is that deference or respect can establish the particular relationship between citizen and legal system that the particularity criterion requires. For Soper, the problem is to show that deference adds anything to the underlying account of political obligation he hopes to bolster. But it does not do this. I may decide that the legal system of Norway or Canada is more worthy of deference than that of the United States. Does that mean that I am under a political obligation to one or both of those countries rather than to my country of citizenship, the United States? Soper might reply that I am wrong somehow to conclude that Norway or Canada is more worthy of my deference, but it is difficult to see how he can justify this claim without appealing to a preexisting relationship between me and the United States that requires my deference to the laws of *my* country. In that case, though, it is the preexisting relationship, such as a fair-play obligation, that is doing the work, not deference. Or Soper could say that owing more deference to Norway or Canada does not entail that I owe *no* deference to the United States. But in that case, we still would need a reason other than deference to satisfy the particularity requirement by showing that my political obligation is to the United States.

Higgins faces the same problem with regard to respect, but she may well see this openness to the possibility of considering foreign legal systems to be more

---

[38] Simmons, *Moral Principles and Political Obligations*, pp. 31–35.

worthy of respect than one's own as a virtue of her theory. In a way, she even seems to balk at the particularity requirement, living as we now do in a world of porous boundaries and overlapping jurisdictions.[39] Hence her "theory of respect" is "only pragmatically relativized to the parochial and is at all times capable of extension where our legal or moral duties transcend territorial boundaries."[40] However, Higgins also suggests that there is a sense in which one's *own* legal system is fundamental, or has a prior claim on one that must always be given attention. This claim traces to what one owes to those who share membership in a legal system, for it is our "fellow legal subjects, as people," who "deserve our most basic respect."[41] "As citizens," furthermore, "our fellows deserve a proper reciprocity."[42] This is a welcome conclusion, of course, from the fair-play point of view. But it is welcome because Higgins is invoking a fair-play account of obligation in order to handle the particularity problem. Respect is doing nothing here beyond what the obligation to obey the law of one's polity does.

Similar problems arise with regard to punishment. Here the problem is to determine the proper response to those who fail to show deference to or respect for the law. If respect for the law is in most cases tantamount to obeying it, as I have argued, then punishment presents no special problem; but that is because the duty to respect the law, and thereby to respect one's fellow citizens, is at bottom the same as the duty to abide by the principle of fair play. To punish someone for breaking the law and to punish someone for failing to respect the law are virtually the same. Suppose, though, that there is a significant difference between respecting the law and obeying it, so that the duty of respect calls either for less or more than the duty to obey. In those cases, punishment proves troublesome indeed for the argument from respect.

In the first case, the duty to respect the law would be less stringent than the duty to obey it, or "less extensive" in Higgins's words, with the implication being that someone who respects the law without obeying it presumably should go unpunished.[43] The problems of such an approach are not hard to foresee. One of them will be the problem of determining how sincere are the claims of those who have been charged with an offense when they protest that they truly do respect the law. Another will be to determine what counts as respect for law when respect is regarded as less demanding than obedience. Will it be enough to say that one respects the law when she briefly considers the likelihood of being caught before breaking it? Is it enough to respect the laws of her polity

---

[39] Higgins, *The Moral Limits of Law*, pp. 32–34.
[40] Ibid., p. 246.
[41] Ibid., p. 246.
[42] Ibid., p. 246.
[43] Ibid., p. 245.

in general even though she does not respect those laws she finds onerous or obtuse? There are reasons to find the latter conception of respect attractive, of course, as examples of justified civil disobedience attest. But in those cases the disobedience still counts, and it counts even if we think that one's overall respect for the law should temper our judgment of what response this particular act of disobedience deserves. More broadly, we may begin with sympathy for those who profess to respect the rule of law in general while having nothing but scorn for laws that, to their minds, unjustly limit their liberty. How far this sympathy should extend, though, is not at all clear. Jones believes that laws that proscribe the use of certain drugs deserve no respect while Smith believes they do; Smith maintains that laws regulating what he may do with his livestock's waste violates his liberty while Jones disagrees. As these and many other examples indicate, what counts as an unjust limitation on one's proper liberty is a highly controversial matter, and the attempt to confine punishment to those only who act out of *disrespect* for law will simply exacerbate the controversy.

Such problems may seem to vanish if one takes the view that respect for law is more demanding than mere obedience to it, but this prospect is also illusory. In this case the problem is that obeying the law would not be enough to keep one free from punishment. Someone who grudgingly or unthinkingly obeys the law could be subject to punishment simply because he did not demonstrate respect for it. Such would certainly be the case for someone who obeys the law while expressing his contempt for it, whether it be contempt for a particular law or for law in general. Not only would the prudential anarchist need to obey the law, then, but he would also have to keep his hatred or even disdain for the law to himself if he wants to remain free from punishment. Surely this is taking respect for law too far. Whether we think of respect for law as less demanding than obedience, as Higgins does, or as more demanding, the approach simply cannot provide the basis for an acceptable theory of punishment.

Conclusion

To be sure, Higgins and Soper could say that providing a justification of punishment is not part of the project that either of them undertakes. But if I am right about the connections among political authority, political obligation, and punishment that I have tried to establish in this book, then any theory of law and obedience that fails to provide satisfactory guidance on all three points will be, at best, inferior to one that will. Such is clearly the case with the deferential turn with regard to both political obligation and the practice of punishment.

I conclude, then, that this new approach to the ancient problem of political obligation does not constitute the theoretical advance that its proponents claim.

Like the service conception and other revisions of the standard account of authority, it fails to provide a middle ground between the claims of the philosophical anarchists, on the one hand, and the defenders of political obligation, on the other. That is not to say that the deferential turn is without merit; but whatever merit it does have is owing largely to its implicit reliance on considerations of fair play.

9

Political Obligation, Punishment, and the Polity

Is there a general obligation to obey the laws of a reasonably just polity? Is there any justification for inflicting suffering, in the form of punishment, on those who break the law? In the preceding pages I have given affirmative answers to these longstanding questions of political and legal philosophy, and in both cases the answer has been grounded in the principle of fair play. Moreover, in Chapter 7 I have tried to show how fair-play theory helpfully addresses not only the justification of punishment but also other problems posed by that practice, particularly the proper treatment of recidivists, the place of restitution within a punitive scheme, the problem of excessive incarceration, and the question of whether felons should be denied the vote. What remains, to complete the case for fair-play theory, are two final tasks. The first is to explain how the two aspects of this theory—that is, the one concerned with political obligation and the one concerned with punishment—relate to each other. The second is to fill out and sharpen the picture I have been sketching throughout the book of the polity as a cooperative meta-practice. In doing so, I hope to show how fair-play theory provides practical guidance in conditions that fall short of the ideal of the polity so conceived.

Two Aspects of Fair-Play Theory

If the arguments in Part I of this book are correct, then the principle of fair play is the basis for a compelling theory of political obligation. If the arguments of Part II are correct, then the same principle justifies the legal practice of punishment and points toward the resolution of problems associated with that practice. To show that the appeal to fair play underpins both a general obligation to obey the laws of a reasonably just polity and the justification of punishment within it, though, is not simply to reveal a coincidence or testify to the versatility of fair-play theory. If it were, proponents of the theory could still claim the extra value that I noted in the Introduction, for a theory that resolves two longstanding problems is at least twice as good as a theory that responds, at best, to one. But it is not merely coincidence or even versatility that gives fair-play theory its added value. It is, instead, the interlocking and mutually reinforcing nature of its two aspects, with one directed toward political obligation and the other toward punishment.

Examples of these mutually reinforcing aspects of the theory have appeared in previous chapters, but the nature of this reinforcement requires explanation here. To begin with the most fundamental point, the application of fair play to the justification of punishment reinforces the fair-play argument for political obligation by addressing the assurance problem—that is, by providing those who would happily play fair in a cooperative endeavor the security they need in the face of potential free riders, double-crossers, and parasites. Fair-play theory appears to be vulnerable on this point because one's obligation to bear one's share of the burdens of a cooperative practice is sensitive to how others act, or even how they are likely to act. If you have reason to worry that the cooperative practice will fail, and your cooperative efforts be wasted, because too many others will try to take advantage of you and the other cooperators, then whether you truly have an obligation in these circumstances becomes an open question. But if there is an effective system of coercion, such as legal punishment typically affords in the case of the polity, then you have the assurance you need to recognize that your fair-play obligation is in force and thus to act on that knowledge. In that way the fair-play approach to punishment undergirds the fair-play argument for political obligation.

Turning the relationship around, it is also true that the fair-play argument for political obligation establishes the fundamental justification for punishment. That is, if it is right, in general, to punish those who break the law, it is right because they have violated their *prima facie* or *pro tanto* obligation to obey it. But it is also true that the fair-play argument for political obligation elaborated in this book reinforces the fair-play approach to punishment in another way. As we saw in Chapter 6, the idea of playing fair with punishment can be understood as a matter of either *general* or *partial compliance*. If we take it to be the latter, then we must proceed on a case-by-case, law-by-law basis to determine whether there has been a disturbance of the properly balanced distribution of benefits and burdens that warrants the punishment of lawbreakers. The problem with this approach is that there are serious crimes that do not easily fit this description, for there are laws that supply no benefit to some people and laws that impose no burden on some. Most people do not find the laws against rape and murder to be burdensome, for example, so how are such laws to be justified as ways of balancing the benefits and burdens of compliance? How, furthermore, are we to justify the punishment of the homeless trespasser who receives no apparent benefit from laws proscribing trespass? Such questions present serious problems for the fair-play account of punishment, but they do so only if we take that account to be a matter of partial compliance. What I have argued for, however, is a general compliance theory of punishment, according to which the benefits and burdens in question are those that follow from general obedience to the laws of a cooperative practice—or, to be precise, from the rule of law in a polity. Understood in this way, everyone engaged in the cooperative meta-practice of the polity is to enjoy the benefits of security under law while bearing the general burden of obedience to the law whenever such obedience is disagreeable. Moreover, this general compliance conception is itself grounded in the fair-play argument for a general obligation to obey the laws of one's polity, at least when the polity is itself reasonably just. Because the obligation to obey is general, in other words, and not something that varies from one particular law to another, the justification for punishment also must be a matter of general rather than particular compliance. In this way the fair-play argument for political obligation reinforces the fair-play approach to punishment.

It is also important to note that this system of mutual reinforcement extends beyond obligation and punishment to political and legal authority. As I pointed out in Chapter 8, the traditional understanding of authority as the right to rule has been challenged by various philosophers who believe that having legitimate authority does not entail even a *pro tanto* obligation to obey the law as such on the part of those who are subject to the authority. In the case of Joseph Raz's much-discussed *service conception* of authority, as we saw, both authority and the obligation to obey it operate in a piecemeal manner, so that the laws the authority enacts are likely to bear on some citizens but not on others—and this outcome is likely to occur even when the laws do not specify to whom they apply and who is exempt. In contrast to this piecemeal approach, the fair-play theory insists on generality. If it makes sense to think of the obligation to obey the law as a duty of fair play within a cooperative meta-practice, and to think of punishment as justified because it helps to secure that practice, then it also makes sense to think that those who bear the authority of the practice have a right to promulgate laws that members of the practice *qua* members have a general obligation to obey.

When we talk about the fair-play theory of political obligation and the fair-play justification of punishment, in short, we are not referring to two separate theories that coincidentally appeal to the principle of fair play and simply happen to be mutually reinforcing. These are, instead, two *interlocking* aspects of a shared conception of the polity. Both aspects are grounded in the principle of fair play, of course, and by extension grounded also in the idea of the polity as a cooperative practice—to be precise, a cooperative meta-practice that advances and administers the rule of law. For that reason, the fair-play account of political obligation and that of punishment stand or fall together. In my view, for the reasons set out in this book, the interlocking and mutually reinforcing nature of the two aspects of fair-play theory is clear evidence of the strength of the fair-play theory of political obligation and punishment.

Fair Play and the Cooperative Threshold

Whether they are taken individually as separate theories or together as two aspects of the same theory, the question of the plausibility of fair-play accounts of political obligation and of punishment has yet to be settled. Appeals to fair play are all well and good in the appropriate circumstances, objectors may insist, as they are in games played among friends. But how can we take seriously the claim that the polity is a cooperative practice that not only imposes on ordinary citizens an obligation to obey its laws but also has the right to punish those citizens who fail to comply? When the threat of coercion is necessary to secure compliance and when relations among citizens are marked as much by competition and contention as by cooperation, as they typically are in modern polities, can we reasonably regard the polity as a cooperative practice? When injustice and unfairness are so obviously present and persistent in all of the political and legal systems of which we have record, how can we do anything other than dismiss fair-play accounts of political obligation and/or punishment as idle exercises in ideal theory that have no bearing on the real world of politics and the law?

I have responded to this fundamental challenge in various ways in earlier parts of this book. In Chapter 2, for instance, I have tried to show that cooperative practices make room for both competition and coercion. Another instance is my response in Chapter 6 to the objection that the fair-play account of punishment is self-subverting because it fails to apply to actually existing societies. Other instances include the reminders, scattered throughout this book, that fair-play theory contains a critical and aspirational element that enables us to call attention to the ways in which present arrangements fall short of the cooperative ideal while pointing toward the realization of that ideal. Indeed, one may say that the principle of fair play has its place in the real world of partial compliance rather than in ideal theory; for if no one were tempted to be a free rider, double-crosser, or parasite, and if everyone cheerfully took up her part of the cooperative labors, there would be no need for considerations of fair play. Between the presumably unattainable ideal of complete and unstinting cooperation, however, and the threshold below which a political or legal system cannot sink without ceasing to qualify as a cooperative meta-practice, there is ample room for fair-play theory to do its work.

One may accept this point, though, while continuing to question the practical value of fair-play theory for the problems of political obligation and punishment. One may agree, that is, that a polity need not be perfectly just in order for considerations of fair play to bear on the question of whether one has a general obligation to obey its laws, or whether punishment is justified within it; but what does it mean to say that a polity must be *reasonably* just? Or how do we know when a political or legal system has fallen below the threshold that distinguishes cooperative meta-practices in which political obligation obtains and punishment is justified, on the one hand, from insufficiently cooperative practices in which neither condition is present, on the other?

Perhaps the best response to the challenge posed by questions such as these would be to devise a fair-play index that would enable us to calculate precisely the extent or dearth of cooperation in any political or legal system. The attempt to devise such an index, however, would surely run afoul of Aristotle's dictum that we should not seek greater precision than the subject matter allows (*Nicomachean Ethics*, 1094b13–15). Even if such an index were available, moreover, we still would be faced with the question of where to draw the line that establishes the cooperative threshold. So far as I can see, there is no obvious point of demarcation in this regard, just as there is no chronological age that obviously distinguishes the mature from the immature. Some informal and vague point that will remain subject to contention is almost certainly the best we will be able to do. Even so, having some sense of where such a threshold will fall seems not only possible but sufficient for the support of fair-play theory. To indicate how we might develop such a sense, I offer here some brief remarks on the general considerations that are pertinent to establishing a cooperative threshold.

If the polity is, as I have argued, a cooperative meta-practice charged with administering the rule of law, it follows that any attempt to establish a sense of the cooperative threshold must focus on that administration. If there are no rules at all, then there is no cooperative *practice*, and thus no point in worrying about a threshold. If the rules are patently unjust or unfair, such as "Heads I win and tails you lose," or "Do as I say or else," then there is no *cooperative* practice, and again no reason to worry about a threshold. As a first condition, then, we must be able to say the political or legal system in question is a rule-governed enterprise and its rules must be, at least on their face, ones that respect the equal standing of every member of the enterprise. To say that a polity is a rule-governed enterprise is to say, again, that it is responsible for administering and remaining true to the rule of law. Within the polity there may be exceptions of a kind to the principle of equal standing, as there are in a constitutional monarchy that grants privileged positions to members of the royal family, but even those persons must be subject to the law—and thus subject to the loss of their privileges should the laws be changed in lawful manner.

Once we are satisfied that the laws are at least superficially consistent, as a whole, with fair treatment of the members of the polity, the next consideration is whether those who hold positions of authority—or others who are in a position to control or manipulate those who hold authority—are indeed playing fair in their interpretation or enforcement of the law, or whether they fail to do so by somehow distorting the laws in their own favor, or even by ignoring them altogether. Of course, isolated incidents of this kind of injustice are not enough to plunge a political or legal system below the cooperative threshold. In his *Unfair*, for example, Adam Benforado recounts the story of an assistant district attorney in New Orleans who withheld evidence in order to secure the conviction of an innocent man.[1] Benforado also suggests that this miscarriage of justice was in part the result of pressure within the prosecutor's office to win convictions with little concern for how they were won.[2] A single instance of prosecutorial misconduct is a serious matter that requires redress; a number of such instances indicates a pattern of misconduct that calls out for reform. But how large does that number have to be, and how widespread must the misconduct be, before we should conclude that the legal system in question has fallen below the cooperative threshold? Benforado himself notes possibilities for correction in cases such as the one from New Orleans. First, there is the possibility of correction imposed by some higher authority within the legal system—in this case, condemnation and correction of the injustice in New Orleans by officials of the State of Louisiana and by the US Department of Justice. Second, there is the possibility of self-correction within prosecutors' offices through a shift of emphasis away from courtroom victories and toward a more careful handling of cases—and perhaps through the systematic reexamination of cases in which the defendants' guilt seems to have been in doubt.[3]

When considering instances of injustice, in other words, we must try to assess the extent to which they represent the systematic corruption of what should be a cooperative practice. We must also ask whether that corruption goes so far as to deprive some significant number of people of the benefits of the rule of law—a number large enough, that is, to suggest that something more than an occasional miscarriage of justice is occurring. In this respect, our situation is akin to that which Jean-Jacques Rousseau depicts in his *Discourse on the Origin of Inequality* when he explains how the rich and powerful persuade the poor and weak to join with them in forming a political society. According to Rousseau's scathing account, "the origin of society and laws . . . gave new fetters to the weak and

---

[1] Benforado, *Unfair: The New Science of Criminal Injustice* (New York: Broadway Books, 2015), chap. 4.
[2] Ibid., esp. pp. 80–81.
[3] Ibid., pp. 88–89.

new forces to the rich ... and for the profit of a few ambitious men henceforth subjected the entire human race to labor, servitude and misery."[4] But it is also true that Rousseau notes, in the same context, how even "easily seduced men" could "realize the advantages of a political establishment," and especially so as they "had too many disputes to settle among themselves [in the lawless state of nature] to get along without arbiters, and too much greed and ambition to be able to get along without masters long."[5] Setting aside Rousseau's reliance on the ideas of a state of nature and a social contract, the problem for someone seeking to determine whether her political society is above or below the cooperative threshold is to determine whether the corruption is widespread and serious enough to outweigh "the advantages of a political establishment" by thoroughly vitiating the rule of law itself. If so, it falls below the cooperative threshold and is no longer fit either to be the subject of political obligation or to carry out the justified punishment of lawbreakers. If it rises above the cooperative threshold, however, the question then becomes: What must be done to move it closer to the ideal of a fully cooperative practice in which the members owe duties of fair play to one another? In the meanwhile, as that question is pondered and debated, one should continue to regard this polity as a cooperative meta-practice in which fair-play obligations remain in force and punishment is generally justified.

A third consideration concerns the attitudes and actions of ordinary citizens who are not in positions of authority. Do they think of the law as something to obey whenever the police are watching, so to speak, but disobeyed whenever they safely can gain some personal advantage through disobedience? Is the law-abiding citizen widely regarded as someone who contributes to the public good or as a simple-minded sucker? Again, we must be careful to distinguish disobedience of a particular law or set of laws from a general attitude of disrespect for the law, for it may be, as I noted in Chapter 7, that one or more laws within an otherwise just legal system imposes an unfair burden on members of the polity. In such a case, disobedience of that particular law need not threaten the polity with the imminent danger of falling below the cooperative threshold. When obeying the law as such is commonly taken to be nothing more than a mug's game, however, the danger is quite real.

A final consideration, implicit in the foregoing remarks, is whether there is a genuine possibility of reform when things have gone wrong in one or more of the above ways. Estimating this possibility may be as difficult as determining where the cooperative threshold lies, especially when one faces a situation in which two or more of the preceding considerations interact with one another.

---

[4] Jean-Jacques Rousseau, *On the Social Contract; Discourse on the Origin of Inequality; Discourse on Political Economy*, trans. D. A. Cress (Indianapolis, IN: Hackett Publishing, 1983), p. 150.
[5] Ibid., pp. 149–50.

If obeying the law when disobedience is advantageous is widely regarded as a mug's game, for example, that attitude may simply reflect the truth of the matter when the laws are routinely ignored or perverted by those who hold power. In such circumstances, the possibility of reform is likely to be remote and the cooperative threshold out of reach. There are many other circumstances, though, in which the rule of law is sufficiently strong, and cooperative attitudes are sufficiently widespread, to support a reasonable belief in the possibility of removing or reforming a law or set of laws that fail to play fair with some members of the polity. The same point holds, *a fortiori*, if we are talking about particular acts of injustice, such as the prosecutorial misconduct mentioned above, rather than unjust laws. For an enterprise to be a cooperative practice, it must be open to the possibility of correction. A political or legal system that is not open to this possibility is almost certainly one that has sunk below the cooperative threshold.

Other considerations also may bear on this question of how to determine where the cooperative threshold lies, but the four set out above should be sufficient for present purposes. It may help, though, to illustrate these considerations by means of an example. Taxation provides a particularly apt example, for it is an area in which the topics of compliance and fairness frequently arise. Briefly, then, we can note that the tax code must comprise rules that are at least formally just. There is much room for disagreement on this point, of course, with proponents of various schemes—the flat tax, the progressive income tax, sales taxes, value-added taxes, the progressive consumption tax, and so on—all contending for the superior fairness of their favored form of taxation. The main points, though, are these two: first, no polity can administer the rule of law without levying taxes; and second, any tax scheme that baldly exempts those who hold power from the burden of paying taxes while imposing the burden on ordinary citizens is not operating in accordance with the principle of fair play. Any system that taxes in this baldly unfair fashion must fall, therefore, below the cooperative threshold.

To be sure, few political or legal systems have declared their disdain for fair play so openly. In most cases the problem will be to discover whether the tax scheme operates as fairly in practice as its formal statement promises. Here again there is room for a remarkable range of possibilities, from conscientious implementation of formally just tax provisions at one end to a system shot through with loopholes granting tax relief to a special few, and on to systems that amount in effect to kleptocracies or extortion rackets. In the part of that range that extends from conscientious implementation through the loophole-ridden situation, there is likely to be lively debate over the fairness or efficiency of various provisions, and the principle of fair play does not require that there be one clear-cut resolution to this debate. There must be a genuine concern for the equal standing of all members of the cooperative meta-practice, however, and that concern is clearly absent in those political or legal systems that are little more than the aforementioned kleptocracies and extortion rackets—systems that clearly fall below the cooperative threshold.

There is also the question of how willing ordinary citizens are to pay their taxes. Coercion, particularly in the form of punishment, is a perfectly appropriate means of assuring those who would voluntarily bear their share of the burdens of a cooperative practice that their efforts will not be in vain, as we have seen. The more willing the citizens are to bear their share of the tax burden, though, and the less need there is to call on coercion, the better. When taxes are easily evaded, and especially when such evasion is widely considered to be both the sensible and the normal course of action, then the citizen who would be willing to comply with the tax laws must ask whether she is being simply naïve or even foolish to contribute to an enterprise that is in danger of falling below the cooperative threshold.

What should we say to such a citizen? My answer is that she should pay her taxes as long as she has reason to believe that the cooperative threshold has not been breached and that the slide toward that threshold may be slowed, halted, and eventually reversed. The same point holds with regard to obeying the law in general. As long as there is reason to believe that the cooperative meta-practice of the polity, and the rule of law it administers, is providing significant benefit without imposing an overwhelming burden of obedience, then fair play requires that one continue to do her part. In such circumstances, moreover, the cooperative citizen should understand that doing one's part includes doing what one can to encourage others to bear their shares of the cooperative burdens as well.

There is, however, a serious objection to reliance on the idea of a cooperative threshold that remains to be considered. This is an objection, moreover, that can be raised from within the fair-play camp, as Tommie Shelby illustrates in his recent *Dark Ghettos*. "The legitimacy of a political order," Shelby says,

> is to be judged by how well it maintains a fair system of social cooperation. . . . It would violate fair-play principles to take advantage of the freedom and social benefits made possible by a just legal order without accepting the constraints of the law and contributing our share to maintaining the material conditions of social life.[6]

But when there are serious doubts about the justice of the social and legal order, then the notion of a cooperative threshold is troubling. To speak of a threshold implies a single line of demarcation that applies equally to everyone within the

---

[6] Shelby, *Dark Ghettos: Injustice, Dissent, and Reform* (Cambridge, MA: Harvard University Press, 2016), p. 231.

legal order; but when there is abundant evidence that racial discrimination and other forms of bias render the dispensation of justice far from equal, it is hard to see that there is a single line—even a vague and contested one—that separates an order treating its citizens justly from one that does not; for there may be many citizens who stand above that line while others fall below it. As Shelby says,

> in an affluent society with a recent history of overt racial domination and civic exclusion, no reasonable standard for tolerable justice is compatible with persistent ghetto conditions. If this conjecture is correct, then when the ghetto poor in the United States refuse to respect the authority of the law qua law, they do not thereby violate the principle of reciprocity or shirk valid civic obligations.[7]

Some people within the United States, perhaps even a substantial majority of them, will have "valid civic obligations" that flow from considerations of fair play, in other words, while others do not. Such a situation is one that the idea of a cooperative threshold seems unable to handle.

As Shelby sees it, the proper approach to social and political systems in which justice is unevenly distributed is to draw a distinction between two types of legitimacy, which he calls *legitimate authority* and *justifiable-enforcement legitimacy*, or simply *enforcement legitimacy*.[8] The first, in keeping with the idea of a cooperative threshold, obtains when a state satisfies "certain minimum standards of social justice"; but a state that "fails to meet these standards *lacks the legitimate authority to punish disobedience to its laws*."[9] In this case, though, it would be unwise to deny the state any kind of right to punish wrongdoing, especially as it often happens that those who are victims of social injustice steal from and do violence to other victims of social injustice. Shelby's conclusion, then, is that a state may enjoy enforcement legitimacy even when it lacks legitimate authority. As he says,

> Those who are most burdened by the injustices of a society may lack an obligation to obey the law (on reciprocity grounds); however, the state that claims jurisdiction over the territory within which the oppressed live may still have the right to impose penalties for certain crimes. That is, it may have enforcement legitimacy.[10]

---

[7] Ibid., p. 218.
[8] Ibid., p. 223–30.
[9] Ibid., p. 232; emphasis in original.
[10] Ibid., p. 232; see also p. 248.

Shelby's case for a version of fair-play theory that rests on two distinct kinds of authority is thus at odds with my claim that the fair-play theory of political obligation and punishment is properly grounded in the idea of a cooperative practice, which in turn entails the idea of a cooperative threshold. Among other points of difference, Shelby believes that those "who claim jurisdiction over a territory" may have a right to enforce their claims even though they have no legitimate authority to do so; whereas I believe it is a mistake to divorce the right to enforce laws from the legitimate authority to issue them—a form of authority that entails, for both Shelby and me, a correlative obligation of obedience on the part of the citizenry. I think his view mistaken for two main reasons.

The first is that such a divorce is bound to raise problems about the legitimacy of those who seek to enforce their commands. That is, if enforcement legitimacy is not grounded in legitimate authority, then what is the source of its legitimacy? If it is simply a matter of having the power to enforce commands, then this kind of legitimacy is open to the devastating objections that H. L. A. Hart brought against "the command theory of law" in *The Concept of Law*.[11] In the bluntest terms, the problem is that the gunman may have the power to enforce his commands, but this is not to say that he has the right or authority to do so. To put the point more broadly, it looks as if Shelby's desire to invest enforcement legitimacy in some people is akin to the claim that the ship's officer or flight attendant who is in a position to lead passengers to safety after a wreck has the right to issue and enforce commands even though none of the passengers has a duty to obey the officer or attendant. Whether this is a matter of right, though, or merely a matter of prudence, is the important question. Even the ordinary citizen who steps up to direct traffic in the aftermath of an automobile accident appears to have this kind of enforcement legitimacy. But if that is what enforcement legitimacy is, it seems to be nothing more than a right to issue directives that prudent people will follow. Nor is it easy to see how those who exercise this kind of authority will have the *right* to punish those who refuse to go along with their orders.

Of course, Shelby has something more in mind than the exercise of informal authority in times of emergency when he speaks of enforcement legitimacy. As we have seen, his reference is to "the state that claims jurisdiction over the territory." If the state's claim is not supported by legitimate authority, however, then we face the question of why we, as citizens or subjects, should honor its claims to jurisdiction. Shelby's answer is that we should recognize and go along with the state's enforcement of its laws because of "the need to protect the vulnerable from unjustified harm. A state can sometimes be in a position to provide this

---

[11] Hart, *The Concept of Law*, 2nd ed. (Oxford: Oxford University Press, 1994), esp. chaps. 2 and 3.

protection in a way that is justifiable to those who wrongly threaten others."[12] Not only prudence but justice is at issue, then. But suppose that there are two states, or two rival claimants to the title of state, and both seem to be in a position to enforce, say, laws against murder, robbery, and rape in a way that will protect the vulnerable from unjustified harm. In such a case, how are we to know which of the two has enforcement legitimacy? Or is it possible that both do, so that the right to enforcement simply attaches to whichever can put its enforcement regime to work first? In practical terms, chaos would seem to be the result of relying on a notion of enforcement legitimacy that is divorced from legitimate authority. In theoretical terms, we can see once again the *particularity problem* discussed in earlier chapters at work. If we are going to say that some state or agency has enforcement legitimacy with regard to us, in other words, then we need also to be able to say that it is in some sense *our* state or agency. Without such a sense of a particularity, we could find ourselves in the position of people who are caught between two or more mobs that are seeking to extort "protection money" from us.

The second main reason to think that Shelby's attempt to distinguish enforcement legitimacy from legitimate authority is mistaken is that it would undercut efforts to revise and reform the means by which enforcement of the laws proceeds. That is to say, if the state or polity lacks legitimate authority, and if the legitimacy of authority is disconnected from the right to enforce laws, then what is the motive—or the proper avenue—for improving enforcement mechanisms and procedures? Attempts to reform plea-bargaining procedures and to eliminate prosecutorial misconduct certainly are of significance to the just enforcement of the laws and the protection of the vulnerable, but the pursuit of such reforms is not simply a matter of concern for the enforcement branch of government. Such concerns have broader implications for the justice of the society and legal order as a whole, and these implications at some point will have to be addressed in the legislative arena through the passage and revision of laws. To do that, though, will require some sense of legitimate authority on the part of those who pass and revise—and interpret and enforce—the laws. If the point of enforcement legitimacy is to protect the vulnerable, in other words, then it will require the guidance and reinforcement of legitimate authority.

For these reasons, it would be a mistake for fair-play theorists—or for anyone, in my view—to insist on a strict distinction between legitimate authority and enforcement legitimacy. The latter is properly subsumed in the former, and legitimate authority itself is best understood as the authority a cooperative metapractice enjoys as long as it surpasses the cooperative threshold I have tried to

---

[12] Shelby, *Dark Ghettos*, p. 248.

define, albeit imprecisely, in this chapter. There may well be reasons for granting exceptional treatment under law to those whose criminal acts seem in some way to spring from injustices to which they have been subject, but these are best treated case by case in terms of justifying, excusing, or mitigating circumstances. That is the best approach, at least, when the political and legal order does indeed rise above the cooperative threshold.[13]

Conclusion

Early in his first term as president of the United States, Bill Clinton provoked much derision when he referred to taxes as "contributions" that citizens make to the public treasury. The scornful reaction to Clinton's apparent euphemism is easy to understand: people who are accustomed to thinking of contributions in the context of charity will find it hard to conceive of paying taxes under penalty of law—that is, under the threat of punishment—as a kind of contribution. The tendency to think of government or the state as some alien but looming coercive force no doubt also played a part in the derisive reaction. According to the fair-play theory developed in this book, however, there is nothing necessarily objectionable about Clinton's use of "contributions" in this context. Indeed, when taxes provide a government with the funds needed to maintain the polity as a cooperative meta-practice administering the rule of law, it is perfectly proper to regard the payment of taxes as contributions—that is, literally as shared payments—to the public good.[14]

This is true, furthermore, even when these contributions are elicited somewhat grudgingly under the threat of coercion. One reason is that the presence of this threat does not free one from the obligation to contribute one's fair share to the cooperative meta-practice; contributions may be either voluntary or involuntary. Another reason is that the coercive threat secures the assurance, in H. L. A. Hart's words, "that those who would voluntarily obey shall not be sacrificed to those who would not."[15]

There are, of course, problems of both appearance and reality in these matters. To many people, it is simply quite difficult to conceive of taxes as their fair share

---

[13] Here, as in the related discussion in chap. 6, valuable guidance may be found in Stuart Green, "Just Deserts in Unjust Societies: A Case-Specific Approach," in *Philosophical Foundations of Criminal Law*, ed. R. A. Duff and Stuart Green (Oxford: Oxford University Press, 2011), pp. 352–76.

[14] On the need for taxes not only to provide public services but also to sustain individual liberty, see Stephen Holmes and Cass R. Sunstein, *The Cost of Rights: Why Liberty Depends on Taxes* (New York: W. W. Norton, 1999), esp. chaps. 3 and 4.

[15] Hart, *The Concept of Law*, p. 198.

of the burdens that must be borne if the polity is to provide the benefits of the rule of law. It is also possible that their difficulties are well founded, either because the tax burden is not apportioned fairly or because tax monies are diverted to the pockets of the rulers and their friends rather than to the support of the rule of law. In the latter case, the perception of the government as an alien and threatening force is also likely to be accurate. In happier circumstances, though, in which the government is an agency of a polity that rises above the cooperative threshold analyzed in this chapter, the problem is to help the citizens grasp the cooperative nature of the polity that they may have difficulty perceiving.

In these happier and not uncommon circumstances, citizens will have a general obligation to obey the laws of their polity and will be liable to punishment, *ceteris paribus*, for their failure to obey. Those conclusions are grounded, as I have argued, in the principle of fair play. In the unhappy circumstances of an oppressive and exploitative regime that falls below the cooperative threshold and effectively denies its subjects a fair chance of not becoming criminals, there is neither a fair-play obligation to obey the law nor a fair-play justification for punishment. Even in these circumstances, however, there is a sense in which considerations of fair play are still at work; for it is as important to know when conditions of fair play do not prevail as when they do.

INDEX

abolitionism
  philosophical, 37, 170–75, 228
  political, 163–70, 175
  therapeutic, 160–63, 175
acceptance of benefits, 117–20
anarchism
  communal, 28–30
  individualist, 30–32
  philosophical, 3, 32–40, 69, 72, 74–75, 89, 111, 136, 171, 261–62, 273, 279
  political, 28, 69
anarcho-capitalism, 29–39, 36, 98
anarcho-communism, 29
Antigone, 15, 16, 17, 140
Aquinas, St. Thomas, 179
Aristotle, 287
Arneson, Richard, 55n23
associative theory, 10, 72–90. *See also* membership theory
assurance, 143, 155–56, 168, 195, 251, 284, 295
Austen, Jane, 78

Barnett, Randy, 164, 229–30, 234–39, 246–47
Bell, Nora, 110n20
Benforado, Adam, 288
Benn, S. I., 142–43, 146–47, 245
Bennett, Christopher, 202, 247, 269
Bentham, Jeremy, 144, 146–47
Beran, Harry, 72n8
Bianchi, Herman, 166–67
Bibas, Stephanos, 205n3
Boonin, David, 144–45, 171–74, 182, 189–91, 194, 204, 239–44, 247
Boston Marathon, 114
Braithwaite, John, 148

Broad, C. D., 42
Brooks, Thom, 7n15, 7n17, 256n99
Burgh, Richard, 4n8, 185n14, 185n16
Bush, George W., 46
Butler, Samuel, 160

Canada, 91, 107–8, 156–57, 279
Carr, Craig, 48–49
Casal, Paula, 53n18
Cholbi, Michael, 242n72
Christiano, Thomas, 96–98, 269–70
Christie, Nils, 164
Clinton, Bill, 295
Clinton, Hillary Rodham, 140
Code of Hammurabi, 140
communicative aspect of law and rules, 66, 179, 260
communicative theory of punishment, 8, 142, 149, 151, 167–69, 174, 180, 182, 184, 199, 223, 243, 247, 253, 255
communitarianism, 18, 25–27, 36, 37, 50, 68, 159, 164–66, 169
consent, 18, 25–27, 36, 37, 50, 68, 159, 164–66, 169
content independence of obligations, 19, 129, 271
cooperative practice, 43–67, 98–111, 113–19, 124–26. *See also* meta-practice
cooperative threshold, 57, 102, 134, 198–200, 286–96
Copp, David, 271
Cottingham, John, 148

Dahl, Robert, 212n14
Davis, Michael, 200–201
Deigh, John, 253–55

democracy, 33, 96–98, 203, 212–14, 264, 269–70, 272
deterrence, 6, 7, 155–58, 189, 195–96, 207
Dickens, Charles, 77–78
double effect, doctrine of, 173
Duff, R. A. (or Antony), 8, 141–45, 167–69, 171–73, 184–85, 191–94, 197, 199, 242–43, 245, 248
Durning, Patrick, 118n36
Dworkin, Ronald, 72, 75–76, 82–83, 85
Dzur, Albert, 217n18

Edmundson, William, 262, 273n32
electoral college, 46
Ellin, Joseph, 232n49
Estlund, David, 96–97, 264–65

Feinberg, Joel, 142, 149
Filmer, Sir Robert, 76
Fingarette, Herbert, 187–88
Finnis, John, 104
Fire Department of New York, 114
Flew, A. G. N., 142–43, 245
France, Anatole, 106
franchise, 8, 157, 212, 252–56. *See also* voting rights
Friedman, David, 30n34
Frye, Harrison, 98n77
Fuller, Lon, 104

Gandhi, Mohandas, 16
Gardner, John, 147n16, 166
Gauthier, David, 55n22
Gilbert, Margaret, 20–21, 69n1, 72n10
Golash, Deidre, 143–45, 170–72
Goldman, Emma, 29–30
Gore, Al, 46
Green, Leslie, 9n19, 32n38
Green, T. H., 15, 17, 27, 201, 211
Green, Stuart, 201n42
Greenawalt, Kent, 17n6
Greene, Abner, 15n3

Hajdin, Mane, 230–33, 235–38, 246
Hampton, Jean, 142, 148–59, 167–68, 171–72, 174–75, 178, 182, 185, 187, 196, 245, 247–48
Hardimon, Michael, 73–75, 83, 85, 119
Harding, Tonya, 193
Harris, Edward, 24n21
Hart, H. L. A., 1, 2, 5, 42–43, 50–51, 54–55, 57–58, 63–65, 67, 69, 101, 114, 117, 139, 142–43, 146–47, 168, 176, 183, 245, 293, 295
Hartogh, Govert den, 43n4
Hawking, Stephen, 122

Hershenov, David, 249–52
Higgins, Ruth C. A., 262, 273–74, 276–81
Hobbes, Thomas, 16, 23–24, 57, 70, 87, 214, 250
Holmes, Stephen, 295n14
Holmgren, Margaret, 229n41
Horton, John, 34n42, 54–62, 73–75, 85–90, 115
Hoskins, Zachary, 3n5, 4n9
Huemer, Michael, 30n34, 35n44
Hume, David, 71
Husak, Douglas, 206

incarceration, 8, 11, 204–17, 242–43, 252, 257, 283
Intergovernmental Panel on Climate Change, 268

Jackson, Shirley, 46–47, 58, 60. *See also* "Lottery, The"
Jackson, Shoeless Joe, 210
Janeites, 78

Kant, Immanuel, 94–97, 113
Kavka, Gregory, 31n36
Keller, Helen, 122
Kerrigan, Nancy, 193
King, Martin Luther, Jr., 16
Klimchuk, Dennis, 244n76, 250
Klosko, George, 6, 16, 43, 44, 51–53, 77, 101, 110, 118, 120, 126, 128–34, 270
Kramer, Matthew, 135

Lacey, Nicola, 210n10
Lee, Youngjae, 218–27
Lefkowitz, David, 25n22
Legality, 103–5, 134, 266
libertarians, 29, 31, 32, 36, 65, 159, 163–64, 230–39, 240–45
Locke, John, 16, 25, 37, 38, 70–71, 127
"Lottery, The," 46–47, 58, 60. *See also* Jackson, Shirley

Mackie, John, 148
Mafia, 82–84
mala in se offenses, 8, 206
mala prohibita offenses, 8, 206, 215
Mapel, David, 107n11
Markel, Dan, 3n5
Martin, Casey, 46, 62
Matravers, Matt, 195–96, 200
membership theory, 5, 18, 23, 26, 36, 61–62, 72–90, 98, 99, 119, 120, 127, 159, 225, 228, 252, 256, 280. *See also* associative theory
Menninger, Karl, 160, 162–63
meta-practice, 65–67, 101–8, 183–91, 285–87, 289–91. *See also* cooperative practice

Index

Mill, John Stuart, 213
Miller, Franklin, 230n42
Mokrosińska, Dorota, 121–22
Montague, Philip, 191n29
Moore, Michael, 146
Morison, Samuel, 191n30
Morris, Herbert, 2, 150–54, 156, 161–62, 167, 171, 172, 176–78, 182, 187–88, 192, 195, 228, 247, 249–52
Mozart, Wolfgang Amadeus, 53
Murphy, Jeffrie, 148, 149, 167, 177–79, 186, 197, 243
Murphy, Mark, 72n8

Natural duty, 5, 10, 18, 36, 68, 70, 85–86, 90–101, 131, 132, 214
Neuhouser, Frederick, 59n30
New Orleans, 288
Normore, Calvin, 123–24
Norway, 199, 279
Nozick, Robert, 3, 31, 50, 68, 70, 109–11, 117, 118, 125

O'Brien, Rachel, 211n12
Olsaretti, Serena, 53n18

particularity requirement, the, 26–27, 87, 91–99, 108, 132, 279–80, 294
Pateman, Carole, 27n28
Pecksniff, Seth, 77–78, 81
penal populism, 5, 212–16
Pettit, Philip, 148
Pilon, Roger, 246n79
Pinch, Tom, 77–78
Pitkin, Hanna F., 27n28
Plato, 42, 140, 165, 172, 264
polity, 7–10, 20–23, 25–28, 63–67, 87–90, 97–103, 105–8, 113–16, 119–23, 126–28, 133–35, 156–58, 177–86, 212–18, 223–28, 247–53, 268–71, 283–97
presumptive goods, 110, 118, 120, 126, 270

Rawls, John, 2, 3, 18, 43–44, 47, 50, 54, 56, 58, 59, 62, 67, 69, 90–91, 94, 97, 101–4, 114, 117, 120, 139, 176, 178, 214
Raz, Joseph, 9, 22, 263–70, 272, 276, 285
recidivism, 156, 211, 213, 217–27
recidivist premium, 217–27, 252, 257
Renzo, Massimo, 79–82, 126
Restitution, 227–52
  punitive, 4, 171, 228, 240, 245–52
  pure, 164, 171, 228–44

retributivism, 6, 147–57, 178, 182–83, 189, 199, 246, 249–50
  expressive, 149–57, 168, 175
Roberts, Julian, 217n19
Rothbard, Murray, 229n38
Rousseau, Jean-Jacques, 288–89
Royal Society for the Arts, 211
rule of law, 56–57, 63–66, 101–8, 120–22, 133–35, 177–79, 183–85, 188–91, 287–91

Samaritanism, 69, 92–94, 100
Sartorius, Rolf, 9n19, 32n38
Saudi Arabia, 93
Sayre-McCord, Geoffrey, 171–74
scale, the problem of, 113–17
Scott, David, 160n52
Shapiro, Scott, 266, 269, 272
Shelby, Tommie, 291–94
Sher, George, 2
Sigler, Mary, 253, 255–56
Simmons, A. John, 3, 26, 28, 32, 36–40, 56, 71, 91–93, 111, 113–15, 118, 120, 127, 261, 279
Smart, J. J. C., 147
Smith, M. B. E., 19, 56, 111–17
Socrates, 15, 16, 42, 140, 165, 172
Song, Edward, 55n23
Soper, Philip, 262, 273–76, 277, 279, 281
Sophocles, 15, 17, 140
Steinberger, Peter, 72n8
Stilz, Anna, 94–97
Sunstein, Cass, 295n14
Sweden, 93
Switzerland, 93

Tadros, Victor, 7n17
Tamanaha, Brian, 103, 104, 134
Tamir, Yael, 77–79, 83–85
Thoreau, Henry David, 16, 127–28
Tocqueville, Alexis de, 40
Tosi, Justin, 2n3
Trump, Donald, 46

United Kingdom, 199
U.S. Conference of Catholic Bishops, 268
U.S. Congress, 268
U.S. Department of Justice, 288
Utilitarianism, 26, 36, 148, 156

Von Hirsch, Andrew, 196
voting rights, 5, 156–58, 204, 210, 252–57. *See also* franchise

Waldron, Jeremy, 91–92, 94, 97, 268
Wellman, Christopher Heath, 37–38, 92–95, 97, 100
Will, George, 205
Williams, Andrew, 53n18
Wolff, Jonathan, 6
Wolff, Robert Paul, 3, 33–36, 40, 261, 262, 273

Wood, David, 7n15
Wootton, Barbara, 160

Yankah, Ekow, 211n13

Zaibert, Leo, 241n70
Zimmerman, Michael, 171–73